This book is a timely and stimulating addition to the international marketing and consumer behaviour canon, highlighting sometimes quite spectacular aspects of accommodation, integration and contradiction across social, political and consumerist culture domains. For those who do not understand how business works in present-day Russia, this is where to start.

Charles McIntyre, Senior Lecturer, Bournemouth University, UK

Roberts' rigorous cultural and historical analysis provides a fascinating and unique insight into post-socialist Russian consumer culture. Laying particular emphasis on the political context in which that culture has emerged, this book will be essential reading for anyone seeking to understand Russia today.

Philippe Odou, Professor, The University of Reims
Champagne-Ardenne, France

Offering rich descriptions and novel insights into the rapid development of consumerism in Russia, this book explores aspects of contemporary society in the process. The author provides a detailed, analytical perspective on the ways in which specific brands and retailers have rapidly become embedded within Russian culture.

Helen Goworek, Lecturer, University of Leicester, UK

Consumer Culture, Branding and Identity in the New Russia

As shopping has been transformed from a chore into a major source of hedonistic pleasure, a specifically Russian consumer culture has begun to emerge that is unlike any other. This book examines the many different facets of consumption in today's Russia, including retailing, advertising and social networking. Throughout, emphasis is placed on the inherently visual – not to say spectacular – nature both of consumption generally, and of Russian consumer culture in particular.

Particular attention is paid to the ways in which brands, both Russian and foreign, construct categories of identity in order to claim legitimacy for themselves. What emerges is a fascinating picture of how consumer culture is being reinvented in Russia today, in a society which has one, nostalgic eye turned towards the past, and the other, utopian eye, set firmly on the future.

Borrowing concepts from both marketing and cultural studies, the approach throughout is interdisciplinary, and will be of considerable interest to researchers, students and practitioners wishing to gain invaluable insights into one of the most lucrative, and exciting, of today's emerging markets.

Graham H. Roberts teaches Russian Studies and International Business at the University of Nanterre (Paris Ouest). He is a member of the CECILLE research centre at the University of Lille 3, and an associate member of the REGARDS research centre at the University of Reims Champagne-Ardenne.

Routledge Interpretive Marketing Research

Edited by Stephen Brown and Barbara B. Stern
University of Ulster, Northern Ireland and Rutgers, the State University of New Jersey, USA

Recent years have witnessed an 'interpretative turn' in marketing and consumer research. Methodologists from the humanities are taking their place alongside those drawn from the traditional social sciences.

Qualitative and literary modes of marketing discourse are growing in popularity. Art and aesthetics are increasingly firing the marketing imagination.

This series brings together the most innovative work in the burgeoning interpretative marketing research tradition. It ranges across the methodological spectrum from grounded theory to personal introspection, covers all aspects of the postmodern marketing 'mix', from advertising to product development, and embraces marketing's principal sub-disciplines.

1. The Why of Consumption
Edited by S. Ratneshwar, Glen Mick and Cynthia Huffman

2. Imagining Marketing
Art, aesthetics and the avant-garde
Edited by Stephen Brown and Anthony Patterson.

3. Marketing and Social Construction
Exploring the Rhetorics of Managed Consumption
By Chris Hackley

4. Visual Consumption
By Jonathan Schroeder

5. Consuming Books
The Marketing and Consumption of Literature
Edited by Stephen Brown

6. The Undermining of Beliefs in the Autonomy and Rationality of Consumers
By John O'Shaugnessy and Nicholas Jackson O'Shaugnessy

7. Marketing Discourse
A Critical Perspective
By Per Skålén, Markus Fellesson and Martin Fougère

8. Explorations in Consumer Culture Theory
Edited by John F. Sherry Jr. and Eileen Fisher

9. Consumer Culture, Branding and Identity in the New Russia
From five-year-plan to 4x4
Graham H. Roberts

10. The Practice of the Meal
Food, families and the market place
Edited by Benedetta Cappellini, David Marshall and Elizabeth Parsons

Also available in Routledge Interpretive Marketing Research series:

Representing Consumers: Voices, views and visions
Edited by Barbara B. Stern

Romancing the Market
Edited by Stephen Brown, Anne Marie Doherty and Bill Clarke

Consumer Value: A framework for analysis and research
Edited by Morris B. Holbrook

Marketing and Feminism: Current issues and research
Edited by Miriam Catterall, Pauline Maclaran and Lorna Stevens

Consumer Culture, Branding and Identity in the New Russia

From five-year plan to 4x4

Graham H. Roberts

Routledge
Taylor & Francis Group

LONDON AND NEW YORK

First published 2016 by Routledge

2 Park Square, Milton Park, Abingdon, Oxon OX14 4RN
605 Third Avenue, New York, NY 10017

Routledge is an imprint of the Taylor & Francis Group, an informa business

First issued in paperback 2021

Publisher's Note

The publisher has gone to great lengths to ensure the quality of this reprint but
points out that some imperfections in the original copies may be apparent.

British Library Cataloguing in Publication Data
A catalogue record for this book is available from the British Library

Library of Congress Cataloging-in-Publication Data
Names: Roberts, Graham H., author.
Title: Consumer culture, branding and identity in the new Russia : from
five-year plan to 4x4 / Graham H. Roberts.
Description: Abingdon, Oxon ; New York, NY : Routledge, 2016. |
Series: Routledge interpretive marketing research | Includes
bibliographical references and index.
Identifiers: LCCN 2015035187| ISBN 9780415722407 (hardback) |
ISBN 9781315858302 (ebook)
Subjects: LCSH: Consumers--Russia (Federation) | Consumption
(Economics)--Social aspects--Russia (Federation) | Marketing--Russia
(Federation) | Branding (Marketing)--Russia (Federation) |
Group identity--Russia (Federation)
Classification: LCC HC340.12.Z9 C6235 2016 | DDC 306.30947--dc23
LC record available at http://lccn.loc.gov/2015035187

ISBN: 978-0-415-72240-7 (hbk)
ISBN: 978-0-367-34063-6 (pbk)

Typeset in Bembo
by Taylor & Francis Books

Il n'y a pas d'image en soi. Son statut et ses pouvoirs ont varié au gré des révolutions techniques et des croyances collectives.

Régis Debray, *Vie et Mort de l'Image*

Contents

Acknowledgements   xii

Introduction   1

1   From Red Square to Nike Town: Re-enchanting the
retail experience   10

2   From Superman to the Invisible Man: Imagining the male
body in contemporary Russian advertising   45

3   The politics of packaging in post-socialist Russia: Labels,
logos, locations   81

4   The final frontier: Brands and branding on social media in
the new Russia   115

Afterword, or the cautionary tale of Diana, Lada, Myusya – and Vlad   154

References   156
Index   193

Acknowledgements

Special thanks go to: Jacqueline Curthoys at Routledge, for the enthusiasm with which she accepted my initial proposal; the three anonymous reviewers of that initial proposal, for their very helpful comments; my editor Sinead Waldron for her constant encouragement; Andy Baxter for his invaluable copy-editing skills; my colleagues Jean-Robert Raviot and Sergueï Sakhno for arranging my teaching timetable so as to maximise my research time; Jean-Robert for taking on the arduous task of reading through the penultimate version of this book; my colleagues at Nanterre University's Centre de Recherche Pluridisciplinaire Multilingue, for generously funding a research visit to Moscow in 2013; Elena, Galina, Sasha and Tatyana for their hospitality on that and other trips; my students for the Dahlgren book; Aleksandra Shcherbakova for Smirennyi; Philippe Odou for his early-morning discussions on brands on the motorway to Reims; Charles McIntyre for graciously sharing with me his paper on shop façades; Yuliya Checheneva, Anna Louyest, Laurence Roche-Nye and Serge Rolet for the boxes, packets and wrappers; Alain Brunet for his wisdom; J. B., D. L. and K. Z-Q. for listening; Bill Evans for keeping me company during so much of the writing; The Ghost Rider for helping me see the broader perspective during the revision stages; mum and dad for their culture (and my identity); Mathieu for the Wednesdays; and Béa – for so much more than I can ever say.

An earlier version of part of chapter one appeared in Roberts (2013a) 'I love theatre! Branding Russia's "Mega Mall" shopping centres', *The Marketing Review*, 13, 3: 255–69. An earlier version of part of chapter three appeared in Roberts (2014a) 'Message on a bottle: Packaging the Great Russian Past', *Consumption, Markets and Culture*, 17, 3: 295–313. An earlier version of part of chapter four appeared in Roberts (2014c) 'On the Trans-Siberian with Sylvester Stallone: National identity and brand identity in post-socialist Russia', *Quaestio Rossica*, 3, 2: 197–208.

Introduction

I can remember the day I finally understood why I had decided to write this book. It was a hot afternoon in July 2013, and I was on the Moscow metro, on my way to see an Arctic Monkeys concert in Gorky Park. The distances between metro stops in Russia's capital city are often quite considerable, so I had plenty of time to look around at my fellow passengers. The first person to catch my eye was the young woman sitting immediately opposite me. With her Dorothy Perkins bag, her Adidas training shoes and the tablet on which she was reading a novel, she would have been at home in any number of the world's big cities. It was only when I looked at her elderly neighbour that I remembered where I was. While the shopping bag she was carrying was from French hypermarket chain Auchan, the retailer's logo was emblazoned across it in large red Cyrillic letters. She was also leafing through one of the most popular Russian TV magazines, reading an article about Russian state-owned Channel One's latest game show. At that moment, we pulled into a station, and as the doors opened, a middle-aged man got off, his hands reaching for the top pocket of his shirt, from which he pulled out a pack of 'Russian Style' cigarettes, on which I could clearly see the double-headed Romanov eagle. A pre-recorded voice urged passengers 'not to forget anything when leaving the train'. As we moved off, I mused to myself that I had never heard this gentle reminder being given during my numerous trips to the country when it was still the Soviet Union, and continued to look around the carriage. To my right, a teenage boy carrying a Fred Perry bag and dressed in a Sex Pistols T-shirt was engrossed in the soccer game he was playing on his Gameboy (Russia, I noticed, were thrashing Brazil 6–0), while opposite him sat an elderly gentleman busily doing the crossword in his copy of the free *Metro* newspaper. Sitting next to the latter was a woman in her mid-30s, sporting a pair of stars-and-stripes earrings, Diesel wristwatch and Coco Chanel handbag, and looking at an ad for Moscow's TsUM department store in the latest issue of Russian *Vogue*. While I had witnessed scenes such as this many times before in the previous few years, the afternoon and evening spent in Gorky Park was a completely new experience for me. The park had undergone a complete transformation since the last time I had visited, in the autumn of 1986. Back then, I had sat and watched a solitary accordionist perform a free concert to a dozen or so Muscovites who looked as downcast as the weather. Today, at a rock festival ironically called 'Subbotnik' (the name given to volunteer shifts of work in the USSR, so called because they often took place on a Saturday – 'subbota'), I wandered around the Samsung tent marvelling at the wonders of the new Galaxy S4 Zoom smartphone, before spending the evening standing behind rows of Russian teenagers filming an entire rock concert on their iPads.

What I saw that day in Moscow were so many fragments of the rich, variegated, perfectly recognisable and yet highly distinctive consumer culture that has emerged in Russia in the last twenty years or so. What struck me most, however, was not that culture itself, but rather the fact that it had attracted so little scholarly attention in the West, at least in the form of an academic monograph. Book-length studies have appeared on consumer culture in other emerging economies, such as India (Mazzarella 2003), Nepal (Liechty 2005) and China (Wang 2008; Zhiyan, Borgerson and Schroeder 2013). There has also been a steady rise of works on consumption under socialism, both in the USSR (Gronow 2003; Hessler 2004; Randall 2008; Hilton 2012; Chernyshova 2013) and elsewhere (Patterson 2011; Bren and Neuburger 2012). One notable exception is Jennifer Patico's (2008) engrossing study of consumption patterns among teachers in St Petersburg in the late 1990s. Patico's approach is however rooted firmly in social anthropology. Olga Gurova (2015), in a monograph on the 'consumer revolution' in the new Russia which appeared as we were putting the finishing touches to our own book, also examines consumption in the new Russia. She looks exclusively at the fashion sector, however. Like Patico, she adopts an ethnographic approach to examine how Russian consumers negotiate the 'revolution' in their everyday lives. The subject of this book is much broader, while our approach is fundamentally interdisciplinary, bringing together strands from marketing, critical theory and Russian cultural history.

Our main objective is to analyse the nature of the quite specific consumer culture that has emerged in Russia since the fall of the Soviet Union at the end of 1991. Before we proceed, we ought to say something here not just about our approach to the subject of consumer culture, but also about how we understand the term itself. This is extremely important, as one finds in the literature, alongside the term 'consumer culture' (Featherstone 1991; Slater 1997; Sassatelli 2007; Lury 2011), others, such as 'consuming cultures' (Brewer and Trentmann 2006), 'consumerist culture' (Bauman 2007), 'consumer society' (Baudrillard 1998; Smart 2010), and the 'world of consumption' (Fine 2002). Moreover, as Lury (2011: 5) points out, consumer culture is itself characterised by a fundamental heterogeneity, made up as it is of a rich diversity of 'things, processes, values, norms and practices'.

The first point to make is that we draw a clear distinction between 'consumer culture' on the one hand and 'consumer society' on the other. Put simply, a consumer society is a society in which the problem of mass production has been solved to such an extent that the issue is no longer how to produce enough of the things people need, but rather how to persuade them to purchase enough of what is produced (Bauman 2007). If it is a society which, as Clarke (2003: 23) puts it, 'both cultivates and thrives upon a sense that one can, ultimately, always buy oneself out of trouble', it is also one in which, in Giddens' famous formulation, 'we have no choice but to choose' (Giddens 1994: 75; on the emergence of a consumer *society* in post-Soviet Russia, see Althanns 2009). The term 'consumer culture', on the other hand, refers to the range of methods used to encourage consumers to 'choose', to purchase what is produced (Smart 2010: 23–24). At the heart of consumer culture then, are signs, designed to 'cultivate' consumers (Smart 2010), and indeed the act of consumption itself.[1] As Slater has put it: 'Consumer culture […] involves an aestheticization of commodities and their environment: advertising, packaging, shop display, point of sale material, product design etc.' (Slater 1997: 31). This process has accelerated to such an extent with the arrival of Web 2.0 technology that we have now definitively entered the era of what Schroeder has termed 'visual consumption', in which 'the real skill of marketing management and consumer research' has moved 'from the production of goods to the production of images' (Schroeder 2002: 5). Baudrillard's contention that we no longer live in an age of production, but rather one of signification, characterised by what he calls 'the conversion of economic exchange value into sign exchange value' (Baudrillard 1981: 113), is truer today than ever before.

The kind of consumer society of which Bauman, Clarke, Giddens, Smart and others speak has well and truly arrived in Russia, as the exponential growth in consumer credit over the last few years demonstrates (Weaver 2013; Trading Economics 2015). Before we turn to look at Russia, and some of the many different forms 'visual consumption' is taking there, we need to say more about one of the key themes in this book, namely identity. As Moran (2015) has pointed out, the question of identity is often raised in the literature on consumption (see for example Miller 1998b; Hackley 2001; Arnould and Thompson 2005; Sassatelli 2007; Lury 2011; Muthar 2013; Ruvio and Belk 2013; Schroeder 2015b). As she notes, there are essentially two schools of thought. On the one hand, there are those who argue that one's possessions play a fundamental role in creating one's sense of identity (Belk 1988; Giddens 1990; Bauman 2007; Sassatelli 2007).[2] As Sassatelli (2007) notes, this idea is rooted in the work of anthropologists Douglas and Isherwood (1996) and sociologist Pierre Bourdieu (1984), for whom goods structure social space, and my purchasing of those goods testifies to, and indeed reproduces, my relative location in that space. A number of writers have also used the work of Michel de Certeau (1984), and in particular his notion of 'bricolage', by which consumers reappropriate everyday objects, actively and indeed subversively transforming them as part of their own highly personal identity project. Arnould and Price (2000: 150–51) for example, discuss how mass-produced boots may, thanks to consumer agency, become what they call 'repositories of personal meanings' (see also McCracken 1988). On the other hand, there are those, writing from a Marxist perspective, who argue that marketing consists in constructing specific lifestyles, and then presenting certain products and services as a way of attaining them (Slater 1997; Fine 2006). In other words, consumption is itself marketed to the individual as a way – or rather *the* way – of achieving 'distinction' (Bourdieu 1984). For her part, Moran cogently argues that while both viewpoints may be justified, they nevertheless miss the crucial point that the concept of identity itself did not predate the emergence of consumption as a means of 'identity construction'. Rather, as a comparatively recent concept in Western thought, it in fact developed alongside consumption (Moran 2015: 127–28).

One of Moran's most significant contributions lies in her distinction between 'personal' identity on the one hand, and 'social' identity on the other (see Moran 2015: 42–46). While the former, she maintains, refers to that which makes me *different* from everybody else, the latter signifies those characteristics which I have *in common* with the other members of my social group(s). If we accept Moran's distinction (and it is a crucial condition), then we might rephrase her argument by saying that in a consumer society, consumer *culture* appeals to my sense of social identity in order to encourage me to construct my personal identity. In doing so, it presents me with the illusion – the 'simulacrum' (Baudrillard 1994) – of personal agency (Warde 2005). This is one of the main paradoxes of consumer culture, in contemporary Russia just as much as elsewhere.

The question of identity is central to our study of consumer culture in today's Russia. It is an important theme in all four chapters, although approached differently in each. In *A Theory of Shopping* (Miller 1998b), anthropologist Daniel Miller explores the relationship between shopping and sacrifice. In essence, he argues that in the very act of shopping, the consumer sacrifices her time, her money and ultimately herself up to the object of her devotional duty (this may be her partner, an infant, or indeed a purely idealised, non-existent 'other'; Miller 1998b: 149). In so doing, Miller argues, she constructs the other as the 'desiring subject' (Miller 1998b: 148) – indeed, for Miller, this is the true purpose of shopping. The point is, however, that if shopping is a way of constituting the other, and entering into a relationship with that other, then it follows that it must also be a means of constructing the other half of that relationship, namely the *self*. This argument is made, albeit in a rather different context, by Bauman, for whom the choices I make as shopper are part of my investment in my 'social membership' (Bauman 2007: 56). As many scholars working in a variety of disciplines have commented, however, the role shopping plays in identity construction (my 'social membership') is not just a function of what I buy or even for whom I buy it, but also *the place in which* I buy it, and indeed how that place is physically designed (Miller *et al.* 1998; Mansvelt 2005; Cairns 2010; McIntyre 2014; Wrigley and Lowe 2014). In other words, my social identity as consumer may very much be shaped by the different physical surroundings in which I shop (what Miles 2010 refers to as 'the architectures of consumption') – a point which follows on from Veblen's (1925) work on 'conspicuous consumption', and in particular his suggestion that social status is measured not just by what one consumes, but by the manner in which one consumes it (Moran 2015: 128–31). The ways in which the relationship between shopping and consumers' subjectivity may actually be articulated in contemporary Russia is one of the main themes in chapter one. We begin that chapter, however, by presenting an overview of the development of retailing in Russia between the late Imperial era and the end of the Soviet period. This enables us first and foremost to place post-Soviet retailing in a historical context. Such contextualisation is crucial to our argument, since it enables us to show the different ways in which retailing has been 're-enchanted' (Badot and Filser 2007) since the end of the USSR. Retailing – part of what Thompson (2000: 129) refers to as 'Capitalism's holy trinity' – is crucial to the 'cultivation' of the consumer, a process that Smart (2010) sees as an essential feature of any consumer society. As we shall see, the re-enchantment of retailing in post-socialist Russia involves not only the redesign of store space, but also the implosion of space and time (Ritzer 2010). As a result, stores themselves become invested with precisely the kind of 'symbolic meanings [and] mystical, transformative powers' that in Thompson's view are ascribed to the goods on sale in consumer society (Thompson 2000: 129). Those symbolic meanings are then, as we argue following Bitner (1992), offered to the consumer to be used as part of her own identity construction project.

Miller's (1998b) point about shopping as sacrifice reminds us that there is a performative aspect to identity construction (see also Featherstone 1991; Arnould and Price 2000; Elliott and Davies 2006). We mean 'performance' in the sense understood by Goffman, namely 'the way in which the individual in ordinary […] situations presents himself and his activity to others, [and] the ways in which he guides and controls the impression they form of him' (Goffman 1990: 9). Sassatelli, for her part, argues, first, that the performance in which shoppers often engage is essentially the negotiation of the tension between freedom and constraint (what she calls 'pleasure and social order': Sassatelli 2007: 166), and second, that this negotiation is often determined by the fundamentally gendered way in which consumers regard shopping. These two concepts – performativity and gender – are at the heart of chapter two, which looks at how masculinity has been 'performed' in advertising in Putin's Russia. This chapter is informed by two fundamental assumptions. First, advertising presents the consumer with an idealised view of himself (Berger 1972, Williamson 1978). Second, advertisements are intertextual by nature (Gibbons 2005; Gee 2013). In other words, they very often function like a palimpsest (Genette 1997), drawing on the stock of images, narratives and myths germane to the culture in which they are produced. A cultural–historical approach can, therefore, be a useful way of teasing out some of the meanings of a given advertisement (Schroeder 2002; 2005; 2012), although those meanings will always and inevitably be contingent (McFall 2004). Taking this as our starting-point, we discuss the re-emergence of the Soviet trope of hegemonic masculinity in recent Russian advertising, via the male body. For Baudrillard (1998), the body is, of course the 'finest consumer object'. Our own reason for focusing on the male body in advertising in Putin's Russia is rooted more in contemporary Russian politics. Since Putin came to power at the very end of 1999, he has consistently per-formed masculinity in a way which has not just sexualised Russian politics (Sperling 2015), but has also put the question of what it means to be a man at the heart of his quest to assert his own particular notion of Russianness. The at times symbiotic relationship between two forms of social identity, namely gender and ethnicity, that has emerged in Russian public discourse is as apparent in advertising as in other areas of the country's popular culture. Indeed, given the general, and indeed increasing, politicisation of consumer culture in post-socialist Russia, the fact that Putin's highly gendered political agenda has found its way into advertising should come as no surprise (see for example Cassiday and Johnson 2013). What is especially noteworthy, however, is the contrast between the figure of the 'super-hero' as seen both in Putin's various publicity shots and in much mainstream Russian advertising during Putin's reign, and the way in which Putin is himself represented in much political advertising. This is especially true of Putin's electoral campaign in 2012, with which we close chapter two.

One other area of contemporary Russian consumer culture in which the politics of national identity are played out is packaging. This, a particularly under-researched area of consumer culture, is the subject of chapter three. We begin by tracing the move in the literature away from the notion of 'packaging as marketing' through the concept of 'packaging as branding' to the idea of 'packaging as ideology' (Kravets 2012). Pointing out that packaging design has a long and rich tradition in Russia, we focus in this chapter on the representation of Moscow on the wrappers and boxes used in one product category in particular, chocolate. This is not, however, quite the narrow topic that at first glance it might appear to be. As Smirennyi (2007) demonstrates, Moscow has con-tinually appeared on Russian FMCG (fast-moving consumer goods) packaging ever since the end of the nineteenth century. That it has done so reflects the enduring political, cultural, social and economic importance of that city, despite the fact that for much of Russian history the country's capital has been located elsewhere. In twenty-first century Russia, Moscow appears to be searching for a new identity (Clowes 2011; Roberts 2014b; Walker 2015), an issue we explore ourselves by looking for example at the logos used in recent city branding initiatives. As we show, there is a stark contrast between the duality under-pinning the way the city has been presented publicly, and the representation of the city that appears so consistently and so prominently on chocolate packaging. Discussing the extent to which these images of old, pre-Soviet Moscow can be said to appeal to consumers' nostalgia, or patriotism, we conclude by suggesting that their primary function is to 'objectify' (Miller 1987) social relations between Russian consumers themselves.

With its conceptual roots firmly in cultural studies, and indeed cultural theory, our analysis has much in common with the heterogeneous branch of marketing scholarship known as Consumer Culture Theory ('CCT'), the 'family of theore-tical perspectives that address the dynamic relationship between consumer actions, the marketplace, and cultural meanings' (Arnould and Thompson 2005: 868; see also Sherry Jnr and Fischer 2007; Belk, Price and Peñaloza 2014; Schouten, Martin and Belk 2014). Many of the assumptions of CCT inform our own work – not least the idea that consumption contexts should be studied not only for themselves, but also for what they tell us about existing theoretical models. At the same time, however, our study of post-socialist Russia focuses far more on the marketplace, and the cultural meaning circulating within it, than on consumer (re)actions to those meanings. Absent from our first three chapters, Russian consumers nevertheless make their voice heard in the fourth and final chapter. In this chapter we move from the materiality of packaging to the immateriality of social media. The recent proliferation of the Internet, and in particular the arrival of Web 2.0 technology, has given consumers new opportunities to express their identity – or rather a multiple, shifting plurality of identit*ies* (Schau and Gilly 2003; Belk 2013; Wallace, Buil, de Chernatony and Hogan 2014; Kozinets 2015). One of the ways in which social media contributes towards consumers' identity projects is by providing them access to 'brand communities' (Muñiz Jnr and O'Guinn 2001; Schau, Muñiz and Arnould 2009), in Russia as elsewhere. This is particularly evident in the first of the two cases we examine in this chapter, that of AB-InBev's 'Siberian Crown' beer. Using concepts drawn from Appadurai (1996) and Anderson (2006), we show how this brand's Facebook page constructs a 'grand narrative' (Lyotard 1984) around the myth of the Great Russian Past, and invites consumers to write themselves (literally) into that narrative (Giddens 1991). The second brand we look at in this chapter, Levi's, functions rather differently. Representing a particularly interesting example of the challenges facing 'iconic' (Holt 2004) US brands abroad, Levi's functions effectively as an 'ideoscape' (Appadurai 1996; Askegaard 2006), carnivalising the Russian blogosphere by erasing the ontological distinction between the brand and its customers in an attempt to portray itself as the very embodiment of global democracy. In this sense, it represents the latest – perhaps the ultimate – stage in the development of 'postmodern' branding that for Holt (2002) began with the counter-culture revolution in the US in the 1960s. Representing what one might call the 'final frontier' for branding, Levi's is a fitting way to end our analysis of consumer culture in the new Russia.

Our last chapter in particular lends weight to Lury's (2011) point about the increasing visibility of brands in consumer culture. The trope of the brand is a constant thread in the book. Indeed, one of our secondary aims is to contribute to contemporary debates on the nature of brands (and branding) in a general sense. A major shift has occurred in marketing as an academic discipline over the last twenty-five years or so – a shift that has crystallised around approaches to the question, 'what is a brand?' This fundamental change, epitomised by a radical move away from Kotler's original emphasis on marketing's '4 "P"'s' (Kotler and Armstrong 2015), has been influenced by work in related disciplines such as cultural theory, anthropology and semiotics (see for example McCracken 1988; 2005; Brown 1995; 1998; Arvidsson 2006; Schroeder and Salzer-Mörling 2006; Merz, He and Vargo 2009; Manning 2010). One of the most prolific, and influential, writers on brands today is Jonathan Schroeder. Pointing out that branding in emerging economies such as post-Soviet Russia is one of the 'central issues' in contemporary research on brands (Schroeder 2015a: 4), he notes that there are currently four different perspectives on brands in the literature (for a useful short history of thinking on brands, see also Bengtsson and Ostberg 2008). These perspectives are (in the order in which he lists them): cultural, corporate, consumer and critical. The cultural perspective considers brands as part of the broader social, cultural and historical context, rather than merely a management tool. The corporate perspective, which according to Schroeder still dominates the branding literature, emphasises issues such as brand equity, brand identity and brand valuation. The consumer perspective focuses on the role played by brands in the everyday lives of consumers, while the critical perspective reveals 'how brands function as ethical, ideological, and political objects, beyond their strategic roles' (Schroeder 2015a: 7). Schroeder's own approach to branding is symptomatic of the broader shift in the branding literature from a focus on 'brand identity', seen as a reflection of the organisation's strategic concerns (Kapferer 2012), to a preoccupation with 'brand culture'. The latter is defined by Schroeder himself as 'the cultural codes of brands – history, images, myths, art, theatre – that influence brand meaning and value in the marketplace' (Schroeder 2009: 124) Schroeder's call to explore the cultural and ideological aspects of brands (see also Eckhardt 2015) is particularly germane to post-socialist Russia, where consumer culture is increasingly politicised, as we shall see.

Before we conclude, we need to make it clear that our aim is not to produce an exhaustive account of consumer culture in post-socialist Russia. Such an account would stretch to several volumes. While preferring depth of analysis over breadth, we have nevertheless sought to include a wide variety of industrial sectors and brands, both Russian and foreign. Since we discuss very different aspects of Russian consumer culture, from sex shops to electoral campaigns, chocolate boxes to football supporters' video selfies, our methodology is inevitably interdisciplinary. Our visual analysis method is based first and foremost on the work of semiotician C.S. Peirce (1931–58). In Peirce's oft-quoted definition, a signs stands for something to someone in some capacity (either iconically, indexically or symbolically). Of course for Peirce, as Manning (2012: 11) reminds us, signs 'assert nothing' in and of themselves. Rather, how we interpret them will depend on two things. First, there is our 'semiotic ideology', the term Keane (2003: 419) uses to describe 'our basic assumptions about what signs are and how they function in the world'. Second, there is the sign itself. Here we need to mention two other theorists of the sign, Yury Lotman and Roland Barthes. Images that draw on what Lotman (2001: 125) calls a culture's 'semiosphere' (i.e. 'the whole semiotic space of the culture in question') may generate myth thanks to (second-order) connotation (Barthes 1973). Thus, the Senegalese infantryman on the front cover of *Paris Match* points iconically towards France's colonial subjects, and symbolically towards French imperial power. To return to Peirce, this notion is fully consonant with his view that a sign can have more than one capacity, serve more than one function, at the same time. It can, to be more precise, be both an icon, mimetically representing something material (an object, or indeed a – colonial – subject), and a symbol, metaphorically standing for something immaterial (a concept). The Senegalese infantryman highlights one especially salient feature of Peirce's semiotics; as Keane (2005: 186) puts it, for Peirce 'signs give rise to new signs, in an unending process of signification [which] entails sociability, struggle, historicity, and contingency.'

The new Russia is itself a site of struggle, an unending process of signification – as illustrated by the fate of the St George Ribbon, the highest military honour in tsarist Russia which had been banned by the Soviets but was rehabilitated by Yeltsin in the 1990s and has become under Putin as emblematic of Russia as the country's flag itself (see in particular chapter three). The struggle over the 'brand meaning' of Russia has given rise in recent years to a significant and multi-faceted rise in nationalist sentiment that has been well documented elsewhere (Laruelle 2009; Daucé, Laruelle, Le Huérou and Rousselet 2015). Brundny in particular notes that 'surveys consistently show the spread of illiberal, imperial, anti-market, and xenophobic notions of Russian identity in Russian society' (Brundny 2013: 139). This trend has increased in the last two years or so, as Russia has found itself more and more isolated from the West, politically, economically and culturally, in the wake of the Ukrainian crisis which at the time of writing (summer 2015) shows no signs of ending. It has led to the growing politicisation of everyday life in Russia today (Oushakine 2013, Sokolov 2014). It has also had an important impact on Russian consumer culture, to which we now turn.

Notes

1 Our understanding of 'consumption' is taken from Campbell (1995: 102), for whom it involves not merely the act of buying a commodity, but 'the selection, purchase, use, maintenance, repair and disposal of any product or service'.
2 For a critique of this view, see Warde (1994).

1 From Red Square to Nike Town

Re-enchanting the retail experience

Introduction: The curious tale of the giant steamer trunk in the night

In November 2013, Muscovites awoke to find a bizarre and unfamiliar structure, the size of a small block of flats, installed in the middle of Red Square. The object in question was a giant replica of a Louis Vuitton steamer trunk, designed to accommodate an exhibition tracing the French luxury brand's history. Both the exhibition and the trunk were the brainchild of managers at GUM, the department store lining one side of Red Square, who intended it to be part of the celebrations marking the store's 120th anniversary (Vuitton's GUM store currently extends over two floors). Historical items belonging to the Romanov family were to be among the exhibits of 'Soul of Travel', a show organised to raise funds for a children's charity run by Russian model Natal'ya Vodyanova, the girlfriend of Antoine Arnauld, son of LVMH's chairman, Bernard. Plans for the exhibition were quickly abandoned, however, and the Vuitton trunk dismantled, after a series of complaints. Muscovites and tourists alike objected to the fact that the structure blocked the view of iconic landmarks such as St Basil's Cathedral and the Kremlin. Some Russian MPs lambasted Vuitton for installing the trunk next to Lenin's mausoleum, thereby trivialising a 'sacred space'. One Duma deputy went so far as to accuse the firm of undermining the very foundations of the Russian state by 'deriding and mocking' Red Square. Not even the (rather incongruous) presence of the Russian flag running all the way down the sides of the trunk could prevent public figures such as media celebrity Maksim Vitorgan from describing it as a 'symbol of vulgarity'.[1]

The furore surrounding Vuitton's installation tells us much about contemporary Russia. For one thing, it reminds us of the ever-widening gulf between rich and poor in the country today. A report by investment bank Credit Suisse published just a month prior to the Vuitton controversy found that Russia had the highest rate of income inequality anywhere in the world, with 35% of household wealth in the hands of just 110 individuals (Credit Suisse 2013). It also highlights the fact that in post-socialist Russia, political considerations often have a significant impact on both the shape and the direction of consumer culture. It is true that this was also a feature of late

Imperial Russia (West 2011; Hilton 2012), and even of the USSR at certain key moments (Gronow 2003; Hessler 2004; Randall 2008; Chernyshova 2013). One might also add that it is by no means an exclusively Russian phenomenon; as Cohen (2003) and others have argued, ideological considerations were key to the emergence of mass consumption in post-War America (on post-War France, see Pulju 2011). Nevertheless, the politicisation of consumer culture (and its corollary, the commodification of political culture) has reached unprecedented levels under Putin's leadership (Kravets 2012; Goscilo 2013a; Roberts 2014a; Sperling 2015; on this process in China, see Zhao and Belk 2008). Vuitton's steamer trunk, and the controversy it sparked, is symptomatic of this process. The French brand's choice of Red Square is itself highly significant. To paraphrase Miles (2010), as under Stalin, so under Putin, Red Square has become the ultimate 'space for consumption' in contemporary Russia. In recent years, it has been the site of open-air equestrian shows, live opera performances, music festivals and – since November 2011 – Soviet-style military parades (Oushakine 2013). Whatever their differences, both these parades and Vuitton's ill-fated exhibition put on display the Great Russian Past, something Russians are currently being invited to consume without moderation on an almost daily basis.

As for Vuitton's over-size trunk itself, it can be read in a number of different ways. On the one hand, it points metonymically to the enduring popularity of luxury, and foreign luxury brands, in Russia today (Kulikova and Godart 2014). At the same time, it serves as a metaphor for the spectacular excess at the heart of contemporary Russian consumer culture. Indeed, Vuitton's installation is emblematic of the extent to which post-socialist Russia has transformed itself into Guy Debord's 'society of the spectacle'. This is a society in which 'the commodity [la merchandise] *completely takes over* social life [… and] is all we see' (Debord 1992: 39, author's italics, our translation). As spectacle, Vuitton's trunk may be viewed as an attempt to introduce the mythical and indeed the sacred into the mundane and profane arena of Muscovites' daily lives (Belk, Wallendorf and Sherry Jnr 1989). One could argue that the trunk re-enchants not just consumers' day-to-day existence, however, but also consumption itself, in the sense understood by Badot and Filser. As they put it: 'Re-enchantment of consumption can be defined as a set of practices initiated by both manufacturers and consumers to incorporate non-functional sources of values in goods and services, and turn them into hedonic, symbolic, and interpersonal value' (Badot and Filser 2007: 167). The trunk neatly encapsulates the three different 'sources of value' mentioned here; designed as an essentially hedonic experience, the trunk symbolises new Russia's break with the (increasingly distant) Communist past, while at the same time promoting interpersonal links between individual Russian consumers via an appeal to a shared heritage, namely the Romanov dynasty. In effect, these consumers are invited to consume this heritage, just like any other 'product'.

It is this 're-enchantment' of consumption in contemporary Russia, and more specifically the re-enchantment of retailing, that will be the focus of this chapter. However, before we look more closely at some of the many forms this re-enchantment has taken, we need to explain how we understand the concept itself. Essentially, it involves downplaying the mercantile, transactional nature of consumption, and focusing instead on the consumer's emotional experience. Holbrook and Hirschman (1982) were among the first to point out that consumption does not merely involve rational information processing in the search for goods or services. Instead, they argue, many consumers also look to indulge their creativity and feel positive emotions when out shopping. It is only, they maintain, by looking at this experiential aspect of consumption – shoppers' 'fantasies, feelings, and fun', as they put it – that researchers and indeed retailers themselves can reach an adequate understanding of consumer behaviour (Holbrook and Hirschman 1982: 139; see also Babin, Darden and Griffin 1994).[2]

This insistence on the need to focus on the more intangible aspects of consumption – the aesthetic, the ludic and the hedonic – nods implicitly to an earlier article by Kotler (1973), which foregrounded the importance of store atmospherics in the retail marketing mix. What is especially interesting, however, is that it coincided not so much with the rise of new retail experiences, as with the coming into fashion among cultural theorists of the concept of 'postmodernism' (see for example Jameson 1984 and Lyotard 1984).[3] While Holbrook and Hirschman do not refer explicitly to 'postmodernism', this concept was central to the article, inspired by their work, in which the notion of 're-enchanting consumption' first appeared, almost a decade and a half later. In that article, Firat and Venkatesh claimed that in the 'modern' era (which they suggest runs from the late sixteenth or early seventeenth century up to the present day), the consumer has been reduced to 'a reluctant participant in a rational economic system that affords no emotional, symbolic, or spiritual relief' (Firat and Venkatesh 1995: 240). Reminding us that the postmodern age is supposed to sound the death knell for all metanarratives, they continue: 'the postmodern quest is therefore to "reenchant human life" and to liberate the consumer from a repressive rational/ technological scheme' (Firat and Venkatesh 1995: 240). As this comment makes abundantly clear, re-enchanting consumption and re-enchanting life are for Firat and Venkatesh ultimately the same thing. Citing not just Holbrook and Hirschman, but also the work of Debord, and Baudrillard (1994) they maintain: 'as the consumption sector turns more and more toward the consumption of images, the society at large becomes more and more a society of spectacle' (Firat and Venkatesh 1995: 250). And, they argue, it is precisely by embracing the spectacular, the symbolic and the experiential aspects of consumption, that the consumer will become the producer of her own experience, and thereby of her own self/ves (see also Firat and Dholakia 1998; Kozinets *et al.* 2004). For Firat and Venkatesh this is where the 'liberatory' potential of postmodern consumption ultimately lies.

While some have criticised Firat and Venkatesh's narrative (see for example Holt 2002), their faith in the power of consumer agency has nevertheless found a significant echo among marketing academics and practitioners alike. As Carù and Cova have put it:

Since the 1960s and 1970s, consumption has progressively disengaged from its essentially utilitarian conception, one that was based on products' and services' use value. Consumption has become an activity that involves a production of meaning, as well as a field of symbolic exchanges. (Carù and Cova 2007: 4)

This notion of the consumer as 'producer' recalls de Certeau's (1984) claim that individuals continually re-appropriate objects in new and unintended ways, actively transforming their cultural meanings via a process of customisation (or 'bricolage') as part of their personal self-identity project (see also Miller 1987).[4] More recently, the relationship between the 'productive' consumer and the re-enchantment of consumption has been explored by George Ritzer (see for example Ritzer and Jurgenson 2010). Ritzer takes up Max Weber's point that modern society is driven by the move towards rationalisation, and as such is characterised by disenchantment (Weber 1978). More specifically, he describes the relentless drive for efficiency, predictability, calculability and control in today's, post-Fordist (Western) world. He takes McDonald's as the archetypical example of this process, which he labels 'McDonaldization' (Ritzer 1993). For Ritzer, McDonaldization has produced widespread disenchantment, since it leaves no room for the magical or the mysterious in consumption (Sassatelli 2007: 174–77). In response, stores, malls, and indeed many other forms of what Ritzer calls 'new means of consumption', such as casinos, cruise liners and even sports stadia, all attempt to re-enchant the consumer. They do this by various means, collectively described by Ritzer (2010: xiv) as 'spectacle and extravaganza through the use of simulations, implosion, and manipulations of time and space' (see also Lipovetsky 2006). In other words, in an increasingly wide variety of settings, the consumption experience is designed so as to give the consumer the impression of transcending time and space (Miles 2010: 177). However, these commercialised and pre-packaged 'simulations', the purpose of which is to create an almost religious sense of wonder for the consumer, are never enough, and ultimately leave the consumer continually dissatisfied with the show on offer in these 'cathedrals of consumption'. The result, Ritzer maintains, is an endless cycle of enchantment–disenchantment–re-enchantment (Thompson 2006).

A rather different view of the re-enchantment of consumption has been put forward by Badot and Filser (2007). Their approach is at once narrower than Ritzer's (since they focus on retailing), and deeper, since they maintain that re-enchantment does not necessarily involve the extraordinary or the spectacular (Badot and Filser 2007: 167–68). On the contrary, they suggest that it may be produced by quite 'ordinary' experiences, such as discovering special price promotions in a hard-discount store, or interacting socially with other shoppers (Badot and Filser 2007: 168). As part of their argument, they propose a typology of four re-enchantment strategies. These are organised along two axes, first, contingent/non-contingent, and second, street corner/conspicuous. This gives the following four strategies:

- Strategy 1: non-contingent and conspicuous
- Strategy 2: contingent and conspicuous
- Strategy 3: contingent and street corner
- Strategy 4: non-contingent and street corner

The second axis, street corner/conspicuous, is particularly noteworthy, as it runs from those strategies designed to produce a 'euphoric' experience more or less independently of the consumer's needs (as in the Mall of America in Minneapolis for example) – to those, 'rooted in the microevents constituting our daily lives' (Badot and Filser 2007: 170). The latter strategy may, Badot and Filser argue, be seen for example in Wal-Mart, whose stores are designed to reproduce the various stages of the life cycle, to romanticise popular culture, and to promote ordinary shoppers as 'local heroes' (Badot and Filser 2007: 172–73). Crucially, Badot and Filser do not share Ritzer's pessimism concerning the capacity of the consumer to be endlessly 'enchanted'. They focus (implicitly) on the liberal democracies of North America and Western Europe – as indeed do virtually all those who have written on the re-enchantment of consumption. Yet their point about the possibility of 'ordinary' re-enchantment, and their strategy typology, are particularly relevant to the development of retailing in post-socialist Russia.

It would of course be simplistic in the extreme to assume that Russia – and indeed the other former Soviet republics – have spent the last few years merely aping Western consumer culture wholesale (indeed, part of the interest of looking at Russia lies in exposing the limits of a set of theories developed in an almost exclusively Western context). As Sassatelli observes, 'each of these countries has come to confront global commodities, commercial processes and consumerist discourses in a particular moment and from a particular position, concocting its own culture of consumption' (Sassatelli 2007: 47). Post-socialist Russia in particular is characterised by what Mansvelt (2005: 52) refers to as a 'hybridity of forms, practices and constructions of consumption' that do not always conform to the 'standard framework' discussed in much of the literature. Nevertheless, Russia has a long, and well-documented history of trying to 'catch up with', and ultimately overtake the West economically, going back at least to Peter the Great (Kochan 1962; Hughes 1998). Nowhere has this desire to outplay the West at its own game been more evident in recent years than in the high streets, shopping malls and outlet villages of Moscow, St Petersburg, Yekaterinburg, Samara, Rostov-on-Don and countless other Russian cities. This is perhaps not surprising, since, as Twitchell (1999: 240) wryly observes, 'of all the freedoms demanded by Central [sic] Europe in the 1980s – freedom of individual speech, freedom of religion, freedom of assembly, freedom of the press – the most cauterizing was the freedom to shop.' Indeed, given the recent huge rise in consumer credit mentioned in our introduction, nowhere in Central and Eastern Europe does Twitchell's 'freedom to shop' appear to have been more coveted (and more enthusiastically exploited), than in Russia. To quote Kramer (2013a):

Russia has a flat 13 percent income tax rate. Most Russians own their homes, a legacy of post-Soviet privatizations, and so pay no mortgage or rent. Health care is socialized. Not surprisingly, then, Russians have become fanatical shoppers [spending] 60 percent of their pretax income on retail purchases.

It is to Russia, and the re-enchantment of retailing under way in that country since 1992, that we now turn.

Retailing in Russia, 1885–1991: From enchantment to disenchantment

The Vuitton steamer trunk with which we began was erected in 2013 to celebrate the 120th anniversary of GUM,[5] the department store which extends along one side of Red Square, directly opposite the Kremlin. GUM was not actually founded 120 years earlier in 1893, however. In that year, the 'Upper Trading Rows' – the building that eventually came to be known as GUM – reopened in Moscow. By the 1880s, the Rows had become a place of 'dirt, darkness, and general disrepair' (Hilton 2012: 37). As Hilton has observed, when they reopened in December 1893, they were intended to be 'a new kind of civic space where merchants could pursue an enlightened, ethical trade and residents, a civilized way of life' (Hilton 2012: 50). GUM was not the first Russian department store, however. This honour went to Muir and Merrilies, which opened in Moscow in 1885 (it is today one of Moscow's most chic stores, although it is still referred to by its Soviet name 'TsUM', which stands for 'Tsentralnyi Universalnyi Magazin', or 'Central Universal Store'). In the late nineteenth century, Muir and Merrilies closely resembled the numerous department stores that had begun to appear in North America and Western Europe ever since Aristide Boucicaut's Le Bon Marché had opened in Paris in 1852. Like its counterparts elsewhere (and indeed GUM), it saw its role not just as selling goods to the growing urban middle class, but also and most importantly as bringing enlightenment to society (Smith and Kelly 1998).[6]

If anything, this desire to ascribe a *mission salvatrice* to sites of consumption intensified during the Soviet period, and especially under Stalin. As Randall (2008: 1) notes: 'retail trade and consumption were heralded as not only central to the socialist revolution but also the stage upon which the limits of capitalism would be exposed'. As a result, a series of model shops were opened in the 1930s in cities throughout the country – many in the sumptuous buildings of pre-revolutionary stores (Hilton 2012). They were filled with a dizzying array of the latest Soviet consumer goods, alongside luxury items such as smoked fish, caviar and champagne (Gronow 2003; Hessler 2004). Standards of service too were raised to unprecedented levels, in a drive to encourage 'cultured' consumption (Randall 2008). A mail order service was even introduced in some stores in the 1950s (Goldman 1960: 14–15).

However, even the visit to Moscow in 1959 of Christian Dior, invited to show off his latest collection (Fitzpatrick 2012) could not hide the fact that consumption was by this time slipping rapidly down the Soviets' list of priorities. For Khrushchev, catching up with the West could only be achieved through massive investment in agriculture and heavy industry (Nove 1984). Manufacturing consumer goods, and creating an efficient distribution network for those goods, now came a poor second to producing tractors, tanks and space rockets, as French retail historian Étienne Thil once famously put it (Thil 2000: 254). As a result, black markets arose in every Soviet city (Ledeneva 1998: 87–92). Paradoxically, the obligation to overcome adversity in order to find what one was looking for had unforeseen consequences. As Verdery notes, in a comment relating to the Communist bloc as a whole but which is especially relevant to the USSR of the late socialist era:

> The arousal and frustration of consumer desire and East Europeans' consequent resistance to their regimes led them to build their social identities specifically *through consuming*. Acquiring consumption goods and objects conferred an identity that set one off from socialism. To acquire objects became a way of constituting your selfhood against a regime you despised. (Verdery 1992: 26)[7]

In the words of Masha Lipman (1999), the Soviet Union was by and large 'a consumer society without consumer goods' (quoted in Neidhart 2003: 123). The problem was not just the lack of items in the shops, however; as Chernyshova (2013) points out, the Brezhnev era actually witnessed a consumer boom in areas such as televisions and refrigerators. What made life especially difficult for consumers was more the shops themselves. Cramped and insalubrious, many stores in the late Soviet period were the antithesis of the 'dream worlds' of the 1930s and 1940s. Shopping in the Soviet Union, especially in the 1970s and 1980s when there were frequently shortages of even the most basic consumer goods, could be a very claustrophobic experience, since, as Neidhart points out, 'wherever scarce goods were available, the place was packed and people pushed and shoved' (Neidhart, 2003: 117–18).

As well as the shortages and the lack of space, one of the chief characteristics of Soviet shops was the abysmally poor levels of service. Harassed, generally underpaid and frequently ill-trained shop assistants were notoriously uncivil, while in the overwhelming majority of sectors, the concept of self-service was unknown.[8] This meant that even when items were available, the actual process of buying was often time consuming, and invariably stressful. Part of the problem was the way in which the purchasing system was organised. As Wilson and Bachkatov (1988: 30) noted at the very end of the Soviet era:

> A housewife can spend up to two hours a day shopping. This is partly because of shortages, partly because of a lack of sales staff, but also because of the rarity of self-service arrangements. In most shops it is necessary to queue three times: to inspect the goods, to buy a ticket for them, then to receive them at the counter. More time can be lost as the customer heading the queue examines every item for soundness. Since housewives seldom carry a list or stock up, shopping becomes an almost daily chore.

In 1985, barely months after becoming Communist Party General Secretary, Mikhail Gorbachev introduced his dual policy of glasnost ('openness') and perestroika ('[economic] reconstruction'). At the heart of the latter was the promise to fill the shops with consumer goods people would actually want to purchase (Wilson and Bachkatov 1988: 93). One of the problems was the store managers, who were often incompetent, since many had absolutely no experience, and owed their position to patronage. The 1986 'stores' trial', involving the top managers from a number of Moscow's 'model' shops such as GUM, uncovered all sorts of illegal practices, such as overcharging, tampering with the scales, or selling low-quality produce at high-quality prices (Wilson and Bachkatov 1988: 107–8). In the late 1980s, the situation began to change, as private shops slowly emerged on Soviet streets. In the state-owned stores, foreign goods such as Scotch whisky began to appear, although as the goods in question frequently came from the illegal personal stockpiles of government bureaucrats working in the import–export sector, one never quite knew what one would find – or indeed how much one would be expected to pay for it. In Moscow, the historic Arbat quarter became one of the main locations of this nascent consumer revolution. Alongside the street vendors hawking Russian dolls featuring the Soviet leaders from Lenin to Gorbachev, one could also find shops selling diamond bracelets and necklaces, although prices – over three hundred times the average monthly salary – proved prohibitive for most Muscovites (Barnett and Bielski 1998: 230). Throughout the country, huge open-air weekend markets began to appear in public parks and sports stadia, selling anything from locally made arts and crafts to imported leather jackets (the latter often cost the equivalent of ten months' salary: L'vov 2014).[9] For the average Soviet citizen, however, the Gorbachev years were most closely associated with severe restrictions on the sale of vodka, and the rationing of basic food items such as meat, flour and butter. In the words of one woman, a scientist from the Siberian city of Tomsk:

> When my children were born, in 1984 and 1988, it was at the very height of the shortages when you couldn't find even the most basic items in the shops. And I can remember all those terrible queues, when I had to wait for hours to buy food for my baby, all the while holding on to the hand of the other child, who was four at the time, because they always gave out more food if you had two children. And it was terrible when you went into a shop, and there was nothing but empty shelves with nothing but tins of sea-kale. Yes, it was really scary.[10]

The re-enchantment of retailing in post-Soviet Russia: Privatisation and the arrival of the pre-fabricated kiosk

On 25 December 1991, the Russian tricolour replaced the Soviet flag above the Kremlin, and Boris Yeltsin became de facto President of the new, post-Soviet Russia. Those hoping that the political revolution would make shopping less 'scary' for consumers were to be disappointed, however. On the contrary, as the new regime began to find its feet, one of the first things Russian shoppers noticed was hyperinflation. Between January and March 1992, prices on most items were freed. As a consequence, by the end of the year, they had risen by a factor of twenty-six (Goldman 2003: 186). As Christoph Neidhart (2003: 194–95) points out, the Russian consumer had to master very rapidly skills which she had never needed before, such as the ability to compare prices, and to negotiate directly with the seller. As Shevchenko (2002) has observed, her lived experience at this time was marked by what Bourdieu (1977) calls the 'hysteresis of habitus', a term used to describe a situation in which there is a significant gap between the socio-economic conditions an individual has learnt to negotiate, and the actual conditions with which she is faced on a daily basis (see also Patico 2008). Between January 1992 and October 1993, the average monthly inflation rate was 25% (Shleifer and Treisman 2000). To make matters worse, firms often went for months without paying their staff salaries. And when they did pay, it was frequently in the form of payment in kind.[11] As a result, when in 1992 the Yeltsin government gave each and every Russian citizen a voucher worth 10,000 roubles with which to buy shares in the newly privatised state companies, most of them immediately exchanged them for cash (frequently for a sum way below their face value; Blasi, Kroumova and Kruse 1997: 39–43).

Given this chaotic economic context, it is hardly surprising that the emergence of what we would recognise as a modern distribution system started very slowly. Indeed, to begin with, it appeared to many as if the decades-old black market system was merely being formalised. In 1991, the last year of Soviet power, vendors would appear on city streets, after the shops had closed, selling at inflated prices items usually obtained from connections in stores or factories. Goods for sale in this manner, often passing through several traders before reaching the streets, included vodka, Soviet champagne, sausages and flowers (Humphrey 2002). Then, from 1992, hordes of small traders began appearing on street corners, near railway stations or in the collective farm markets, displaying their merchandise – a handful of dried mushrooms, for example, or second-hand tea towels – on little camping tables. Soon, 'shuttle trading' emerged, with imports from as far afield as China being sold in bulk out of trucks or freight containers (Neidhart 2003: 191–93).

One of the first tangible signs of the new, post-Soviet consumer culture came in the form of the kiosks that began sprouting up on the streets of most major Russian cities as early as 1988. While street kiosks had existed under the Soviets, their number was limited, they usually sold only one type of item (theatre tickets, flowers or cigarettes for example), and they were all state-controlled.[12] The new kiosks – for the most part merely ramshackle aluminium booths – were very different indeed. Moreover, they could scarcely have been more emblematic of the consumer culture emerging in the new Russia. Like Vuitton's steamer trunk, they signified, both metonymically and metaphorically. First, they signalled the official legalisation of Western goods, since they sold such items as Italian shoes, French tights, Dutch liqueurs and American cigarettes – the very products that just a few years earlier would have marked one out as a danger to society (Yurchak 2005). Second, with their astonishingly eclectic range of goods – from washing powder to tampons, perfume to chewing gum, beer to underpants – piled high and in glorious disorder, they embodied the very chaos of the country's new capitalist regime. Third, since they were by nature so small, they exemplified the reorganisation of space in Russia, its atomisation and privatisation.[13] Fourth, since it was common knowledge that they were mostly controlled by the mafia (Varese 2001; Humphrey 2002: 48–49), they epitomised the authorised lawlessness of the country's nascent consumer culture. Fifth and finally, since many of them remained open through the night, they heralded the arrival of 24/7 shopping. They may have been dingy, and indeed filthy, and it may well be true that one never quite knew what one would find in them. Nevertheless, by offering Russians for the first time the opportunity to shop whenever they liked, and blurring the boundary between 'day' and 'night' as never before, they contributed towards the implosion of time (and indeed space) that Ritzer (2010: 137) places at the heart of the re-enchantment of consumption.

Of course, Ritzer himself finds nothing especially 'enchanting' about all-night shopping, or many other features of late modern consumer culture. As Sassatelli (2007: 175) reminds us, he is highly critical of that culture's 'dehumanising' effects. And he shares with Baudrillard a distrust of the kind of excessive abundance that these street kiosks represented. Such suspicion was generally not shared by Russian consumers themselves, however. Indeed, these structures proved so popular and sprang up so fast that soon there was not a street corner in any Russian city that did not have its own kiosk. As Varese (2001: 230) has pointed out, by April 1994 there were 16,000 in Moscow alone. They quickly spread throughout the country, stretching from St Petersburg in the extreme north west (Papadopoulos and Axenov 2006), via cities such as Perm, located 800 miles to the east of Moscow (Varese 2001: 85–92), to Siberia and the Russian Far East (Hudgins 1997). While many sprang up in isolation on street corners, it was not uncommon to find them clustered together to form makeshift markets around metro stations or in suburban residential areas, where they proved extremely popular. As Axenov, Brade and Bondarchuk note, in their study of the development of retailing in 1990s St Petersburg, kiosks and other mobile trading forms (such as lorries or pavement counters) became 'the main tool for the exploration of urban space by the retail trade and services during the first phase of transformation' (Axenov, Brade and Bondarchuk 2006: 75). By 1996, there were 26–29 kiosks per 10,000 inhabitants in the city's socialist-era residential areas, as against just eight to nine fixed space shops (Axenov, Brade and Bondarchuk 2006: 77).

For a variety of reasons – including their rapid numerical growth, their unsightly appearance, their unsanitary nature, their connections to criminal elements, the threat they posed to more organised, 'modern' distribution networks, and their owners' general ability to evade corporate tax – many populist local politicians have made a career out of trying to get rid of these kiosks. In

1994, Moscow mayor Yury Luzhkov famously declared that the 'age of the kiosk is over' (Varese 2001: 230). Here as elsewhere, however, it has proved impossible completely to eradicate these structures. At the same time, today's kiosks bear little resemblance to the ad hoc affairs of the early 1990s. They tend to be much more solidly built, and frequently sell one specific kind of good, such as newspapers and magazines, flowers, fruit and vegetables, or mobile phones. Foreign retailers such as French bakery chain Paul also use them. They are also much more tightly regulated, as a result of which their number has significantly decreased in recent years, at least at street level. Underground, however, the picture is very different. In cities such as Moscow and St Petersburg, the low-ceilinged, dimly lit underground walkways leading to metro stations are lined with tiny booths where one can buy anything from a hot dog to a suspender belt, a packet of cigarettes to a pair of tights, a USB stick to an alarm clock. Furthermore, a blow to many street kiosk owners was struck on 1 January 2013 in the shape of a federal law declaring beer an alcoholic beverage and completely banning its sale from kiosks, which at the time accounted for approximately 30% of all beer sales in Russia. While the ban on beer sales has not spelt the end for kiosks in Russian cities, many kiosk owners believe it would be a different matter altogether if they were also forbidden to sell cigarettes (Herszenhorn 2013). At the time of writing (summer 2015), Moscow city hall is putting further pressure on kiosk owners, discussing plans to 'rationalise' the newspaper kiosk sector in the city, which include raising the rate of tax they have to pay, and reducing the total numbers by up to 20% (Girin 2015).

While the authorities reluctantly tolerate these kiosks at best, they remain extremely popular with Russian consumers. On a visit to Moscow in the summer of 2013, I counted no less than three flower-shop kiosks, open 24/7, within 200 metres of my local metro station. Stores such as these bear out Badot and Filser's point that re-enchantment does not have to be 'spectacular'. Rather, it may be based around what they call 'the microevents constituting our daily lives', and emerge thanks to the particular creativity of the entrepreneur involved. The example they give of this kind of re-enchantment – which they refer to as 'non-contingent and street corner' – is the Parisian café, in which, as they put it 'the operator enacts the re-enchantment almost blindly [in a context] where there is no room for maneuver' (Badot and Filser 2007: 171–72). Our discussion of the emergence of kiosks – often located literally on 'street corners' – shows that Badot and Filser's point is just as relevant to emerging markets as it is to more mature consumer societies. Further evidence of this will be provided in our next section, on the development of the fast-food sector in the new Russia.

The politics of fast food in the new Russia: From Big Macs to pineapple milk shakes

One of the immediate attractions of the kiosks was that they tended to sell much sought-after foreign goods. Russian consumers' attitudes towards foreign goods and brands went through a number of 180 degree turns during the

1990s, however. Many of the Muscovites Humphrey interviewed in 1993 told her they would 'rather go without, or restrict their food to a few repetitive items, than buy foreign produce.' Something happened to alter attitudes towards foreign goods quite radically between the spring of 1993 and 1995, however. As Goldman (2003: 57) points out, by 1995, imports made up as much as 70% of the goods sold in some of Russia's largest cities. Even Russian firms sought to 'Westernise' themselves. When in 1992 entrepreneur David Yakobashvili and his associates founded Wimm-Bill-Dann, one of the country's most abidingly popular fruit juice and dairy product brands, they deliberately chose a name which would evoke the West (or more specifically the West London suburb of 'Wimbledon'). Domestic industry was given a boost how-ever in 1998, when the devaluation of the rouble and the subsequent financial crisis rendered foreign imports prohibitively expensive for Russian consumers, thereby making local produce that much more attractive (Supphellen and Gronhaug 2003). When Vladimir Putin, the then Prime Minister of the Russian Federation, declared in 1999, 'the 20-year old, down-to-earth dream of Soviet paradise – with sausage and freedom as its main symbols – is almost fulfilled now; we have plenty of both' (quoted in Oushakine 2000: 97–98), the sausage he was referring to was very definitely of the Russian variety.

In the fifteen or so years since Putin made that statement, there has been a steady influx, not only of foreign sausage but also of foreign retailers. One of the very first retail sectors to welcome foreign firms was fast food. The arrival of fast-food restaurants in Russia can actually be traced back to the very end of the Soviet era, to 31 January 1990, when McDonald's opened its first restaurant in downtown Moscow.[14] Its location, just off Moscow's Pushkin Square, a hundred metres or so from the statue of Russia's national poet and a rallying point for demonstrators of all political hues, was deeply emblematic of the new Russia. Since there was still officially a Cold War between the USSR and the USA, the restaurant was originally run by McDonald's *Canada* (rather than the US arm of the company). The head of McDonald's Canada, George Cohon, had spent twelve years trying to persuade the Kremlin to let the company enter the Soviet market, before finally succeeding in 1988. In that year, he formed a joint venture with Soviet company Glavobshchepit, the food service operator for the city of Moscow (Goldman 2003: 227).[15] Less than eighteen months later, the first store opened its doors. The brand was an instant success, serving over 30,000 customers on its first day, a world record at the time. With 28 cash registers and a seating capacity of around 700, it was the largest McDonald's in the world. In its early years, it was not unknown for Muscovites to hold wedding receptions there. Such enthusiasm was not confined to the customers, but was also shared by many of the company's employees. One worker, in an unconscious reference to Zola, spoke of the restaurant 'as if it were the cathedral in Chartres [...] a place to experience "celestial joy"' (quoted in Ritzer 2010: 7). In the early months and years of its existence, people regularly queued up for several hours in sub-zero temperatures, just to get their hands on a burger – despite the fact that at the time a Big Mac cost four roubles, making it more expensive than a monthly bus pass (Grozny 2010). McDonald's revolutionised consumption in Russia by compressing time and space as nobody had done before them.[16] Indeed, the restaurant proved so popular that when the second McDonald's opened, in 1993, the then Russian President Boris Yeltsin, desperate to share in the brand's success, and acutely aware of its metonymic value for the socio-economic changes sweeping the country, had himself photographed in front of the restaurant, waving one of the company's red and gold flags.

While McDonald's undoubtedly heralded a revolution in customer service in the country, it is not this that makes it such an important example of the re-enchantment of retailing in post-Soviet Russia, however. Rather, it is the way in which, as Caldwell (2004) notes, Russians have 'domesticated' McDonald's, blurring – 'imploding', as Ritzer (2010) might put it – the distinction between the local and the foreign in ways that have muddied the waters in the debates about global business (on McDonald's and globalisation, see for example Mansvelt 2005: 49–52, Sassatelli 2007: 174–82, and Smart 2010: 120–22). As Caldwell puts it, in a comment on consumers in the Russian capital but which could refer to anywhere else in the country:

> Muscovites have incorporated McDonald's into the more intimate and sentimental spaces of their personal lives: family celebrations, cuisine and discourses about what it means to be Russian today. In so doing, Muscovites have drawn McDonald's into the very processes by which local cultural forms are generated, authenticated and made meaningful. It is by passing through this process of domestication that McDonald's has become localized. (Caldwell 2004: 6)

As Caldwell observes, in an attempt to attract new customers, McDonald's positioned itself from the outset as a 'local' brand, to an extent rarely seen anywhere else in the world. First, it stressed not its novelty or its foreignness, but what Caldwell (2004: 12) calls 'its very ordinariness'. Indeed, it speaks volumes about the appalling state of customer service in the USSR in 1990, that simply cultivating an image of what Caldwell (2004: 12) calls 'familiarity, responsiveness and accessibility' – to which she might have added 'providing clean toilets' – was enough to spark a consumer revolution.[17] Second, mindful of the fact that Russian shoppers set great store by the cultural heritage and ethnic origins of food producers and their products (Caldwell 2004: 7), it began actively surfing the 'Buy Russian' campaign of the late 1990s. In particular, the company emphasised the local origins of their produce (it opened a meat-processing factory, dairy and bakery, just outside Moscow).[18] In the summer of 2002, it commissioned a series of posters to remind customers that the company was 'Our McDonald's' ('Nash Makdonalds').[19] To quote Caldwell, 'this move enabled McDonald's to position itself within the parameters of the imagined – and, more importantly, *trusted* – collectivity to which its Muscovite customers belonged' (Caldwell 2004: 14).

Debates about the 'McDonaldization' of local consumer cultures rage on (Ritzer 1999; Mansvelt 2005; Sassatelli 2007; Smart 2010). In the case of

Russia, the brand appears to have been so successful in blurring the boundaries between the 'local' and the 'foreign' that it has prompted many Russians to revise their view of what exactly constitutes 'Russian' food. When, for example, in the summer of 2012, Russia's chief sanitary officer and head of consumer protection, Gennday Onishchenko, began recommending people stop eating hamburgers, as they were 'not our kind of food', his comments were derided by many Russian bloggers (Lally 2012). Despite – or perhaps because of – such criticism, McDonald's flagship restaurant on Moscow's Pushkin Square had the highest sales and served the most customers of any of the company's outlets anywhere in the world in 2012. In 2013, McDonald's had 42% of the total Russian fast-food market by value (Euromonitor 2014a), despite the arrival of Burger King in January 2010. In late summer 2014, however, the chain saw a dozen of its 451 Russian-based restaurants closed (some temporarily, others permanently) by the country's consumer watchdog Rospotrebnadzor, in what some commentators see as retaliation against Western sanctions following Russia's annexation of Crimea (Popov 2014; Russia Today 2014). Nevertheless, at the time of writing, the chain is planning to open 60 new outlets in Siberia (Popov 2014).

The rapid success of McDonald's in the 1990s encouraged other foreign fast-food retailers to enter the Russian market. One such was Pizza Hut, which opened two restaurants in the Soviet capital later in the same year (1990), followed in quick succession by Dunkin' Donuts and Baskin-Robbins.[20] Next came a host of home grown fast-food chains. There are now over 1,000 such outlets in Moscow alone, most of which are no more than glorified street kiosks, serving more than three million customers per month. One of the most successful is Stardog!s (sic), a company founded in Moscow in 1993, which sells hot dogs in over 400 outlets in 13 regions in Russia and Ukraine. Another is Kroshka Kartoshka, which first began trading in 1998, sells baked potatoes, and has outlets throughout Russia. According to Grozny (2010), it is 'the only example of a successful Russian fast-food chain'. Unfortunately, in the early twenty-first century, these stalls have fallen foul of the authorities in just the same way that the kiosks did in the late twentieth century. In November 2010, hundreds of these on-street restaurants, including forty of the 150 Stardog!s outlets alone, were forcibly closed down by the new Moscow mayor, Sergey Sobyanin. In a series of statements uncannily echoing those made by his predecessor, Yury Luzhkov, Sobyanin variously claimed that these kiosks caused traffic jams, were unsightly, or unsanitary, were too close to metro stations, or to criminal elements, were operating on expired permits, or blocked the view of particular historical monuments (Taranova 2010).

There was perhaps another, murkier, political agenda behind these closures, however. A high proportion of these kiosks were run, and staffed, by people who were originally from former Soviet republics such as Azerbaijan, and who had moved to Moscow with their entire families. Many of them were given just forty-eight hours to vacate kiosks they had been running for several years. As Taranova (2010) points out, the closures in Moscow in November 2010 were reported to have left 7,000 of these people out of work and effectively homeless. This incident is a perfect illustration of just how politicised the fast-food business has now become in Russia. Surely the best indication of this, however, is provided by the chain known as 'Russkoe Bistro'.

This chain of fast-food restaurants, perhaps the best-known 'domestic' by-product of McDonald's success, and nicknamed the 'Russian McDonald's' by many Russians themselves, opened in the country in the mid-1990s. The idea to open a fast-food chain with a distinctly Russian menu came personally from Luzhkov, who wanted to develop a home-grown firm to compete with McDonald's – thereby confirming the point made by Appadurai (1996: 32) that standardisation is inevitably complemented by heterogenisation, globalisation by localisation. In the words of Dorozhkin (1997), Russkoe Bistro was part of Luzhkov's grand 'Russian idea', which also included the restoration of the Cathedral of Christ the Saviour. The restaurant chain which emerged was controlled by his 'Mosrestoranservis', just as Pizza Hut had been, while Luzhkov even personally registered patents for two of the items on the menu (Grozny 2010).[21] The links with Moscow politics by no means ended there, however. It soon emerged that the restaurants were equipped and supplied by a company owned by the son of the man running the Consumer Affairs office in Moscow City Hall. The disposable tableware and cutlery was all provided by a company run by Luzhkov's wife, Elena Baturyna. Despite the fact that Russkoe Bistro was a publicly owned company, all the shares found their way into the hands of relatives of Moscow City employees. After the financial crisis of 1998, Luzhkov even insisted that all new shopping centres opening in Moscow reserve a space in the food court for Russkoe Bistro. Despite such staunch political support – the company was given credit at preferential rates by Moscow City Council, as well as tax breaks and prime city-centre locations – Russkoe Bistro found life very difficult after the financial crisis of 1998. It barely survived into the early years of the twenty-first century, and was sold at auction in 2005 (Goldstein 2011: 274), whereupon it re-emerged briefly in the shape of rough-and-ready kiosks on the streets of Moscow. Unfortunately, however, it went to the wall at the end of the decade, victim of the low quality of the food on offer, poor service, a flawed business model (in particular, its inability to achieve economies of scale owing to the small size of its outlets), and intense competition. Part of the problem is that, as overall levels of wealth have risen, Russkoe Bistro's target market has correspondingly dwindled. In today's Russia, relatively protected from the current global financial crisis thanks to its petrodollars (at least until now), Russkoe Bistro is merely an irrelevant anachronism, something left over from what already seems like a bygone age. As Goldstein (2011: 264) has argued: 'The new generation of affluent Russians has travelled more, has more money, and is not wedded to things Russian. Thus the trendiest places [...] announce their foreignness, and the real signs of the times are sushi and hookahs'. One should also mention the company's failure to achieve a clear brand positioning; as Dorozhkin (1997) wryly observes, from the outset not everything on the menu was Russian, not least the pineapple milk shakes.[22]

Russkoe Bistro's failure may be contrasted with the continuing success of 'Elki-Palki',[23] another domestic chain similarly positioned around the notion of 'traditional Russian food' – a positioning supported by a mise en scène designed to evoke a peasant's hut (a feature of many 'ethnic' restaurants in today's Russia, such as Ukrainian chain Taras Bul'ba: Caldwell 2009). As for McDonald's, its continued success further underlines the paradox – or rather the blind spot – at the heart of Ritzer's theory of the re-enchantment of consumption. On the one hand it lends support to his view that consumers appreciate predictability – or as Ritzer himself puts it 'they want to know that the "big Mac" they order today is going to be the one which they ate yesterday and will eat tomorrow' (1999: 84–85). At the same time, however, its success, and the success in Russia of other fast-food chains, raises the question of the importance for re-enchantment of the 'extravaganza' and the 'spectacle' by which Ritzer lays such store. Indeed, this point serves to underline the tension at the heart of Ritzer's theory of re-enchantment as 'cold and utilitarian fantasy'. In other words, the kind of rationalised service system underpinning fast food may be perceived by the consumer not as 'utilitarian' but rather as 'utopian', to paraphrase Badot and Filser (2007) – especially in relatively young emerging markets where the sector concerned (here, fast food) may be in a much earlier phase of development than in the kind of Western liberal democracy on which Ritzer focuses. This point will become even clearer in our next section.

Space invaders: The arrival of IKEA

However 'kitsch', restaurants such as Elki-Palki, Russkoe Bistro and Taras Bul'ba are nevertheless important for the way they represent that form of retail re-enchantment described by Badot and Filser as 'contingent and street corner' (strategy 3). In this form, the consumer's 'ordinary well-being' is encouraged via entertainment, escapism and aesthetics (Badot and Filser 2007: 171). This strategy is also employed by a very different kind of retailer, namely the furniture giant and 'category killer' IKEA. The Swedish retailer first established a presence in Russia in the late 1980s, when it set up an office in St Petersburg and began sourcing Russian-made furniture (Dahlgren 2010: 18).[24] The company opened its first Russian outlet, in the town of Khimki just north of Moscow, in March 2000. That same year, Rachel Bowlby was arguing that the retailer's stores, with their characteristic guided-shopper flow – what she called 'the over-stark contrast between movement and stoppage, dream and reality' – were nothing less than the embodiment of 'the staple metaphor of shopping as hellish confinement' (Bowlby 2000: 3). Few Russians appeared to see it that way, however. As the Moscow journalist Irina Sandomirskaya (2000) eloquently put it at the time, 'Ikea [sic] is a guest from the future. It has landed at the fringe of Moscow's ideological landscape like a spaceship from another world with a message of lightening public spaces, open personal relations, and a predictable healthy life' (quoted in Neidhart 2003: 221–22). Russian consumers proved especially receptive to this message; on the day of its opening, IKEA's first store welcomed over 37,000 visitors, and two weeks later the store had almost been emptied (Cockburn 2000).

At the time of writing, Russia is the company's fourth largest market by revenue, after Germany, the US and Sweden. IKEA recently announced it would invest 2bn€ as part of a five-year expansion plan (Malls.com 2014). IKEA's continuing success in Russia can be put down to a number of factors. Its logistics expertise, its vertical integration, its business model, its ability to leverage economies of scale – all these have enabled it to gain significant market share in whichever market it has entered. As far as Russia is concerned, Cockburn himself suggested that the key was IKEA's relatively low prices; as he pointed out, even in 2000, buying furniture in Russia often absorbed several months' salary. IKEA also had the advantage of entering the country at a time when Russian consumers were beginning to find credit easier to come by (Bush 2004). Like their Chinese counterparts, IKEA's Russian customers 'like to show they have money to spend', according to the company's Head of Design, Kristina Petersson-Lind (Belot 2013). As this last point suggests, the chain's appeal in Russia may be just as symbolic as it is economic. Writing three years after IKEA's arrival in Russia, Neidhart opined: 'By buying furniture from Ikea, people distance themselves from the masquerade of the bragging New Russians, from the governing elite, and not least from the Soviet past' (Neidhart 2003: 230).

One should of course be careful not to present the transition from socialism to post-socialism as an absolute break; as Patico and Caldwell (2002: 291) have argued, for Russian consumers 'the "exit from socialism" is far from unitary or complete'. Nevertheless, to return to Neidhart, part of the 'Soviet past' from which IKEA's customers sought to 'distance themselves' was the experience of visiting the country's furniture stores themselves. As Chernyshova (2013: 180) notes, if the quality of the goods on offer radically improved in the 1970s, obtaining decent furniture in the late socialist period still largely depended on one's personal connections – connections which often had to be spelt out to the store manager before he or she would admit to having a particular item in stock (see also Ledeneva 1998). Furthermore, the physical design of Soviet stores imposed rigid restrictions not just on customers' physical movement but also on their imagination. As one Russian customer put it, when interviewed by Cockburn, in a comment that contrasts starkly with Bowlby's reference to shopping in the store as 'hellish confinement': 'You can walk around here. You can see how you would design your house' (Cockburn 2000).

The kind of internal layout favoured by IKEA for its stores – where customers can not only 'walk around' unimpeded by shop assistants, but can also handle the merchandise and are even encouraged to try out the sofas and mattresses for themselves – had never been seen before in Russia. If McDonald's and the other fast-food chains essentially imploded time, IKEA collapsed space. In that sense, it revolutionised furniture shopping for Russians, and heralded more clearly than anything else hitherto the emergence of a new consumer culture in Russia. With its self-service ethos and theatricalised store design, IKEA was to

Moscow what Habitat had been to Chelsea's King's Road in 1964 (Beckett 2011). Indeed, the Swedish firm represented a further stage in the re-enchantment of retailing in post-socialist Russia. If fast-food restaurants had given Russians a glimpse of what Badot and Filser (2007) describe as 'contingent and street corner' re-enchantment, IKEA offered them for the first time the full-blown version, namely 'a shopping experience that is based on discovery, entertainment, escapism, and esthetic' (Badot and Filser 2007: 171). The Swedish retailer's success shows just how powerful this strategy can be, since in theory at least, the uniformisation on offer in IKEA's warehouse-cum-theme-parks in March 2000 went directly *against* the desire, so prevalent especially among young Soviets in the 1980s, to use furniture to distinguish themselves from their neighbours (Chernyshova 2013: 180).

'Pleasure domes with parking': The rise of the mall

IKEA's success in Russia has not only come from its self-service based business model, however. The company has also been able to leverage competitive advantage from the chain of shopping malls that it has opened in Russia. There are currently fourteen such centres, which collectively make up the 'Mega Mall' brand stretching from Moscow in the West to Novosibirsk in the East (1,745 miles and three time zones from the capital).[25] Moscow is the city with the highest number of such malls (it currently has three – plans for a fourth were scrapped after mayor Sobyanin decided in 2012 to limit the number of shopping malls in the city; Chesnokova 2012).[26] While these malls are built to a virtually identical format and floor plan, they are not all the same size. The trading area ranges from 43,000 to 182,000 m^2, while the total area can be anything from 92,000 to 330,000 m^2. The Mega Malls have up to 2 km of shop fronts. The largest such mall, at Belaya Dacha in Moscow, is the same size as the biggest US mall, the Mall of America (Kramer 2008). Another, the very first Mega to be opened, situated at Teplyi Stan in south-west Moscow, registered almost 60 million customers in 2007. This figure is twice as much as that of the previous most popular mall in Europe, Bluewater near London (Dahlgren 2010: 97), and 50% more than the number of annual visits at the Mall of America (Kramer 2013a). Russia's 14 Mega Malls attracted a total of 270 million visitors in 2014 (Malls.com 2014).

These retail parks are not just huge; they also offer a comprehensive range of retail formats and categories. Their brand positioning is very much that of a 'one-stop shopping complex'. Alongside the obligatory IKEA store, one can almost always find an Auchan hypermarket[27] and 'category killers' in DIY (the German OBI or the French Leroy Merlin), electronics (Russian retailers Tekhno-sila or M-video), and sports goods (home-grown Sport-master). There is usually a department store, such as the Finnish Stockmann or Debenhams, and a multiplex cinema. Smaller, specialised retailers cover a broad range of sectors, and usually include Accessorize, Mothercare, Hallmark, Benetton, Zara, Reebok, Sony and Marks & Spencer, as well as many Russian retailers, such as bookstore Bukberi and lingerie chain Palmetta. As well as the shopping, there is also a wide assortment of complementary services on offer. Customers can enjoy a meal at the sprawling food court, with its steel and glass canopy roof, complete with KFC, Pizza Hut and McDonald's, or skate on the indoor rink. Moreover, all this can be enjoyed at any time between 10am and 11pm, seven days a week (every Friday and Saturday, the cafes, restaurants, bowling alley, pool tables, cinema, mini-golf course and climbing wall at the largest Mega, at Belaya Dacha in Moscow, stay open until 5am).

In the West, as Kent, Warnaby and Kirby (2009) point out, malls have come to be regarded by many as the very epitome of soulless 'non-places', and provide the visitor with a wide array of opportunities for entertainment precisely in order to overcome this perception. Indeed, Bloch, Ridgway and Nelson (1991: 445) argue that the mall is 'the most common site for recreational or hedonic consumption' (see also Gottdiener 1995; Csaba and Askegaard 1999). A more balanced view might be that they seek to maximise their attractiveness by offering both 'thrift' and 'treat' (Bardhi and Arnould 2005). This is very much Mega Mall's strategy too. Very often, the 'treats' on offer extend beyond the cinema or the bowling alley to the numerous events the chain organises. In February 2010, for example, the participants in that year's Miss Russia contest gathered in the Belaya Dacha mall to take part in a demonstration of ice skating on the mall's rink, before spending time painting toys for patients in a children's hospital. Alongside such spectacles, Mega Mall also proposes other, more participatory events. As in certain themed brandstores, these events are designed primarily to encourage active, interpersonal experience connecting customers who might not otherwise meet (Borghini *et al.* 2009). Many are comparatively low key, such as the games of basketball or volleyball organised during the summer. A large number of these are designed specifically for children, such as talent shows, origami classes, and English lessons. Clearly, Mega Mall sets out to blur the distinction between various forms of consumption. This can be seen as an attempt to differentiate itself from the competition, to stand out from what Arnould (2005), Levy, Grewal, Peterson and Connolly (2005) and others refer to as the 'Big Middle', the market space in which the largest retailers compete in the long run. This is especially crucial in a country where as early as 2004 analysts were suggesting that shopping mall developers were merely 'cloning' existing models (L'vova, 2004).

By their lavish architectural design and social role,[28] the Mega Malls look back to the great department stores of the late nineteenth century, including Moscow's GUM and Muir and Merrilies (Smith and Kelly 1998). One could even argue that these vast, crystal palaces of light, play, fashion parades, beauty shows and the like constitute just the kind of 'aestheticized, consumer dream worlds' of which Walter Benjamin spoke in his treatise on Parisian shopping arcades (Benjamin 2002). Indeed, in some respects the way the post-Soviet consumer is invited to move freely around these spaces calls to mind Benjamin's archetypical *flâneur*, whose very existence is, to quote Clarke (2003: 87), 'a reaction to, and a mode of coping with, the otherwise disorienting, agoraphobic spaces of the city'. Yet while consumption spaces such as these may appear to be sites of freedom (freedom *from* labour, just as much as freedom *to* consume), the 'empowerment' they offer (Zukin and Maguire 2004) is nevertheless rigidly codified. In this respect, as in many others, Mega Mall bears the hallmark of its parent-company, IKEA, whose stores are also both vast and enclosed, and who also invest so heavily in theatricalisation (Dahlgren 2010). Indeed, if Belk and Bryce (1993) argue for a definition of the mall as theatrical spectacle, Mega Mall sometimes takes this idea to its literal limit; on the day in December 2004 when a Mega Mall opened in the north Moscow suburb of Khimki, after several lengthy delays due to Russian bureaucracy, the company even arranged for a real circus to show up, complete with orchestra, clowns and elephants (Dahlgren 2010: 179). We would contend, however, that the tension between freedom and rules, improvisation and order, self-expression and externally imposed direction, characteristic of the way the consumer must (learn to) negotiate these malls, transforms shopping itself into nothing less than a theatrical *performance* (Elam 1980: 49–97). Theatre, both literally and meta-phorically, occurs on a daily basis at the Mega Malls, with the shopper invited constantly to fluctuate between passive spectator and active participant (Sit and Birch 2014). This lends weight to Badot and Filser's (2007: 176) contention that 'the marketplace in general, and malls in particular, are [today] becoming a theater where consumers can create their own world and fantasize and deliver their parts in a play; retailers provide the staging, props, lighting, etc.' (see also Langrehr 1991: 428).

While Ritzer (2010) sees the mall as one of the most important types of the new cathedrals of consumption at which we worship in today's postmodern, post-theistic world (see also Zukin 2004),[29] a number of writers have suggested that the mall is in decline, in the face of stiff competition from, for example, non-mall-based category killers such as Toys"R"Us and Office Depot, the rise of e-commerce, growing homogenisation, and the presence of what Twitchell (1999: 269) euphemistically refers to as 'the young and the rowdy'; see Scharoun 2012).[30] While this may be true of some parts of the US for example (Glancey 2014), it is definitely not the case in post-socialist Russia. One might not necessarily wish to go quite so far as Kramer (2013a), for whom Russian malls are the places 'where the secrets of Western capitalism [are] finally peeled open and laid bare'. It is nevertheless true that by their size, their popularity, and their ubiquity, Russia's malls (of which the Mega Mall chain is merely the tip of the iceberg) are deeply symbolic of the country's new consumer culture (Makhrova and Molodikova 2007: 108). However, their popularity is not due to the fact that 'there simply is nowhere else to go', as Moss (2007) claims for many malls in the West. Rather it is because they are at the forefront of the re-enchantment of retailing in today's Russia. Promoting what Badot and Filser (2007) describe as 'ordinary well-being' through (active) discovery, entertain-ment and escapism, the shopping mall in Russia is still the kind of 'pleasure dome with parking' that the very first North American mall, Southdale Mall, was meant to be for the consumers of Minneapolis in 1956 (Miles 2010: 105).

Collectively, Russia's malls – often called in Russian 'Torgovo–razvlekatel'nye tsentry', or 'Shopping–entertainment centres' – represent one of the most dynamic areas of the country's economy.[31] At the end of 2014, Russia became Europe's largest shopping mall market, with some 17.7 million m² of floor-space, out of a total of 152.3 million (Cushman and Wakefield 2015). As Kramer (2013a) points out, many Russian malls have a hypermarket as an anchor, rather than a department store as in the US (or indeed the UK). This is not because, as Kramer claims, Russians often struggle to find groceries in their local neighbourhoods. Rather it is more likely to be part of a deliberate strategy to make Russian malls as attractive as possible, since a large food store in a mall tends to act as a 'locomotive', helping to maximise traffic. The presence of the hypermarket – frequently *alongside* a department store, another 'locomotive' – points to something else, too, something with which we began this section of our chapter. This is that the re-enchantment practised in many of Russia's malls corresponds to the third strategy in Badot and Filser's typology, namely 'contingent and street corner'. In this strategy, as they put it, the 'discovery, entertainment, escapism, and esthetic' is often 'hidden within a day-to-day environment that does not appear at first glance to be re-enchanted' (Badot and Filser 2007: 171).

The problem with a concept such as 'day-to-day environment' is, of course, its very subjectivity; your 'day-to-day environment' may be very different from mine. While Badot and Filser do not explain how they themselves understand the concept, in their classification it covers a range of (North American) retail contexts, from discount hypermarket chain Wal-Mart through wholesaler Costco to Canada's West Edmonton Mall. What these different contexts have in common is their 'invitation for the buyer to participate in a treasure hunt process', thereby promoting a sense of 'ordinary well-being' (Badot and Filser 2007: 171). Many malls in Russia fit this description, not just IKEA's Mega Mall chain. This is particularly true of the countless city centre malls that have sprung up all over the country over the last decade and a half, and which devote the overwhelming majority of their floorspace to retail, rather than entertainment facilities. These include Moscow's Gagarinskaya shopping centre (home to one of Russia's largest Auchan hypermarkets), the Tandem mall, opened in the Tatarstan capital Kazan in 2014, or the 80,000 m² 'Murmansk Mall' that began trading in the eponymous northern city on 30 April 2015.[32]

These are not the only kind of mall to have appeared in the new Russia, however. Another very different type is exemplified by 'Crocus City', one of the most extraordinarily extravagant shopping centres anywhere in Russia. This luxury mall, opened in 2001 and located in a north-western suburb of the Russian capital, covers 61,000 m².[33] On its corporate web site, it is described as a 'fully fledged metropolis, visited by 100,000 to 1 million people each day' (Crocus Group [n.d.]). Alongside 200 boutiques, cafés and restaurants, it has a 225-room Aquarius hotel, a 10,000 m² casino, a 6,000-seater concert hall, Crocus Hall, and even its very own yacht club. Like London's Canary Wharf, Crocus City has its very own purpose-built metro station, Myakinino, the first ever such station in Russia co-financed by a private company, according to the mall's web site (Crocus Expo [n.d.]). Adjacent to Crocus City is the Crocus Expo exhibition complex, which covers 549,000 m^2, and includes three pavilions, and 49 conference halls. It is here that the annual Moscow Motor Show is hosted, an event rapidly gaining popularity on the world circuit. Russia's Millionaire's Fair was also held there annually between 2005 and 2009.[34]

With its marble-lined aisles, its tropical plants and fountains, and its eccentric location, Crocus City illustrates supremely well the point made by Backes (1997: 12), that 'the mall, a beautifully imagined and uninhabitable city, satisfies those conflicting desires to build cities and escape them' (see also Jacobs 1986). This impression is enhanced by the very entrance to Crocus City, a rather incongruous looking portal made of pale stone. This is the kind of structure which might look more at home in the United Arab Emirates, or perhaps in Las Vegas. 'Vegas' is itself the name of what was Russia's biggest shopping mall when it opened in the summer of 2010. Like Crocus City, Vegas is also owned by the Crocus Group. Unlike Crocus City, however, this mall does have amusement rides. In fact, it houses a two-level, 5,000 m^2 park of extreme attractions called 'Happylon', which includes an ice rink, its own 5D theatre, an 18 m Ferris wheel and a 19 m drop tower – these last two located right underneath the mall's steel and glass roof (Vegas City, n.d.a, SkyscraperCity.com n.d.b). Vegas is home to more than 300 stores (including the 17,000 m^2 DIY and furniture store, Tvoi Dom) and fifty cafés and restaurants, as well as the nine-screen, 3D and 5D 'Luxor' cinema. It covers 4.15 million square feet (386,000 m^2), making it larger than the Mall of America, excluding the Nickelodeon Universe amusement park (Kramer 2013a). The shopping area at the Vegas mall is divided into lavishly decorated 'streets', with names such as 'Jewellers' Street' and 'Fashion Avenue'. Perhaps the most visually striking street is the one known as 'Ginza', the 130-m-long and 12-m-high 'night street', described on the mall's web site as 'the most luxurious shopping street in the world' (Vegas City n.d.b), complete with omnipresent neon lighting and miniature skyscrapers. Ginza (named after Tokyo's exclusive downtown shopping district) is home to the boutiques of luxury retailers such as Swarovski, Baldinini, VASSA and Co., and Enrico Marinelli. Ginza is much more than a mere shopping arcade, however. It also contains the Museum of Show Business, where one can marvel at the stage costumes of various local celebrities, such as ageing Soviet pop star Alla Pugacheva and camp 2007 Eurovision runner-up Verka Serdyuchka, and its very own 'Walk of Fame'. The latter, like its Hollywood namesake (and the Las Vegas 'Walk of Stars'), features five-pointed stars embedded in the pavement, and signed by celebrities such as Robert de Niro, Moby, John Cusack, Bryan Ferry, Gloria Gaynor and Carlos Santana. There is also a 'Graffiti Alley', featuring work by US rapper Xzibit, Ukrainian street art duo Interesni Kazki and even the American wrestling star known as The Miz. In its kitschy vision of consumerist excess, Vegas is perhaps the closest contemporary Russia has come to having its own theme park. In this respect, it represents one step – not to say several steps – up from the Mega Mall shopping centres. The various forms of leisure and entertainment organised at Vegas – indeed, the very existence of this particular 'shopping-entertainment centre' – bears out Ritzer's wry observation: 'The distinction between shopping and fun has completely imploded. The fun of shopping for goods and services is no longer enough but must be supplemented by other amusements' (Ritzer 2010: 121; on the role of leisure in the attraction of shopping centres, see also Howard 2007).

Vegas functions like a theme park in that it is very much designed as a replicated 'elsewhere' (on malls as 'simulated elsewheres', see for example Hopkins 1990). If, as Huxtable (1997: 2) notes, 'surrogate experience and surrogate environments have become the American way of life', then the Vegas mall suggests that a similar process has begun to grip post-socialist Russia. Its very name is evocative of a non-space that mimics a plethora of other spaces, with its ersatz pyramids and fake Arc de Triomphe (Begout 2003; see also Miles 2010: 17). Indeed, the Vegas mall might best be described as a non-space which alludes to another non-space (Ryan 2007), namely the 'real' Las Vegas, a city artificially constructed in the middle of the Nevada desert, an area that Miles (2010: 144) has described as 'the ultimate in themed space'. In doing so, it reminds us that, as Baudrillard (1996) notes, consumption is based not on objects themselves, but rather on signs, and the systematic manipulation of those signs. Indeed, like the French out-of-town hypermarkets of the 1960s, Vegas and malls like it in today's Russia take us into the heart of Baudrillard's 'hyper-real', in that they simulate what is in itself a simulation, thereby setting up a self-enclosed world of duplication and reduplication (Baudrillard 1994). In this sense, the Vegas mall constitutes a particularly interesting form of utopia.[35]

The idea of a mall as a utopian space was first discussed by Maclaran and Brown (2005). They argue, following Levitas (1990), and with more than a nod towards Firat and Venkatesh (1995), that the term 'utopia' designates not just an idyllic place, but also an emancipatory process, since it 'draws attention to the gap between what is and what could be' (Maclaran and Brown 2005: 312). This would certainly apply to the Vegas mall, with its wide range of escapist entertainments. At the same time, Maclaran and Brown's contention that utopian forms of retailing tend to appear in consumption-saturated societies, together with their focus on festival malls – marketplaces such as London's Covent Garden or Dublin's Powerscourt Townhouse Centre which typically occupy a refurbished building of acknowledged architectural merit, are tenanted largely by independent retailers and mix craft activities with designer goods – are far less relevant. To understand just how the Vegas mall might be seen as a 'utopian' space, we need to turn once again to Badot and Filser. A shopping mall, an amusement park, a cultural and sacred[36] site and a tourist location all rolled into one, the Vegas mall is perhaps the archetypical 'utopian island', in the sense understood by Badot and Filser – 'overcolored and funny "urban islands" in urban archipelagos [...] oriented to a prophylactic society of hedonic and spiritual values as well as leisure and friendliness, full of simulacra, where the ideas of fear and death will be absent' (Badot and Filser 2007: 177). This utopian aspect of the Vegas mall, combining as it does the two etymological strands of the word, namely a 'good place' ('outopia') and 'nowhere' ('eutopia'; see Maclaran and Brown 2005: 311), may help explain its popularity with Russian consumers: it currently welcomes 50,000 visitors in weekdays, and close to 80,000 at the weekend. Indeed, the concept has proved so successful that in the summer of 2014 the Crocus Group opened a new 'Vegas' mall in Moscow. This mall, 'Vegas Crocus City', is even larger than the first, and features scaled copies of New York's Rockefeller Centre and Times Square, together with a theatre complex called 'Vegas City Hall', designed to hold circus performances and concerts for children (Izakowski 2014).

Many of Russia's malls are visually stunning, few more so than Moscow's 'Avia Park'. With 377,000 m^2 of enclosed space, a 17-screen multiplex and a 70-foot tall aquarium of tropical fish rising up in the middle, 'Avia Park' is currently the largest mall in Europe (at the time of writing it is also largely empty of customers, a reflection of the country's current economic downturn: Kramer 2015). It should be pointed out, of course, that Russian malls are neither the biggest in the world, nor the most 'spectacular' in terms of the opportunities for entertainment they offer.[37] Their significance, we would argue, lies elsewhere. Partly it is in the speed with which they have arisen in the country, and spread to virtually every city, from St Petersburg in the north to Sochi in the south, from Moscow in the west to Vladivostok in the east (on the last of these cities, see KidsReview.ru [n.d.]). Another point to note is that many Russian malls have American-sounding names. This is very different from what one finds in more established markets such as the UK, where malls are frequently given bucolic names in order to suggest authenticity (Morrison 2012), or indeed other emerging markets, where malls tend to take the name of the place in which they are located (such as the 'South China Mall' or the 'Dubai Mall'). In Russia, alongside 'Vegas', one finds for example the 'Grand Canyon' and 'Atlantic City' malls (in St Petersburg), and the 'Greenwich' mall (named after New York's Greenwich Village), in the Urals city of Yekaterinburg. This practice does more than merely take the consumer 'elsewhere'; it has unquestionable political significance, assimilating as it does mass consumption with the adoption of an explicitly Western lifestyle. Other malls in post-socialist Russia have a very different kind of political resonance. One such is St Petersburg's Galeriya, with which we shall conclude this section.

Designed by British architects Chapman Taylor, the Galeriya mall was opened in November 2010, just a few hundred metres from Insurrection Square, which is situated at the end of the city's most famous thoroughfare, Nevsky Prospect, and is home to the city's main railway station, Moskovsky Vokzal ('Moscow Station'). Located on the site of a former block of flats, it covers over 19,000 m^2, making it St Petersburg's largest inner-city mall. Built at a cost of 0.5 billion dollars, it houses 285 stores over five storeys, together with what have now become standard features of Russian malls, namely a fitness club, swimming pool, cinema, bowling alley, billiard hall, and 'Happylon' children's fairground. There is also a 1,000 m^2, children's interactive science museum and discovery centre, 'Umnikum'. The inside is a model of modern, minimalist architecture, with its gently curving shopping galleries stretching far into the distance, reached by a network of overhead walkways, under a high, glass-ceilinged nave. The interior design is reminiscent of that of many recent inner-city Russian malls, such as the Moremall, opened in Sochi in October 2012, just over a year before the 2014 Winter Olympics. Outside, however, the picture is very different indeed.

Unlike the malls we have so far discussed, Galeriya is an inner-city complex close to an area of inestimable architectural and historical significance. Consequently, when the city authorities first saw the plans, they demanded the exterior be redesigned 'in the classical Petersburg style' (Fontanka 2012). This involved replacing the plate glass façade with stone of a similar colour to that of the nearby Moscow Station (SkyscraperCity.com [n.d.b]). The designers went much further than this, however. The mall has a slightly concave, neoclassical façade at an angle to the street on which it is situated. This façade contains an imposing row of square columns, at the top of which are bas-relief sheaves of corn. Positioned either side of the main entrance, on recessed platforms about four metres above the ground, are two statues, one of a maiden carrying a sheaf of corn, and the other a winged male figure carrying a quiver containing an arrow, representing 'Allegory' and 'Genius' respectively (Berezkin 2010). Each figure holds out a laurel wreath, as if about to place it on the head of a victorious athlete just out of the viewer's range of vision. Other sides of the building – the one that looks out over the main street on which the mall is located, and the other, facing the railway line leading to and from the Moscow Station – are designed in the same vein, except that this time they feature several statues of the goddess Flora and the god Hermes (the latter is the god of, among other things, trade). This neoclassical style is reminiscent of high Stalinism (on Stalinist Socialist Realist architecture as neoclassical, see Aman 1992, and Mumford 2009). Indeed, according to Yasinskaya (2012), the façade design recalls the kind of grand Soviet-style architecture to be found at the entrances to collective farm markets. To this extent, the Galeriya mall can be seen as a typical example of the 'Stalin Empire' architecture that has recently enjoyed a revival in many post-socialist Russian cities – a trend which has even extended to the kiosks in Moscow's underground stations (Shevchenko 2013). It is also resurrecting the neoclassical architecture that was typical of late Imperial Russian malls such as Odessa's 'Passazh' mall that opened in January 1900 (Hilton 2012: 66).[38]

The question is, of course: how precisely might Galeriya's neoclassical architecture be said to re-enchant retailing? To answer that question, we must first examine the connection between architecture, consumption and the consumer. While not wishing completely to overlook the planning context mentioned above, the point is that architectural structure is never innocent, but always signifies.[39] Moreover, that signification is dialogic, as architecture 'speaks' to the viewer, addressing her in a way which solicits a particular kind of response (Bakhtin 1981). As architectural historian Kim Dovey (2008: 12) has argued: 'architecture necessarily plays on our desires, the task is to understand rather than to eradicate its seductive capacities'. Writing on the role of architecture in consumer culture, Schroeder echoes this sentiment. As he puts it: 'architecture is more than the place that we shop, the building that we visit, or where we have our office – architecture expresses psychological, and cultural, and consumer values' (Schroeder 2002: 91). The expression of values of which Schroeder speaks is particularly intense in the case of neoclassical architecture of the kind embodied in the Galeriya mall. For Etlin (1991), such architecture signifies rationalism and order (see also Barshak 2011). And as Conway and Roenisch (1994: 16) have observed, classical forms such as those found in Ancient Rome and Greece 'visually reinforc[e] the power structure in any period' (quoted in Schroeder 2002: 100; on the ideological symbolism of neoclassical architecture in Mussolini's Italy, see Kirk 2005).

To return to Putin's Russia, Adams (2008) in particular has persuasively argued that the monumental architecture of certain recently built public buildings serves to define and legitimise state power. The classical forms on Galeriya's imposing exterior, we would suggest, fulfil a very similar function. They do so, moreover, in a way which inevitably impacts both upon consumers, and on how those consumers see themselves. To understand precisely how, we need to look more closely at some of the work that has been done on the ways in which shopping realms interact with shoppers. As McIntyre (2014) has shown, shopping realms – and in particular storefront design – contribute to local 'social capital' (Bourdieu 1984) – defined by Putnam (1995: 664–65) as 'social connections [... involving] features of social life – networks, norms, and trust – that enable participants to act together more effectively to pursue shared objectives.' In doing so, as McIntyre points out, they may help shape, in a literal sense as well as a metaphorical one, local social identities (see also Miller *et al.* 1998; Clarke 2003; Wrigley and Lowe 2014; O'Brien and Harris 2013). In particular, McIntyre suggests – and this is crucial to our own argument – storefronts have experiential importance for the consumer, and for the consumer's social identity, by the way in which they 'become part of an attractive visitor experience economy that offers [her] distinction in terms of socio-culturally valued judgement, taste and utility'. In other words, façade design can help to define both a place, and by extension those people who circulate within that place.

To see more clearly how Galeriya's façade may help to 'define' those people who circulate within and indeed around it, we need to introduce one more concept. This is Bitner's (1992) 'servicescape', a notion which covers the physical environment in which a service is provided, including ambiance, function and design. Bitner's contribution was to show how perceptions of that environment have an impact on consumers' emotions and beliefs (see Kent, Warnaby and Kirby 2009). In the case of Galeriya, by reflecting, and indeed perpetuating the 'architectural identity' (Miles 2010) of Russia's pre-Soviet capital city, the mall functions like many other thematised environments which, as Firat and Dholakia (1998: 97) argue, give consumers the chance to experiment with alternative selves and self-images. It 'hails' the consumer (Althusser 1969), 'seductively' inviting her (Dovey 2008) to co-create the physical shopping environment (Baker, Grewal and Parasuraman 1994), by investing it with local, symbolic (and often deeply political) meaning (Sherry Jnr 1998; Healey 2002; Julier 2005). More specifically, it visually constructs a particular form of Russian national identity, rooted in a mythical, reassuringly regimented (Stalinist) past, and invites the shopper to participate in that identity in the (Putinian) present. It is first and foremost in this, deeply political sense that Galeriya re-enchants retailing for today's Russian consumer. To borrow Balina and Dobrenko's (2011) expression, the Galeriya mall becomes a 'petrified utopia' in a very literal way.

Architecture's role in the 'experience economy' is not of course unique to Russia (Klingmann 2007). Neither is the desire to use buildings to reinforce political legitimacy and give expression to a particular vision of national identity (see for example Vale 2008). Nevertheless, Russian history is awash with examples of the politicisation of architectural form, not least during the Soviet era. As the architecture critic Rowan Moore has rather starkly observed, the marbled stations of the Moscow metro (inaugurated at the height of Stalin's Terror in the mid 1930s) did not merely 'speak' – they personified 'force with charm, the twinkling eyes with the mailed fist' (Moore, 2012: 82; see also Ryklin 2003). St Petersburg's Galeriya mall was, of course, designed by a private firm of British architects who were not working to an explicitly political agenda. Nevertheless, both this mall, and Moscow's Vegas, are undeniably attention-seeking symbols of economic, cultural and political regeneration. In this sense, they are 'iconic' buildings of the kind discussed by Toderian (2008) and others (see Miles 2010: 83–87). 'Iconic' buildings are, to quote Miles (2010: 85), 'product[s] of a world in which architecture is more about a physical statement than the realisation of functional intent'. Numerous recent examples can be found in other former Soviet republics, and indeed throughout the BRICS economies, as politicians and public planners alike seek to reassure citizens that revitalisation is in full swing (on Kazakhstan's capital Astana, see Koch 2010). The point Russia's new malls so eloquently reinforce is that, just like sports stadia, railway stations, business parks, concert halls, museums or cathedrals, for example, retail environments can also 'signify' (Brauer 2002; Wrigley and Lowe 2014). Moreover, that significance is very often ideological, so deeply enmeshed as these sites of (and *for*) consumption are in issues of political legitimacy and cultural identity (Scharoun 2012). As Hilton (2012: 2) has elegantly put it, 'stores, shops, retail arcades, and marketplaces [are] not simply sites where buying and selling [take] place, but also agents and mediums of political transformation, social organization, and cultural training.' Hilton's point is eloquently borne out by the last retail space which we shall examine in this chapter, Russia's Tochka-G sex shops.

The Russian sex shop market and the branding of Tochka-G

The sex shop industry has undergone fundamental change throughout the world in recent years. To quote an article that appeared in April 2011 in *The New York Times*:

For years, vibrators were bought quietly in sex shops, and later online, arriving in discreet unmarked packages. They were rarely discussed, other than perhaps during a late-night girl-talk session fueled by many glasses of pinot grigio. But now you can find them advertised on MTV and boldly displayed at Duane Reade, Walgreens and other mainstream drugstores, mere steps from the Bengay and Dr. Scholl's. (quoted in Hewson Group 2012a: 17)

In Russia, the industry has recently been subjected not only to the kind of vulgarisation discussed in *The New York Times* article, but also to a certain 'spectacularisation', as we shall see. Although it was possible to find literature of varying degrees of eroticism in some Soviet bookstores (to say nothing of what one could find on the black market), sex shops were completely banned in the USSR, as were pornographic magazines (Kon and Riordan 1997). Moreover, communal living in many Soviet cities helped produce a culture of taboo and embarrassment surrounding sex. As Boym (1994) notes, the lack of privacy in such places, and the concomitant fear of being discovered 'in the act', was a major source of sexual dysfunction in the Soviet era. Pornography, which had a long tradition in pre-Soviet Russia, returned to the country around 1987 (Goldschmidt 1999: 319). Often this was in the form of relatively hard-core newspapers such as the spuriously entitled *SPID-Info* (*AIDS-Info*; see Condee and Padunov 1995: 169; and Goldschmidt 1999: 323–24). By the mid-1990s, however, this had been largely replaced by something softer, if a good deal more widespread. The top-shelf magazine *Penthouse* first appeared in Russia in December 1992, although not yet as a monthly (Condee and Padunov 1995: 152–53, 169).

As far as sex shops are concerned, many of the first examples in post-socialist Russia were very different from the stereotypical image one might have in the West. As Goldschmidt (1999: 334) observes:

> Sex shops *à la russe* are in themselves a strange experience. The store Intim in Moscow is the hangout not of seedy-looking men in trenchcoats but of white-smocked doctors. It is located at a birthing hospital. The prospective customer must first discuss his or her problem with a licensed sex-opathologist. The doctor then 'prescribes' some sort of regimen for the patient (dildo, inflatable doll, lubricant, etc.), which the patient can have 'filled' at the store with the help of a specially trained pharmacist.

The industry has come a long way in Russia in the fifteen years or so since these words were written. Most importantly, it has become 'de-medicalised', as doctors and pharmacists have been replaced by trained sales staff, and the product range has considerably expanded. Russia is typical of the BRICS economies, which 'offer vast possibilities but [in which] there are inevitable questions about social change, cultural inhibitors and legal prohibition' (Hewson Group 2012a: 5). The number of sex shops in the major Russian cities has risen exponentially since the first opened there in 1992. In Moscow alone, rapid growth in the sector saw the number rise from five to 150 in the first decade of the twenty-first century (Schwirtz 2010). Moscow now hosts an annual sex shop convention, the X'Show. Ignorance about sexual matters remains in many areas of Russian society (Schwirtz 2010). Nevertheless, one million sex toys were sold in Russia alone in 2010 (Hewson Group 2012a: 33), and there is now a host of on-line sex shops in the country, such as mysextoys.ru (My Sex Toys [n.d.]).[40] The most striking example of this metamorphosis of the industry comes in the shape of the 'Tochka-G' ('G-Spot') chain, which at the time of writing has two stores, one in downtown Moscow (opened in the summer of 2011), and another on St Petersburg's Nevsky Prospect (opened in the autumn of 2012). The Moscow store covers 300 m^2, and has its very own 'Museum of Erotic Art'. This museum covers 800 m^2, contains 3,000 exhibits, and is open 24 hours a day, seven days a week. In Moscow, as in St Petersburg, customers also have the opportunity to lose themselves in an elaborate, and brightly coloured mirrored maze.[41]

Tochka-G may claim on its web site to be the largest sex museum anywhere in the world, but it is far from being the only such museum, of course. Sex museums can be found in various guises in cities such as Berlin, New York, Las Vegas, Paris, Amsterdam, Athens, Warsaw and Copenhagen. The first sex museum in Russia opened in St Petersburg in 2004, and even claims the pre-served penis of Rasputin among its exhibits.[42] Neither is Tochka-G the only consumption space in the world to blur the distinction between shop and museum/theme park. This strategy is a central pillar of the positioning of 'themed brandstores' such as Chicago's Nike Town (Peñaloza 1998) and New York's American Girl Place (Borghini *et al.* 2009). It is, however, one of the most remarkable, and successful brands in this sector, something which is largely down to the way it positions itself around the concept of 'spectacular consumption'.

The first thing to say about Tochka-G is that, blurring the distinction between shop, museum, and play space, it operates very much as a 'themed environment' as defined by Miles (2010: 147). Indeed, on its web site it describes the combined shop and museum space of its flagship store as nothing less than 'a Disneyland for adults in the heart of Moscow' (Tochka-G [n.d.]). At the core of the Tochka-G brand is the spectacularisation of consumption. Moreover, Tochka-G encourages customers to *actively* consume the spectacle on display. One example of this is the mirrored maze, which is the setting for late-night parties.[43] More importantly, consumers also offer *themselves* as spectacle. Among posts on the brand's Facebook page, one can find videos showing: consumers interacting with a male model, naked but for a fig leaf, during a show with live snakes; customers riding a giant, bucking phallus, rodeo-style; a lesbian 'wedding' ceremony in a makeshift registry office set up inside the store; and an invitation to participate in an in-house collective installation (this particular call, posted on 19 November 2013, was for 'naked men and women between 18 and 100').[44] The company's web site contains several photo galleries featuring consumers, such as one purporting to show 'The party of Mrs. Lotta "Auction of slaves"'.

It is precisely by becoming part of the show in these and many other ways that consumers engage with their own sense of identity – not only sexual, but also, we would argue, national. This sense of *national* (rather than sexual) identity is reinforced by the presence of kitschy allusions to Russian iconography, such as the BDSM Russian matryoshka dolls for sale, or the giant phallus decorated with the blue and white swirls of a Gzhel ceramic which stands next to the museum entrance.[45] There are also visual allusions to the Soviet Union, both in the shop (where one can purchase an Aeroflot stewardess or Communist-era Pioneer[46] uniform), and the museum (where one can marvel at Soviet-era condoms and watch a documentary on 'Sex in the USSR'). Above all, Russia and Russian identity was evoked by the central exhibit when the museum opened in Moscow. This item, a painting by St Petersburg artist Vera Donskaya-Khilko entitled 'Wrestlers', portrayed a naked Obama and Putin, facing each other as if about to do battle, the former endowed with one giant phallus, the latter with two (Elder 2011).

With its heavy reliance on experiential, fantasy-based marketing (Holbrook and Hirschman 1982), its emphasis on the ironic, the spectacular, the interactive and the ludic, Tochka-G certainly aims to 're-enchant' retailing by creating a sense of consumer agency via play (Firat and Venkatesh 1995; Kozinets *et al.* 2004). It does so, crucially, in ways which engage consumers' sense of identity, allowing them to customise 'alternative selves and self-images' (Firat and Dholakia 1998: 97) in a much more active sense than Galeriya's neoclassical façade. Combining the 'ordinary' and the 'extraordinary' (in highly original ways), the brand encourages customers actively to re-enchant the retail experience. In essence, Tochka-G's strategy corresponds to what Badot and Filser, in their four-part typology of re-enchanted consumption, describe as 'non-contingent and conspicuous'. As they put it (Badot and Filser 2007: 171), this form of re-enchantment is designed to promote the brand or the site more or less independently from consumers' needs or desires. They continue: 'the objective is to attract the highest number of visitors by the extraordinary originality of the commercial proposition (assortment, design, events, etc.) and to make them buy impulse [...] products as a result of the euphoria of the experience' (Badot and Filser 2007: 171). Blurring the distinction between a shop, a museum and a play space, Tochka-G also embodies the notion of 'edutainment', first used by Podesta and Addis (2007), meaning the convergence of learning and entertainment. To paraphrase McCracken (2005: 143), the museum's function is no longer to civilise the consumer through culture, but rather to provide 'new experiences, emotions and participations'. Moreover, by ensuring that consumers *share* these experiences, either in the 'real' world of the maze for example, or in the virtual space of its social media, Tochka-G contributes towards the recreation (in both senses of the word), of certain specific type(s) of 'consumer tribe' (Maffesoli 1996; Langer 2007). To paraphrase Cova, Kozinets and Shankar (2007: 4), it is almost as if Tochka-G's customers could not 'consume' without engaging in a (tribal) dance within Tochka-G itself – even if in this context, the 'dance' in question takes place atop a giant bucking phallus.

Conclusion

The narrative underpinning our discussion of the re-enchantment of retailing in post-socialist Russia has been both chronological and conceptual. To trace the development of the retail sector in Russia from the late 1980s to the mid-2010s is not just to run through the four categories of re-enchantment as discussed by Badot and Filser, but to do so *in reverse numerical order* (Badot and Filser themselves do not discuss the question of chronological order). In other words, with the kiosks and the fast-food chains we have strategy 4, 'non-contingent and street-corner', with IKEA and the Mega Malls (and indeed French hypermarket chain Auchan) we have strategy 3,[47] 'contingent and street corner', with Crocus City and other luxury malls we have strategy 2,[48] 'contingent and conspicuous' (in which 're-enchantment is fully contingent on the characteristics of the demand – which in this case is composed of the aristocratic class [...] and the middle class, which projects itself in upper-class lifestyles'; Badot and Filser 2007: 171), and finally with the 'Vegas' mall and Tochka-G we have strategy 1, 'non-contingent and conspicuous'.

Before we continue, we need perhaps to expand briefly on the reason why the re-enchantment on offer in Tochka-G falls into strategy 1. Badot and Filser include as an archetypical example of this strategy retailer Nike. As Peñaloza has argued elsewhere, Nike Town, the US sportswear manufacturer's original concept store/museum founded in 1990 in Portland, Oregon, promotes a form of 'spectacular' consumption designed to offer the subject – and especially although not exclusively the male subject – the opportunity to ease what she calls his 'existential anxiety about [his] place in the hegemonic order' (Peñaloza 1998: 437). At the risk of sounding reductivist, such anxiety is, we would argue, precisely what Russia in general and Russian men in particular have been experiencing ever since the loss of the Soviet empire (Thornhill 1999; Sperling 2015; Gillespie forthcoming). What better way, then, to defuse this anxiety than by offering the consumer the chance to perform the spectacle (Deighton 1992; Arnould 2007) of his ideal self – or rather to 'consume' (Bauman 2007) his multiple alternative selves – and then to offer those selves up to be consumed in turn? This is precisely what characterises Tochka-G, and what links it to Nike Town. Combining a retail space, a museum, a play area and a social media experience, the brand provides the consumer with endless opportunities for re-enchantment, by allowing him the freedom both to be seduced by the spectacular consumption the market has to offer, and to subvert the rules imposed by that market (Firat and Venkatesh 1995) – to both 'play along' and 'play around' (Grayson 1999; Kozinets *et al.* 2004). It is in this sense that the mode of re-enchantment proposed by Tochka-G can be described as 'non-contingent and conspicuous'.

Of course, the picture is not quite as simple as this. Most importantly, there is a certain chronological overlap between the different stages. Our discussion nevertheless suggests that there may be a diachronic element to Badot and Filser's model, especially in emerging markets. Our account also reveals the limitations of that model, in particular its failure to take account of the social, political and economic context of re-enchantment. As we saw, in a situation where everyday shopping has become 'scary', street corner kiosks, no matter how ramshackle their structure or how unpredictable the goods for sale, can be just as 'enchanting' as a Parisian café. And as our reading of St Petersburg's Galeriya mall shows, re-enchantment can be highly political, bound up as it may be with issues of personal, local and national identity. That particular case also suggests that the exterior of a store can play just as much a role in the re-enchantment of retailing as the interior – a point not discussed by Badot and Filser. Our findings nevertheless raise two important questions. First, is there any particular reason why the chronological narrative and conceptual evolution should run in parallel? And second, is the diachronic pattern of retail re-enchantment evident in Russia also seen in other emerging markets – indeed, could it even be used as an alternative way of defining such markets? The answer to the second question is the subject for another book. As for the first question, there may be a certain social and economic logic to the way these different forms of re-enchantment have followed each other since the late 1980s; political and economic instability favours the establishment of ad hoc distribution structures run by criminal elements, a situation which slowly gives way to an investment climate that encourages foreign retailers to offer tried-and-trusted formats such as the hypermarket and the mall, before economic prosperity prompts domestic brands to experiment with new and innovative formats. Clearly, however, this is a complex question, where there is much research still to be done.

In his discussion of themed consumption environments, Miles (2010: 151) comments: 'crucial here is the way in which such spaces offer the stability of a recognisable and often life-affirming identity in a world which is potentially characterised by the individual's experience of isolation and self-doubt'. Miles' remark is especially germane to a Russia which is still undergoing rapid change, and where questions of identity – national, sexual, etc. – remain extremely thorny (Clowes 2011; Bassin and Kelly 2012). And it is something which brand managers at Tochka-G in particular would do well to remember, as its sector – what one might call its 'theatre of operations' – becomes more crowded in Russia over the years to come. It is in Tochka-G, more than anywhere else in contemporary Russia's retail landscape, that shopping merges with performance, the real with the fake (Ritzer 2010). It is also in Tochka-G that the related issues of gender identity and performativity are most central to that of retailing. We propose now to turn our attention to advertising, a branch of consumer culture in which these two issues are inextricably intertwined.

Notes

1 For more details on the installation, see Krainova (2013).
2 The consumer's emotional experience may be shaped by the need for a sense of belonging and personal worth, related to ownership, care and sacrifice (Miller

1998b), or by the desire to shape her personal identity, via interaction with other shoppers in a shared environment (Schouten 1991; Arnould 2000; Wrigley and Lowe 2014; Mansvelt 2005; McIntyre 2014). For a review of the literature on the re-enchantment of retailing, see Antéblian, Filser and Roederer (2013).

3 One might add that there are important homologies between Holbrook and Hirschman's valorisation of the individual consumer's intangible, unstructured and unrepeatable experience on the one hand, and postmodernism's insistence on the fragmentary, decentred and unpredictable nature of subjectivity on the other (see Brown 1998: 44–49).

4 De Certeau and Miller are not alone; this notion has in fact become one of the cornerstones of postmodern marketing theory (Thompson 2000).

5 The acronym 'GUM' stands for 'Gosudarstvennyi Universal'nyi Magazin', or 'State Universal Store'.

6 On the socialising role of the department store see for example Williams (1982), Crossick and Jaumain (1999) and Whitaker (2006).

7 Shevchenko (2002) argues that in the early post-Soviet period, the ability to 'beat' the chaotic distribution system and obtain what one wanted was also a source of personal distinction.

8 Although, as Goldman (1960: 14) claims, self-service was first introduced in the USSR in late 1954, in a Leningrad food store, it was a feature of very few Soviet stores, especially outside the food sector. As Neidhart (2003: 195–96) points out, practically the only places in the USSR where shoppers were allowed to touch the goods were the foreign currency stores, the so-called 'beriozkas' selling souvenirs to tourists.

9 On the rise, and fall, of open-air markets in St Petersburg, see also Zhelnina (2009).

10 Personal interview, December 2011. Other interviewees in Tomsk claimed that it was common for Soviet shoppers in the late 1980s to 'borrow' children from friends, as the more children one appeared to have, the more food one was given.

11 One firm in Volgograd went so far as to pay its employees in sex toys (*The Economist* 1997).

12 One could also buy ice cream from mobile freezers, mineral water was available on tap from the 1960s from machines which provided a single glass tumbler designed for collective use, and kvas (a popular and highly refreshing low-alcohol drink made from fermented bread) was sold from small roadside trucks. As Papadopoulos and Axenov (2006) point out, kiosks were a central part of on-street trade in nineteenth century Russia.

13 As Neidhart notes: '[In 1992 p]eople began to erect private barriers and close doors. Their demand for privacy increased. In apartment buildings, neighbors got together to install metal grates or iron doors at the entrances to their corridors, barring the unwanted from even reaching their apartment doors. Thus, for the first time, people shared control over space' (Neidhart 2003: 144).

14 On the Soviets' experimentation with on-street hamburger stalls in the late 1930s see Gronow (2003).

15 For Cohon's own account of his experience of taking McDonald's to Russia, see Cohon (1997).

16 Ritzer suggests that it is precisely this ability that makes the new means of consumption such as fast-food restaurants so spectacular, or as he puts it rather ambivalently, 'so phantasmagoric' (Ritzer 2010: 129)

17 For a discussion of the insalubrious nature of Soviet-era canteens see Nérard (2015).

18 As Goldman recounts, a lack of high-quality contractors meant that for the first time anywhere in the world, McDonald's had to build its own food-processing plant. The facility, set up in the Moscow suburb of Solntsevo, cost the company US$40 million to complete (Goldman 2003: 227).

19 'Nash' (literally 'Our') is a very interesting concept in Russian food culture. As Caldwell points out, it is 'more exclusive than labels such as "domestic" or

"Russian" because it delineates subgroups within larger national or ethnic groups, it in fact supersedes concrete origins and identities because of its emphasis on trust and familiarity' (Caldwell 2004: 14).

20 Pizza Hut and Dunkin' Donuts have since withdrawn from the Russian market.

21 According to Dmitriev and Yurev (1997), Luzhkov financed Russkoe Bistro by selling 31% of the shares in McDonald's owned by the city of Moscow. On Russkoe Bistro, see also Beumers (2005: 333–34).

22 Russkoe Bistro was by no means the last episode in the politicisation of fast food in post-socialist Russia. Film director, outspoken Russian nationalist and staunch Putin ally Nikita Mikhalkov, together with his brother Andrei Mikhalkov-Konchalovsky, recently approached the Kremlin with a request for 971.8 million roubles (£12.5m) to help launch a 'Russian alternative to McDonald's' (Pechenkin 2015).

23 'Elki-palki', which in Russian literally means 'fir trees and sticks', is an idiomatic phrase that may be used to express surprise, dismay or pleasure, depending on the situation.

24 As head of IKEA Russia from 1998 to 2006, it was Dahlgren who oversaw the company's entry into the country.

25 On Mega Mall, see also Roberts (2013a).

26 In September 2014, however, IKEA once again announced plans to build a fourth Moscow Mega (Malls.com 2014).

27 Imploding both space and time, the 'everything-under-one-roof' concept introduced into Russia by Auchan and other hypermarket chains has also contributed to the re-enchantment of retailing in the country (Roberts 2005).

28 With so many child-oriented services and events, Mega Mall not only encourages families to go shopping together, but also helps create what Whitaker (2011: 7), in her discussion of department stores such as Le Printemps in Paris, calls 'a new culture of childhood'.

29 Miles (2010: 118) argues that malls are 'the primary physical form through which consumers enter the world of consumption'.

30 For an overview of recent academic literature on the shopping mall, see Miles (2010, chapter six).

31 The same could be said about the outlet villages which have begun to appear in the country (the first opened in a northern suburb of Moscow in August 2012: Smirnova 2012). By offering opportunities for the discovery of bargains, these complexes embody precisely the kind of 'contingent and street-corner' re-enchantment of which Badot and Filser speak.

32 On the Tandem shopping centre, see BusinessGazeta.ru (2014). On the 'Murmansk Mall', see ShopandMall.ru [n.d.].

33 Crocus City was one of the first of a series of luxury malls to be built in Russia. Another is the 80,000 m² Barvikha mall, opened in 2005 on the Rublevsko–Uspenskoe highway to the north of Moscow – known colloquially as the 'Rublevka', the most exclusive residential area in Russia and home to the country's rich and powerful, including Vladimir Putin (see Kulikova and Godart 2014: 57).

34 British photographer Martin Parr famously shot a series of pictures at Moscow's Millionaire's Fair in 2007: see Parr and Healey (2010).

35 On the 'real' city of Las Vegas as a degenerate form of utopia, see Jameson (1984).

36 Unlike Madrid's Xanadu mall, which as Badot and Filser (2007: 178–79) point out resembles a holy site thanks to its architectural design, the Vegas mall is reminiscent of a sacred shrine by the way in which it offers the costumes of iconic Russian and Ukrainian popular culture stars, contained in a row of glass cases, for contemplation by passing shoppers.

37 For a list of the twelve largest malls in the world in terms of gross leasable area, see Federigan (2014).

38 Galeriya's imposing façade suggests that the days when urban interventions in post-socialist St Petersburg were 'defiantly antimonumental' (Boym 2001: 167) are long gone.

39 On the complex social and cultural politics of urban planning in post-Soviet St Petersburg, see Yurchak (2011) and Dixon (2015).

40 Russia represents approximately 1% of the global sex toy market: Hewson Group (2012a).

41 While the Tochka-G sex shop can for the time being only be found in Moscow and St Petersburg, the company has recently opened versions of its mirrored maze in a range of Russian cities, including Yekaterinburg, Voronezh, Chelyabinsk, Arkhangelsk and Volgograd. In a neatly ironic twist, one such maze recently opened at VDNKh, the site of the former Soviet Park of Economic Achievements, in one of Moscow's northern suburbs: see Tochka-G [n.d.].

42 In February 2013 a second sex museum opened in the city, the 'MuseEros', which houses a branch of the leading Russian sex shop chain, 'Rozovy krolik' ('Pink Rabbit').

43 At its inception, the maze was reserved exclusively for gay men on Thursdays, lesbians on Fridays, and heterosexuals on Saturdays. The company has recently undertaken a major brand repositioning, however, and now targets much younger age groups, including children. Moreover, many photographs of children can be found on the web page dedicated to the maze: see Pikabolo [n.d.].

44 The brand's Facebook page also makes a 'spectacle' of many its opponents. For example, it recently posted a video of an in-store anti-porn demonstration by members of a Russian Orthodox group, a demonstration which forced the store to close temporarily. As this incident suggests, organising gay weddings, even fake ones, is dangerous in a country notorious for its widespread homophobia (in a trend reminiscent of the anti-jazz sentiment whipped up in the USSR in the 1950s, LGBT associations are increasingly being accused of taking part in foreign-led conspiracies to destroy Russia: Baer 2013a). Gay Pride marches are still banned in Moscow.

45 Decorated with distinctive blue and white floral motifs, Gzhel porcelain comes from the area around the eponymous village, going back to the fourteenth century.

46 The Pioneer movement was the children's organisation run by the Communist Party.

47 While the fact that the Mega Malls organise special events might appear to place them in Badot and Filser's strategy 1, the relative affordability of the experience, together with the standardised design of the malls themselves, puts them in strategy 3.

48 While Crocus City opened before the first Mega Mall, it opened after IKEA, and more importantly after such malls as 'Hunter's Row', an underground shopping centre inaugurated in 1997 alongside the Kremlin (Neidhart 2003; Goscilo 2011). On the development of malls in post-socialist Russia, see also Gurova (2015).

2 From Superman to the Invisible Man

Imagining the male body in contemporary Russian advertising

Introduction

A young woman, caught in mid-shot, stands darkly silhouetted against a brooding sky, her long robe billowing in the stiff breeze. As a soaring guitar solo begins, the camera angle suddenly shifts to reveal the upper half of her face, its features thrown into sharp relief by the picture's high-contrast monochrome. Eyes framed by strands of loose blonde hair gaze calmly up towards something off camera. We barely have time to look at her, however, before the image changes once again, to reveal the object of her gaze – a housing estate in an unidentified Russian suburb. This is not just any ordinary estate, however. There is something post-apocalyptic about the whole scene, in the dilapidated condition of the buildings, and the litter-strewn streets, not to mention the isolated man sitting aimlessly by the side of the road as anonymous individuals move silently past him, as if sleepwalking. The figure from the original shot now reappears, removing her coat and gently placing it around the shoulders of another young woman, sitting in a silent daze on a bench on a patch of wasteland, surrounded by all kinds of detritus. Next, as the solo guitar gives way to a soothing sequence of rising chords on an electronic keyboard, we see a young man step off a bus. He too is blond, and he too removes his coat, this time to smother a fire burning in a litterbin. There is something almost angelic about this strikingly beautiful youth, with his porcelain-white skin, his flowing locks, and beatific aura. This impression is generated not just by his extraordinary beauty, but also by the graceful, silent poise with which he moves, by the low camera angle from which he is filmed, and by the flock of white doves which fly symbolically up into the sky as he moves away from the bin, as if in recognition of the peace and harmony he brings. It is an aura that unites each of the main characters in this clip, almost as if they were benign visitors from another, very distant planet. It is certainly present in the sleek, blond creature who in the very next scene removes her jacket, using it to wrap up some fruit and a loaf of bread that have appeared as if by miracle, and which she hands to a rather bemused old woman, before gazing up enigmatically at the sky (perhaps she's thinking of the spaceship that brought them here and that even now is hovering just above the earth's atmosphere, waiting to take them back home once they've completed their mission?). A shimmering vision in luminescent white, she joins the other two 'visitors', as they begin to walk together in silent procession, seemingly heading towards a pre-arranged rendezvous spot. As they do so, they pass a middle-aged resident of the estate, sweating over the engine of what appears to be his broken-down Lada. Suddenly, as if from nowhere, another youth appears, just as stunningly beautiful as the other three. Exchanging nothing more than a silent, and rather cursory glance with the Lada owner, he removes his shirt and hands it to the man, who gratefully clutches at it and immediately uses it to wipe the grime and sweat from his face. The appearance of this fourth youth heralds the end of the film. This climactic dénouement comes in the three stages. First, a voice-over exhorts the viewer to 'give up your last shirt, and buy a new one in a "Savage" store'. Next, the camera focuses on this young man's face. If the three previous youths resembled angels, this individual, with his shoulder-length hair, piercing eyes, and three-day-old beard, is reminiscent of Christ himself. And finally, in the film's closing shot, he stands alone, his head and naked torso shot from a low angle and silhouetted against a sky in which the sun can now be seen to be piercing the once menacing clouds, as if presaging a bright new dawn. As he does so, he gazes up at, and moves slowly towards a banner suspended high above the pavement, on which one can read the following text: 'SAVAGE: New Collection'. This, it would appear, is where the ad's bright young things have been heading – nothing less than shopping heaven, courtesy of one of Russian's most dynamic new clothing brands.

This ad for the 2006 spring collection of Russian retailer Savage (a company founded in 2000, targeting the 25–35 age group) is remarkable for a number of reasons. First, it reveals a very different Russia, an urban landscape that diverges as radically as possible from the marble-lined malls described in chapter one. Second, with the slick editing, short shot length and high-end, pop-video production values, it demonstrates particularly clearly that Russian brands – and indeed Russian-based ad agencies – have found a way of embracing the visual grammar of Western-style advertising while at the same time producing something distinctively Russian. What is distinctively Russian about this ad – and this is the third point of note here – is not the setting itself however, but rather the way in which it blithely skirts around the not inconsiderable ethical issues involved in representing class; the ad in effect exploits the growing social divide in the new Russian consumer society, patronising the have-not's (most of whom are associated with the old, Soviet order) in order to appeal to the have's, the country's young, upwardly mobile urban professionals. Fourth, the ad raises questions about the representation of gender in advertising, most importantly in the final shot, with its aestheticisation – and indeed eroticisation – of the male body. Thanks both to that body itself, and to the way that body is filmed, the male subject – or more precisely the male *consuming* subject – emerges here as super-hero, gliding effortlessly through the world and bestowing peace and harmony on all those he meets. It is this 'heroic' representation of the male subject in contemporary Russian advertising, and the political subtext of that representation, which will be the subject of this chapter.

Masculinity in contemporary Russian culture

Russian society is currently undergoing a fundamental transformation. Historically, debates about societal change in Russia have gelled around questions of masculinity and masculine identity. As Evans Clements has cogently argued:

> Tsarist bureaucrats, Stalinist economic planners, intellectuals and social reformers from the eighteenth to the twentieth century understood that they could not change Russia unless and until they changed Russian men. Fundamental to this task was defining what men were and what they should become. (Evans Clements 2002: 12)

Evans Clements' observation is especially relevant to today's Russia, a country run by a man, Vladimir Putin, who has personally overseen a return to the deeply patriarchal values of earlier times (Goscilo 2013a).[1] In a process aptly described by Sperling (2015: 63) as the 'sexualization of politics', Putin has constantly sought to frame debates about what it means to be Russian with the question of what it means to be a (heterosexual) man (see also Cassiday and Johnson 2013). Borenstein (1999a) has argued that this conflation of masculinity and national identity began in the pages of Russian men's magazines in the 1990s. While this is undoubtedly the case, it has nevertheless gathered significant momentum since Putin was first elected President in March 2000, and especially since the introduction in January 2013 of legislation introducing a nationwide ban on homosexual 'propaganda' to minors (Sperling 2015: 73–74).[2] A number of Russian politicians have been very willing to collude in this process, as demonstrated by the homophobic criticism of 2014 Eurovision Song Contest winner, Austrian transgender Conchita Wurst. In a thinly veiled reference to the desire of many Ukrainians to see their country join the EU, Russia's Deputy Prime Minister Dmitry Rogozin tweeted, '"Eurovision" showed European integrators their Euro-prospect – a bearded girl'[3] (Huffington Post 2014; on homophobic discourse in the construction of national identity in contemporary Russia, see also Baer 2009; Healey 2010). Ol'ga Batalina, member of Putin's United Russia party and Deputy Chair of the Duma Committee on the Family, Women and Children, suggested that Wurst's victory highlighted the moral division between Europe and Russia (*Interfax* 2014).

As Lehman (2007) has observed, a central role in the social construction of masculinity is played by the body. This is because, as Butler (2007, 2011) argues, in her Foucauldian re-reading of Freud and Lacan, it is through the body, rather than through language, that the subject enters the Symbolic Order. It is onto the body and the body's 'contoured materiality' (Butler 2011: xxv) that gender is projected, and through the body that the subject's identity is ultimately 'performed'.[4] When it comes to Russia, the body occupies a central place in that country's culture (Costlow, Sandler and Vowles 1993), thanks in no small measure to the Russian Orthodox belief in the corporeal reality of the resurrection, not just of Christ on Easter Sunday, but of all the dead on Judgement Day (Merridale 2000). It is perhaps not surprising then that if, as Goscilo and Hashamova (2010) and Gillespie (forthcoming) have shown, male identity has come under increasing scrutiny in recent years in Russian visual and literary culture, in response to the perceived 'crisis' of post-Soviet Russian masculinity (Zdravomyslova and Temkina 2002), much of that scrutiny has centred on the male body (see also Larsen 2003; Borenstein 2007; Moss 2013; Ioffe and White 2014).

The body, and its 'spectacularisation', is central to Putin's personal myth, as Goscilo (2013c), Sperling (2015) and others have noted. As Sperling in particular has argued, Putin's physical, bodily brand of masculinity, which involves fishing bare-chested, shooting wild animals and unceremoniously throwing judo opponents, transforms him into a modern-day 'muzhik'. The very incarnation of the down-to-earth male Russian peasant, characterised by a rugged physicality and coarse language to match, the figure of the 'muzhik' has achieved positive valency in post-Soviet Russia. In particular, he is opposed to the rational, practical, cool-headed manager type seen as emblematic of Western-style mas- culinity (Sperling 2015: 36–38). As Sperling (2015: 36) observes, the 'muzhik' figure has found its way into a number of recent Russian advertisements, including those for certain national brands of beer (Morris 2007). While Morris is totally justified in analysing the representation of Russian national identity in these ads, he nevertheless overlooks what they have to say about Russian masculinity. This is all the more surprising given that, as Hirschman (2014: 237) notes, 'virtually all beer advertising targets men' (see also Tungate 2008). Indeed, as the 'Savage' example with which we began this chapter demonstrates, images of masculinity circulate just as much in advertising as in other branches of contemporary Russian visual culture. In many Russian ads, to paraphrase Butler (2007), the male body is very much a 'bod[y] that matter[s]'. This is because the way that body is represented not only reflects the predominant view in Russian society on what constitutes 'normal' masculine behaviour (White and Gillett 1994); it also helps disseminate, and thereby reinforce, that very view (Schroeder and Borgerson 1998; Schroeder and Zwick 2004). How, then, is the male body displayed in contemporary Russian advertising? Before we answer that question, we need to say something about the way the representation of masculinity has been approached in the advertising literature.

Masculinity in/and advertising

As Bourdieu (1998) has observed, in so many cultures and at so many times throughout history, the masculine perspective has been so dominant as to become entrenched as the default position from which all value judgements are made. As he puts it: 'The strength of the masculine order can be seen in the fact that it does not feel the need to justify itself: the androcentric vision imposes itself as neutral and does not need to draw attention to itself in discourses which aim to legitimise it' (Bourdieu 1998: 15; our translation; see also Mort 1988). For many years, the 'androcentric vision' of which Bourdieu, Mort and others speak informed studies of gender, and especially those of the body. As recently as 2012, Jeff Hearn commented: 'Oddly, many sophisticated gendered analyses [of the body] are often explicitly about women [...] and only implicitly about men. [...] Men and men's bodies often remain unnamed, decisively *unmarked*, in a similar, but different, way to "white bodies" in Western societies' (Hearn 2012: 307).

Hearn's comment notwithstanding, recent years have seen an upsurge of interest in masculinity. As French psychoanalyst Élisabeth Badinter put it in 1992: 'Because women have begun to redefine themselves, they have forced men to do so too' (Badinter 1992: 10; our translation). Like Badinter, scholars working in a variety of disciplines, from psychology to sociology, cultural studies to political science, sports studies to anthropology, marketing to musicology, have begun to re-examine many centuries-old truths about men and male identity (see for example Brod and Kaufman 1994; Clare 2000; Faludi 2000; Benwell 2003; Connell 2005; Brownlie and Hewer 2007; Mangan 2012; de Boise 2015). An increasing number of scholars have approached the question of masculinity through the related issue of the male body and its evolving representation (these include Bordo 1999; Kon 2002; Edwards 2006; Lehman 2007; Woodward, K. 2007). In marketing too, a number of recent studies have focused on the various ways in which men use consumption to construct their own particular, often alternative 'masculine' identities (see for example Schouten and McAlexander 1995; Belk and Costa 1998; Holt and Thompson 2004; Coskuner 2006; Moisio, Arnould and Gentry 2013; Östberg 2013).

As far as advertising is concerned, the rise of scholarly interest in issues of gender and gender representation can be traced back to the mid-late 1970s. Goffman's analysis of the ways in which advertising constructed 'femininity' and 'masculinity' (Goffman 1979) was followed by a series of other studies, by for example Courtney and Whipple (1983), Barthals (1988), Schroeder and Borgerson (1998), Nelson and Paek (2008) and Knoll, Eisend and Steinhagen (2011). While pointing out the necessity to examine how women are objectified in advertising, several scholars have nevertheless bemoaned the relative lack of discussion of the representation of men and masculinity in advertising research (see for example Kolbe and Albanese 1996). In the last twenty-five years or so, however, there has been a steady rise in the number of studies focussing exclusively on the representation of men and masculinity in advertising, in a range of formats, and across a variety of disciplines. These include White and Gillett (1994); Nixon (1996); Kates (1999); Patterson and Elliott (2002); Whitehead (2002); Hirschman (2003); Schroeder and Zwick (2004); Warrington and Gourgova (2006); Feasey (2008); Gee (2009); Cole (2010); Stern (2012). Alongside the studies of the ways in which masculinity is depicted in advertisements, there has also been considerable interest in how men as men *look at* advertisements (see for example Stern and Holbrook 1994; Brown, Stevens and

Maclaran 1999; O'Donohoe 2000; Elliott and Elliott 2005; Tuncay 2006). It should be pointed out, however, that relatively little has been written on men and masculinity in contemporary *Russian* advertising. Shaburova (2002) has commented on the myth of tough, resilient masculinity underpinning Russian beer advertisements in the late 1990s. Generally speaking, however, scholars either discuss masculinity alongside femininity (Yurchak 1997), or ignore the issue of masculinity altogether, choosing instead to focus exclusively on the question of femininity (Yurchak 2000), or national identity (Morris 2007) – even when examining advertisements in which issues of masculinity could be said to be central.

As the way in which men appear in advertising has itself developed, becoming more ironic, self-reflexive, intertextual and visually sophisticated (see for example Phillips and McQuarrie 2008; Reichart and Lambiase 2012), so research into how masculinity is depicted in advertising has also evolved. In particular, there has been a steady move away from what one might call 'stereo-type studies' to take in concepts and theoretical frameworks from other dis-ciplines.[5] In his analysis of an ad for Toyota aimed at the male homosexual market, for example, Kates (1999) builds on the work of Butler, by demon-strating that masculinity (and indeed male heterosexuality) is not a given, but is in fact socially constructed, a product of power relations visually inscribed into the ad itself. In Kates' reading of the Toyota ad, advertising emerges as one of the many cultural institutions and practices designed to reproduce and indeed perpetuate the sexual status quo (see also Borgerson, Schroeder, Bloomberg and Thorssén 2006). Kates' queer-theory-inspired work, with its roots in French post-structuralism, lesbian–feminist writing and psychoanalysis, constitutes a master class in the application of Derridean deconstruction to advertising imagery. It also explores the relationship between spectatorship, subjectivisation, and power. In doing so, it is can be compared to that growing body of work on gender in advertising that centres around the issue of the gaze.

The concept of the gaze comes from psychoanalysis. For Lacan, the gaze plays a fundamental role in the formation of the subject, alongside the process of language acquisition (Kuhn 1993: 45–49). The first to apply this concept to visual culture was Laura Mulvey. In a groundbreaking essay in 1975, Mulvey argued that inscribed within mainstream narrative cinema was a mode of spec-tatorship that was both gendered, and based on patriarchal power relations. As she put it (Mulvey 1999: 837): 'In a world ordered by sexual imbalance, pleasure in looking has been split between active/male and passive/female' (see also Berger 1972). In other words, mainstream visual culture is designed in such a way as to enable the male viewing subject to gaze voyeuristically on the female object. For Mulvey (1999: 838), this gives the male viewer 'a satisfying sense of omnipotence' – a point echoed by Kaplan (1983: 311): 'men do not simply look, their gaze carries with it the power of action and of possession that is lacking in the female gaze' (see also Bordo 1999).

Mulvey's original thesis has attracted much criticism in recent years (she herself subsequently refined it: Mulvey 2009). In particular, it has been argued that contemporary visual culture, including advertising, posits a multitude of different spectators, gazes and subject positions (Sturken and Cartwright 2009). These may be male or female, homosexual or heterosexual, voyeuristic or narcissistic (Gamman and Marshment 1988; Mort 1988; Merck 2007). Writing on masculinity in advertising in the UK in the 1980s, Nixon (1996) criticised Mulvey's account of the gaze for being ahistorical and totalising. He retains an interest in spectatorship and subjectivisation, however, although his *maître à penser* is Foucault, rather than Lacan. As Nixon points out, Foucault's account of the 'gaze' relates to the power exerted on the individual by institutions operating in specific social and historical contexts. For Foucault, the ultimate example of the powerful gaze, forcing the body to 'emit signs' (Foucault 1979: 25), is the eighteenth-century Panopticon designed to allow a single watchman to observe all the inmates of a prison. The concept to which Nixon draws particular attention, however, is that of the 'technologies of the self' (Foucault 1985). These are techniques or practices of self-formation and individuation, such as shopping, grooming or dressing, at the heart of which are what Nixon (1996: 18–19) refers to as specific techniques or 'technologies' of looking.

Nixon's Foucauldian insistence on the power dynamic linking spectatorship, the body and subjectivisation takes us back to our earlier point about Putin's performance-based personality cult. The association Nixon posits in relation to the construction of male identity between 'technologies of the self' and 'technologies of looking' anticipates two more recent articles on advertising and masculinity. Patterson and Elliott (2002) have argued that by inverting the gaze, certain advertisements encourage male consumers to adopt unorthodox subject positions, and thereby view their bodies as sites of an on-going process of identity construction. The gaze is also central in an article on three US ads published two years later by Schroeder and Zwick (2004). While their understanding of the gaze is a rather literal one, this article is nevertheless important for our own study, for a number of reasons. First, it focuses on the male body and that body's central role, both in the representation of masculinity, and in consumer culture more generally (on the body and its representations in consumer culture, see also Featherstone 1982). Second, Schroeder and Zwick argue for an approach to advertising research that views advertisements not just as managerial tools but also as cultural artefacts, and that draws attention to the cultural, aesthetic and historical contexts in which the images on display are produced (see also Stern and Schroeder 1994; Gibbons 2005; Gee 2013). Third, they examine how advertisements aimed at men may be designed to reassure male consumers that consumption does not necessarily lead to emasculation. We shall have occasion to return to this idea later on in this chapter. For the time being, however, we should point out that the studies of masculinity in advertising that we have been discussing here virtually all involve Western scholars looking at Western ads. The question is, then: what of contemporary Russian advertising? Before we answer that question, we need to say something about our own approach to reading advertisements.

Key assumptions and methodology

It is our contention that advertising, like any other form of visual culture, not only serves a commercial, rhetorical purpose (Scott 1994a; McFall 2004), but also has an important social function (Goldman 1992; Cathelat 2001; Zhao and Belk 2008; Wharton 2013). Put simply, advertisements are as inherently political as any other form of visual culture (Gombrich 1999; Bartmanski 2013). To paraphrase Lacan, advertising is one of the most important ways in which the subject is exposed to the Symbolic Order. Socialisation, the transformation of consumers into 'cultured' individuals, was a key function of advertising in Russia, not just in the Soviet era (Hanson 1974; Tolstikova 2000; Cox 2003; Cox 2006), but also in the late Imperial age (West 2011; Sheresheva and Antonov-Ovseenko 2015).

Furthermore, as Williamson (1978), Goffman (1979), Goldman (1992), Goldman and Papson (1996), Schroeder (2002), Gibbons (2005) and others cogently argue, advertising does not exist in a socio-cultural vacuum, but is part and parcel of the broader semiotic landscape. In the words of Schroeder and Borgerson (1998: 191), 'advertisements are not just pictures, they are cultural texts informed by the social, political, and artistic worlds that produces [sic] them' (see also Artz and Venkatesh 1991). Outside advertising scholarship, French philosopher and art historian Régis Debray has argued that advertisements are inevitably inscribed within both an iconographic tradition and a specific technological context. As he puts it, in his 'Twelve theses on the new [cultural] order': 'We are *innovating inheritors*, encumbered by myths but also provided with certain tools, and our culture is a negotiated transaction which we undertake as best we can between our mythological heritage and out technological milieu' (Debray 1992: 495; our translation, author's emphasis). Our own approach follows from the above. More specifically, it is premised on the notion that many of the most effective advertisements function intertextually, like palimpsests. A palimpsest, in the sense defined by French literary theorist Gérard Genette, is 'any text derived from a previously existing text by transformation which is either direct [...] or indirect (imitation)' (Genette 1982: 16; our translation). Whereas to describe advertisements as 'palimpsests' is relatively new (see however Roberts 2008), our point echoes Scott who has argued, quoting Bakhtin (1989), that 'ads are crafted by people who share a social milieu with the audience, and thus reflect collective cultural knowledge' (Scott 1994b: 468).[6]

While mindful of the cultural contexts in which advertisements are produced, we also focus on the role of advertisements in what Hirschman (1993) refers to as 'consumer ideology', namely the collective mechanisms by which consumer culture influences consumers in order to defend dominant interests in society. In particular, we examine how Russian advertising has contributed to the circulation of images of masculinity that reinforce Putin's own patriarchal politics. In order to do so, we have chosen a range of advertisements from the Putin years, from a variety of product categories and brands, which target the male consumer and foreground the male body. Like Nixon (1996) and Schroeder and Zwick

(2004), we focus on product categories usually associated with the masculine. These are clothing, alcohol, male grooming products and motor vehicles. For benchmarking purposes, however, we also look at ads shown outside Russia, as well as briefly discussing an advertisement for a product from a traditionally non-masculine category (drinking yoghurt). As well as constituting particularly interesting examples of the representation of the male body, our corpus also contains two of each of Northrop Frye's four basic mythic orientations that operate in creative advertising design, according to Johar, Holbrook and Stern (2001). These are: the comic, which usually features a happy ending (Philips and Gillette); the romance, with a nostalgic ending (Savage and Nivea);[7] the tragic, with an ambiguous ending (the Dodge Caliber and Russian Ice vodka), and the ironic, with a surprise ending (Tinkoff Zooom and Putin's campaign ads). Apart from demonstrating the range of 'marketplace mythologies' (Thompson 2004) at work in contemporary Russian advertising aimed at men, this also has the advantage of enabling us to inscribe our discussion of masculinity within a broader account of branding as myth-making (Holt 2004). Finally, the order in which we present these advertisements is thematic, rather than chronological, since while there are common threads within them, there is no neat linear narrative at work here. This owes much to the fact that advertising representations are not merely 'the result of changing social and cultural practices' (Schroeder and Zwick 2004: 24), but also the reflection of specific briefs given to advertising agencies by brand managers seeking ever more effective ways to segment an increasingly complex marketplace (Hackley 2002, McFall 2004).

Throughout what follows, we also need to remember the crucial point demonstrated by Brown, Stevens and Maclaran (1999), following Bakhtin (1981), that we cannot avoid approaching ads from subject positions (positions which are very often gendered, and are indeed inscribed in those ads themselves, as Williamson 1978, Mick and Buhl 1992, and O'Donohoe 2000 among others have argued). As Scott (1994b: 472) points out, citing Bakhtin (1981), as readers of texts such as advertisements, we are ourselves composed of multiple, and frequently conflicting voices. In our specific case, this is a masculine position (for a feminist critique of the masculine bias in marketing research, see Bristor and Fischer 1993). This point chimes in with Scott's (1994b) reminder, as part of a call for marketing scholars to use reader-response theory when analysing advertisements rather than more formalist or structuralist concepts, to be ever mindful of the fact that different viewers respond to advertisements differently (see also McFall 2004). It is also consonant with the views of Stern, the scholar who has done most to show the usefulness of literary theory to marketing. Almost two decades ago, Stern (1996) was already arguing that literary-theory-inspired advertising criticism needed to move beyond the semiotics of Williamson (1978) to embrace reader-response theory and deconstruction (see also McQuarrie and Mick 1999). Those positions include gender (Otnes and Zayer 2013), but may also include nationality, ethnicity and sexuality. Indeed, as Bordo (1999) sagely observes, not only do we all see different things in ads, but we also view other people's bodies differently too. Throughout the rest of the chapter then, the reader needs to remain aware that the readings presented are those of a white, middle-aged male.[8] And as Haynes (2003: 14) reminds us, quoting de Lauretis (1984: 38–39), 'entrenched as it is in "the encompassing context of patriarchal ideologies" [,] men's discourse has largely been constructed with no apparent awareness of how their position as men within the same context may have inflected that discourse'. It is precisely that lack of awareness that we will seek to guard against in what follows. This is because, as Schroeder (2002) has cogently argued, semiotic analysis is not just about analysing meaning (Mick 1986); it is also very much concerned with the process of meaning *construction*.

Back to the (Soviet) future: The Dodge Caliber and the cult of the male body

Initially at least, advertising was one of a number of cultural spheres characterised by continuity rather than rupture between the Soviet and post-Soviet eras. As Kelly (1998: 225) points out, however, Russian advertising began to develop its own, 'naturalised' visual and textual codes alongside Western ones around 1995 (see also Mickiewicz 1997: 232–41; Borenstein 1999b; Padgett 2002; Beumers 2005; Ciochetto, 2011). The two have continued to exist side by side ever since, with many Western brands choosing not to adapt their advertisements to the Russian market. This is especially true of those sectors where Russian brands are under-represented, such as haute couture, high-tech or perfume. In 2002, for example, when Lacoste launched a global poster campaign advertising its perfume for men, featuring an entirely naked man staring at the camera while sipping a cup of coffee, the image also appeared on the streets of Moscow. Other foreign brands considerably adapt their advertising for the Russian market, however. One such is the US car manufacturer Dodge, the ad for whose Caliber SUV, from 2006, will be our first case study here.

The car is perhaps the ultimate iconically male product, consuming cars one of the most common ways in which men express their identity, both individually and collectively (Hirschman 2003; Belk 2004; Schroeder and Zwick 2004; Thomas 2013). While Seiler (2008) has discussed the societal importance of the automobile in US society, the car arguably played an even more important role, both economically and socio-culturally, in the USSR. Indeed, as Siegelbaum (2008) has astutely noted, one of the unintended consequences of the lack of state-run garages in the USSR was the male bonding it encouraged. In the main, with the arrival of car showrooms and car-repair garages, most Russian men no longer need to spend the 162 hours per year their Soviet counterparts devoted to car maintenance (Siegelbaum 2008). Nevertheless, the importance of the car, both for contemporary Russian consumer culture and for the way the post-Soviet male constructs his social identity, is indisputable. If one takes a stroll down any city centre street anywhere in Russia on any evening, one is struck by the number of imposing, tinted-windowed vehicles parked outside banks, casinos, night clubs and restaurants. The 4×4 in particular rapidly became a popular accessory of conspicuous consumption for wealthy New Russians after 1992. The first official Russian 4×4 owners' club was founded as early as 1993, followed in 1994 by the country's first national off-road competition, and the country's first national off-road magazine, *4×4*, a year later (4×4Club.ru [n.d.]). General Motors' Hummer, the preferred mode of transport of global stars such as US rapper Eminem (Ebrahim, A. [n.d.]), soon became a regular feature of Russia's clogged inner-city arteries. Since 2004, the iconic Hummer H2 has been built at the Avtotor plant in the Russian enclave of Kaliningrad (Ebrahim, A. [n.d.]). Production of the Hummer H3, a mid-size sports utility vehicle, began two years later, in 2006 (Motor1.com 2006). The brand currently has two online fan clubs in Russia (hummerclubrus.ru, and rushummer.ru) each with approximately 1,000 members. As for the Dodge Caliber, it too has an online owners' club in Russia (caliberclub.ru), which at the time of writing (summer 2015) boasts over 7,000 members.

The Caliber's arrival in Russia in 2006, was marked by a thirty-second advertisement.[9] The ad starts with a screen split vertically in two. In the left half, we see the circular combination lock of a safe, and in the right half, the knob of what appears to be an in-car radio, magnified so as to appear the same size as the lock. The images immediately come to life, as fingers begin hurriedly twirling both knobs. Sound arrives, in the shape of a steady, up-beat, drum rhythm leading into heavy rock guitar. As it does so, the image changes on both sides of the screen. On the left, we now have an overhead view of a black car, travelling diagonally across the frame, while on the right, we have another aerial shot, this time of a bare-chested man in shorts lying across a bench engaged in weightlifting exercises. Man and vehicle now switch sides, the former's naked, muscular back now appearing on the left, while the interior of the car, also seen from behind, with the rear door raised, emerges on the right. As it does so, a deeply masculine extradiegetic voice pronounces three words in a tone as measured as it is assured: 'Strong – Insolent – Muscular'. The male athlete remains in the left hand of the frame, as the camera focuses successively on various body parts – his face and bare shoulders, his open mouth, his face and hands (as he launches into yet another sit-up), his (rippling) torso, his head and arms as he repeatedly hits a punch ball, and his face. Simultaneously, on the other side of the screen, we are shown different parts of the car, including the front grille with the unmistakeable Dodge ram's head logo. All the while, a visual association is suggested between man and machine – nowhere more so, perhaps, than when we are simultaneously shown the former's legs jumping over a skipping rope, and the moving pistons of the car's engine. Just as the framing and fragmentation of the athlete's body becomes so insistent as to run the risk of dehumanising him, however, the visual style of the film changes. We now see him from behind, back in the right-hand side of the screen, running away from us (in the left-hand side, we see the rear of the car as it moves away). The voice-over reinforces the shift in tone: 'He is of a completely new calibre', it tells us, 'when he's told "you can't" [nel'zya'], he replies "yes I can" [mozhno]'. This theme of defiant resistance in the face of adversity is reinforced visually; as the word 'mozhno' (literally 'it is possible') is pronounced, we see him vigorously striking a punch ball. In the next shot, we follow him as he runs up a series of zig-zagging metal stairs, before returning to exert himself once more with the punch ball. As he does so, the voice-over continues the theme of (male) power: 'Can it really be true that he fears nobody – nobody and nothing?'. For most of the ad, the camera moves seemingly randomly between car and athlete. At times the car is on the left and the athlete on the right, at other times this is reversed. In some shots, we see only the athlete, while in others we are shown only the car. A sudden shift of emphasis occurs in the final scene, however, taking us away from the male athlete and focusing our attention on the car. The screen is no longer split, the athlete disappearing to reveal the car screeching to a halt in front of us. As it does so, the voice-over concludes triumphantly: 'The Dodge Caliber – "you can't" means "yes I can"' ('Dodzh Kaliber – "nel'zya znachit mozhno"').

If, as Bordo (1999: 19) has argued, the arrival of Calvin Klein underwear ads in 1977 meant that Western consumer culture had finally begun to 'develop the untapped resources of the male body', the Dodge ad represents a similar milestone for Russia. In one sense, of course, the boxer who spends most of the ad working out can be seen as a reference to the fitness craze that has spread throughout the country in the last fifteen years or so (and to which Putin himself is no stranger: Goscilo 2013d). The cult of bodybuilding has re-emerged in post-Soviet Russia, with the arrival of specialist magazines, and countless fitness centres (Beumers 2005). Recent years have also seen the rise of the security industry, for which physical strength is one of the most important pre-requisites (Mikhel [n.d.]). As well as alluding to a growing trend in Russian culture, the Dodge Caliber ad, with its association between masculinity and a particularly dynamic physicality, is typical of many Western advertisements. As Sturken and Cartwright comment, for example, discussing a 1990s advertisement for Range Rover which features a man punting across a river on a raft, 'men [in advertising] have been traditionally depicted in action [...] which negates attempts to objectify them because they are shown as powerful within the frame' (Sturken and Cartwright 2001: 88). Another feature which the Dodge ad shares with many recent Western ads is the prominent presence of the well-honed muscular body. As Warrington and Gourgova (2006) argue, the athletic male body is now one of five idealised images of the masculine subject in advertising in the US (see also Elliott and Elliott 2005).

In their study of advertisements in the popular US bodybuilding magazine *Flex*, White and Gillett (1994) argued that the muscular male body is quite literally the embodiment of patriarchal power, offering conservative resistance to progressive change in society. It would be simplistic to make the same claim for the Dodge ad in the case of Russia. Nevertheless, with his powerful, muscular physique, and single-mindedly 'insolent' refusal to submit to any authority other than that of his own free will, Dodge's sporting hero is the very embodiment of hegemonic masculinity (Gee 2009). Our understanding of 'hegemonic masculinity' is taken from Gramsci (1971), via Connell (2005: 77):

Hegemonic masculinity can be defined as the configuration of gender practice which embodies the currently accepted answer to the problem of the legitimacy of patriarchy, which guarantees (or is taken to guarantee) the dominant position of men and the subordination of women. This is not to say that the most visible bearers of hegemonic masculinity are always the most powerful people. [...] Nevertheless, hegemony is likely to be established only if there is some correspondence between cultural ideal and institutional power, collective if not individual. [...] It is the successful claim to authority, more than direct violence, that is the mark of hegemony (though violence often underpins or supports authority).[10]

Connell's definition of the practice and process of hegemonic masculinity, with its reference to 'patriarchy', 'institutional power' and 'authority', immediately calls to mind Vladimir Putin (Goscilo 2013a, Sperling 2015). In many ways, Putin's vision of masculinity, as indeed his entire world view, looks back to the communist past, to the Soviet era in which he grew up and received his professional training as a spy, a time for which he has publicly expressed regret (Goscilo 2013c; see also Roxburgh 2012). The hegemonic masculinity on display in the Dodge ad, with its emphasis on peak physical fitness, can also be traced back to the Soviet era, to Soviet ideology and in particular to Soviet iconography. As Starks (2008) points out, in the USSR a strong association was made between a healthy, vigorous body and political purity. And as Riordan (1999: 54) reminds us, in the USSR, physical culture had several functions: it was encouraged as a way of preventing the spread of infectious diseases; it was seen as a way of combatting alcoholism and religion; and it became an adjunct of the various Five-Year Plans, since in most branches of the economy, and certainly in those most valorised by the State, if one wished to become a 'hero of labour', one had to be physically extremely strong (on the politicisation of sport in the USSR, see also O'Mahoney 2006). Gilmour and Evans Clements (2002) also suggest that this emphasis on physical sport and training was part of the attempt to encourage 'culturedness' ('kul'turnost") in Soviet men – a policy which went back at least to various advertising campaigns of the 1920s (Kelly and Volkov 1988), if not earlier. As they observe, the Soviet state strongly encouraged men to engage in bodybuilding. This was the case more or less throughout the Soviet era, but especially in the period between 1945 and 1960, when the newspaper *Soviet Sport* frequently published biographical sketches of elite male athletes. One edition of the newspaper, published in 1950, contained one of the most iconic Soviet posters of all time (Gilmour and Evans Clements 2002: 211). In the poster, a Soviet athlete can be seen showing off his rippling muscles to a young Pioneer, who is sitting on his knee and admiringly feeling one of his impressive biceps. The text below the picture reads: 'If you want to be like me, TRAIN!'.[11]

There is more in the Dodge Caliber ad than an allusion to the benefits of physical exercise, however. By the way in which the voice-over is deliberately designed to conflate the athlete and the car (since the Russian masculine singular pronoun 'on' can mean both 'he' and 'it'), this ad also looks back to a key myth about men, masculinity and the male body that underpinned mainstream Soviet ideology for so long. This was the association between the masculine ideal and an 'iron' will and determination. This link found its most important expression in the flesh-to-metal myth of high Soviet culture, especially in the early Soviet period (Kaganovsky 2004). As Hellebust (2003: 3) puts it, this idea, absolutely central to Soviet mythology, involved nothing less than 'the metal-lization of the human body as a metaphor for the creation of the communist New Man'. This symbiosis between man and machine was a central aspect of the Bolsheviks' utopian belief in man's capacity to triumph over the natural world. It can be seen not just in the early works of Soviet literature discussed by Hellebust, but also in photographs of strapping young proletarian males working heavy machinery of one sort or another, such as Arkady Chajhet's (1931), 'A Komsomol at the Wheel' (Walker, Ursitti and McGinnis 1991: 34), or Boris Ignatovich's 1930 series 'At the press' (Lavrientiev 2006: 214 and 219). One of its most explicit expressions came in a physical culture poster of 1955, in which a naked man shown from the waist up can be seen lifting up a new-born baby, accompanied by a text reading: 'Fear neither the heat nor the cold, temper yourself like STEEL' (reproduced in Gilmour and Evans Clements 2002: 216).[12]

The Dodge Caliber ad, then, is not merely designed to sell a car that can go wherever its driver wants. It also looks back to, and reproduces, the Soviet myth that physical exercise ultimately affords the male subject mastery over nature.[13] As a result of the confusion – or rather *fusion* – between man and machine, flesh and metal, the car becomes a metaphor for the male consumer's idealised self, capable of boldly going where no man has gone before, as it were. The ad, then, projects back at that (narcissistic) consumer his ideal self, *both* visually (the image of the boxer in training) *and* linguistically. Viewed in this light, the Dodge ad presents consumption as not just liberatory (Firat and Venkatesh 1995), but also compensatory (*pace* Schroeder and Zwick 2004), and indeed emancipatory (Holt and Thompson 2004). In other words, the ad marshals hegemonic masculinity in order to reassure the male consumer that consumption – specifically consumption of the Dodge Caliber – will not involve any loss of power. To paraphrase Thompson and Holt (2004), it allows Russian men to 'grab the phallus' while keeping hold of the steering wheel.

It is possible that this assertion of power, and the re-emergence of hegemonic masculinity on which it is based, reflects Russian men's collective need to feel strong again after the debacle of two unsuccessful wars in Chechnya (on the re-emergence of 'muscular' masculinity in post-Vietnam US popular culture, see Jeffords 1989). There are other, just as probable reasons, however – reasons, moreover, linked with consumption itself. First, for Russian men at the start of the post-industrial twenty-first century, the act of consumption itself may be just as 'tainted' with femininity as it was for their American counterparts at the end of the twentieth-century (in her study of masculinity in the US, Faludi (2000: 517) refers to 'the conformism, passivity and consumerist mirror-gazing traditionally held to be feminine'). Second, the product itself – the Dodge

Caliber – is a 'crossover' between a saloon and a 4×4, not much bigger than most family cars. As such, it is smaller than the average 4×4 (and certainly a good deal smaller than the Hummer H2), a point which is potentially problematic for those Russian male consumers for whom 'size really does matter', as it were.[14]

Russia was not the only market in which Dodge brand managers sought to reassure the male consumer concerned about potential loss of both social and sexual status in purchasing such a small family car. In its home market, the US, the company launched two TV ads for the car in 2006, the same year as the Russian ad. In one, a Tinkerbell-like fairy floats above a city, transforming first a tower block and then a train into their miniaturised, 'toytown' equivalents with the aid of her magic wand. When she tries to do the same to a Dodge Caliber, however, she is unable to do so. Instead, the car throws her unceremoniously onto the sidewalk. In another US ad from the same year, the Caliber is unveiled to a panel of life-sized stuffed toys. They are asked in turn to give their opinion on the new car. Eventually, it is the turn of a Furby-like creature, named 'Binky', who says simply 'It scares the ★★★★ out of me'. At this point, an unidentified man (presumably a representative of the company) says 'That's just the reaction we were looking for', at which point the ad ends. Both these ads conclude with the strapline, 'The new Dodge Caliber – it's anything but cute'. If in the US, Dodge brand managers appear to have believed that consumers needed reassuring that driving such a 'small' car would not pose a threat to their masculinity, this does not seem to have concerned their Belgian counterparts. Indeed, the ad for the car published in the country's Flemish-speaking magazine, *Autowereld* (*Auto World*), in 2006, uses a very different kind of humour altogether. A black and white photograph, covering the entire bottom half of a page, shows the vehicle in question in profile, its rear-end raised and perched atop a photocopier from which a light can be seen emerging. The Dodge Caliber, it would appear, is behaving like so many men at drunken office parties the world over, namely taking a picture of its rear end. Indeed, the caption in the top left-hand corner of the photograph reads simply, 'Men at Work'.

The way in which the brand (Dodge), and indeed the anthropomorphised product (the Caliber), express radically different personality traits in different national cultural contexts is an example of what Kates and Goh (2003) refer to as 'brand morphing'. Each market highlights a different approach to the problem of reassuring the male consumer that to buy a Caliber is not to compromise his sexual or social status. Only in Russia, however, is there such emphasis on the male body. And only in Russia is the problem addressed with such a degree of seriousness. Ultimately, the Russian advertisement for the Dodge Caliber draws on Soviet iconography and mythology to encourage the male consumer to gaze narcissistically at his ideal self in order to gain reassurance – reassurance primarily about the consequences for his masculinity of buying such a relatively 'small' car. In our next case study, the male consumer is invited to gaze at another embodied version of his ideal self (and indeed another 'boxer'), in the shape of Hollywood actor Sylvester Stallone. This time, however, the ideal fails spectacularly to live up to expectations.

On 'Russian Ice' with Sylvester Stallone

If for many the 4×4 has come to symbolise the new, opulent Russia, vodka remains the Russian national product par excellence. As Kravets (2012: 363) observes, 'vodka is a symbolically dense, sociomaterial artefact that prominently figures in Russia's economic history and cultural politics'. As such, it, it has throughout the ages been inextricably bound up with Russian politics and the vexed question of Russian national identity (Herlihy 2012; Schrad 2014). Indeed, with over 600 national vodka brands currently on the Russian market, associating the brand with the notion of 'Russianness', however spurious, can give a brand the legitimacy required to gain competitive advantage. One such brand which has tried to do precisely that is Russian Ice ('Russki Led').

On the brand's official website, Russian Ice is described as: 'a genuine Russian vodka, conveying the soul, strength and old glory of Russian victories' (Russian Ice [n.d.]). As if in support of this claim, etched onto the bottle itself is a representation of one of the most famous battles in Russian history, namely that fought against the Teutonic Knights on a frozen Lake Peipus in 1242 (see Roberts 2014a). The victory on the 'Russian ice' is deeply imbricated with Russian national identity, since Russia's defeated enemies were finally forced to recognise the inviolability of her frontiers (its significance prompted Eisenstein to make it the centrepiece of his film *Alexander Nevsky* in 1936). In an attempt to underline still further the brand's patriotic credentials, a horizontal band of white, blue and red (the colours of the Russian flag) was added around the base of the bottle during a rebranding in 2008 undertaken just three years after the brand's initial launch. In the same year of 2008, Russian Ice vodka launched a press and TV advertising campaign, using Sylvester Stallone.

The ad appeared in two versions, one in the press, and the other a video broadcast on TV and YouTube. The two versions present a number of similarities, but also certain key differences, which we shall examine presently. In the press photo, we see a youthful Stallone, in what is very probably a publicity photograph taken in the 1980s to publicise the 'Rocky' series of films (1976–2006), in which he played the eponymous hero, a small-time boxer who makes it big. Stallone is photographed in high-contrast monochrome (rather like the boxer in the Dodge Caliber ad). As well as harking back to old black-and-white TV images of bouts from the 1950s and 1960s (not to mention iconic boxing movies such as Martin Scorsese's *Raging Bull* of 1980), this also reinforces Stallone's imposing presence. This is further enhanced by the angle at which he is shot; he appears to us slightly from below, at mid-distance, so that the clenched fist, on the end of his outstretched arm, fills virtually the whole of the bottom quarter of the picture, the knuckle of his index finger especially prominent. He is in fact taking up the stereotypical pose of the boxer throwing a punch – indeed, his other hand, his left, is also clenched into a fist, and raised under his chin, as if he were taking guard.

The pose is clearly meant to remind us of Stallone's 'Rocky' persona, in a way which blurs the distinction between the actor and the film character. The image itself, however, is light years away from the gritty, and at times very bloody, pictures from the films. For one thing, the torso, adorned in plain grey t-shirt, is straight, not bent forward as it would be if Stallone/Rocky were really about to throw a punch. Moreover, there is more than the hint of a grin on Stallone's face. What the pose suggests in fact is not so much a punch as the kind of friendly, 'manly' greeting that one man might give another in any number of social settings. Of course, Stallone is also well known, in Russia as elsewhere, for his role as the eponymous hero of the 'Rambo' series of films (1982–2008). There is an allusion to this aspect of Stallone's career too, although this time it is textual, rather than visual; the text in the top right-hand corner of the ad, which informs us 'Sylvester Stallone's great-grandmother was born in Odessa' is reproduced in a stencilled, pseudo-military type of the kind one might find on boxes of ammunition or other field supplies.[15] The ad is finished off at the bottom of the page (cutting across Stallone's clenched fist) with the caption 'There is something Russian in everybody', in angular white lettering on a red background – a typographic style reminiscent of Soviet constructivism (Kiaer 2005) – and the bottle of Russian Ice vodka.

This campaign also featured a one-minute video (YouTube 2008b). At the beginning of the film, we see Stallone getting up in a room bathed in light, getting dressed (he has a range of identical expensive suits in his wardrobe), stepping into his Aston Martin, and arriving on the set of what is presumably the latest movie he is filming, where he is surrounded by adoring fans. At each stage, Stallone explains the provenance of the various objects he owns, or the people who surround him: 'The coffee', he tells us, 'only from Brazil. The suits, only from Italy. The car is an English classic. The computer, of course, is from China. My fans are from Japan. The work – pure Hollywood. My friends are all from Beverly Hills' (at this point, a party appears to break out, and we see a waiter carrying a tray of Russian Ice vodka). Throughout the video, the camera cuts between the scenes of Stallone's working day and Stallone himself, whose head and upper torso are bathed in evening light as he stands with his back to an out-of-focus landscape. In the final scene, the light-hearted mood changes completely, however. It is now night-time, and in a darkened alley, Stallone comes face to face with a group of three burly figures who block his path and stare at him menacingly, as if aching for a fight. While Stallone has hitherto restricted himself to English, at this point he suddenly breaks into Russian. As he confronts his potential assailants, he utters the words 'Budet bol'no' ('This is going hurt'), half to the hoodlums, half to himself, twisting his face into a very Rocky-like grimace, and deftly slipping his expensive watch off his wrist and putting it in his pocket for safety – he obviously intends to put his fists to good use.[16] As he does so, he delivers (speaking in English once again) the punch line so to speak: 'My personality, I get from my great-grandmother, so it must be Russian'. At this point, the clip jumps forward and ends, with Stallone back at home, very much intact, and symbolically slipping his watch back over his wrist – he is shot in the mid-distance, a bottle of Russian Ice vodka now filling the foreground.

In one sense, both the press ad and the video reproduce the kind of hege-monic masculinity we saw in the Dodge Caliber ad. Boxing, which also featured prominently in that ad, is one of the sports most associated with hegemonic masculinity, not just in the West (Woodward, K. 2007), but also, and perhaps especially, in the USSR (Guedel 2006). The sport was also ideologically loaded during the Soviet era; throughout the period, boxing remained unprofessionalised, partly so that Soviet boxers could compete on an international stage with their US counterparts. Far more experienced, they tended to win more often than not, something which the Soviet authorities were never slow to exploit in order to demonstrate the apparent ideological superiority of Communism over capitalism.[17] Indeed, as Gilmour and Evans Clements (2002: 212) point out, Soviet boxers, alongside wrestlers and weightlifters, were often compared in the Soviet press to 'bogatyrs', mythical heroes from Russian medieval epic poetry, precisely in an attempt to reinforce patriotic pride among Soviet sports' fans.

The Russian Ice campaign, then, uses Stallone to construct a neo-Soviet version of hegemonic masculinity. Yet there are a number of ironies at the heart of this campaign – ironies, furthermore, which serve to deconstruct the version of masculinity on which that campaign rests. Perhaps most obviously, the ads rely on an iconic Hollywood star, albeit one who can purportedly trace his ancestry back to the Russian Empire (the fact that at the time the campaign was launched – 2008 – Odessa was no longer in Russia, but rather in neighbouring Ukraine, is itself richly ironic). It is true that in *Rocky 4* (1985), the boxer spends a lot of time training in and around a remote cabin in Siberia, in scenes redolent with symbolism. At the same time, however, he does so in order to pit himself against the 'evil' Soviet boxer Ivan Drago. Moreover, defeating Drago by a knockout in the final scene of the movie enables him to avenge his friend, the symbolically named Apollo Creed. And in *Rambo 3* (1988), Stallone's character does not merely knock out one Russian, but personally kills several Soviet soldiers, while fighting alongside the Afghan mujaheddin. As if aware of the discrepancy between his on-screen personae on the one hand, and his purportedly Russian heritage on the other, Stallone gives a wry chuckle at the end of the video, in a gesture which unexpectedly, and completely undercuts the seriousness of the clip's final scene in the dark alley. Another, perhaps no less significant, irony involves Stallone's body as represented in the ads. For there is a remarkable discrepancy between the youthful, well-honed (and almost certainly photo-shopped) figure in the photograph, and the ageing, post-aesthetic-surgery actor in the video, whose face is so swollen as to be almost unrecognisable. Indeed – and this is perhaps the most notable irony here – there is much evidence to suggest that Stallone himself was never comfortable with the kind of body which he was required to develop for his most famous on-screen roles. In an interview with Susan Fauldi, he associated the gym-bred physique not with hyper-masculinity, but with its very opposite. As he put it:

> The guy with the eighteen-inch arms, the thirty-one inch waist, the male-model, chiselled, Calvin Klein-ad type of person, he is, for the nineties,

the woman with triple E [breasts]. He's taking the place of the blond bombshell of the fifties. And the blond bombshell woman, they don't even do that any more! The woman on the street doesn't want to be Jayne Mansfield. (Faludi 2000: 583–84).

With its juxtaposition of two very different images of Stallone's body, and Stallone's own self-deprecating chuckle, the Russian Ice campaign deconstructs the very hegemonic mode of masculinity that it purports to promote. The irony at the heart of the campaign distinguishes it as far as possible from the Dodge Caliber ad which we looked at earlier on in this chapter. Instead, it links it to another series of ads, for a very different kind of alcoholic drink. It is to one of these ads, designed by Oliviero Toscani for Russian micro-brewery Tinkoff, that we now turn.

From abject to subject: Tinkoff's 'Zooom' alcopop and a story of everyday heroism

In his excellent study of the semiotics of drink and drinking, Manning (2010: 210) points out that beer is 'stereotypically associated with a domain of plebeian, informal, non-ritual, non-domestic masculine sociability'. In the USSR, beer was indeed a central element of 'plebeian masculinity' in a number of Soviet republics, not just in Georgia (the focus of Manning's study), but also in Russia. Nevertheless, in terms of the quantities consumed, it lagged way behind vodka, even during the late 1980s, when Mikhail Gorbachev's infamous 'dry law' made obtaining the latter far more difficult (Schrad 2014: 256–73). This may be because, as Morris (2007: 1385) points out, beer was never a staple good in Russia, and was generally only brewed for special occasions such as festivals. The situation changed rapidly throughout the 1990s and early 2000s, however, with the restructuring and development of domestic brewers such as Baltika (in part helped by the boost to domestic production in the wake of the 1998 financial crisis: Morris 2007: 1390), and the arrival of foreign giants such as Indo-Belgian joint venture SUN–Interbrew, Britain's Scottish and Newcastle, Denmark's Carlsberg, the South African–US giant SABMiller and the Dutch Heineken (many of whom bought local production facilities at knock-down prices).[18] A number of these brands lost no time in hiring leading Western advertising agencies to explain the benefits of beer drinking to the post-Soviet male, as a result of which the Russian beer market was growing at 30 per cent per annum by the start of the twenty-first century (Sostav.ru 2001).

As far as domestic brewers were concerned, one of the most dynamic Russian brands in the early years of the new century was Tinkoff. In many respects, the very model of the post-Soviet entrepreneur, the company's founder Oleg Tinkoff first entered business by selling jeans to other students while at university, before launching a successful restaurant business serving 'pelmeni' (Russian-style ravioli). In 1998 he opened an American-style micro-brewery restaurant in St Petersburg. Tinkoff rapidly expanded to become Russia's fourth largest independent brewery, opening a two million hectolitre state-of-the-art brewery in 2002 in Pushkin, near St Petersburg. In the following year, the company recorded annual sales of US$35 million (Arvedlund 2004). By 2004, the company had a chain of micro-brewery-style restaurants across the country.[19]

When in 2003 Tinkoff decided to launch a series of ads to promote his brand, he chose not to approach one of the leading foreign ad agencies already present in Russia, however, but instead to go directly to controversial, four-times winner of the Golden Lion at Cannes, Oliviero Toscani (Rybak 2003). Toscani's ads for Tinkoff began to appear in the spring of 2004. Despite their thematic diversity, these ads all function by reassuring the predominantly young, hetero-sexual, male target audience that drinking beer rather than spirits represents no threat to one's masculinity. One of the ads, for example, constructs a binary opposition between two types of man – one who follows the crowd in opting for external status symbols such as prostitutes, powerful cars and armed security guards, and another who demonstrates individuality by preferring to nurture a sense of inner freedom.[20] After an opening sequence showing a call girl arriving at the penthouse suite of an (unseen) oligarch, the scene shifts to a beach, bathed in a bright orange light. The camera flies down over the beach, swooping over the head of a man standing alone on the sand, dressed in a loose white cotton shirt, and listening to the roar of the ocean emanating from deep within a sea shell. The voice-over tells us: 'He's not like everybody else. He has faith in himself. Above all, he values his inner freedom. Tinkoff – he is so unique'. As if to underscore this freedom, the man is shown in a mid-shot, standing with his back to the sun, which forms an aureole around his head, in a way which lends him a certain mystique. In the ad's final image (visually reminiscent of 1980s commercials for men's cologne by Christian Dior such as Dune and Fahrenheit), the man stands alone, the very embodiment of self-reliant individualism, in complete harmony with the natural world, and untrammelled by superficial trappings of modernity such as power, status and bodyguards (and indeed expensive prostitutes). We are invited to gaze at the hero of the ad narcissistically; he is the ideal man, whose 'inner freedom' the viewer is called upon to experience, to paraphrase Lacan, as a lack (Belk, Ger and Askegaard 2000).

The concept of the lack lies at the heart of perhaps the most destabilising of all the Tinkoff ads – at least from the heterosexual male perspective – namely the commercial for Zooom (sic), introduced by Tinkoff in November 2004. Strate (1991) has described beer commercials in general as 'a manual on masculinity' (see also Carah, Brodmerkel and Hernandez 2014). Observing that the theme of challenge is a virtual constant in beer ads, he continues:

> Beer commercials are aimed at a male audience, and challenge is central to the myth of masculinity. According to this myth [...] men demonstrate their masculinity by taking risks, facing danger, and overcoming challenges. External physical threats are supplemented and can be replaced by symbolic tests of strength, skill, and self-control. (Strate 1991: 117)

Zooom was not a beer, but rather a light, citrus-flavoured alcopop made from natural malt, aimed at the 21–35 age group (it was in fact the first such drink to be made in Russia). This detail notwithstanding, the Zooom ad neatly bears out Strate's point about beer commercials. In this case, the 'challenge' for the male protagonist is nothing less than to find a suitable mate – or, as we shall see, to demonstrate the 'skill' necessary to identify a suitable body with which to pair up. In rising to this challenge, he not only becomes an everyday super-hero, a model of super-hero restraint (Tasker 1993) and an unassuming and unwitting foil to Stallone's back-alley boxer, he also transforms himself from object into subject.

The ad's opening scene focuses on this young man in a nightclub. Casually dressed, he stands in the middle of the dance floor, one hand around his bottle of Zooom (an unconscious acknowledgement of its status as phallic symbol and the power it affords?), another planted firmly in his pocket. Hips thrust slightly forward, he is the very personification of youthful self-confidence. Eager to find a mate, he begins to survey the scene in front of him. He does so, however, by looking through his bottle of Zooom, which enables him to see the 'real' reality behind the façade (a device reminiscent of the series of ads for Smirnoff vodka shown in the UK in the 1980s). He soon spots an attractive young woman, only to be disappointed when he sees her lips are full of collagen, her drink contains a chemical identified only as 'E122', and her breasts have been injected with silicon. Not to be put off, he looks up to see another curvaceous figure, silhouetted against a spotlight, descending a flight of steps. Hoping that this woman is the real deal, he takes a closer look, using once again his bottle of Zooom to check out her credentials. This time, however, what he sees is even worse. Everything about her is fake – from the lurid green cocktail in her hand, to the ill-fitting blond-wig and the garish red lipstick framing her mouth, from which there suddenly issues a very husky 'hello there'. Clearly, 'she' is in fact a 'he'.[21] Our hero turns away in a mixture of embarrassment and disgust, before his gaze finally lands on a 'natural' woman (who also appears to be enjoying a bottle of Zooom). The two of them come together in the final sequence, dancing together in the background behind a close-up of a bottle of Zooom.

On one level, the (clumsy) binary opposition that the ad sets up (both between two kinds of men, and between two kinds of women, one fake, the other 'real') serves merely to underscore the fact that the product in question – Zooom – is made from 100 per cent 'natural' ingredients. An increasing number of food and drink brands worldwide are finding that an insistence on how 'pure' and 'natural' their product is can help give them competitive advantage (on the US convenience food market, see for example Kniazeva and Belk 2007). The question of purity was also central to Soviet Socialist Realism, an artistic doctrine originally developed to help Soviet writers better educate the masses, but ultimately used to apply to all branches of artistic culture. As Clark puts it, in her classic study of the genre: 'Central to Socialist Realism [...] was a concern for purity of several sorts – especially the political, literary, geographic (hence simulation of a Gemeinschaft world), and the bodily or sexual; *all these were effectively equated*' (Clark 2000: 280, our emphasis).

Ultimately, however, this ad works not by emphasising the 'naturalness' of the product, but rather by exploiting the power dynamics of the gaze. The male protagonist uses the Zooom bottle to enhance his own gaze, as he looks around the club for a suitable mate. The bottle–phallus enables him to remain in total control of that gaze throughout; as soon as he feels himself becoming the object of the transvestite's gaze, for example, he immediately picks up the bottle and resumes his search, thereby reverting to his status as subject (finally finding a suitable 'object' this time, in the shape of the 'naturally' heterosexual woman). As a result, the vision we are presented with throughout the ad is uniformly masculine and heteronormative: we never get to see the male heterosexual protagonist as the transvestite sees him, for example, and neither are we shown the silicone-breasted woman's perspective. This is because both of these characters embody (literally) the threat of the 'abject' other. This notion, first applied to popular culture by French–Bulgarian feminist thinker Julia Kristeva in 1982, was originally developed in psychoanalysis, where it was associated with the female body and how that body was perceived by the male subject (Creed 1993). For Kristeva, the 'abject' other is a reminder to the subject (and especially the male subject) of the precariousness of his identity *as subject*. He feels revulsion at the threat which bodily fluids such as menstrual blood represent to the clear delimitation between inside and outside the body, without which the child cannot enter the Symbolic Order (Kristeva 1982; see also Gross 1990). In a highly significant critical turn, Butler adapted Kristeva's notion to include under the term 'abject' all that which is excluded by the regulatory imperative of the 'heterosexual matrix'. As she puts it, in her introduction to *Bodies That Matter* (Butler 2011: xiii):

> This exclusionary matrix by which subjects are formed [...] requires the simultaneous production of a domain of abject beings, those who are not yet 'subjects', but who form the constitutive outside to the domain of the subject. [...] In this sense, then, the subject is constituted through the force of exclusion and abjection, one which produces a constitutive outside to the subject, an abjected outside, which is, after all, 'inside' the subject as its own founding repudiation.

The male subject, then, needs an 'abjected' other precisely in order to become a subject. Reading the Zooom ad through Butler enables us to grasp why we can never be allowed to see the male protagonist's body through the eyes of either the transvestite or the silicon-injected woman. Adopting their perspective would result not just in the decentring of the male subject, but in his very disintegration as subject. This is because, if discourse has 'the power to circum-scribe the domain of intelligibility' (Butler 2011: 139), then so does the look, since the look *acts as a discourse*, fixing its object, as we have argued in a dif-ferent context elsewhere (Roberts 1999). As Butler herself puts it: 'The threat of a collapse of the masculine into the abjected feminine [or indeed transvestite] threatens to dissolve the heterosexual axis of desire; it carries the fear of occupying a site of homosexual abjection' (Butler 2011: 155) Like the Dodge Caliber ad then, the Zooom commercial also manipulates the male body, and the male gaze, in order to reassure the male consumer that consumption – of a drink which is not only relatively low in alcohol for the Russian market (4.5 per cent), but which, with its pale yellow colour and narrow bottle looks more like a 'girly' alcopop than a 'real man's' drink, and is also consumed by women – will not result in a loss of power (specifically the power to attract women).[22]

While the Dodge Caliber commercial addresses the male subject's anxiety about his social status as perceived by other men, the Zooom ad on the other hand resolves the tension caused by that subject's potential loss of sexual appeal *to women*. In contemporary Russia, many brands play on this fear to persuade men to purchase products that do not belong to those categories – certain types of car, or kinds of alcohol, for example – that Hirschman (2014) has identified as typically 'masculine'. This strategy is often accompanied by humour, as in the Zooom ad. Another example might be the series of commercials for Danone's Actimel drinking yoghurt that were aired on national TV in 2008. These ads all featured popular film and TV actor Ivan Urgant dressed as a rather ridiculous-looking super-hero in a red and white cape, exhorting a young office worker named Gennady to boost his body's natural defence systems by drinking Actimel. The link between consuming the yoghurt and boosting one's sex appeal is made quite clear in one of the ads, which begins with Gennady coyly exchanging amorous glances with a female colleague before 'Captain Actimel' arrives to remind him of the physiological benefits of Actimel, whereupon he tries to fly off into the sky only to get his body well and truly stuck in the ceiling. The promise of increased sex appeal is also central to at least some of the ads in our next section, where we focus on another product category on which Russian men have historically been reluctant to spend money, namely male grooming products.

Men's grooming products and the return of the 'real' Russian man: Nivea for Men, the Philips body-hair trimmer and Gillette's Fusion ProGlide Razor

In a recent article on make-up for men, Miller (2014: 246) comments: 'Whilst global brands attempt to sell make-up as the next natural progression from skincare in men's grooming routine, whatever their sexuality, there is plenty of resistance to the notion that men should care at all'. Miller is referring here to men's make-up products and their perception in the West. Yet her comment is equally, indeed more applicable to men's grooming products of all kinds in contemporary Russia. A recent survey, for example, found that while 88 per cent of Russian women use skin-care products, only 30 per cent of Russian men do so (CosmeticsBusiness.com 2014; in the US, the figure for men in the 18–24 age range is currently 70 per cent: Boyle 2013). Although the survey found that in Russia 'it is becoming more acceptable for men to include personal care in their daily activities', its authors concluded that when it came to buying such products, many Russian men felt a 'stigma', associating them with femininity. 'Most [Russian] men', they noted, 'will [only] purchase grooming products that convey masculinity, are simple to use and multifunctional' (CosmeticsBusiness. com 2014).

In 2013, as if conscious of the difficulty of promoting men's grooming products in Russia, three leading Western brands – Nivea, Philips and Gillette – launched advertising campaigns exclusively for the Russian market, each of which centred precisely on the notion of 'masculinity', as mentioned in the CosmeticsBusiness.com report. In an ad for Nivea for Men shaving foam, for example, a man appears in close-up in the extreme right-hand side of the image, his head and upper torso framed by an imposing landscape of lake, pine trees and mountains in the background. His lower face covered in gel, he is shaving. As he does so, he stares straight back at the viewer, in a look caught halfway between defiance and recognition. Nothing remarkable about that, one might think – except that the tool he is using is not a razor blade, but rather an axe (the text at the bottom of the image reads: 'use whatever you like to shave with – the most important thing is not to irritate your skin!'). Despite his position at the very edge of the picture, the man is at the very centre of our attention. Occupying the foreground, his head extending vertically outside the frame, he appears much larger than the trees and mountains behind him. The ruggedly sylvan setting may be an implicit allusion to Putin's various Siberian exploits (see Goscilo 2013c). There is nothing in the natural landscape to identify the location, however; it could just as well be Montana as Siberia. Indeed, the location is of secondary importance to the myths that the image itself conjures up. An implicit link *is* made, via both the axe and the backdrop, between masculinity and productive, physical labour (Moisio, Arnould and Gentry 2013), since this man may well use his axe to chop down a few trees once he's shaved (if he hasn't already done so). More obviously, however, the ad creates an association between masculinity and the great outdoors, offering the possibility of flight from the 'civilised', conformist, domestic world of the feminine (Schouten and McAlexander 1995; Belk and Costa 1998). Rather than embracing femininity, then, Nivea appears to be offering the male consumer the opportunity to neutralise the threat that femininity represents.

If Nivea sought to reassure Russian men by suggesting that personal grooming might offer them the chance to 'escape' from the clutches of women and their cloying domesticity, and by the same token find their true, untamed, solitary selves (Hirschman 2003), another leading Western brand, Philips, took a radically different approach to the problem of persuading men to take care of their body image. Their print ad, designed by the Moscow office of Ogilvy and Mather, appeared in April 2013. The image is split vertically in half. On the left-hand side, entitled 'before', we see a well-honed, white male body. Or rather we see a part of that body, namely the torso, across which stretches a band of chest hair in a vaguely Y-shape, from below the navel to just above each pectoral muscle (thereby leaving the man's impressive six-pack exposed for us to admire). In the right-hand half of the picture (the 'after'), we see the same torso, this time covered by a good deal more hair. The abundant curls in question do not belong to him, however (thanks to the Philips body groomer, he no longer suffers the ignominy of being hirsute), but rather to two admirers, locked with him in what appears to be an amorous embrace. These admirers remain just as anonymous as our male subject, however, since all we see is their hair covering his torso as they give themselves up to him in apparently gay abandon. Lest we have any doubts as to their gender identity, however, there is an accompanying text on hand to reassure us: 'Designed for men. Appreciated by women', it tells us.[23]

In her work on the changing images of men in advertising in the UK in the 1980s and 1990s, Gibbons (1999) suggests that by revealing his body readily and invitingly, the so-called 'new man' of ads for Levi's or Diet Coke is sexualised and eroticised in a way that makes a display of him. His body, she maintains, is overtly commodified and he becomes an accessible object of desire, particularly in images that crop head and limbs. In this Philips ad, however, it is the women who are commodified, since their sole function is to serve as proof of the male subject's sexual appeal, thereby enabling him to retain his status and power as subject (in essence, their hair functions as a badge, rather like the 'S' on Superman's tunic, or the star on Captain America's shield). This commodification is underlined by the cropping technique, which in effect erases their identities (Schroeder and Borgerson 1998; on the importance of the face in advertising, see also Ilicic, Baxter and Kulczynski 2015). As far as the male subject is concerned, his 'to-be-looked-at-ness', to paraphrase Gibbons (1999), is nothing more than a masquerade of femininity, since he remains well and truly in charge of his sexuality. While this masquerade renders him desirable both to women and to male homosexuals, it does so in a way that does not alienate the male heterosexual viewer, thanks to its unambiguous strapline.

This 'masquerade of femininity' nevertheless begs the question: are we seeing the emergence in contemporary Russian advertising of the kind of 'new man' who graced UK TV screens in the 1980s and 1990s? The question is especially germane if we remember that for Nixon (1996: 202), this 'new man' imagery involved 'the display of masculine sensuality, the sanctioning of a highly staged narcissism through the codes of dress and grooming and [...] the coding of sexual ambivalence – especially in the organization of spectatorship.' Each of these elements is present, to a greater or lesser extent, in the Philips commercial. Ultimately, however, the answer to the question is very definitely 'no' – as will become clear if we look at an ad (or rather a pair of ads) for another male grooming product, namely the Gillette Fusion ProGlide razor. In these ads, the kind of hegemonic masculinity embodied by Dodge's boxer returns with a vengeance. Moreover, in doing so it establishes a clear link between that masculinity and Russian national identity.[24]

In 2011, Russian ice hockey star Aleksandr Ovechkin signed a long-term sponsorship deal to become the face of Gillette in Russia (Sostav.ru 2013a). Ice hockey is the national sport in Russia, and Ovechkin, a member both of the

NHL's Washington Capitals and of the Russian national squad, is currently one of the country's most popular players. One of Russia's biggest sports personalities, he is often referred to in the media as 'Aleksandr the Great'. In recent years, this popularity, both at home and in the US, has led to Ovechkin endorsing a range of brands, including Reebok, Nike and Coca-Cola. He has also made two ads for Gillette's Fusion ProGlide razors in Russia, diffused both on TV and on social media such as YouTube. Gillette's choice of an ice hockey star such as Ovechkin is not innocent, of course. As we saw earlier with Sylvester Stallone and Russian Ice, certain sports – especially contact sports – appeal to advertisers precisely on account of the image of tough, rugged masculinity they convey (Jackson and Andrews 2005; Whannel 2007). As Gee (2009) argues, societies in which men have lost many of their long-established opportunities to express their masculinity are especially likely to choose sportsmen as modern-day heroes. Post-Cold-War, Post-Chechnya, post-industrialist Russia is one such country, as we have already suggested, and as has been argued elsewhere (see for example Thornhill 1997; Goscilo 2000; Baer 2013b; Gillespie, forthcoming). When it comes to demonstrating 'manhood', of course, ice hockey stars are not just any kind of sportsmen. A close-contact activity, ice hockey relies on a particularly physical, indeed 'aggressive' type of masculinity that can be very reassuring to many men. As Gee suggests, in a comment specifically about the NHL but which could apply to the sport in general:

> Within this subculture, hegemonic masculinity is a form of masculine practice that generates and regulates the following commonsense cultural ideals linked with 'being a man': aggression, heterosexuality, muscularity, the suppression of fear, intentional physical demonstrations of power and dominance, and the subordinated role of women. (Gee 2009: 581)

Ovechkin's first ad for Gillette appeared in January 2013 (see YouTube 2013a). As he picks up his razor, and gazes at his face in the bathroom mirror, a deeply affirmative, masculine voice-off suddenly intones: 'Provided you choose the right weapon, you can win even the most difficult battle'. The 'warrior' theme which this comment explicitly introduces is, as Gee (2009: 579) has argued, 'an often romanticized symbolic expression of hegemonic masculinity'. As 'warrior hero', Ovechkin is potentially even more reassuring than as ice hockey star. As Woodward points out:

> The warrior hero is physically fit and powerful. He is mentally strong and unemotional. [...] He is brave, adventurous, and prepared to take risks. He has the physical ability to conquer hostile environments, to cross unfamiliar terrain, and to lay claim to dangerous ground. (Woodward, K. 2007: 237; quoted in Gee 2009: 582)

The first Gillette ad presents Ovechkin as precisely this kind of 'warrior hero'. It does so by literalising the 'warrior' metaphor alluded to in the opening bathroom sequence; Ovechkin is transported to a vast ice-covered surface inside what appears to be a huge warehouse, on which he stands defiant but alone against the massed ranks of anonymous, faceless figures opposite him, seemingly ready to charge at any moment. As if oblivious to the danger, however, Ovechkin loses no time in slicing fearlessly and effortlessly through his adversaries, in a manner highly similar to the way in which the blades of Gillette's new razor pass through the stubble on his chin, as we now see, in what is the ad's closing image.[25]

The kind of 'warrior-like' qualities as described by Woodward, are even more in evidence in the second Gillette ad, aired in September 2013, four months before the Sochi Winter Olympics, to which it looks forward (see YouTube 2013b). As the ad begins, we see a figure in the middle distance, running swiftly and assuredly through a forest, leaping nimbly and vigorously over logs as snow falls around him. The caption in the bottom right-hand section of the screen identifies the figure as Ovechkin, 'member of the national Olympic ice hockey team'. We can just make out the word 'Russia' on the back of his tracksuit top. Next, we see him from the rear as he dives, bare-chested into a semi-frozen lake. We are then given two underwater shots in quick succession, first of Ovechkin's body plunging into the lake, then of a blade plunging into water (both enter the water at the same angle). The scene then shifts back to Ovechkin's bathroom, as the star, dressed in singlet and pyjama bottoms, lifts his wet face out of the sink, and stares right at us, before picking up his special razor (shot in close-up, with the word 'Russia' and the Russian flag clearly visible on the handle), and proceeding to shave. The link between hegemonic masculinity and Russian national identity apparent in this final shot is also conveyed in the accompanying voice-over:

> You achieve the best results when you temper you character, forged in extreme heat, then tempered with extreme cold. Our finest blades are made to perfection, and are as strong as the Russian character itself. [...] Show your steely character, with the Fusion ProGlide series, specially designed for the Sochi Olympics.

In the two Ovechkin ads, then, we can see a return to the narcissistic representation of Soviet-style hegemonic hyper-masculinity of the Dodge ad. Indeed, both ads reproduce the flesh-to-metal metaphor/myth underpinning the Caliber commercial – the second even more insistently than the first, as Ovechkin's body, plunging into the icy water, is transformed before our very eyes into a steel razor blade. Another feature the Gillette ads share with the Dodge commercial is 'brand morphing'. Ovechkin's tough, physically uncompromising masculinity has little in common with what we see in the Czech ad for the Fusion ProGlide that aired in late 2010, in which the star is largely restricted to skating nimbly around the ice – and scoring a goal – for 'Team Gillette' (YouTube 2011). Neither can it be compared to the earnest sincerity of another NHL star, John Tavares, who starred in the Canadian ad for the same product that aired in January 2014 in which we see him seated in the locker room mentally preparing for the game ahead (YouTube 2014b). And it is extremely different from the comic playfulness of the double act of Argentinian soccer star Lionel Messi and Swiss tennis ace Roger Federer, who starred in a global ad campaign for the razor shortly before the Soccer World Cup Finals in June of the same year (YouTube 2014a). For Gillette in Russia in 2013, however, as for Dodge in 2006, masculinity is clearly no laughing matter. Granting super-hero powers is, it would seem, a deadly serious business. But what about Putin himself, the one Russian male whose own personality cult involves portraying himself as a superhero (Goscilo 2013d)?[26] How is he represented in advertising? It is Putin, and the advertisements for his presidential campaign of 2012, which will provide our final case study here.

The 'First Time' with Putin, or the Lad(y) Vanishes

> My boyfriend got into trouble again
>
> Got into a fight, took some junk.
>
> I'm so tired of him, I dumped him.
>
> And now I want someone like Putin.
>
> Someone like Putin, full of strength.
>
> Someone like Putin, who doesn't drink.
>
> Someone like Putin, who won't hurt me.
>
> Someone like Putin, who won't run away.
>
> I saw him yesterday on the news.
>
> He said that the world was at a crossroads.
>
> With someone like him, things are easy, at home and at friends'.
>
> And now I want someone like Putin.

The song 'Someone Like Putin', by the group Singing Together, reflects not just Putin's current popularity in Russia – among voters of both sexes – but also, and perhaps particularly, the increasing sexualisation of Putin's image in the second half of the 2000s (see Goscilo 2013d: 194).[27] That image has indeed changed – the Putin brand has 'morphed' – quite considerably since the former head of the KGB's Dresden bureau was appointed Russia's Prime Minister by Boris Yeltsin on 3 December 1999, replacing Yeltsin as President a mere twenty-eight days later. On 7 October 2010, as a gift for his fifty-eighth birthday, a group of female students from the Journalism Department of Moscow State University presented him with a calendar composed of photographs of themselves. The lingerie they wore in the pictures, the poses they adopted, and the 'invitations' they addressed to him left little to the imagination. The following year, a video named 'The Army of Putin' ('Armiya Putina'), after an organisation of well over 1,000 female fans, and featuring another female student urging young women everywhere to take their clothes off in support of their hero, was published on the Russian social media network, VKontakte (Goscilo 2013d).

What this last example demonstrates is how important visual media, and the visual image, have become to the personality cult that has grown up around the man who looks set to remain in the Kremlin until at least 2020. As Goscilo (2013b) notes, citing Debord (1992), twenty-first century post-Soviet Russian society has continued the Soviet tradition of theatricalising public life, turning it into a series of empty rituals, little more than a hollow spectacle. The Putin 'spectacle' (Ryazanova-Clarke 2013) is everywhere – on television (Hutchings and Rulyova 2009), on the official Kremlin website (where he can be seen engaged in all sorts of activities, from posing in the cockpit of the TU-160 long-range strategic bomber to piloting a motorised hang glider in order to save a breed of Siberian geese), or in bookstores, where his face adorns countless varieties of 'office supplies' (Goscilo 2013c). Central to that phenomenon, as Goscilo also points out, is not just his performance of hegemonic, hetero-normative masculinity, but the role played by his body in that performance (see also Sperling 2015). The centrality of the body to Putin's particular brand of masculinity can be seen in the numerous physical, and physically challenging, activities in which the Russian President has very publicly engaged in recent years (many of which have a link with sports of one kind or another): con-ducting a judo master class with the then World and Olympic champion, Yasuhiro Yamashita, in December 2005; practising his butterfly stroke – the swimming stroke which most exposes the torso – in the chilly waters of a Siberian lake; scuba-diving in the Black Sea (and 'discovering' two sixth-century AD Greek vases: Goscilo 2013d: 200–1); or working out on bodybuilding machines at home. He tends also to appear bare-chested, even when this is not strictly necessary (such as when fishing in Siberian rivers: Goscilo 2013c: 9; Cassiday and Johnson 2013: 42). Even when trying his hand (literally) at more 'creative' pursuits, these often also involve a certain physicality, not to say dexterity and indeed – a recurrent them here – mastery over nature and the elements. One thinks, for example, of the photographs of his public turn at the potter's wheel in the tourist village of Verkhnie Mandrogi in 2001 (see Cassiday and Johnson 2013: 53). Goscilo has argued that Putin's cult of leadership in a strong masculine body is designed to reassure the Russian public – an argument that Baer (2013b) also makes.[28] Indeed, as Sperling (2015: 117–18) notes, the rumours that emerged in late 2012 that Putin had undergone Botox treatments on his face were widely interpreted in Russia as a sign that he was considering ditching his masculine legitimacy and launching a programme of political reform.

If Putin's public and very physical persona is indeed designed to reassure his angst-ridden male compatriots, then this brings us back once again to advertising. As we have already noted, Schroeder and Zwick (2004) have convincingly argued that advertisers often seek to persuade men that it is primarily con-sumption, rather than production, that guarantees both the male subject's social status, and his sexual appeal. Indeed, as Goscilo (2013d) has herself observed, Putin's own particular brand of masculinity is a combination of toughness and gentleness which means that even when he demonstrates apparent concern for his good looks by taking Botox, this does not appear to threaten the tough-guy image that he has been careful to nurture. To quote Cassiday and Johnson (2013: 43):

> In contrast to Yeltsin and the flabby, flaccid leaders of the late Soviet era, Putin has a political identity and public image characterized by masculine sexual potency. [...] As a result, Putin's popularity among Russian women has been particularly high, with incidents of Putin hysteria reported occasionally in the [Russian] media.

This sexual aspect of his persona is central to our final case study in this chapter, namely Putin's presidential campaign advertisements of 2012. What is particularly remarkable about these ads, however, is that, whereas historically, strong leaders in Russia have portrayed themselves as 'fathers' of the people (Hubbs 1993), here Putin adopts a different masculine role altogether, namely that of lover. The three ads, put out by the pro-Kremlin youth group 'Nashi' (literally 'Ours'), were aired in the spring of 2012.[29] The combined theme of love, sex and democracy which they feature first figured in the campaign for the legislative elections of Putin's Party, 'United Russia' in December 2011, in an ad which showed an anonymous young couple appearing to have sex in a polling booth.[30] In Putin's presidential ads, however, this sexing-up of democracy is given a very personal twist. In one ad, aired in February 2012, a young woman visits a fortune-teller, in order to find out what love has in store for her (viewable at Huffington Post 2012a).[31] In another, aired around the same time, another young woman visits her doctor to obtain advice (see Huffington Post 2012b). In a third, a young woman visits her psychiatrist (YouTube 2012b).[32] Structurally, the scenarios are remarkably similar: a naïve, credulous female seeks guidance from an older authority figure. The ad in the doctor's surgery is typical:

DOCTOR: This is what I want to say to you. You must not forget that the most important thing is to be safe.[33]

YOUNG WOMAN: Yes, doctor, I understand.

DOCTOR: (putting his glasses on): Particularly because it's your first time.

YOUNG WOMAN: (visibly embarrassed): But perhaps [...] I don't need [...] this [...]

DOCTOR: (firmly): Yes, you do. (As he says so, he vigorously stamps what appears to be a medical form, and declares approvingly:) And it's absolutely right that you should want to do it for love. I fully approve your decision (taking off his glasses once again).

YOUNG WOMAN: (with a mixture of relief and excitement): You do?

DOCTOR: (looking up towards the wall, on which hangs a calendar open at a page on which he can be seen shaking hands with Putin): You will be safe with him.

The young woman smiles at him with a mixture of appreciation and relief.

(The scene cuts to a young woman approaching a polling station. As she begins to climb the steps, the picture fades and is replaced by text: 'Putin. The first time – only for ♡'. Putin's smiling face appears, occupying the right-hand third of the screen.)

On a superficial level, these ads appear to exploit traditional authority figures – the fortune-teller, the doctor, the psychiatrist – to offer young female voters reassurance that with Putin they're in safe hands. As Sperling (2015: 296) notes, they also tap into 'a common heteronormative understanding of gender roles whereby women seek out male lovers to protect them.' These ads do far more than merely rehash the traditional folk tale scenario, however. To see exactly what it is they do, we need to return to the notion of the gaze, in other words to turn to Lacan, or rather to Slavoj Žižek's reading of Lacan. We need, in Žižek's famous formulation, to 'look awry' at these ads. In *Looking Awry*, first published in 1991, Žižek used concepts from Freudian, and especially Lacanian psychoanalysis, to read popular culture. In particular, he referred to concepts such as fantasy, trauma and unconscious desire to produce radically new readings of works by Hitchcock, Poe and Ridley Scott among others. Žižek's take on Lacan in particular is not without its flaws, as Parker (2004) for example has noted. Nevertheless, his writing offers novel ways to approach popular culture, advertising, and in particular our three Putin ads.

In his chapter on the figure of the psychotic in relation to the Symbolic Order, Žižek discusses Hitchcock's film *The Lady Vanishes* (1938). He begins by making the important point that 'a psychotic is precisely a subject who is *not duped by the symbolic order*' (Žižek 1992: 79, original emphasis). In Hitchcock's film, as Žižek reminds us, the hero meets a woman who suddenly and unexpectedly vanishes. When he tries to determine where she might have gone, however, he can find nobody who will confirm that she ever existed. The plot, as Žižek points out, is a variation on the archetypical theme of 'the disappearance which everybody denies'. He continues:

> [T]he person who disappears is as a rule a very ladylike woman. It is difficult not to recognize in this phantomlike figure the apparition of Woman, of the woman who could fill out the lack in man, the ideal partner with whom the sexual relationship would finally be possible, in short, the Woman who, according to Lacanian theory, precisely does not exist. The nonexistence of this woman is rendered manifest to the hero by the absence of her inscription in the sociosymbolic network: the intersubjective community of the hero acts as if she does not exist, as if she were only his *idée fixe*'
> (Žižek 1992: 80)

Of course, the existence of such a figure, while understood by the 'big Other', cannot be openly acknowledged by the intersubjective community, for to do so would be to admit that the subject is right, that he is not in fact duped by the Symbolic Order. This in turn would confirm his psychosis, and allow 'foreclosure' from the symbolic – something which cannot be allowed to happen, since it can lead to political regimes such as Nazism, which for Žižek was first and foremost a 'psychotic' system (Parker 2004: 96). Žižek continues:

> [T]he psychotic subject's distrust of the big Other, his [sic] *idée fixe* that the big Other (embodied in the intersubjective community) is trying to deceive him, is always and necessarily supported by an unshakable belief in a consistent Other, an other without gaps, an 'Other of the Other' [...] When the paranoid subject clings to his distrust of the Other of the symbolic community, of 'common opinion', he implies thereby the existence of an 'Other of this Other', of a nondeceived agent who holds the reins. (Žižek 1992: 81)

What, however, is the relevance of Hitchcock's film, or indeed Žižek's reading of Lacan, to the Putin campaign ads? In order to answer that question, we need first of all to point out that, like the woman in Hitchcock's film, Putin performs his very own vanishing act. He hardly appears at all in these ads, his absence in stark contrast to the stubbornly persistent presence of the body of his predecessor and namesake Vladimir Lenin, eternally on display in the purpose-built mausoleum on Red Square (Yurchak 2015). In the fortune-teller film, we see him merely on a Tarot card, in the doctor's surgery, he is reduced to a photograph on the page of a calendar, while in the psychiatrist's office his image peers out from the front cover of *Time* magazine.[34] This is hardly conventional for a presidential campaign film (Mullen 2013), especially when the candidate in question is usually noted for his 'voracious omnipresence' (Goscilo 2013c). The point is that these ads function as a reversal, a negative image, of the classic 'disappearance' plot as summarised by Žižek. In other words, whereas in Hitchcock's film, everybody conspires to deny the existence of somebody whose reality the viewer has been able to verify with her own eyes, in the Putin ads, we have first a fortune-teller and then a doctor discussing as real someone whom we never actually see. The inclusion of these figures of authority (embodying either traditional folk wisdom or modern scientific knowledge) is crucial here. In effect, they embody the 'nondeceived agent', the 'Other of the Other'. As such, their function is precisely to prevent the subject from slipping into psychosis, to stop her realising that she is right to suspect that the omniscient, omnipotent, 'spectacular' Putin (and indeed the vision of benevolent democracy he embodies) might not actually exist – hence the doctor's reassurance that 'you will be safe with him', and indeed the fortune-teller's insistence that 'he will not *deceive* you'. This reassurance is vital if the subject is to be freed of her psychosis and enabled to enter the Symbolic Order (the 'Symbolic Order', or 'big Other' that in psychoanalytical theory is not just the social world of linguistic communication and intersubjective relations, but also the realm of knowledge of ideological conventions, and the acceptance of the law: Smecker 2014). This is the importance of the final scene of each ad; entering the polling station becomes a metaphor for entering the Symbolic Order, as the subject literally no longer maintains a distance from that Order, now that she has been cured of her psychosis – now, in other words, she has accepted her love for the 'big (Br)other'.

In one sense, then, Putin's disappearing act can be explained by his desire for the subject – or rather *us* – to enter the – or to be more precise *his* – Symbolic Order. But there is, we would suggest, something else at work here too. Putin's vanishing act serves two other, equally important functions. First, the 'first love' fantasy helps locate the viewer as (desiring) subject. As Žižek argues:

> [W]hat the fantasy stages is not a scene in which our desire is fulfilled, fully satisfied, but on the contrary, a scene that realizes, stages, the desire as such. [… D]esire is not something given in advance, but something that has to be constructed – and it is precisely the role of fantasy to give the coordinates of the subject's desire, to specify its object, to locate the position the subject assumes in it. It is only through fantasy that the subject is constructed as desiring: *through fantasy we learn how to desire.* (Žižek 1992: 6; original emphasis)

As he puts it even more pithily elsewhere in the same chapter: 'fantasy space functions as an *empty surface*, as a kind of screen for the projection of desires: the fascinating presence of its positive contents does nothing but fill out a certain emptiness' (Žižek 1992: 8, our emphasis).

So much for the desiring subject. What, however, about the object of that desire, Putin himself? In Lacanian terms, Putin's disappearing act, his almost Derridean 'absent presence', enables him to posit himself as the ultimate fantasy figure, the ultimate object of desire (Belk, Ger and Askegaard, 2001). To paraphrase Žižek, he becomes 'the ~~woman~~ man who could fill out the lack in [wo]man, the ideal partner with whom the sexual relationship would finally be possible, in short, the ~~Wo~~[M]an who, according to Lacanian theory, precisely does not exist' (Žižek 1992: 80). To extend this idea further: 'The ~~non~~-existence of this ~~woman~~ man is rendered manifest to the hero[ine] by the ~~absence~~ [presence] of ~~her~~ [his] inscription in the sociosymbolic network: the inter-subjective community of the hero[ine] acts as if ~~she~~ does ~~not~~ exist, as if ~~she~~ were [not] only ~~his~~ [her] *idée fixe*' (Žižek 1992: 80; original emphasis). This is why the 'vanishing lady' plot has to reversed; while it is only by disappearing that the real Putin can escape the loss of power implied by becoming the object of desire, of the desiring subject and of that subject's gaze, it is only by being talked about as if real that the idealised Putin can retain (political) power as subject.[35] In this sense, the ad enables Putin to square the Lacanian circle drawn by Žižek, since it allows him to exist simultaneously as both object and subject (a most 'sublime subject of ideology', to bowdlerise the title of another of Žižek's works). This dual status does not just make him the 'ideal partner', but transforms him into the very embodiment of utopia, that perfect place that does not exist but about which everybody talks as if it just might – or, as Maclaran and Brown (2005: 312) put it, that 'liberating impulse that breaks through current limitations of human existence and anticipates a better future'. The Putin ads, then, represent the perfect fusion of Putin's personal project and his political vision; there really is, it would seem, no difference between voting for him and loving him.

Conclusion

There is a common thread running through the representation of masculinity in advertisements of the Putin era – that of the (Russian) male as super-hero. This heroic representation of masculinity is designed to reassure the male subject that the consumer is not necessarily any less 'master of the object world' than the producer (Slater 1997: 57). *Homo consumens* may be just as 'authentic', and enjoy just as much 'inner freedom' – in the shape of sexual appeal and social status – as *homo faber*. This message, at the heart of so much advertising in the West and elsewhere, is conveyed, at least in those ads we have examined, by a return to Soviet iconography, and the myth of hegemonic masculinity which that iconography was designed to buttress. The (neo-Soviet) Russian male emerges in these ads as Superman. As for that pseudo-Nietzchean übermensch Putin, he is doubly heroic, since he is *both* Superman in his countless publicity shoots (which can also be said to function as advertisements), *and* the Invisible Man in his election campaign. The myth of hegemonic masculinity is proving to be remarkably tenacious in the advertising space of the new Russia, and might even be said to take itself increasingly seriously as Putin himself intensifies his grip on political power. For the moment, when it comes to hegemonic masculinity in Putin-era advertising, the centre, to paraphrase Maclaran and Brown (2005), appears to be holding. Indeed, masculinity comes to constitute a utopian performative space, rather like the shopping malls that Maclaran and Brown discuss, and indeed the Tochka-G sex shop with which we concluded our previous chapter. The body in which Russian masculinity is 'packaged' in these ads is, to paraphrase Butler (2011), the only body that matters in contemporary Russian consumer culture. This brings us to the subject of packaging itself, a realm in which as we shall see in our next chapter, another utopia emerges, that of Russian history in general and its political and economic centre Moscow, in particular.

Notes

1 The position and role of women in the new Russia has of course also been the subject of much debate, and even 'anxiety' (Oushakine 2001) – particularly in the wake of the Pussy Riot affair of 2012, in which the all-girl punk band performed an impromptu number in front of the main altar of the Cathedral of Christ the Saviour in Moscow, and exhorted the Mother of God to 'become a feminist' (Vaissié 2014, Sperling 2015).
2 As Sperling herself notes (Sperling 2015: 72), gay sex was only legalised in Russia in 1993.

3 Ironically, Wurst came third in the SMS votes of Russian TV viewers.
4 For a useful summary of Butler's discussion of gender, and its relevance to research on advertising, see Borgerson (2005).
5 For an overview of research on gender in advertising from 1970 to 2002, see Wolin (2003).
6 If advertisers do borrow conventions from other genres, this may not necessarily be solely in order to pre-empt and overcome potential consumer resistance, as Scott suggests elsewhere in her article (Scott 1994b: 465).
7 In the case of the Savage ad, the nostalgia is rather of the kind described by Boym (2007: 10) as 'anticipatory [...] for the present that flees with the speed of a click'.
8 However we read ads, we should not forget that the majority of them are still produced by men (O'Donohoe 2000: 90), not just in the West, but in Russia too.
9 The ad can be viewed at Kostyakova (2009).
10 For an extended discussion of the concept, see Connell and Messerschmidt (2005). A useful review of the concept of 'hegemonic masculinity' in the context of advertising can be found in Gee (2009: 580–83).
11 On the iconography of the Soviet political poster, see Bonnell (1997).
12 This is a reference to the archetypical Soviet Socialist Realist novel, Nikolay Ostrovsky's *How The Steel Was Tempered* (*Kak zakalyalas' stal'*), of 1932–34.
13 While not an exclusively Soviet myth (see for example Quam-Wickham 1999), it was nevertheless the cornerstone of Bolshevik ideology.
14 The car's very name – 'Caliber' – appears designed to assuage such fears in the mind of (male) consumers. For a perceptive study of how male consumers of another 'unmasculine' product (kilts) 'perform' rugged, physical masculinity, see Reddy-Best and Howell (2014).
15 While by the time of the ad campaign, Odessa had become part of Ukraine, in the nineteenth century, when Stallone's great-grandmother was born, the city was the fourth largest city of the Russian Empire.
16 The seriousness of this particular scene is in stark contrast to the self-deprecating humour deployed by another Hollywood actor, Stallone's co-star from the *Expendables* franchise, Bruce Willis in an ad from 2010 for Polish vodka Sobieski: YouTube (2010).
17 A photo of members of the Moscow Boxing Federation proudly marching across Red Square, taken in 1954 by Henri Cartier-Bresson (and published in *Life* magazine) can be seen at Clock Shout Photo (2010).
18 On the arrival of foreign breweries in post-socialist Russia, see Arvedlund (2004).
19 Tinkoff sold his beer and brewery business to the Belgian–Brazilian group AB–InBev in 2005 for 167 million €. The following year he founded Tinkoff Credit Systems Bank which currently co-sponsors the Tinkoff–Saxo professional cycling team. The Tinkoff beer brand was relaunched in 2014: *Kommersant'* (2014).
20 For an extended discussion of this ad see Morris (2007).
21 It is unclear in the ad whether this figure is a transvestite (a male masquerading as a female by donning women's clothing), or transgender (which implies a physical transformation of the body itself). For the sake of simplicity, however, we refer to this individual throughout as a transvestite.
22 On alcopops as stereotypically 'women's' drinks, see BBC (2004).
23 An English-language version of the ad, posted by the ad agency, can be seen here: AdsOfTheWorld.com (2013).
24 This conflation between national identity and hegemonic masculinity has also been a feature of recent Russian blockbuster movies by directors such as Nikita Mikhalkov and Aleksey Balabanov (Larsen 2003).
25 The 'Battle on the Ice' is a recurrent trope in Russian consumer culture. It can be seen, for example, on the Russian Ice bottle mentioned earlier, and in a 2003 ad for 'Three Bogatyrs' beer.

26 On Russian cartoonist Sergey Elkin's caricatures of Putin as Superman, see Goscilo (2013c, 2013d).
27 The translation is from Borenstein (2007: 225). For a video of the song, with English subtitles, see: YouTube (2008a).
28 While it may well reassure some members of Russian manhood, this policy has also produced countless parodies of Putin's performative brand of masculinity: Goscilo (2013d).
29 While 'Nashi' is officially a non-government organisation, it is nevertheless sponsored by the Kremlin (Sperling 2015: 163). As such, Putin will at the very least have given his personal backing to the videos: see Allnutt (2012).
30 As Sperling (2015: 296) notes, there is a well-established tradition of more or less explicit sexual references in post-Soviet Russian political ads. On the use of sex in an advertisement for Russian far right politician Vladimir Zhirinovsky during the December 1993 presidential elections, see Mickiewicz (1997: 158–59).
31 In post-Soviet Russia, as elsewhere it would seem, politics has now become 'a consumptive, individualised and private sphere' (Mullen 2013: 182).
32 On these ads, and Barack Obama's use of a similar scenario in a campaign ad of October 2012, see Sperling (2015: 296–98).
33 The Russian word used here – 'bezopasnost' – can mean both '(personal) safety' and '(political) security'. It is the 'B' both in 'KGB', and in the acronym of that organisation's post-Soviet successor, the 'FSB' – two organisations closely associated with Putin himself.
34 While it is true that Putin's image appears right at the end of each ad, ultimately this makes no difference. For, as Tisseron (1996) reminds us, since Lacan's work on the mirror stage, identity is inconceivable outside the image. Indeed, as Tisseron (1996: 92) puts it, 'identity is [itself] an image' ('l'identité est une image'). In consequence, Tisseron continues, any image which purports to represent a person's identity (such as, for example, Putin's), is merely the image of an image, rather than the person her/himself.
35 It is interesting to note here the amount of 'talk' generated by Putin's apparent 'disappearance' for several days in the spring of 2015: Luhn (2015).

3 The politics of packaging in post-socialist Russia

Labels, logos, locations

Introduction

As we noted in the previous chapter, Putin appears everywhere in Russia today. As well as on television and the Internet, his face can be seen on a range of consumer goods, from the watches and mugs sold in the kiosks around countless metro stations, to the baseball caps and designer t-shirts available from online stores such as the 'Putin Shop'.[1] One of the companies fuelling this trend is Konfael', a Moscow-based confectioner founded in 2001. In 2003, the company launched a 12″ by 19″ limited edition chocolate portrait of the Russian president, weighing over three pounds and priced at approximately US $700 (Goscilo 2013c). More recently, at the beginning of 2015, Putin's face appeared on one of the company's boxes. The box in question features a close-up of the President's hand raised to his face as he discreetly adjusts his sunglasses. The accompanying text reads: 'To be a king, surrounded by pawns, takes strong nuts!' ('Byt' korolem, kogda povsyudu peshki […] Nado imet' krepkie oreshki!').[2] The Putin box is in fact one of a number contained in Konfael''s 'Political Chocolates' range.[3] The other boxes in the series reproduce Soviet propaganda posters, the original text accompanying the poster at times modified to reflect the current political climate. So for example, one finds the poster from 1941, the year Nazi Germany invaded the USSR, warning people not to mention anything in casual conversation that may be useful to the enemy. The original image featured a woman on her own, her index finger raised tightly against her lips, above a text reading simply 'Don't blab' ('Ne boltai'). In Konfael''s version, however, Barack Obama stands dangerously close to her, his supersized ear cocked towards her. The accompanying text both amends and extends the original, to read: 'Ne boltai muzhik i dama, Tebya podslushivaet Obama' ('Don't blab, ladies and gents, for in your direction Obama his ear has bent').

Konfael' is by no means the only brand in today's Russia using contemporary political references to sell chocolates. Another example occurred in the summer of 2014, in response to the on-going crisis in Ukraine. In July 2013, Russia banned all imports from Ukrainian chocolate manufacturer Roshen, owned by Petro Poroshenko, a self-made confectionery magnate with serious political ambitions who has since become Ukrainian President (Kramer 2013b). By the following April, with the situation escalating (owing notably to Russia's annexation of Crimea), Ukraine banned all imports of products made by Russia's leading brand, United Confectioners (Nieburg 2014a). In the summer of 2014, Russian firm Chocolate Traditions launched two new products. The first, a chocolate bar entitled simply 'A Map of Russia 2015' ('Karta Rossii 2015g'), comes in a wrapper showing a map of Russia. The map is divided into three areas, identified respectively as 'Russian Territories', 'New Territories' (the Crimea) and 'Planned Future Territories' ('Perspektivnye Territorii'), a region which includes all of Scandinavia, the area of Eastern Europe currently occupied by the Baltic States, Poland, Belarus and Ukraine, much of Central Asia, China and even Alaska. Alongside these chocolate bars, the company also launched a new sweet, sold in a wrapper featuring a super-hero dressed in the colours of the Russian flag, standing against a map of the Crimean peninsula, and framed top and bottom by a black and gold ribbon (the Ribbon of St George, one of the most recognised and respected symbols of military valour in modern Russia).[4] The accompanying advertising slogan read 'The Crimea – Just Try and Grab It!' ('Krym – a nu-ka, otberi!'; reproduced in Cogan 2014). Given the graphic visual style in which these wrappers are executed, with their bright colours and bold text, it would be easy to dismiss Chocolate Traditions' new products as a harmless joke. The element of humour is underlined in the promotional poster for the individual praline chocolates, which contains the slogan 'Even at a time when the country is making difficult decisions, we won't stop smiling, because we're Russians!'.[5] If it is meant as a joke, however, it is likely that many Ukrainians would find Chocolate Traditions' humour extremely hard to swallow.

In a sense, of course, Chocolate Traditions is behaving like so many other FMCG (fast-moving consumer goods) brands which seek to connect emotionally with consumers by creating a distinct sense of place. Such a strategy can help 'humanise' the brand, as Hede and Watne (2013) have pointed out – particularly in Russia, where the shifting notion of 'place' has historically been at the heart of the very idea of Russian nationhood (Widdis 2004). Chocolate Traditions does so in a specific way, of course, thanks to its use of particularly striking – not to say highly controversial – historico-military imagery. That chocolate should be politicised in this way in Russia may be explained partly by the particular place it holds in Russians' collective imagination (Patico 2002). While considered 'artificial' by some of the country's cultural elite (Chester 1997), chocolate was nevertheless extremely popular during the Soviet period, with factories throughout the country – as it actually had been in the late Imperial era. Indeed, in post-Soviet society, presenting chocolate as a gift to thank teachers, doctors and other professionals for services rendered is one of the ways in which Russians today 'establish, perceive, and reproduce measures of social commonality and difference in the midst of unsettling economic developments' (Patico 2002: 346). In Putin's Russia, as Patico (2002) notes, giving chocolate is seen by many as a way of bestowing moral legitimacy on the recipient. In the light of Patico's findings, and our own examples, one could argue, *pace* Fehérváry (2009), that in Russia today chocolate plays a particularly important role in materialising not just social relationships, but political subjectivity itself.

In Russia, as in many other countries, the focal point for political subjectivity is the capital city – as the anti-Putin demonstrations on Bolotnaya Square near the Kremlin in December 2011 demonstrated only too clearly (Judah 2013), to say nothing of the more recent Soviet-style military parades across Red Square (Oushakine 2013). Given this, and the persistent politicisation of labels and containers in Russia since the late Imperial age (Hilton 2012; Kravets 2012; Roberts 2014a), it is perhaps no coincidence that there is a rich and long-established tradition in the country of representing Moscow on FMCG packaging (Smirennyi 2007). This is particularly true when it comes to chocolate. As the country's capital city, Moscow frequently appeared on chocolate wrappers and boxes in the Soviet era (especially, but not exclusively, those produced by confectioners based in the capital). Perhaps not surprisingly, the images that predominated were those of the thrusting, forward-looking 'New Moscow' (the title of a series launched by the leading Moscow brand 'Rot Front' in the 1960s). Among these were the monument to the first cosmonaut Yury Gagarin, and the so-called 'wedding cake' buildings closely associated with the architecture of the late Stalinist era.[6]

Russian and Soviet confectioners, then, have used packaging to exploit, and indeed manipulate, historico-political imagery more than those in any other FMCG sector, including vodka (Schrad 2014).[7] This begs the following question: how has the representation of Moscow changed on Russian chocolate packaging since the end of the Soviet era? This question is particularly interesting given the momentous transformation that the city itself has undergone in the last twenty years or so (see for example Kondakov 2008; Lemon 2009; Goldstein 2011; Goscilo 2011; Roberts 2014b; Walker 2015). Analysing the images of Moscow that circulate among Russian consumers on chocolate packaging will provide further insights into the politics of contemporary Russian consumer culture. It will also tell us something about the role played by packaging in today's Russia in transforming brands into 'cultural, ideological, and sociological objects' (Schroeder 2009: 124). More generally, it might also go some way towards highlighting the importance of packaging to brands and indeed to 'brand culture' (Schroeder and Salzer-Mörling 2006), both in Russia and elsewhere. With this in mind, the rest of this chapter is organised in the following way. First, we undertake a review of the literature on packaging. Second, we discuss the historical importance of FMCG packaging design in Russia. Third, we look at the particular place occupied by chocolate, both the product and its packaging, in Russian culture. Fourth, we discuss Moscow, and in particular the ambivalence surrounding the way the city has represented itself in contemporary Russia. Fifth, we examine the different ways in which the city has been represented on Russian chocolate packaging since the 1990s. Sixth and finally, we draw some more general conclusions on the ideological role of chocolate packaging in today's post-socialist Russia.

Packaging: From shelf space to ideoscape

Before proceeding, we should make it clear that by 'packaging', we mean not only 'communicative containers' (Hine 1995: 13), such as boxes, cartons, bottles, wrappers, but also – and crucially – labels. This is because labels are both part of the container, and a means of communicating something about the brand, of telling the brand's 'story' (Heilbrunn and Barré 2012: 54–56). While it is difficult to concur entirely with Hine's somewhat hyperbolic contention that 'packaging is part of human behavior' (1995: 23), boxes, cartons and bottles are nevertheless the guise in which the consumer usually encounters the product for the first time, on the store shelf. This is what makes packaging such an important aspect, not just of branding, but of 'visual consumption' (Schroeder 2002) more generally. As packaging designer Rebecca Foster has so aptly put it: 'brands are conveyed at such speed that their impact has to be immediate and understood' (quoted in Glaser 2014). Indeed, according to a recent study cited in Jarski (2014), as much as one third of consumer decision-making is based on packaging. This makes packaging central to consumer culture; one of the leading writers on branding, Keller, has gone so far as to refer to packaging as the 'fifth P' (Keller 2012).

Despite the views both of practitioners (Foster) and of academics (Keller), packaging is considerably under-researched. It is largely absent from the literature on 'brand culture' (Schroeder and Salzer-Mörling 2006), despite the fact that the art-historical approach underpinning much of this literature lends itself particularly well to a visual analysis of wrappers, boxes and bottles (see however Johansson and Holm 2006). The same is true when it comes to analyses of 'spectacular' consumption (Schroeder 2002), 'aesthetic' marketing (Charters 2006), or the 'visual' organisation (Bell, Warren and Schroeder 2013). General studies of brands also tend to ignore it (Lury 2004, Arvidsson 2006), as do those on consumer culture (Featherstone 1991; Slater 1997; Sassatelli 2007). While Lury (2011: 4), points to 'the growing importance of packaging and promotion in the manufacture, display and purchase of consumer goods' (Lury 2011: 4) as one of the defining characteristics of consumer culture itself, her most extended discussion of packaging is devoted to the problem of how best to *dispose* of it in order to protect the environment (Lury 2011: 169–71; see also Smart 2010).

One reason for the relative absence of packaging in the literature on branding may lie in the fact that packaging itself is both semiotically complex (involving visual imagery, text, colour, texture, shape, size, etc.), and ontologically ambiguous. Packaging is a hybrid phenomenon, neither immaterial (like the brand), nor material (like the product: Manning 2010: 36).[8] As Manning has observed, packaging is by its very nature torn between the 'semiotic' world of brand and the 'functional' world of the product.[9] To paraphrase Moore (2003: 332), packaging – or rather packag*es* – constitutes the 'concrete sensuous reality' of the dematerialised brand. Whatever the reason for the relative absence of packaging in the literature, it is particularly surprising, since as we have already observed, packaging is often the first point of contact – the 'commercial interface' (Heilbrunn and Barré 2012: 10) – between brand and consumer. Packaging is not merely conceptually complex, however – it is also both ubiquitous (it is difficult to conceive of an FMCG product sold entirely without packaging),[10] and as we have seen, a significant factor in the consumer decision-making process (Ambrose and Harris 2011). This is because innovative packaging is one of the most effective ways in which brands can create an aura around themselves and thereby differentiate themselves from the competition (Moor 2007, Ambrose and Harris 2011; Banet-Weiser 2013). Indeed, one only has to think of the amount of visual and textual information contained on the average bottle of French wine – or packet of British crisps[11] – to realise that packaging today is one of the principal vectors both of brand identity and of brand culture.

The academic literature on packaging can be divided into three phases. These are not discrete, but overlap, both chronologically and conceptually. Most early writers discussed packaging as a means of modifying consumer behaviour – or, if you will, as a basic element in the marketing mix, designed to draw attention to the product within and thereby maximise sales (see for example Brown 1958; McDaniel and Baker 1977; Rosenfield 1987; Underwood and Ozanne 1988).[12] A sea change in the literature began to appear in the mid-1980s, however, as scholars started to examine packages not merely as yet another means of seducing the housewife, but also as aesthetic products in their own right, a means by which the brand might express itself, its 'personality', its 'identity' and indeed its 'culture'. One of the first to do so was French semiotician Jean-Marie Floch. His seminal work, *Identités Visuelles* (Floch 1995), is inspired as much by semioticians A. J. Greimas and C. S. Peirce as by Lévi-Strauss' work on myth. The chapter on the visual branding of French restaurateur Michel Bras includes a detailed discussion of the labels on Bras' home-made liqueurs, in which Floch sees echoes of the 'rayographs', the photographs produced by Man Ray in the 1920s. The publication of Floch's book was closely followed by two articles by Florence Dano (1996; 1998). Dano went much further than Floch, however, in using semiotics to analyse the role played by packaging in helping to 'mythologise' the brand (see also Dinwoodie 1997, and Cougénas 2005). Underwood (2003) echoes Dano's point about the centrality of packaging to branding and brand identity, although he takes a radically different approach, one based not on the mythological potential of the box, carton or bottle, but rather on their materiality. As he points out, packaging (unlike advertising) creates a brand–consumer relationship based *both* on mediated *and* lived contact, as the consumer inevitably handles the packaging in question (see also Simonson and Schmitt 1997).

The idea advanced by Underwood (2003), that packaging is instrumental in the construction of identity, both of the brand and (perhaps even more importantly) of the consumer, was taken an important step further by Kniazeva and Belk (2007). In a seminal article on food packages in the US, they examined how brands fill the space on packaging with messages reinforcing the 'natural' aspects of their product. In a comment echoing Hine (1995), Kniazeva and Belk (2007: 52) treat packaging – and more specifically the stories recounted on packages and labels – 'as cultural productions, similar to those of art, literature, and advertising'. Citing Lévi-Strauss (1963), who argued that myth functions by establishing dichotomies ('raw' v. 'cooked', 'natural' v. 'unnatural', etc.) which then serve to explain the world and man's place within it, Kniazeva and Belk (2007: 52) conclude that packaging can play a crucial role as 'a vehicle for mythologizing the brand'. In this way, Kniazeva and Belk reveal just how important packaging can be in brand management, or what Manning (2010: 44) defines as 'regulating, regimenting, and appropriating th[e] two-way flow of associations between brand and consumer'. Heilbrunn and Barré (2012) also discuss the more 'mythical', and 'poetic' aspects of FMCG packaging. They analyse for example the lavishly designed fragrance bottles of French perfumer Guerlain, which they argue fulfil the 'utopian' function of re-enchanting the brand and reinvesting the product with the 'aura' it may have lost in the age of self-service shopping (Heilbrunn and Barré 2012: 113–14; on the 'sacred' nature of brands in the post-religious age, see also Belk, Wallendorf and Sherry Jnr, 1989).

The third phase in packaging scholarship, and the one that has been most frequently adopted in recent studies of the topic in post-socialist Russia (Kravets 2012; Roberts 2014a) involves looking at boxes, bottles and cartons not as aesthetic artefacts designed to attract the consumer, but rather as ideological objects in their own right, embodying and helping circulate a set of ideas supporting the interests of a dominant group in society. This phase can be traced back to the late 1990s, when Schroeder and Borgerson (1999: 46) examined what they saw as the 'sexist and racist representations typical of colonial discourses' characterising the image of Hawaii on covers of albums (and accompanying liner notes) of that island's music released around the time of its assimilation into the US, in 1959 (see also Schroeder and Borgerson 2012). Schroeder and Borgerson discussed these album sleeves neither as marketing tools, nor as elements of a brand strategy (as writers on packaging as 'myth' have tended to do). Instead, their focus was on what they referred to as 'how consumer culture works in a broader context to influence the construction of the world through representation and marketing images' (Schroeder and Borgerson 1999: 46).

Schroeder and Borgerson's highly innovative approach to packaging, emphasising its ethical and ideological dimensions, found an echo some years later in Askegaard's (2006) work on the brand as 'global ideoscape' – itself part of a broader shift in thinking about the ideological nature of brands that occurred around this time (Lury 2004; Thompson 2004; Arvidsson 2006; Holt 2006; Schroeder and Salzer-Mörling 2006; Moor 2007). Askegaard took his inspiration from Appadurai, who first coined the term in an essay written in 1990 (Appadurai 1990). Developing his point a few years later, in a monograph dealing with the twin themes of modernity and globalisation, Appadurai proffered the following definition of the concept:

> *Ideoscapes* are [...] concatenations of images [... that] are often directly political and frequently have to do with the ideologies of states and the counterideologies of movements explicitly oriented to capturing state

power or a piece of it. These ideoscapes are composed of elements of the Enlightenment worldview, which consists of a chain of ideas, terms, and images, including *freedom, welfare, rights, sovereignty, representation*, and the master term *democracy*. (Appadurai 1996: 36; original emphasis)

Ideoscapes, then, are the means by which states shape their citizens' view, both of their own state and of the world beyond that state's borders. One could of course object that Appadurai is writing as if every state had finally signed up to Western-style democracy, as if, in other words, in 1996 we had indeed arrived at 'the end of history' (Fukuyama 1992). Appadurai himself pre-empts this objection by adding the following, rather euphemistic comment:

[T]he diaspora of these terms and images across the world, especially since the nineteenth century, has loosened the internal coherence that held them together in a Euro-American master narrative and provided instead a loosely structured synopticon of politics, in which different nation-states, as part of their evolution, have organized their political cultures around different keywords. (Appadurai 1996: 36)

The question that most concerns us, however, is not so much whether history had indeed come to an end by 1996 (clearly it had not), but rather what all this has to do with brands and branding, let alone packaging. This is where we need to return to Askegaard. In essence, Askegaard suggests that global brands themselves function as ideoscapes, in that they help 'sell' precisely the ideas of which Appadurai argues ideoscapes are composed – democracy, welfare, freedom, etc. – and in so doing, contribute to the construction of the modern global political environment, ultimately reinforcing what Askegaard (2006: 92) refers to as 'the sovereign status of the liberal market economy'. In this view, brands become 'virtually synonymous with global capitalism', to (only very slightly) misquote Manning (2010: 34). The point is, of course, that each state will project – put into circulation, as it were – its own version of reality, its own ideology, in other words, its very own political culture – its very own 'ideoscape'. And it is here that packaging comes (literally) into the picture.

For decades in the UK, Enid Blyton's (in)famous golliwog appeared on jars of Robertson's jams, while in France, a Senegalese infantryman was until recently to be found on boxes of Banania chocolate powder (on the latter, see Heilbrunn and Barré 2012: 56). Both images have long since disappeared, considered as they are to be deeply racist allusions to a colonial past the major Western powers (if not Western consumers) would rather forget. In Russia of the late Soviet era, it was packaging itself, rather than the visual or verbal content of that packaging, that was often ideologically charged. Labels and packages of Western goods beyond the reach of ordinary Soviet citizens – including foreign chocolate brands – often became as sought after as the goods themselves, embodying as they did a utopian, imaginary West (Lemon 1998; Yurchak 2005; Fehérváry 2009; Manning 2009; 2010). As Yurchak poignantly notes:

> Most of these packages and bottles [displayed by Soviet youth] were empty – they could not be purchased in regular Soviet stores and often circulated as pure packaging free of original products. However, this empty status did not matter because their original meaning as consumable commodities (the actual liquor, beer, or cigarettes) was largely irrelevant. They were not commodities but shells of commodities whose role was to link the here and now to an 'elsewhere'. (Yurchak 2005: 194–95; see Manning 2010: 43)

One of the first to discuss the ideological role of packaging in post-socialist Russia was Kravets (2012; see also Makarenko and Borgerson 2009). Like Kniazeva and Belk, Kravets (2012: 363) refers to the mythical function of certain brands that appear to smooth over the contradictions between the individual consumer's daily reality and the dominant ideology of the society in which s/he lives. At the same time, however, she offers a fascinating and incisive account of how vodka labels in Russia have consistently contributed to that country's image of itself – or as she puts it, 'reshap[ed] Russia's ideoscape' (Kravets 2012: 361) since the early 1990s.

As Kravets' article makes abundantly clear, and as we ourselves have argued elsewhere (Roberts 2014a), packages can be 'read' just like any other text (see also Schroeder and Borgerson 2012). It is this idea which will inform our methodology throughout the rest of this chapter. In this respect, we are following not just theorists of myth such as Barthes, but also analysts of packaging such as Zholkovsky (1983), Dano (1996, 1998), Apel (2006), Golec (2008), Makarenko and Borgerson (2009), Manning (2010, 2012), Ambrose and Harris (2011), Bernstein (2011) and, most recently, Heilbrunn and Barré (2012). If, as Scott (1994a: 252) maintains, advertisements are 'symbolic artefacts constructed from the conventions of a particular culture', then so, surely, are packages (see also Hine 1995: 4). To paraphrase Schroeder (2002: 29–30), packaging 'colonizes and appropriates existing referent systems from literature, art, science, or other cultural discourse [...] creates its own referent systems [... and turns] signs into a kind of myth designed to sell'. It is precisely this process which we intend to study here.

FMCG packaging in Russia

Packaging design in Russia today is a highly competitive and very lucrative business: a number of high-profile domestic design agencies include examples of packaging in the portfolios published on their websites (e.g. Artemy Lebedev, Organica, Firma, Just Be Nice, ID Fabrika, Studioin, Lelikov & Partners, and Novosibirsk-based Hattomonkey). There are also a number of Russian-based websites aimed at professionals working in packaging design (see for example Upakovano.ru [n.d.]). The especially dynamic nature of the Russian packaging industry was what struck packaging design guru Peter Clarke on a recent trip to the country. In particular, Clarke noted that since the collapse of the USSR almost twenty years previously, the Russian packaging industry for food and beverages, cosmetics and tobacco products had grown at an average of between 8 and 10 per cent per annum, and was currently seeing rates as high as 10–12 per cent (Clarke 2010). As he also observed, Russia's domestic packaging industry had been given a significant boost in the period immediately following the country's financial crisis of 1998, as the devalued rouble made imported products prohibitively expensive for most of the population (many of whom had also lost their entire life savings: Goldman 2003). Clarke was also impressed by the ways in which Russian brands were modernising their packaging to compete with the numerous foreign brands that by 2010 had re-entered the Russian market, by for example importing the latest technology in an attempt to improve the package decoration process.

Not only is this industry dynamic and innovative, however; the images which feature on the packages themselves – wrappers, boxes, bottles, cartons, etc. – are frequently highly distinctive, deeply rooted as they are in Russian visual culture and iconography, as Clarke found. Innovative and striking packaging design has a long history in Russia, not least among the country's confectioners and chocolatiers. At the beginning of the twentieth century, Russian confectioners competed with each other to produce the most lavish designs, many of which featured historical themes (Upakovano.ru 2008). The particular attention Russian confectioners paid to packaging should perhaps not surprise us, since, as Bowlby (2000: 95) observes in a comment concerning chocolate in general:

> Boxes of chocolates are most often bought to be given; it is already in their chocolate-box nature to show that they are packaged and presented in wrappings that have little to do with utility and much to do with beauty, lavishness, gratuitous excess.

In the late Imperial era, Russian chocolate factories produced packages that doubled as jewellery boxes, wrappers that turned into puzzle pieces and even chocolate eggs with toys inside (predating Ferrero's Kinder Surprise by several decades). It was not uncommon at this time to see portraits of tsars such as Peter the Great on boxes or tins of chocolates (Upakovano.ru 2008). Russians' enthusiasm for collectible chocolate packaging was particularly evident in 1913, during celebrations of the Romanov dynasty's 300th anniversary, when companies released numerous designs bearing portraits of the Imperial family (Neumeyer 2012).

After the Bolshevik Revolution of 1917, designers tended to look forwards, rather than backwards, eager as they were to reflect what Boym (2001: 59) refers to as the 'Communist teleology' of the 'bright new future'. In 1924, poet Vladimir Mayakovsky and artist Aleksandr Rodchenko were commissioned to design a series of toffee wrappers for the Red October factory. The series, entitled 'Our Industry' ('Nasha Industriya'), featured images of such ciphers of modernity as a vice, a locomotive, a tram, a motorised plough and a tractor.

The accompanying texts carried a clear ideological message; the verse for the 'vice' wrapper, for example, read 'The landowner took to whiskey: Outrage, the bourgeoisie was pinched in the vice' (Ankist 1987: 40–41; see also Hilton 2012: 172). While best known for their highly distinctive, 'Constructivist' advertising posters (Kiaer 2005), Rodchenko and Mayakovsky also produced three series of striking sweet wrapper designs in the mid-1920s. Alongside the 'Our Industry' series, for example, in 1924 Mayakovsky designed the text and the images for a series of eleven 'Red Army Star' ('Krasnoarmeiskaya zvezda') toffee wrappers for the Red October factory. These wrappers were numbered sequentially, so that when read in numerical order, the verse told the story of the victory of the Red Army over the Whites in the recent Civil War (Ankist 1987: 42–43). Confectionery was far from the only product category to feature politically correct packaging in the USSR. The packet of 'Belomorkanal' ('White Sea Canal') cigarettes, for example, is surely one of the most famous examples of Soviet-era packaging (Idov 2011: 68–71).[13] The packet, described by Idov (2011: 70) as 'one of the triumphs of Soviet commercial design', was created in the late 1930s to celebrate the completion of the 141-mile canal connecting the White Sea to the Baltic.

Soviet-era large-scale industrial projects and technological acheivements are generally absent from FMCG packaging in contemporary Russia (one notable exception comes in the shape of the Soviet satellite featured on the tubs of Russkii Kholod''s 'USSR' ice cream: Makarenko and Borgerson 2009). Instead, one tends to find historical, natural and folk-based themes (Clarke 2010). At the same time, while many of the images on Russian packaging have their roots in the country's folklore, others have specifically nationalist overtones. Clarke (2010) himself notes the presence of Moscow's Saint Basil's Cathedral (an image to which we shall return shortly), although he sees it essentially as a religious, rather than political symbol. The nationalist nature of much con-temporary Russian packaging can be seen clearly in a comment made by historian Lindsay Hughes in 2004:

> In advertising [sic], Russian Heritage has been utilised to challenge the domination of the market by Western brand names. Thus 'Peter the Great' cigarettes vie with Marlborough [sic] and 'Cupolas of Moscow' and 'Streltsy' chocolate with Snickers and Cadburys. You can buy 'Boyar' frozen food from packaging imprinted with cartoon-like magnates in seventeenth-century costume and Russian ham adorned, incongruously, with the domes of the Dormition cathedral, washed down with 'Epic Warriors' tea. (Hughes 2004: 193)[14]

Hughes makes two important observations in her discussion. First, she points out that this kind of packaging appears on products intended not just for tourists, but also for the domestic market. Second, she claims that the re-emergence of nationalist themes in Russian FMCG packaging is indicative of a specifically 'patriotic consumerism' (Hughes 2004: 193).[15] We shall address this issue in our discussion section, towards the end of this chapter. For the moment, we should point out that Hughes' comment is consonant with Caldwell's (2002) observation on the re-emergence of nationalist sentiment in the late 1990s and early 2000s among many Muscovites, unhappy with the incorporation of so many Western elements – she mentions in particular credit cards, fast-food restaurants, and American business English – into everyday Russian culture. Claiming that these concerns had given rise at the time to what she calls 'nationalist sentiments oriented at cultivating and maintaining an idealized Russianness', she continues (Caldwell 2002: 297):

> One striking by-product of these trends has been the growing appeal of a specialized niche of commodities that draw on Russian linguistic markers and historical–cultural allusions in order to cater to the notion that Russians share a unique set of tastes and values that is not satisfied by imports or other transnational products. (see also Caldwell 2007)[16]

Caldwell's discussion brings us back to Moscow, and in particular Muscovites' eating habits. As we mentioned in our introduction, our own particular focus in this chapter is not the products themselves, but rather their packaging. However, before we examine how Moscow has itself been represented recently on Russian FMCG packaging, we need to place that packaging in its cultural context. We need, in other words, to say something about the city itself, and how it has been historically represented (mythologised) in the Russian collective consciousness. In other words, we need to explore how Moscow has been 'packaged' in the past, and how that packaging is currently changing.

Moscow and myth, Moscow as myth – past, present and future

Through its turbulent history, Russia has had three capital cities, first Kiev, then Moscow, then St Petersburg, then Moscow once again (Franklin 2004). Nevertheless, the city long ago established itself as the symbolic locus of Russian national identity, even before 1918, when it became the capital, not just of Russia, but of the USSR's fifteen republics. In the nineteenth century, as Figes (2002: 151) notes, '[t]here was a sense in which [Moscow] was the nation's "home", even for members of the most Europeanized élite of Petersburg. Moscow was a symbol of the old Russia, the place where ancient Russian customs were preserved.' As Figes' comment makes abundantly clear, Moscow is not just the current capital city of Russia, it has also been the subject of a whole series of myths over the centuries (Figes 2002: 150–216). Moscow has in turn been seen as 'the Third Rome' (for Orthodox believers),[17] the 'city of the apocalypse' uniting the Russian people thanks to its beauty (for nineteenth-century writer Fyodor Dostoevsky), and the capital of the socialist world, opposing the 'evil of capitalism' (for the early Bolshevik leaders; see Groys 1992).

Although founded in 1138, Moscow only became capital of Russia (a very different space from that which we know today, essentially the Vladimir–Suzdal principality) in 1327. When Peter the Great built his great 'Window on the West' that was St Petersburg in 1703, he immediately moved his capital from Moscow – a place with which he associated all that was archaic and backward about Russia (Figes 2002: 152) – to that city. The Bolsheviks' decision in 1918 to move the capital city back to Moscow was, as Widdis (2004: 37) notes, not just a rejection of Imperial St Petersburg but also an attempt to appropriate a new capital with a sufficiently strong sense of history to provide them with the political legitimacy they needed. Even before 1917, Moscow exerted a special, almost mystical pull on Russians from throughout the Empire. The eponymous heroines of Chekhov's *Three Sisters* (*Tri sestry*, 1901) for example, spend the entire play dreaming of moving there, convinced that this will guarantee them a new and infinitely better life (they never do). In the Stalinist era, a number of films reproduced this Moscow-centric motif (examples include the 1930s musicals by Aleksandrov and Aleksandrov, such as *Happy Fellows* (*Veselye rebyata*, 1934) and *Volga-Volga* (1937); Haynes 2003). In the late Soviet era, films such as Vladimir Men'shov's *Moscow Does Not Believe in Tears* (*Moskva slezam ne verit*, 1979) replicated this myth of Moscow as a utopian space where one could overcome whatever life threw at one, realise one's dreams and find true and everlasting happiness. In the Soviet collective imagination, then, Moscow came to embody more than anywhere else the bright new future of Communist teleology (Boym 2001).

In today's, post-Soviet Russia, Moscow continues to look forward, as anybody who has visited the gleaming downtown 'Moscow-City' business centre, or seen the plans for the Skolkovo Technology Park, a 2.5 million m^2 site currently under construction to the south-east of Moscow, will testify. The latter, which is due to house 50,000 people by 2020 (Tass.ru 2014), aptly illustrates Boym's point that Moscow is characterised by 'the perpetual transformation of space, a process of endless repair that ha[s] neither beginning nor end' (Boym 2001: 96). As well as gazing forwards, however, the city looks backwards, too. The catalyst for this retrospection was the 850th anniversary of the founding of Moscow, in 1997 (Boym 2001: 92–100). The year 2000 saw the opening of the Cathedral of Christ the Saviour, an exact replica of the original, which had been completed in 1883, and razed by the Soviets in 1931 (Boym 2001: 100–8). Post-socialist Moscow, then, is a Janus-faced metropolis, gazing at the same time into both the distant future and the far-flung past. On a visit to the city's Park of the Arts in 1997, Boym (2001: 91) put it like this:

> If there is a nostalgia [in Moscow] at the end of the millennium, it seems to be posthistorical; it is a longing for a life of peace and plenty, an invention of another tradition of eternal Russian grandeur complete with marble shopping arcades next to the Kremlin wall, newly built old churches and luxury casinos.

At the same time, however, the city also looks both inwards and outwards, both to its own cultural history and to 'global' culture – in other words, both

East and West (in this respect, the city may be said to encapsulate the debate between 'Slavophiles' and 'Westernisers' about Russian national identity – and in particular Russia's relationship with the West – that has raged in one form or another for the last 200 years or so).[18] This East–West duality was neatly encapsulated on 31 July 2013, when a statue of the *X-Men* super-hero Wolverine, built by Andrey Aser'yants, and funded thanks to the Russian crowdsourcing site www.boomstarter.ru, was installed inside the walls of the 'Izmailovo Kremlin', the ultra-kitsch fake-ancient arts centre opened on the outskirts of the city in 2003 which describes itself on its website as 'the most Russian place in the whole of Moscow' (Kreml' v Izmailovo [n.d.]). It can also be seen if we compare and contrast two very different recent city branding initiatives presided over by Sergey Kapkov, erstwhile Head of Moscow's Culture Department – or rather the respective logos chosen to promote them. After all, logos are rarely iconographically – or indeed ideologically – innocent; as Heilbrunn (2006b) has argued, logos are designed precisely so that members of the organisation may recognise themselves in the sign, and feel a part of the community that sign represents.

The first logo is that of the summer-long popular arts festival entitled 'Moscow – The Best City in The World' ('Moskva – Luschii Gorod Zemli'; see *Moskovskaya Pravda* 2012). Originally launched in 2012, to coincide with the 865th anniversary of the city's founding, it also ran from April to September 2013, and again in 2014 and 2015. With its own dedicated website (see Luchshii Gorod Zemli [n.d.]), and social media pages, the festival has now established itself in the city's cultural calendar. It includes approximately 1,500 events, both local and citywide, ranging from open-air concerts to photography competitions, from cookery workshops to BMX races, and from talent shows to city-sponsored street art and graffiti fests. The logo used in 2013 as the official emblem of this festival was the one originally created to commemorate the official celebrations of the city's 865th anniversary, on 1 and 2 September 2012. It was designed by contemporary artist and co-founder of the 'sots-art' movement Eric Bulatov, better known for his anti-establishment art of the late Soviet period.[19] His logo for Moscow is visually highly evocative of many of the agitational posters produced in the 1920s by Soviet Constructivist artist Aleksandr Rodchenko (Kiaer 2005). This can be seen in its stark geometrical forms (a light blue square set in the middle of a larger, bright red square turned at an angle of 45 degrees to it), on which are superimposed the words 'luchshii gorod zemli' ('the best city in the world'), the first and third stretched horizontally across the logo, and cut vertically by the second. The letters which form each of these words become progressively larger as they approach the edge of the square, in what is a visual allusion to Constructivist typography (Ankist 1987). Last but not least, the three colours that appear in the logo – light blue, red and white – are those of the Russian flag.[20]

The following year saw the inauguration of a very different kind of official logo for Moscow – 'Я ♡ Москву' ('I love Moscow'). On 11 July 2013, the first of a series of monuments was installed in the middle of Gorky Park (Roberts

2014b). This consisted of an angular white 'tick'-shaped structure (a rather stocky version of the famous Nike 'swoosh'), approximately 3 m high and 4 m in diameter, set on a low, 4-m-wide plinth. 'Ya' ('I') appeared as a stencilled letter in the shorter, left-hand leg, with 'Moskvu' ('Moscow') similarly stencilled in the other, longer leg, positioned at right angles to it. Nestling in the angle between the two legs was a 1-m-high bright red heart, so that the entire structure can be read, from left to right, as saying 'Ya lyublyu Moskvu' ('I love Moscow'). This initiative was intended to be a major municipal rebranding exercise, along the lines of similar initiatives in other, 'global' cities. More than anything, it is the project's logo that shows the extent to which Moscow looks to the West as it seeks to (re)construct an identity for itself for the twenty-first century. The original project's website, 'moscowiloveyou.ru', made this crystal clear:

> We have decided to express our love [for Moscow] and help all those who wish to do the same. This is why we designed the logo 'Ya lyublyu Moskvu'. Declaring one's love for one's home city has become a well-established global trend. 'Ya lyublyu Moskvu' is destined to become a world-famous global brand like 'I ♡ NY', 'IAmSterdam', 'cOPENhagen' and others. (I Love Moscow [n.d.])[21]

Moscow, then, is a city currently in search of itself (Clowes 2011). Nowhere has this been more in evidence than on Red Square itself, which in recent years has hosted both ultra-realistic re-enactments of Soviet military parades (Oushakine 2013), and the giant-sized Louis Vuitton suitcase mentioned at the beginning of chapter one. As the city seeks to reinvent itself, it looks both backwards and forwards, inwards and outwards, westwards and eastwards. Indeed, to paraphrase Heilbrunn (2006a), Kapkov's Moscow functions like so many other brands which enshrine contradictory principles, such as the past and the present, the very distant and the here and now. To return to the theme with which we began this chapter – the politics of chocolate packaging in post-socialist Russia – in the pages which follow we propose to focus on the 'branding' of the city, not by City Hall or the Kremlin, but rather by Russian confectioners. The questions we seek to answer in the remainder of this chapter are the following. First, given the rich tradition of representing Moscow on Russian FMCG packaging (Smirennyi 2007), the deeply polyvalent nature of post-socialist Moscow's 'ideoscape' (Appadurai 1996), and the prevalence of political and historical narratives on so much packaging produced by contemporary Russian-based chocolate brands (Roberts 2014a), how is Russia's capital city represented on chocolate wrappers and boxes in Russia today? Second, what does this tell us about the kind of consumer culture that has emerged in the country in recent years? And third, what broader conclusions can be drawn concerning the role played by packaging in FMCG branding? The discussion that follows is based on, first, personal observation during frequent trips to Russia over the last twenty years, second, exchanges with visiting Russian colleagues, many of whom have been generous enough to offer chocolate as a gift, third, the rich resources provided by the Russian chocolate wrapper website (Etiket Konditerskikh Fabrik [n.d.a]), and fourth, the online chocolate wrapper museum based in Prague (Chocolate Wrappers Museum [n.d.]).

Representations of Moscow on Russian chocolate packaging:

As we briefly discussed in our introduction to this chapter, chocolate occupies a particular place in the Russian popular consciousness (Patico 2002). While Chester (1997: 147) observes that 'chocolate, like St Petersburg, is a manufactured product imitated from a Western original', it is nevertheless one of the oldest surviving manufacturing industries in Russia today. As Neumeyer (2012) notes, the country's first chocolate factory was founded in 1826, by the Leonov merchants. After 1917, many chocolate manufacturers fled abroad, while those that remained were nationalised by the Bolsheviks in 1922. The Leonov factory became Rot Front, another leading brand, Einem', was renamed 'Krasnyi Oktyabr'' ('Red October' – the name by which it is still known today), while Abrikosov and Sons, originally founded by a serf known for his apricot fillings ('abrikos' is the Russian word for 'apricot'), was renamed 'Babaevsky', after a local Communist Party committee chairman. At the time of writing (summer 2015), there are over thirty domestic manufacturers, the most important of which, United Confectioners ('Ob'edinenye konditeri'), founded in 1804, owns 19 separate brands, including Moscow-based Red October, Rot Front, Babaevsky and 'Russkii Shokolad' ('Russian Chocolate'), manufactures 4,000 separate products, and is the fourteenth largest confectionery company in the world (statistics obtained from the company's official website: United Confectioners [n.d.]). While Red October, Rot Front and Babaevsky are the three largest chocolate manufacturers in Russia today (Neumeyer 2012), foreign firms Mars, Nestlé, Ferrero and Kraft all have production facilities in the country, the last of these having its own specific brand range. The Russian chocolate market grew by 7 per cent in 2014 (Euromonitor 2014b), and is currently worth over US$13 billion (Nieburg 2014b).

In a crowded market place, many Russian chocolate manufacturers give themselves names designed to appeal directly to consumers' patriotism (Bernstein 2011). Perhaps the most flagrant example is 'Rossiya – shchedraya dusha' ('Russia – a generous heart'). The brand, founded in 1969 in the city of Samara, some 2,500 miles to the south east of Moscow, was originally known simply as 'Russia'. It was taken over in 1995 by Nestlé, who added the phrase 'generous heart' to its brand name two years later. Since the 1970s, one of its flagship products has been 'Rodnye prostory' (a phrase which translates as 'The wide-open spaces of our native land'). Many other brands, however, use packaging, rather than brand name, to evoke a sense of 'Russianness'. Moscow-based confectioners, in particular, exploit images of the country's capital city. While Hughes (2004) mentions the appearance of various famous monuments on

FMCG packaging in today's Russia, one of the first images of Moscow to appear on a chocolate wrapper post-1992 was not a monument at all, but rather the street known as the Arbat. In 1998, United Confectioners' Rot Front produced its 'Old Arbat' ('Staryi Arbat') chocolate bar. The wrapper does not depict the street itself, but rather an old street lamp, set against the upper section of a row of eighteenth-century buildings, in a picture from which all signs of modernity have been expunged. The grainy, sepia-toned image is cut vertically by an ornate red and gold stripe in the middle of which appears the date '1826', the year in which the brand was founded. The Arbat is one of Moscow's oldest and most famous streets. Originally an area populated by artisans of various professions, in the eighteenth century it became home to several families of the Russian nobility, followed in the nineteenth by artists, poets, writers, musicians and intellectuals (including the 'father of Russian literature', Aleksandr Pushkin). As we saw in chapter one, in the late Gorbachev years, the street – pedestrianised in 1986 – became one of the first places in Moscow where private street hawkers were able to ply their trade. Trestle tables crammed with Russian dolls featuring the succession of Soviet leaders (although usually omitting Andropov and Chernenko) and placed directly in front of an old antique bookshop, became a common sight on the Arbat at this time. Indeed, today this street is rather gaudy, and has become a place where one is far more likely to find fast-food outlets, cheap souvenir stalls and even sex shops than poets' corners (Tochka-G is located on one of the Arbat's side streets). In the late 1990s, however, when Rot Front's wrapper was produced, there was still a romantic aura about this street (indeed, the aura can still be felt today, despite the rampant and rather shoddy commercialism it has come to embody). One could even argue that in 1998, in the midst of the worst financial crisis ever to hit the country, there was something reassuring, not just about the Arbat itself, but also about the rather bohemian-feeling area, with its network of tree-lined side streets, at the heart of which it lay. As Boym (2001: 99–100) put it, referring to the Soviet bard Bulat Okhudzhava, a poet and songwriter of mixed Georgian and Armenian descent who lived on the Arbat and whose songs had celebrated the area in the 1960s and 1970s:

> The backstreets near the Arbat [...] became Okhudzhava's 'little patria'. It was devoid of national or state symbolism, with only an occasional monument to Pushkin in the background. The inhuman city suddenly acquired a human scale. Fellow pedestrians with their quotidian trials and tribulations and minor joys and sorrows became the heroes of songs. They took public transportation, made dates in the metro stations and dreamed of a utopian blue trolley that might save them in a moment of despair. This post-Stalinist Moscow celebrated in that tape-recorder culture of Khrushchev's thaw helped to carve spaces for alternative communities of urban dwellers. Rather than escapist, it was a way of inhabiting modern life against all odds.

Today, it is virtually impossible for any Russian born in the Soviet era to hear the Arbat mentioned without thinking of Okhudzhava's songs, rather as in the

UK Liverpool's Penny Lane – or indeed London's Abbey Road – is immediately associated with the Beatles. It is this, Okhudzhavian Arbat that is celebrated in the 'Old Arbat' wrapper, just as much as the Pushkinian one.

Rather than Moscow's streets, however, it is the city's famous buildings that have appeared most consistently on Russian chocolate wrappers and boxes since the late 1990s. This phenomenon can be traced back to 1997, the year of the 850th anniversary of the city, when Babaevsky issued a special commemorative wrapper featuring a number of landmarks in and around the Kremlin, such as St Basil's and the 'Rossiya' hotel (the latter, a huge Soviet building which also contained a concert hall at which the likes of Elton John and Dave Brubeck appeared in the late 1980s, was, demolished in 2007). The trend first became prevalent, however, around the early years of the twenty-first century, something which may be linked to the nationwide 'Buy Russian' campaign launched at the time, and the official encouragement of nationalist feelings towards food that underpinned that campaign (Caldwell 2002, 2004).[22] Indeed, as well as being particularly famous landmarks, many of the buildings featured on chocolate wrappers and boxes serve as reminders of the symbolic role played by Moscow in the emergence of a sense of national identity in the Russian collective imagination (Hughes 2004). St Basil's, for example, which appeared in the early 2000s on a wrapper produced by the firm 'Slavyanskaya', from the town of Serpukhov in the Moscow region (reproduced in Hughes 2004: 190), was founded by Ivan the Terrible in order to celebrate one of his most famous military victories, the capture of the Tatar capital of Kazan in 1552. This victory was extremely significant, both for the development of the Russian state itself, and for the establishment of Moscow at the centre of that state, as it signalled the beginning of the end of Tatar rule in Russia (Figes 2002: 151–52). One also finds the Dormition Cathedral (also known as the Cathedral of the Assumption). The site of the coronation of successive Russian monarchs between 1547 and 1896, and today regarded as the home of the Russian Orthodox faith, the Cathedral can be seen in all its gleaming splendour on the wrapper of Rot Front's 'Golden Domes' ('Zolotye kupola') 100 g chocolate bar. The golden domes of another religious building, the Cathedral of Christ the Saviour, can be seen on the wrapper of the 80 g 'Golden Symbol' ('Zolotoi Simvol') bar, produced by Yasnogorsk-based brand 'Golden Russia' ('Zolotaya Rus'').[23] The site of Pussy Riot's infamous 'happening' in February 2012, the cathedral was originally commissioned in 1812 by tsar Aleksandr I to commemorate victory over Napoleon, constructed on the site of the old Alekseev monastery and consecrated in 1883 (see Boym 2001). Destroyed by the Bolsheviks in 1931 to make way for a planned 'Palace of the Soviets' (in the end an open-air swimming pool was built instead), the cathedral was restored in a project overseen by city mayor and Yeltsin favourite Yury Luzhkov, and officially consecrated in August 2000. Yet another cathedral, the Archangel's Cathedral, can be seen for example on the wrapper of the 100 g dark chocolate version of the bubbly chocolate range currently manufactured by 'Russkii Shokolad' ('Russian Chocolate'), a Moscow-based confectioner launched in

1998 and owned by United Confectioners. Constructed between 1505 and 1508 and also located within the Kremlin complex, it is the burial place for all Moscow's princes and tsars from Ivan I ('Ivan Kalita'; 1288–1340) to Peter the Great (1672–1725), as well as Peter II.

Russian Chocolate's bubbly chocolate bar range also includes an image of the Moscow Kremlin (on the milk chocolate bar). The Kremlin is, of course, the current seat of political power in the country. As Figes (2002) argues, its very construction, in the fourteenth century, symbolised more than anything else the consolidation of the wealth and power of Moscow's princes, and the city's concomitant rise in status at the expense of Kiev. It is much more than that, however. As Yampolsky (1995: 97) points out, it can be read as a monument to political power itself. As he puts it:

> The transfer of the capital to Moscow and the concentration of political power in the Kremlin have their own symbolic aspects. This is, of course, a transfer of power from the periphery to the spatial center, but it is also the placement of power inside walls, as into a core protected by a shell. Power becomes its own monument, symbolically moving beyond the boundaries of time.

Perhaps not surprisingly, given Yampolsky's point, the Kremlin did sometimes feature on Soviet chocolate wrappers, often accompanied by the slogan 'Glory to October' ('Slava Oktyabryu'), or 'Victory' ('Pobeda' – as on a 1985 wrapper produced by the Minsk-based 'Kommunarka' factory, celebrating the fortieth anniversary of victory over Nazi Germany). In the late Soviet era, the Kremlin tended to appear as a crudely coloured photographic image that gave prominence to modern buildings within its sprawling complex, such as the concrete Palace of Soviets, in which successive Party Congresses were held. The way the Kremlin is represented in today's Russia, however, is completely different. This can be seen by examining the image which appears on the wrapper produced by the company Volzhanka based in the provincial city of Ulyanovsk. This is a nineteenth-century sepia-toned engraving on a pale yellow background, bisected vertically by a broad ribbon of Imperial red at the centre of which one can read the words 'Kremlevskii stil'' ('Kremlin Style') enclosed within an ornate silver frame.

The middle of the 2000s saw the emergence of references to another side of Moscow, this time centred around its cultural heritage, rather than its political significance. This trend began with Red October's 'Tretyakovskaya Galeriya' ('Tretyakov Gallery') series,[24] launched in 2004 (the image can be viewed at: Etiket Konditerskikh Fabrik [n.d.b]). At first sold as 100 g bars, this series now comes in a range of six different gold-framed 240 g boxes. It features some of the most famous Russian paintings housed in one of the capital's most important art museums, including I.N. Kramskoi's 'Unknown Woman' ('Neizvestnaya' of 1883), and V.M. Vasnetsov's 'Bogatyrs' ('Bogatyry'), produced between 1881 and 1898.[25] This was followed in 2007 by the launch of the 'Vdokhnovenie' ('Inspiration') series of 100 g bars and 450 g boxes by another Moscow-based

United Confectioners' brand, Babaevsky. In this case, the building in question is not a museum, but rather the Bolshoi Theatre, erected at the heart of the Theatre Square complex in 1824 and designed by St Petersburg architect Joseph Bové. The theatre's famous façade appears in the centre and at the top of each wrapper and box, drawn in a very precise outline in either silver (for the wrapper) or gold (for the box). Contrasting starkly with the very bright, deep blue background against which it is set, the building almost jumps right out at the viewer. In front of the Bolshoi one can see a pair of male and female ballet dancers, performing on a stage framed by ornate silver or gold swirls. Babaevsky's 'Inspiration' was voted 'Product of the Year' in Russia in 2007, and it remains a leading brand in the country today, alongside Red October's 'Tretyakov Gallery' (Euromonitor 2014b).

The above-mentioned monuments and paintings fulfil an important marketing function, as they help differentiate the brand in question from the competition – an especially valuable role in a crowded market such as chocolate. Indeed, as Ambrose and Harris (2011: 15) put it, generating brand loyalty 'represents the packaging designer's real challenge.' At the same time, these images are ideologically loaded. In other words, they may be said not just to mythologise the brand, but also to sacralise the state (Roberts 2014a). In particular, they serve to reinforce the importance to Russian identity of a certain kind of 'high' culture, alongside military prowess, and the Orthodox faith (on religion and Russian national identity, see Franklin 2004, and Shterin forthcoming, 2016). Most importantly, however, they underline Moscow's central place in that identity and its construction, by emphasising its embeddedness in pre-Soviet history and culture (to borrow a phrase used by Yurchak (2011) to refer to St Petersburg).

In most of the cases so far discussed, the brand itself has taken a back seat as it were, visually foregrounding Moscow to such an extent that one has to look very hard to find any mention of the brand at all (as on Babaevsky's 'Inspiration' box, for example). Red October's 'Tretyakov Gallery' series, launched in 2004, broke with that tradition. On the front of the box the brand's logo is displayed prominently above each of the gold-framed portraits. On the back, one finds a text describing not just the chocolates inside as a veritable 'gallery of wonderful fillings', but the company's factory itself as 'a treasure-trove of confectionery chefs d'oeuvre'. In 2009, two years before its 160th anniversary, the brand took this branding logic a stage further. In that year, it released a series of three 280 g boxes of chocolates. The front of each box (the lid) features an image of Moscow, above the legend, 'ANCIENT RECIPES OF THE EINEM' COMPANY' ('STARINNYE RETSEPTY TOVARISHCHESTVA EINEM''), and the date '1851' – the year in which the brand that was eventually to become Red October was founded.[26] The three scenes featured on these boxes are not, however, old photographs of the city in the mid-nineteenth century, but rather paintings of the Moscow of the future *as someone in 1851 might have imagined it*.[27] As such, they evoke more the (utopian) world of Jules Verne than the 'real' space of the Russian capital. Two of the boxes show people travelling through the air on fantastical flying machines, while on the third a number of individuals are floating on the surface of the Moskva river on special shoes, a contraption that looks like a cross between a unicycle and a paddle steamer, and even a horse-drawn carriage. In each case, one can see in the distant background familiar sights of the Moscow skyline, such as the Kremlin or the Cathedral of Christ the Saviour, greatly reduced in size thanks to the effect of perspective. In the middle of all three box lids appears the word 'EINEM'' written in elegant serif capitals and set within an equally stylish florid border accompanied by the italicised, lower case text 'A selection of elegant chocolates made according to ancient recipes'. Immediately above this is the Imperial crest, complete with gold crown, a medieval knight's helmet that calls to mind the founder of Moscow, Ivan Dolgorouky, and the Romanov double-headed eagle. Below the crest one can read, in proud capital letters, 'Purveyor to the Court of his Imperial Majesty' ('Postavshchik Dvora Ego Imperartorskago Velichestva').

On opening each of the boxes, one finds the following text, which we propose to quote in full, in order to convey precisely how packaging can be co-opted into telling the 'story' of the brand (Heilbrunn and Barré 2012), and thereby contribute to its elevation to the status of myth:

> When you taste an Einem' chocolate, you are transported to the amazing atmosphere of the end of the XIX century, when people dreamed about the future, fantasised [about that future], and tried to imagine how the world might look several years hence. In response to the general interest in all things new and original, the confectioner Einem' produced a series of postcards entitled 'Moscow of The Future', showing views of the country's capital in the XXI century. Each card depicts right down to the smallest detail the future as seen by someone living one hundred years ago. Today, these cards can be seen only in private collections and museums, and on boxes of Einem' chocolates. After all, Einem' is a world of chocolate fantasies![28]

This closing strapline is repeated in a similar text on the back of each box, which also reminds the consumer that the company has held 'the secret of making perfect chocolates since 1851'. Unlike the boxes – which were first produced not in the nineteenth century but rather in 2009, and in this sense represent today's view of how yesterday might have imagined tomorrow (the twenty-third century to be precise) – the postcards contained inside are reproductions of a series first released between 1904 and 1918, and currently held in the brand's museum (Sostav.ru 2009). Alongside the recognisable features of the city – Red Square, the Minin and Pozharsky monument,[29] the Central Railway Station and Lubyanka Square (subsequently to become the site of the KGB headquarters), one sees a host of fantastic machines – motorised sledges shooting down the Moscow–Petersburg highway that is now covered in a single sheet of mirror-like ice, fast automobiles, aeroplanes landing alongside the Moskva river, airships, and multi-decked passenger liners. The Moscow of 2259 is a city of bustle and hustle, of intensive, dynamic movement, where 'those who wish to may transport themselves with the speed of a telegram', as one of the cards put it. Perhaps most remarkably, it is a world where commerce has expanded immeasurably, where the Muir and Merrilies department store building has grown 'to mythical proportions' and Moscow, or rather the Moskva river, has now become 'the centre of world trade'.

Rather like Rot Front, and the other brands we have mentioned so far, Red October (the modern avatar of Einem') is also seeking to exploit Moscow's 'cultural capital' in order to gain 'economic capital' (Bourdieu 1984). One might even say that it is capitalising on the 'love' for Moscow felt by Russians consumers – the 'love' of which Sergey Kapkov spoke so effusively in July 2013 – in order to make itself more 'likeable' (Nguyen, Melewar and Chen 2013) as a brand. At the same time, however, the Einem' box functions in a rather different way from all the other examples we have so far looked at. The focus here is not the city of Moscow (since the Moscow presented is 'a figment of our wild imagination', to quote yet another of the postcards), but rather the Red October brand itself. As Underwood (2003) has argued, the use of nostalgic imagery in packaging often creates nostalgia for *the brand*, rather than for a mythical, shared past. Indeed, the 'Einem' 1851' series of boxes demonstrates just how packaging may be used to emphasise a brand's cultural heritage. We should say immediately that it is not a question of the brand trying to throw off its 'Soviet' past by returning to its pre-1917 name (the name 'Red October' appears at the bottom of the back of the box, albeit in extremely small type). Rather, it is a case of the brand both reminding consumers that it has a rich cultural heritage – a 160-year old heritage to be precise – while at the same time suggesting that it has always been forward-looking and innovative. As Urde, Greyser and Balmer (2007) argue, 'cultural heritage' brands – a category in which they include 'brands' as diverse as Siemens, IKEA and the British Royal Family – seek actively to embrace the past, the present *and* the future.

Positioning itself as a 'cultural heritage' brand, Red October operates a neat sleight of hand; in effect, it presents 1851 (the year in which it was founded) not as some distant *past*, but rather as a time when people looked to the *future*. The brand's own past, by analogy, appears to contain its future within it – indeed, the two become indissociable from one another. In a sense, using packaging to suggest that as a brand it has a well-established tendency to look to the future (in other words, it has a long tradition of innovation), Red October wants to have its (chocolate) cake and eat it. Put simply, it wants to be *both* 'Krasnyi Oktyabr'' (a question of *identity*, since this is the name by which generations of Soviet and post-Soviet consumers have come to know and love it), *and* 'Einem'' (a name which contributes to the brand's *legitimacy*, since it enables the brand to remind those very same consumers of its long experience as a confectioner). Packaging becomes a central pillar of this positioning strategy.

Discussion

This last example notwithstanding, what emerges from our survey is that packaging is not just a marketing or branding tool; it may also play a significant ideological role (Askegaard 2006; Kravets 2012), thanks to the way in which it promotes certain myths (Kniazeva and Belk 2007). These may be myths about a given brand, or about the society in which that brand circulates and from which it takes its meaning. When it comes to post-socialist Russia, the politics of packaging are especially evident in the way a number of brands allude, either textually or visually, implicitly or explicitly, to key moments in the country's history. They may do so by referring to certain key figures or battles (Kravets 2012; Roberts 2014a), or by presenting the consumer with images of historically significant monuments. Showing such monuments means of course showing urban space, and indeed, the representation of the city on Russian chocolate packaging has undergone a 180 degree shift since the mid-1980s, when photographs of modern, Soviet buildings were the norm. Nowhere has this change been more in evidence than in the case of the capital city, Moscow. Today's Russian chocolate boxes uniformly look to Moscow's past (even when pretending to look to the future), in a way seemingly at odds both with the forward-looking images on Soviet wrappers, and with the deeply ambivalent manner in which the city has itself been 'packaged' in recent years. This is nowhere clearer than on the series launched by the brand 'Russian Chocolate' in 2002, just four years after its creation. The images of Red Square which feature on the wrappers are accompanied by the wording 'Moscow 1860', in a reference to what many historians see as the most important decade in nineteenth-century Russian history, a period whose botched reforms led indirectly to the Bolshevik Revolution of 1917 (see for example Schapiro 1984).

The image of the city conveyed on post-Soviet chocolate packaging is in no sense homogeneous, however. At times, the building in question is historically significant (St Basil's), while at others it is far less so (the eighteenth-century façade on the Arbat). And while most of the images conjure up the past, a minority (featured on the Einem' special '1851' boxes and cards) look to the future. Whereas some buildings are primarily religious (the Dormition Cathedral), others are essentially political (the Kremlin), while a third set are cultural (the Bolshoi). And if some images function metonymically (Kramskoi's portrait of 'The Unknown Woman' is a synecdoche for the Tretyakov Gallery), others can be read as metaphors for the new Russia itself (none more so than the 'resurrected' Cathedral of Christ the Saviour; Remnick 1997: 169–73). Finally, while the brand is sometimes foregrounded (as on the 'Einem' 1851' series), elsewhere it is the monument itself that takes centre stage (as with Rot Front's 'Golden Domes'). At the same time, there has been a chronological evolution; the relatively apolitical 'Old Arbat' of 1998 was followed in the late 1990s and early 2000s by images of ideologically significant monuments (political, religious or cultural), before the arrival in the mid-2000s of products alluding to the city's cultural heritage, and the emergence towards the end of the decade of packaging that focussed on the brands themselves. These phases are not neatly sequential, however, but rather overlap each other. Chocolate may not yet embody the 'Russian dream', in the way that chewing gum has come to embody the 'American dream' (Redclift 2004). Nevertheless, it is far more involved in generating a sense of place than other snacks sold in Russia, such as crisps; despite its name, and the fact that it is one of the few national brands of potato crisp, the packets of 'Moskovskii kartofel" ('Moscow Potato'), founded in 1963 and still on sale today, contain no visual reference to the city of Moscow.[30]

The retrospective view of Moscow to be found on so many chocolate wrappers and boxes is singularly at odds with the temporal duality of the 'real' Moscow discussed earlier in this chapter. It also contrasts, both with the manner in which Moscow is represented on for example contemporary Russian vodka bottles – where one finds the fifteenth-century Kremlin, the nineteenth-century Arbat and the twenty-first-century Moscow City – and indeed with the way the capitals of some other former Soviet Republics are depicted on chocolate packaging (one finds, for example, the modern buildings of Kazakhstan's new capital Astana on wrappers of the country's confectioner Rakhat). In a previous article on packaging in contemporary Russia (Roberts 2014a), we suggested that the use of images of historically significant monuments might be read as an appeal to consumers' nostalgia, driven by a desire to encourage them to see continuity between the 'great Russian past' and the post-Soviet present – thereby reiterating and developing a point made briefly by Holak, Matveev and Havlena (2008: 174; see also Bernstein 2011). There is certainly a good deal of retrospection in today's Russia, as Cassiday and Johnson (2013: 50) rightly observe, much of it caused by what they call 'the acute dislocation that has characterized Russians' lives since the collapse of the Soviet Union'. This tendency to look to the past as a 'golden age' can be seen throughout Russian society today (Mazur 2015). Scholars have identified nostalgia in a number of areas, including: the public sphere (Boym 2001; Oushakine 2013); restaurants and gastronomy (Caldwell 2006); television (Hutchings and Rulyova 2009; Gorbachev 2015);[31] advertising (Morris 2005, 2007; Holak, Matveev and Havlena 2008); the Russian blogosphere (Morenkova 2012); video games (Strukov 2012); literature (Marsh 2007); contemporary art (Oushakine 2007); and cinema (Larsen 2003; Hashamova 2004, 2007; Roberts 2013b).[32] As Gorbachev (2015) points out, however, while in the 1990s the subject of much of this nostalgia was pre-1917 Imperial Russia, more recently the focus has switched to the Soviet era.

Nostalgia, as Holak, Matveev and Havlena (2008) point out, has long attracted the attention of marketers, in Russia and elsewhere. However, we have to tread extremely carefully when talking about nostalgia, as to do so begs a (large) number of questions. Do all historical monuments, for example, necessarily evoke the past? This question is particularly germane to the Cathedral of Christ the Saviour. Some have argued that this monument is deeply ambivalent, both semiotically, and ideologically. As Boym (2001: 106–7) has suggested:

> [T]here are many ironies in the new mammoth cathedral. While commemorating the glory of the Russian past, the new cathedral strives to obliterate Soviet history and restore the continuity between pre-revolutionary and post-Soviet Russia. Inadvertently, it reveals a clear

continuity between the Soviet and post-Soviet times in terms of power structures and authoritarian fantasies.

(on the original cathedral's 'double semiotics', see also Yampolsky 1995: 100–1). Are all representations of the past necessarily appeals to nostalgia? As Fehérváry (2009) has astutely noted, what at first sight appears to be nostalgia for the former socialist state is frequently nothing more than the re-contextualisation of mass-produced goods and popular culture of the time, as part of the conscious reconsideration of the capitalist commodities once so admired. And even if nostalgia is involved, then whose nostalgia is it, and whose interests does it serve (Todorova and Gille 2012; Angé and Berliner 2014)? As far as the link between brands and nostalgia is concerned, it is unclear whether brands react to nostalgia, or actually contribute to the emergence of nostalgia in a given society (Brown, Kozinets and Sherry Jnr 2003; Holt 2006). This raises the prospect that consumers may not actually respond in the way brands hope to the wave of nostalgia they may seek to surf – a point Morris (2005) eloquently makes about reactions to appeals to patriotism in contemporary Russian cigarette advertising. Indeed, a number of the informants in the study by Kravets and Örge (2010) into attitudes towards certain iconic Soviet brands on sale in today's Russia expressed their unease at what they saw as brands' manipulation of their childhood tastes and feelings of nostalgia.

Most importantly of all, perhaps, nostalgia itself is a particularly complex concept. As Brown, Kozinets and Sherry Jnr (2003: 20) argue, and as Angé and Berliner (2014) also suggest, we need a more nuanced notion of nostalgia than simply 'things were better back then'. The problem is, the concept of nostalgia has been with us for such a long time – since at least Odysseus's yearning for Ithaca – that it is easy to forget the many different ways in which the concept has been approached. Drawing attention to what they see as a lack of 'a solid theoretical structure' in discussions of the concept, Kessous and Roux observe (2008: 195) that nostalgia has been variously described in the literature as an evocation (Davis 1979), a mood (Belk 1990), a preference (Holbrook and Schindler 1991), an emotion (Bellelli 1991), an emotional state (Stern 1992), or an affective reaction (Divard and Robert-Demontrond 1997). One of the most frequently drawn distinctions in discussions of nostalgia is that between 'private' nostalgia based on the individual's direct experience, and another, 'collective' mode generated via that individual's interaction with other members of his or her community (see for example Davis 1979; Turner 1987; Stern 1992). In their discussion on nostalgia and advertising in Russia, Holak, Matveev and Havlena (2008) see evidence of both private and collective nostalgia. They expand on Davis (1979) however, by distinguishing between four types of nostalgia in the country, namely: 'personal nostalgia […] based on direct experience'; 'interpersonal nostalgia […] based on interpersonal communication concerning the memories of others'; 'cultural nostalgia […] where members of the group share a similar response that helps to create a cultural identity'; and 'the nostalgic equivalent of "virtual reality," with the emotion based upon shared indirect experience' (Holak, Matveev and Havlena 2008: 173; for a similar discussion on nostalgia as a melancholic sense of loss of values in contemporary mass consumer culture, see also Turner 1987).

Citing 'Russia's craze for nostalgic products', Holak, Matveev and Havlena (2008: 173) argue that a number of brands in post-socialist Russia use one or more of these types of nostalgia, and that this has met with a positive response from those Russian consumers whom they interviewed (this contrasts markedly with the findings in Kravets and Örge 2010, cited above). They note that their respondents frequently referred to feeling a 'loss of security', and conclude (Holak, Matveev and Havlena 2008: 177) that in the years to come nostalgia 'may become a more common positioning strategy in Russia'. Problems remain with their study, notably in the way in which they conflate, first, advertising and packaging, second, explicit and implicit appeals to nostalgia, third, nostalgia generated by historical monuments such as St Basil's Cathedral and that produced by a cultural reference such as Pushkin's fairy tales, and fourth, nostalgia for the USSR and a yearning for the tsarist era. Nevertheless, they make the very important point that nostalgia may be related to the issue of cultural identity.

This connection between nostalgia and shared identity links their work to that of the scholar who has perhaps contributed most to discussions of nostalgia in post-socialist Europe, namely Svetlana Boym. Writing just two years after the break-up of the USSR, Boym saw two fundamentally distinct forms of post-socialist nostalgia, 'ironic' and 'utopian'. While the former 'acknowledges the displacement of the mythical place without trying to rebuild it', the latter seeks actively to rebuild the past and lies at the heart of many nationalist ideologies (Boym 1994: 16; see Sabonis-Chafee 1999: 367). In a subsequent study of the subject, Boym renamed these categories as 'reflective' and 'restorative' nostalgia respectively. 'Reflective' nostalgia, accepting the irrevocability of the past, may allude to it with irony and humour (Boym 2001: 49). 'Restorative' nostalgia, on the other hand, seeks to present the past as new – to 'patch up the memory gaps', as Boym (2001: 41) puts it. It 'evokes [the] national past and future', and in doing so 'takes itself dead seriously' (Boym 2001: 49). In our earlier article on FMCG packaging in today's Russia (Roberts 2014a), we took our cue from Boym, contrasting what we saw as the unambiguously serious, 'restorative' nostalgia of the country's chocolate boxes (and vodka bottles) with the far more playfully ironic references to the past to be found on much packaging in contemporary Britain.

The question remains, however, despite what Holak, Matveev and Havlena (2008) suggest, and what we ourselves have argued: does the packaging of Moscow and other cities we have been discussing here necessarily represent a call to Russian consumers' nostalgia? After all, is the portrait of Queen Victoria on the label of Bombay Sapphire gin necessarily designed to appeal to my nostalgia as a UK consumer for the British Empire (for that matter, am I necessarily more nostalgic if I choose to drink gin, a spirit closely associated with the long-lost days of that Empire, than another spirit such as whisky, tequila or rum?)?[33] Rather than depicting national monuments – or former monarchs – on their packaging, brands that seek to appeal to consumers' nostalgia often do so instead via 'retro' style packaging. Such packaging often features a logo or other visual markers that evoke a relatively recent past (one example is Pepsi's 'Throwback' can, launched in 2009). In cases such as this, the 'retro' look may also serve to underline the brand's longevity, and hence its authenticity, in a crowded marketplace (Brown, Kozinets and Sherry Jnr 2003). In Russia, where memory-driven authenticity can also play an important role in consumer choice (Kniazeva and Charters 2014), such 'retro' packaging is increasingly popular. One example is the can launched in 2013 by the AB–InBev-owned Zhigulevskoe brewery from the city of Samara, featuring a picture of a couple of dancing 'stilyagi' (Soviet hipsters from the 1950s; see Sostav.ru 2013b). Others use Soviet-style visual design. One such brand is the Moscow-based Ostankino company that manufactures pelmeni. In a promotional video designed primarily to appeal to the consumer's personal nostalgia, rather than any communal sense of history (Stern 1992), the company declares 'we pack pelmeni in the same cardboard box with the spoon familiar to you from childhood' (ostankino.ru, quoted in Soviet Is in the Details [n.d.]). Some Russian confectioners do this too; the face of the little girl adorning the immensely popular line of 'Alenka' chocolates has remained virtually unchanged since its launch in 1966 (see Adme.ru [n.d.]). Other brands go so far as to place the now obsolete Soviet quality mark on their packaging – this can be found on the range of 'USSR' ice creams made by the company 'Russkii Kholod'' (Makarenko and Borgerson 2009), or on the label of Zhigulevskoe's 'Original'noe' ('Original') beer, first issued in 2013 – a design which also features one of Moscow's seven iconic Stalinist, 'wedding cake' buildings, the apartment block on Kotel'nicheskaya Embankment (see Sostav.ru 2013c). Sabonis-Chafee (1999) has argued that such packaging amounts to nothing more than 'ironic-nostalgic-kitsch'. Makarenko and Borgerson (2009) on the other hand suggest it has a far more serious function, namely to solidify collective memories in an era characterised by the rapid and wholesale commodification of human relations.

We shall have more to say about the concept of 'collective memory' in the next chapter. For the moment, we wish merely to point out that Makarenko and Borgerson's point is extremely interesting, as it suggests that it might be more accurate to say that the images we have been discussing involve not so much an appeal to consumers' nostalgia as to their *patriotism*. An emotional attachment to the 'imagined community' (Anderson 2006) of the nation state, patriotism so often relies on the generation of collective memories for its legitimation. After all, as we noted earlier, some Russian chocolate manufacturers give themselves names designed to appeal directly to consumers' patriotism (as do many Russian brands in other food sectors: Bernstein 2011). Of course, nostalgia and patriotism are not unconnected, as Morris (2005) demonstrates, in his discussion of nostalgia in Russian cigarette advertising in the early 2000s, which he sees as an expression of increasing anti-American feeling in the country after the events of 9/11. Holak, Matveev and Havlena (2008) themselves suggest that certain forms of nostalgia may help create a sense of shared cultural identity (see also Wallendorf and Arnould 1991; Holak and Havlena 1992). And Boym, in a follow-up article to her monograph on modern nostalgia, makes the following chilling observation:

> In extreme cases [nostalgia] can create a phantom homeland, for the sake of which one is ready to die or kill. [...] While claiming a pure and clean homeland, nostalgic politics often produces a 'glocal' hybrid of capitalism and religious fundamentalism, or of corporate state and Eurasian patriotism. (Boym 2007: 9–10)

Boym's comment is not directly related to Putin or his politics. Nevertheless, it certainly calls to mind the society over which Putin has reigned, which has seen a distinct rise in patriotic sentiment (Laruelle 2009), of which the Ukrainian crisis may be seen as the latest episode (Daucé, Laruelle, Le Huérou and Rousselet 2015). This trend has been accompanied by a deliberate attempt by the Kremlin to revisit the country's past, to expunge all 'countermemories' (Thompson 2004; Thompson and Tian 2008) that do not correspond to the official version of the country's history (see for example Oushakine 2013; Thom 2015). At the time of writing (mid-2015), there is every possibility that MEMORIAL, the Russian non-governmental association founded in 1989 by Andrei Sakharov in order to rehabilitate the victims of Stalinism and promote reflection on the Soviet era, may be forced by the Russian courts to close (Bérélowitch *et al.* 2014). In a meeting with young Russian researchers and teachers of history in November 2014, Putin went so far as to suggest that there were forces at work seeking to reshape Russian society specifically by writing the country's history in order to further their own 'geopolitical interests'. He also expressed regret that so few Russians knew the names of the principal Soviet heroes from the war, and argued that it was the State's direct responsibility to rectify this situation (for the full transcript of the discussion, see Kremlin.ru 2014). Putin's use of national history for his own ideological ends was especially evident in May 2015, during the celebrations marking the 70th anniversary of the Soviets' victory over Nazi Germany (Kobrin 2015).

Russian confectioners' exclusive focus on the past cannot be viewed outside this social and political context. Support for our argument comes from Jahn (2004). As Jahn points out, in the late Imperial era, Einem' issued two series of free card pictures entitled 'Views and Types of Old Moscow' and 'Scenes from Russian Life'. This kind of promotional material was a result of the momentous socio-economic changes taking place in the country at the time, including the mass migration of peasants to cities in search of work in the new factories:

> Such material was likely to be sold predominantly in [Russian] cities, where it catered to the nostalgia of people who had recently moved there from the country and who were now struggling for a new identity in a different and quite hostile environment. (Jahn 2004: 69)

Most importantly, Jahn argues that these idealised images, not just of Moscow but indeed of 'Russianness', reflected a growing sense of national identity in nineteenth-century Russia. Pre-Soviet Russian chocolate brands, then, were deeply implicated in what Jahn (2004: 69) refers to as 'defining oneself and categorising the other'. It is perfectly possible to read those more recent images analysed in this chapter in the same way, that is to say as encouraging consumers' emotional attachment to an 'imagined community' that draws a clear, and qualitative, distinction between 'us' and 'them'. Indeed, as Oushakine observes, 'the main task of impeccably imitated old structures is to produce an already known and previously encountered effect of recognition, to evoke a *shared experience*, to point toward a *common vocabulary*' (Oushakine 2007: 469; our emphasis). The same could be said of St Petersburg's leading brand, Krupskaya, which has a range of wrappers and boxes evoking the founding of the Russian navy in the city in 1703, as well as an extensive series devoted to paintings in the city's Russian Museum (see note 24).

However, as with nostalgia, so with patriotism, we need to be careful how we read these packages. As a British consumer, for example, am I more of a patriot if I choose to eat my fish and chips with HP brown sauce, which features the Houses of Parliament (the 'HP' in the brand's name) on the label, rather than with Daddies sauce, which contains no such image? Of course, the real reason I prefer it may have nothing to do with my 'patriotism', and everything to do with the fact that it reminds me of my childhood (Kessous and Roux 2008) – in which case, I may not even notice the image on the bottle, or even make the connection between that image and the acronym from which the brand's name derives. The issue at stake here, of course, is not my own (inevitably idiosyncratic) response to the images under discussion in this chapter, but rather how they contribute to reshaping post-socialist Russia's 'ideoscape' (Kravets 2012). On the one hand, the capacity for signs such as these to construct consumers' identity depends precisely on their 'iterative normativity' (Schroeder and Borgerson 2003: 3). The danger is, however, that as with the Houses of Parliament on my sauce bottle, so the very ubiquity of St Basil's, the Kremlin, the Dormition Cathedral and even the Cathedral of Christ the Saviour may merely turn them into what Barthes (1984) refers to in his discussion of the Eiffel Tower in Paris as 'empty signs'. These are signs so full of meaning(s) that they become meaning*less*, such a 'must-see' element of any visit to the city that one ends up no longer seeing them at all – or at least no longer seeing them for what they once were (rather like the Arc de Triomphe on Lindt's popular 'Champs Elysées' chocolate box, which is graphically presented not as the military monument it originally was, but rather as merely the culminating point of Paris's most glitzy shopping avenue). In a recent article on contemporary Russian art, Oushakine makes the following point:

> The difficulty with finding adequate signs for expressing new situations – 'expressive aphasia,' in Jakobson's terms – is compensated by extensive manipulations with available elements *within* adopted visual or textual

borders ('ready-to-wear past'). Elaborate rituals of *combination* of borrowed signs become the main condition and the main content of symbolic production. (Oushakine 2007: 467; see also Lotman 2000)

Yet given the profusion of so many 'borrowed', and potentially 'empty' signs of Moscow on chocolate packaging there is every possibility that one may end up with nothing more than what Morris (2005: 650) eloquently calls 'a vague but compellingly viscous "Russian idea"'.

To suggest that the images we have been discussing here are designed to appeal to consumers' sense of nostalgia, or patriotism (or indeed both) raises, then, a number of rather complex questions. Nevertheless, it would be extremely difficult to deny these images an ideological subtext (Schroeder 2009), as indeed we have already suggested. Urban artefacts, whether one considers them as 'works of art' (Rancière 2004) or as 'the soul of the city' (Rossi 1982), inevitably carry political meaning – not least in today's Russia, where planning projects often provoke fierce public opposition (Yurchak 2011). As such, their representations are just as politically loaded as many of the Imperial *objects* that circulate in post-Soviet space (Buckler, forthcoming) – or indeed as the images of Putin and the Crimea with which we began this chapter. Indeed, rather like the images to be found on many post-Soviet vodka labels, those representations we have been discussing necessarily contribute to contemporary Russia's 'ideoscape', inasmuch as they 'distribut[e] ideological images and views of the state' (Kravets 2012: 361). As such, they inevitably shape Russian consumers' views both of their own world, and also, by implication, of the 'other' world beyond (since like all myths, they function according to a logic of duality: Lévi-Strauss 1963). To see precisely how they might do so – how they might construct 'a bridge from text to [collective] mind' (Scott 1994b) – we need to return to Appadurai (1990, 1996), who first developed the concept of the 'ideoscape'. We need, in fact, to look at another of Appadurai's concepts, namely the mediascape. Appadurai (1996: 35) defines the concept as follows:

Mediascapes, whether produced by private or state interests, tend to be image-centered, narrative-based accounts of strips of reality, and what they offer to those who experience and transform them is a series of elements (such as characters, plots, and textual forms) out of which scripts can be formed of imagined lives, their own as well as those of others living in other places.

In other words, if brands contribute to a society's ideoscape, they do so primarily *thanks to the mediascapes which they put into circulation in that society*. These mediascapes then generate a sense of community among consumers, by presenting them with a canvas of 'shared experience, [... and] a common vocabulary of symbolic gestures', as Oushakine (2007: 469) puts it, and inviting them to project their own identity onto that canvas (on the link between consumers' preference for 'nostalgic' products and their need for a sense of belonging, see

Loveland, Smeesters and Mandel 2010). These mediascapes may manifest themselves in the 'architectural identity' (Miles 2010) of the Galeriya mall discussed in chapter one. They may also come in the form of packaging. Indeed, if packaging, to quote Hine (1995: 202) 'provides a way in which people define and understand themselves', it is primarily because, like consumption itself, it is a 'critical site in which identities, boundaries and shared meanings are forged' (Kates 2002). To return to Appadurai, it is surely no coincidence that in his discussion of what he calls 'nations and their narratives', he mentions that foremost theorist of the nation state as 'imagined community', namely Benedict Anderson (2006; Appadurai 1996: 161). As Appadurai (1996) himself points out, feelings of belonging to a community are first and foremost generated by signs. Ironically, this is nowhere more in evidence than in Red October's 'Einem' 1851' series, which despite not quite being a 'retro brand' in the sense meant by Brown, Kozinets and Sherry Jnr (2003), nevertheless evokes, with its utopian images of fantastical flying omnibuses and horse-drawn carriages gliding effortlessly across the Moskva river, what they call 'the arcadian ethos of the retro brand [...] strongly associated with the upstanding individuals and caring-sharing society of a dear departed golden age' (Brown, Kozinets and Sherry Jnr 2003: 24).

Mention of Anderson takes us even further back, to the debates surrounding packaging itself and the question of its materiality. By evoking the imagined community of the nation state (for which 'resurrected' Moscow stands as both metonym and metaphor), these wrappers function like so many of the products of late Socialism. That is to say, they materialise social relations (Fehérváry 2009). Occupying, as we saw earlier, that middle ground between dematerialised brand and material product, these wrappers and boxes nevertheless constitute material culture by virtue of their the capacity to 'objectify' the consuming subject (Miller 1987). They become objects in which the consumer 'recognises again his own self' (Hegel 1975: 31–32; quoted in Miller 1987: 28). Indeed, as Miller (2008: 287) has polemically argued:

> [O]bjects create subjects much more than the other way around. It is the order of relationship to objects and between objects that creates people through socialisation whom we then take to exemplify social categories, such as Catalan or Bengali [or Russian as against Ukrainian, or Muscovite as distinct from Petersburger], but also working class, male, or young.[34]

Of course, consumers, in today's Russia or elsewhere, may respond positively (Holak, Matveev and Havlena 2008) or negatively (Kravets and Örge 2010) to this materialisation of their social relations. As Appadurai (1996: 145) himself observes, thinkers such as Gramsci, Williams, de Certeau and Hebdige have all noted that, rather than passively accepting the ideologies of identity to which they are exposed, many individuals consciously 'invent' (de Certeau 1984) daily life via a complex system of negotiation, using irony and subversion to create their own identities. In other words, to return to Boym's (1994) original distinction, there is every likelihood that the 'utopian nostalgic' images of Moscow on display may be read 'ironically' by consumers themselves. Of course, the mediascapes offered by packaging give them less scope for such invention and self-creation now than in the late Soviet era (Yurchak 2005). This may be why the range of images on offer, while often distinctively Russian (Hughes 2004; Clarke 2010; Kravets 2012) is nevertheless relatively narrow (the latter observation may in fact follow from the former). If we want to see how Russian-based brands are using mediascapes to construct 'imagined communities' – both around themselves and around the 'nation state' – and how consumers are responding, we need to look elsewhere. We need, in other words, to look at social media. As we have argued elsewhere (Roberts 2014b), the way in which social media can be exploited by brands to promote a sense of community among consumers is directly analogous to the 'print capitalism' which was central to Anderson's original argument (on computers as 'electronic capitalism', see Appadurai 1996: 161). Moreover, social media are a particularly rich source of mediascape. As Appadurai (1996: 4) noted with such foresight twenty years ago, 'electronic media provide resources for self-imagining as an everyday social project' (see also Miller 2011). This is especially the case in Russia, in which two thirds of Internet users have at least one social media account, a proportion far higher than the global average (Shklovski 2013). With this in mind, it is to social media branding in Russia that we now turn our attention.

Notes

1 See Putin Shop [n.d.]. The site, which is not official, describes itself on its home page as 'an international store for all those who love Russia'.

2 See Rainsford (2015). The Russian word 'oreshki' has a double meaning, rather like 'nuts' in English.

3 The original range, including lollipops featuring caricatures of the three Western politicians perceived to be behind the economic sanctions that hit Russia in 2014 – Barack Obama, François Hollande and Angela Merkel – can be viewed here: Sostav. ru (2015). The text on the lollipops reads: 'Oni khotyat nas s'est' nakhal'no ... S'edim-ka ikh luchshe bukval'no!', which might be translated idiomatically as: 'The cheeky beggars want to eat us – we'll eat them first, without a fuss!'

4 Established in 1769 as the highest military decoration of Imperial Russia, the Ribbon of St George ('Georgevskaya lentochka') was re-introduced by Boris Yeltsin in 1998. The Ribbon appeared on a number of chocolate wrappers in the Soviet era, usually to mark anniversaries of military victories. Most recently, it was particularly prominent on giant hoardings on Red Square on 9 May 2015 during the ceremony commemorating the seventieth anniversary of victory over Hitler's Germany. For an insightful discussion of the recent re-emergence of the Ribbon in contemporary Russian political iconography, see Oushakine (2013).

5 'Dazhe v to vremya, kogda strana prinimaet neprostye resheniya, my ne perestaem ulybat'sya. Potomu chto my – Rossiyane'. The choice of 'Rossiyane' for 'Russians' is significant here, as the word, which became largely obsolete under the Soviets, refers to residents of the country known as 'Russia', rather than to ethnic Russians (referred to collectively by the term 'Russkie'). In effect, the word 'Rossiyanin' is based on an imperial–multinational notion of Russian identity, rather than an ethno-cultural one (see Jahn 2004).

6 Moscow is home to seven such buildings, all constructed between the late 1940s and mid-1950s. They are so nicknamed because, as they are constructed in ever-narrower stages as one moves towards the top, their form resembles that of a wedding cake. These buildings, still standing today, include the main corpus of Moscow State University, The Ministry of Foreign Affairs and the Ukraine Hotel, as well as an apartment block. The predominance of politically correct and ideologically symbolic buildings and monuments on chocolate packaging during the Soviet era was in no sense limited to Moscow, but occurred in other Soviet cities too.

7 Images of Moscow were largely absent from vodka labels during the Soviet era. The most notable exception was 'Stolichnaya' (literally 'Capital [vodka]'), which since its launch in 1944 has featured on its label the Moskva hotel on Manezh Square next to the Kremlin, one of central Moscow's most famous landmarks, although of relatively little political significance. As Schrad (2014: 408) notes, the hotel's presence on the label is purported to be due to the personal intervention of the head of Stalin's secret police, Lavrenti Beria.

8 It is perhaps this hybrid nature of packaging, and the space it consequently occupies somewhere between materiality and immateriality, that lies behind the relative silence on the subject by writers otherwise interested in the relationship between material culture and consumer culture (see for example Miller 1987, 2005, 2008; McCracken 1988, 2005; Woodward, I. 2007).

9 Private comment received via email.

10 Hine (1995: 193) quotes a study that found that 'although shoppers simply do not see a lot of the packages in a[n average US] supermarket, they are still aware of about eleven thousand different packages during the 1,800 seconds they spend walking the aisles'.

11 In a recent interview, one of the co-founders of UK brand Corkers Crisps commented 'everything you see on the packet has a story behind it' (Dann 2015).

12 This utilitarian approach to the question of packaging was symptomatic of the way marketing was thought of in the post World War II period (Hackley 2001, especially chapter 3).

13 Belomorkanal cigarettes are a distinctively Russian product known as a 'papirosa', whereby instead of a filter, there is merely a hollow cardboard tube. They remain a popular (and very cheap) brand among Russian smokers even today (Kravets and Örge 2010; Levinskaya 2014). The pack design, like the product itself, remains virtually unchanged since the Soviet era.

14 The 'streltsy' were units of Russian guardsmen from the sixteenth century to the eighteenth. The first such units were created by Ivan the Terrible around 1550. A 'boyar' was a member of the highest rank of Muscovy aristocracy, from the tenth century to the seventeenth. Hughes' conflation of advertising and packaging – or rather her implicit view of packaging as merely a sub-category of advertising – illustrates the difficulty packaging has to be seen by scholars as a discrete category of consumer culture.

15 For a more recent study of Russian consumers' patriotic ethnocentrism, see Puzakova, Kwak and Larsen Andras (2010).

16 Caldwell (2002: 297) makes the intriguing point that such preference amounts to subverting market capitalism in order to preserve typically 'socialist' values, by which she understands 'the ethics of sociality and collective responsibility'. On the enduring popularity among Russian consumers of archetypical Soviet products such as the bologna-type 'Doktorskaya' ('Doctor') sausage or 'Druzhba' ('Friendship') cheese, see Kravets and Örge (2010).

17 After Constantinople fell to the Mongols in 1453, Moscow saw itself as the last surviving centre of Orthodoxy, in effect as the heir to Byzantium and Rome, and as such as nothing less than 'the saviour of mankind' (Figes 2002: 152). This idea, and the belief on which it is built, is one of the defining elements of Russian cultural history.

18 In essence, the Slavophiles believed that all Russia's problems could be traced back to the reign of Peter the Great (1696–1725), when a Europeanised elite rejected age-old Russian traditions in favour of Western notions such as rationalism and private property. The Westernisers, on the other hand, maintained that Russia's future lay in emulating Western social and political models. As Jahn (2004: 62) notes, the ideas of the Slavophiles and the Westernisers can still be heard in contemporary debates on Russia's identity and destiny.

19 Founded by Soviet artists Vitaly Komar and Aleksandr Melamid in 1972, sots-art began as a non-conformist movement mixing Soviet iconography with motifs from US Pop Art. On Sots-art, see for example Oushakine (2007), and on Bulatov, see Chramtchenko (2014).

20 While not denying the Constructivist allusion, Bulatov himself has claimed the logo looks back to the work of another Soviet avant-garde artist, namely Kazimir Malevich (1878–1935) and in particular his 'Red Square' of 1915: Afisha.ru (2012). Malevich, and his 'Red Square', belong to another, equally home-grown Russian early twentieth-century artistic movement, namely Suprematism (Gray 1986).

21 The use of the English word 'brand' to refer to Moscow is itself significant: as Yurchak (2005) notes, in the Soviet era, the word was used by Russians to refer exclusively to *foreign* brands.

22 Moscow was by no means the only Russian city to have its famous buildings appear on chocolate wrappers at this time. On Cadbury's 'Gold Reserve' range, launched in 2001 and which included the image of a fourteenth-century church in the ancient northern city of Novgorod, as well as a reproduction of Rostov-on-Don's seventeenth-century kremlin, see Roberts (2014a). With the exception of Leningrad, images of historical monuments were virtually absent from Soviet chocolate packaging.

23 For a discussion of the use in contemporary Russian FMCG packaging of gold and other symbols of material prosperity as part of the construction of a new, post-Soviet national identity see Bernstein (2011).

24 One can compare this with the series of wrappers entitled 'Vernissage' issued in 1998 by St Petersburg brand Krupskaya, to celebrate the centenary of the city's Russian Museum, and again in 2008 for the museum's 110th anniversary (the museum houses the second-largest collection of art works in the city after the Hermitage, and contains a far higher proportion of Russian, rather than Western art). Like those in the 'Tretyakov Gallery' series, Krupskaya's wrappers also featured a range of famous paintings, all by Russian artists.

25 We are not suggesting a complete break in the representation of the city before and after 1992. Red October for example, produced a wrapper in the 1970s, featuring a photograph of the front of the Gallery. At around the same time (1976), the brand also issued a wrapper showing the Bolshoi Theatre, on the occasion of the bi-centenary of the theatre's opening.

26 The word 'Einem'' is written with a final 'hard sign' ('ъ'), which corresponds to the old, pre-Revolutionary spelling. This convention – placing a hard sign at the end of every noun ending in a consonant – has become extremely popular among Russian companies in a number of sectors, especially restaurants and hotels, which see it as a means of giving themselves a certain legitimacy.

27 Each of the three boxes, along with the series of eight reproduction postcards contained within them, can be viewed here: Mail.ru [n.d.].

28 All translations of the 'Einem'' boxes and postcards are our own.

29 In 1612, during the war against Poland and Lithuania known as The Time of Troubles, Prince Dmitry Pozharsky and the merchant Kuz'ma Minin gathered an all-Russian volunteer army and expelled the Polish garrison from the Moscow Kremlin. The monument was erected in 1818 soon after the victory over Napoleon, symbolising a rise in patriotic consciousness.

30 This is in stark contrast to the practice of UK brands such as Yorkshire Crisps or Kent Crisps, which feature a variety of visual and textual references to their respective regions on their packaging.

31 The satellite TV channel 'Nostalgia' was launched in 2004. It shows re-runs of old TV programmes from the 1960s to the 1990s, as well as its own retrospective programmes, such as 'Made in the USSR' ('Sdelano v SSSR'). On the channel, see Kalinina (2014). The channel uses the hammer and sickle to form the 'st' in its logo, as can be seen on the home page of its website: Nostalgia TV [n.d.].

32 On post-Soviet Russian nostalgia, see also the special edition of the journal *Neprikosnovennyi Zapas*, available on line at: *Neprikosnovennyi Zapas* (2010). As Angé and Berliner (2014) note, most of the recent literature on nostalgia in anthropology has focused on post-socialist contexts. See for example Berdahl (1999); Blum (2000); Bach (2002); Nadkarni and Shevchenko (2004); Boyer (2006); Ghodsee (2011); Todorova and Gille (2012); Rabikowska (2013); Angé and Berliner (2014); Louyest and Roberts (2015).

33 On gin's close association with the British Empire see for example Manning (2012).

34 On the link between materiality and intersubjectivity, see also Woodward, I. (2007) and Borgerson (2014).

4 The final frontier

Brands and branding on social media in the new Russia

Introduction: Social media, brand communities and value co-creation

In the previous chapter, we saw how the images put into circulation by a number of Russian confectionery brands contribute to the materialisation of social relations. In doing so, they create a sense of community – not just around the nation as 'imagined community' (Anderson 2006), but ultimately around the brand itself. The phrase 'brand community' was first coined by Muñiz Jnr and O'Guinn (2001), in an article focussing on three brands in particular, Ford Bronco, Macintosh and Saab. Taking their cue from a raft of nineteenth- and twentieth-century theorists of identity and community (including Anderson), they argued that in today's fragmented, and 'distanced' (Giddens 1990) consumer society, it is now brands, rather than physical places or religious groups, that create a sense of belonging (see also Belk, Wallendorf and Sherry Jnr 1989).[1] It is worth quoting in full Muñiz Jnr and O'Guinn's definition of brand community, since it makes explicit not just the despatialised, mediated and commercial aspects of these communities, but also their moral dimension – a point to which we shall return:

> A brand community is a specialized, non-geographically bound community, based on a structured set of social relationships among admirers of a brand. It is specialized, because at its center is a branded good or service. Like other communities, it is marked by a shared consciousness, rituals and traditions, and a sense of moral responsibility. Each of these qualities is, however, situated within a commercial and mass-mediated ethos, and has its own particular expression. Brand communities are participants in the brand's larger social construction and play a vital role in the brand's ultimate legacy. (Muñiz Jnr and O'Guinn 2001: 412)

For Muñiz Jnr and O'Guinn, creating such communities can help strengthen the emotional bond between consumer and brand, and thereby enhance consumers' commitment and attachment. This point is echoed by Cova who argues, in his study of Nutella's online 'My Community', that brand communities are part of a three-point 'virtuous circle' in which consumers' passion for a brand favours the formation of a brand community, whose members then generate the kinds of myths about the brand likely to increase consumers' passion towards the brand, which in turn feeds into the brand community, and so on (Cova 2006: 55; see also for example McAlexander, Schouten and Koenig 2002 (on Jeep's 'brandfests'); Ballantyne and Aitken 2007; Stokburger-Sauer 2010). Muñiz Jnr and O'Guinn are careful to draw a distinction between 'brand communities' and the subcultures of consumption, such as that centred around Harley Davidson and analysed by Schouten and McAlexander (1995), which crystallise into lifestyles characterised by an 'outlaw' ethos of marginality.[2] This point notwithstanding, Muñiz Jnr and O'Guinn (2001: 415) maintain that a community may form around any brand, especially one 'with a strong image, a rich and lengthy history, and threatening competition'. Many scholars have seized on this last point to apply the concept to 'underdog' brands such as (ironically) Harley Davidson itself (O'Sullivan, Richardson and Collins 2011). However, the concept of 'brand community' has increasingly come to be used in relation to market leaders, such as Apple and Nike (Kilambi, Laroche and Richard. 2013), Coca-Cola and Red Bull (Allen, Fournier and Miller 2008), and Pampers (Aaker 2013).[3]

As this last point suggests, the original concept has been applied in a wide range of fields – especially since the advent of Web 2.0,[4] which has generated a marked increase in interest in online brand communities.[5] This interest, among brands, consumers and indeed marketing scholars, should come as no surprise. Social media in general lend themselves particularly well to community formation, thanks to the 'sociality' which they encourage, via processes of cognition, communication and co-operation (Fuchs 2014; Kozinets 2015). Indeed, as Fuchs (2014: 59) notes, social networking sites such as Facebook, Google+ and LinkedIn (to which we would add the Russian VKontakte) are precisely oriented towards community building. Alongside Cova's (2006) study of Nutella (see also Cova and Pace 2006), Amine and Sitz (2007) were among the first to seek to extend Muñiz Jnr and O'Guinn's original concept to the realm of online branding, in an article analysing three consumer-led discussion groups, devoted to Nikon, Canon and Apple's now defunct Newton personal assistant respectively. Reminding readers that brand communities of shared values and behaviours arose as a direct result of market globalisation, they insist on the need to fine tune Muñiz Jnr and O'Guinn's original thesis. In particular, they convincingly argue (Amine and Sitz 2007: 65) that there is in fact a continuum of brand communities, ranging from those sharing specific geographic location at one end to those whose members interact exclusively online at the other. Amine and Sitz's most important contribution, however, was to suggest that online brand communities emerge in three distinct stages: first, the creation of a community space in which consumer interactions are both facilitated and regulated; second, the construction of symbolic identity, during which consumers work together to establish rules and resolve conflicts between group members; and third, stabilisation of the group's hierarchical structure, a phase which may include the organisation of physical meetings between group members.

An increasing number of scholars, focussing on a wide variety of industry sectors, have investigated the potential for brand communities to develop online, and the opportunities for brands to generate value from customer involvement in those communities (see for example Schau, Muñiz Jnr and Arnould 2009; Gummerus, Liljander, Weman and Pihlström 2010; Kaplan and Haenlein 2010, 2012; Brodie, Ilic, Juric and Hollebeek 2011; Kietzmann, Hermkens, McCarthy and Silvestre 2011; Healy and McDonagh 2013; Wirtz *et al.* 2013; McCarthy, Rowley, Ashworth and Pioch 2014). In recent years, scholars have also begun to look at this phenomenon in emerging markets (see for example Zhou, Zhang, Su and Zhou 2012). The research agenda has slowly shifted to take into account not just consumer-led discussion groups, but also brands' official platforms. Habibi, Laroche and Richard (2014) are among an increasing number of researchers who look at how communities form around brands' social media pages. They argue that it is precisely the social and net-worked nature of such pages that makes them an ideal environment in which such communities can develop, by fostering mutual trust between brands and consumers (see also Wallace, Buil and de Chernatony 2012; Zaglia 2013).

Much of the literature on social media branding raises the issue of the 'co-creation' of the brand's value by consumers themselves (Etgar 2008; Cova and Dalli 2009; Christodoulides, Jevons and Bonhomme 2012; Singh and Sonnenburg 2012; Aaker 2013; Healy and McDonagh 2013; Habibi, Laroche and Richard 2014; See-To and Ho 2014; Wallace, Buil, de Chernatony and Hogan 2014). In this view, social media have now become central to brands and branding, since as Pongsakornrungslip and Schroeder (2011) persuasively argue, the 'brand value' they can help generate is not just about the bottom line, but relates in a more general sense to the ways in which consumers understand the brand's very meaning (see also Arvidsson 2006). So, for example, Muñiz Jnr and Schau (2005) show how Apple's 'defunct' brand of Newton personal assistants was resurrected by bloggers interacting in discussion forums (see also Allen, Fournier and Miller 2008). At other times, this process is initiated by the brands themselves. The analysis by Cova (2006) and Cova and Pace (2006) of the interactive site *my nutella The Community* demonstrates how Ferrero successfully used it to help shape its brand image in Italy. Bough and Agresta (2011) discuss Ford's use of videos made by consumers – so-called 'Fiesta Angels' – on its YouTube channel to help promote the launch of a new product range. And Singh and Sonnenburg (2012) show how consumers' own stories and images on Harley-Davidson's Facebook page feed into the brand's myth-making process.

The notion of consumers 'co-creating' the brand – its 'value' and thereby its meaning – goes back to the work of Prahalad and Ramaswamy (2004) who were among the first to argue that interaction between brands and consumers could help create value for the brands themselves (for an alternative view, see Foster 2007). Their focus was on how brands might gain competitive advantage by co-creating with the consumer personalised experiences in line with her or his specific circumstances. This idea itself harks back to the concept, so central to postmodern marketing theory, of consumer agency (and indeed consumer empowerment: see Cova and Pace 2006). Building on the work of postmodern theorists of consumption such as Firat and Venkatesh (1995), Arnould and Price (2000) argued that in the postmodern era, with its challenge to the concept of the unified self, consumers (re)construct a sense of self by reappropriating various commodities and using them in new and original ways (the reference here is to de Certeau's (1984) concept of 'bricolage'). The 'self' then, becomes a narrative (Giddens 1991; Hall 1996) – or rather a series of narratives (Clarke 2003) – which, if shared with others via what Arnould and Price (2000) refer to as 'authenticating acts' and 'authoritative performances', enables individuals to come together and form communities.

A decade or so ago, Thompson and Arsel (2004) discussed the fragile tension at the heart of the relationship between certain iconic US brands and their foreign markets. They showed that while local consumers often *collectively* (rather than individually) reappropriated and even directly contested brand meanings (see also Miller 1998a, and Askegaard and Csaba 2000), a company such as Starbucks could nevertheless hope to go some way towards countering such 'cultural heterogeneity', maintaining some measure of control over brand meaning by establishing what they called a 'hegemonic brandscape'. Today, with the emergence of a whole gamut of social media, the balance appears to have significantly shifted towards the consumer, however. Christodoulides (2009), for example, maintains that the Internet and related e-technologies have upset what he calls the asymmetry of information between brand managers and consumers (see also Champoux, Durgee and McGlynn 2012; Quinton 2013). Thanks to the arrival of Web 2.0, the latter are now, he believes, empowered to participate more actively in the branding process, and thereby to emerge as 'guardians' of the brand. Fournier and Avery paint a far darker picture of the implications of Web 2.0 for brands. Arguing that the rise of digital media has heralded an age of absolute transparency, they issue this dire warning to managers: 'In Web 2.0, the brand message and source no longer provide claims to authority. Brand culture is authenticated by the masses; cultural populism determines how messages are interpreted and what value brands afford' (Fournier and Avery 2011: 200). In the Web 2.0 era, then, brand managers ignore at their peril the threats posed by what Pongsakornrungslip and Schroeder (2011) refer to as 'co-consuming brand communities' (see also Denegri-Knott, Zwick and Schroeder 2006).

This warning is particularly relevant to brands in Russia, since not only does the country have its own home-grown social media alongside the foreign networks such as Facebook, Instagram, YouTube and Twitter,[6] but social media use is far higher than the global average (Shklovski 2013). How, then, are Russian-based brands using Web 2.0? In what follows, we look closely at two specific examples, each of which involves a brand using social media to meet a specific challenge. First, we examine how a regional brand ('Siberian Crown' lager) has used Facebook to help turn itself into a national brand.[7] Second, we analyse the social media strategy of a foreign, global brand (Levi's) as it attempts to maintain market share in Russia against strong competition (both foreign and local). Our close textual and visual analysis of these pages is based on an 'observational netnography' methodology (Kozinets 2006, 2015). While Kozinets (2006: 132) suggests that ideally, netnographic research should be multi-method, we generally avoided taking part in online discussions, since we analyse these media primarily as aesthetic objects (McQuarrie, Miller and Phillips 2013). Since the purpose of these pages is to promote their respective brands' mythology, we propose to 'read' them rather as Lévi-Strauss read myth, not following them line by line (or post by post), but rather apprehending them 'as a totality', teasing out their 'basic meaning' by looking at 'bundles of events' that 'appear at different moments in the story' (Lévi-Strauss 2014: 40). In the case of Siberian Crown, we look at the brand's social media pages in their entirety. As far as Levi's is concerned, however, given the length of time that the brand has been present on social media in Russia, and the high number of images (several thousand) contained on its pages, we focus on one year in particular. The year in question is 2013, the 160th anniversary of the company's founding.

Siberian Crown's 'Map of Russian Pride' on Facebook: Collective memories, imaginary geographies, brand identity

In a sense, analysing a beer brand is a neat way of bringing together some of the themes from chapters two (masculinity) and three (packaging). For example, it could be argued that beer is the ultimate collective tipple for men, and as such helps them construct their social identity (Manning 2012). This is especially true in the West, where most beer advertising tends not just to target men, but also to encourage them to see the drink as an essential element in the male bonding ritual (Tungate 2008: 182–86). To refuse to drink beer is to run the risk of exclusion from the group, as the character Andy nearly finds to his cost in the recent film *The World's End* (directed by Edgar Wright in 2013). This socio-cultural connotation of beer is by no means confined to Western Europe, however. In recent years, it has become closely associated with national identity both in Russia (Morris 2007) and other ex-Soviet republics such as Georgia (Manning and Uplisashvili 2007). Manning (2012: 206) refers to the countless 'beer-mediated masculine solidarities' fuelled by Georgian advertising, and enacted on a daily basis in the country. His findings confirm the point made by Shanks and Tilley (1992: 208): 'Beer is not just any consumable item, it has strong historical and social links with community life'.

A number of alcoholic beverages function by (re)creating a common history, and a shared sense of identity, underpinned by the notion of authenticity (on French champagne, see Guy 2003, and on Mexican pulque, see Toner 2015). Few alcoholic beverages do this more, however, than beer (White 2009). Many beer brands create an identity for themselves by evoking a sense of both time and place (Hede and Watne 2013). As Shanks and Tilley (1992) have argued, beer packaging – bottles, cans, labels – often embodies important social values.

In doing so, it frequently constructs a particular image – a 'mediascape' (Appadurai 1996) – of that society and its history (in much the same way as the chocolate wrappers and boxes we looked at in our previous chapter). This phenomenon has increasingly become a feature of Russian beer can and bottle design in recent years – as we suggested in our brief discussion of 'retro' packaging in chapter three. Russia is currently the world's fourth largest beer market (Schultz 2012), having seen sales rise by more than 40 per cent between 2001 and 2011, at the same time as vodka sales have fallen by nearly 30 per cent (BBC 2011). In recent years, however, the sector has been the target of draconian advertising and retailing restrictions in Russia. The crackdown on advertising began in 2008. In 2011, the beverage was officially reclassified as an 'alcoholic drink', in a state-backed attempt to curb alcoholism in the country (Walker 2011). The law restricting the sale of beer from kiosks introduced on 1 January 2013 (see chapter one) also concerned railway stations, airports and a number of other public places (Schultz 2012; Herszenhorn 2013). Beer sales in the country fell by 9 per cent between May 2014 and May 2015, partly in response to these restrictions, but also as a consequence of the country's current economic woes (MyTradeGroup.com 2015). Faced with this increasingly difficult context, Russian brewers have had to find ever more creative ways to attract consumers' attention. Distinctive packaging has been one such way, as indeed it has been for the country's vodka industry (Kravets 2012). One example of this is AB–InBev's 'Zhigulevskoe original'noe', which we discussed briefly in chapter three. Its distinctive, Soviet-style label is very possibly designed as an attempt to associate the brand with 'Russianness', and thereby gain competitive advantage over the many foreign beers that have recently flooded the market (on this practice in Georgia, see Manning 2012). It may also help it distinguish itself from the dozens of other beers currently sold under the same name in Russia.[8]

Our focus in this chapter is not, of course, packaging, but rather social media. Before we look at how one particular Russian beer brand has used social media to 'cultivate' consumers (Smart 2010), however, we need to say something about the concepts 'collective memories', and 'imaginary geographies'. The term 'collective memory' has been used in a variety of different contexts in recent years. While the literature on the topic may not be as exhaustive as that on nostalgia, it is nevertheless vast. It was first used by Maurice Halbwachs (1877–1945), a sociologist and student of Émile Durkheim, who had studied the role of shared rituals in providing the sense of continuity and connection with the past necessary for social cohesion. Halbwachs himself argued that collective memories are used by groups to explain the present, and that further-more they are often manipulated by elites within a given group to protect their privileged status and source of power (Halbwachs 1992, 1966). Much of the recent literature on collective memory centres on the notion of trauma, especially in relation to the Holocaust (see for example Zeruvabel 1995; Bal, Crewe and Spitzer 1999). In recent years, scholars have begun to examine the different ways in which collective memories are being constructed on social media (see for example Neiger, Meyers and Zandberg 2011).[9]

The notion of 'collective memory', rather like 'nostalgia', has also been much exploited in studies of post-socialist Europe (Berdahl 2010; Rabikowska 2013). This last point should come as no surprise, since, as Olick (1999: 333) put it at the very end of the twentieth century:

> [T]he term collective memory has become a powerful symbol of the many political and social transitions currently underway, though there is something broadly epochal about our seemingly pervasive interest in memory. New regimes seek to 'settle' the residues of their predecessors, while established systems face a rise in historical consciousness and increasingly pursue a 'politics of regret'.

The 'politics of regret' of which Olick speaks is often pursued via what Zeruvabel (1995: 3) calls 'commemorative narratives and rituals in contemporary social life', since it is through them that individuals come to imagine themselves as part of the same social group, be that a family, a 'tribe' (Maffesoli 1996), an organisation, or that broader 'community' known as the nation state (Anderson 2006; see also Climo and Cattell 2002). As we saw in our previous chapter, this aptly describes the mechanisms of power at work in today's Russia, as Putin actively engages in what Oushakine (2013) – in an article that makes explicit reference to the work on 'collective memory' by Winter and Sivan (1999) – has called the 'affective management of history'. Indeed, as we mentioned in our introduction and have observed elsewhere (Roberts 2014b), recent political debate about Russian national identity has seen the emergence of certain key founding myths of the Russian nation (Brundny 2013), myths which have at times involved the construction of very selective, anti-Western kinds of collective memory.

Mention of history brings us to geography. The term 'imaginary geographies' goes back to the work of Edward Said, who originally used it in the singular to refer to the way in which the 'Orient' has historically been constructed as the exotic 'other' in the Western cultural imagination (Said 1978). More recently, Said's concept has been fruitfully exploited by Manning (2012), in reference to that most iconic of English drinks, gin. As Manning observes, referring specifically to Said's work: '[G]in bears the afterimage of an orientalist imaginary geography [...], its erstwhile sphere of circulation and consumption, which is now a lost, nostalgic world found mostly on the labels of gin bottles'.[10] Manning's point, however – and this is crucial to our argument – is that *all* alcoholic drinks function in this manner, not just gin. He continues: '[d]rinks [...] construct elsewheres within space and time, imaginary geographies that make their consumption meaningful in a way that transcends here and now' (Manning 2012: 20).

In recent years, a number of Russian beer brands have used advertising to construct the kind of spatial and temporal 'elsewheres' of which Manning talks, precisely in order to issue a 'call to solidarity' (O'Shaughnessy and O'Shaughnessy 2004: 56) among their predominantly young, male target market. Many of them emphasise either the country's rich history, or the vastness of its territory. One of the best examples is 'Siberian Crown' ('Sibirskaya korona'), a non-descript, middle-of-the-road lager that launched an aggressive marketing campaign in the early 2000s. As Morris (2007: 1399) notes, the series of ads made for the brand at the time 'presented Imperial Russia in all its luxurious glory: candle-lit balls, splendid military uniforms and the Russian tricolour flying from every available pole'. The brand is a market leader in Russia, and was voted 'No. 1 beer in Russia' in 2007 and 2009 (SunInBev.ru [n.d.]). It was launched at a local brewery, 'Rosar' in the Siberian city of Omsk in 1996, before being acquired by Russian brewer SUN–Inbev in 1999. SUN–Inbev in turn became part of the brand portfolio of the Belgian–Brazilian Anheuser Busch–Inbev ('AB-InBev') group in 2005. According to SUN–Inbev's Russian company website, 'The brand's contemporary image is based on concepts such as quality, style, pride in one's country, prosperity, generosity of spirit, and nobility' (SunInBev.ru [n.d.]). The notion of 'pride' is central to the brand's positioning; its advertising slogan has traditionally been 'We've Got Something to Be Proud of' ('Est' chem gordit'sya').

In June 2012 Siberian Crown sought to accelerate its transition from a regional to a national brand. And it chose to do so first and foremost via a quite extraordinary use of Web 2.0. Its social media pages – both on Facebook, where it reached just over 10,000 'friends' before being closed down in June 2015,[11] and VKontakte, where it currently has more than 12,748 (having peaked at around 25,000 in late 2013)[12] – are packed with facts, images and quotations all designed to make the viewer feel proud to be Russian. The original title of both pages is 'The Map of Russian Pride' ('Karta rossiiskoi gordosti'), which echoes its advertising slogan.[13] The introduction to the VKontakte page makes this abundantly clear: 'Every day is a new reason to feel proud of our country' ('Kazhdyi den' – novyi povod dlya gordosti svoei stranoi'). Despite the fact that its VKontakte page has consistently had more followers than its Facebook account,[14] throughout its existence the latter consistently contained a higher number of posts, and can therefore be said to have been the main vehicle for the brand's repositioning. For this reason, we propose to focus on the Facebook page, although we will highlight any significant differences between the two accounts. If Siberian Crown generates so imaginary a geography and marshals so many collective memories on its social media pages, it does so in order to mythologise both Russia as a country and itself as a brand. Myths, as Halbwachs, Olick, Zeruvabel, Anderson and others have all shown, both work off, and feed into collective memories and imaginary geographies. One could also mention here the work of Slotkin (1973) on the ideological construction of the American West – the ultimate mythical 'elsewhere' for so many US brands, including Levi's, as we shall see later on in this chapter (for a discussion of Slotkin's work on myth, see Thompson 2004). As Slotkin (1973) has argued, all myth rests on a particular duality; while it involves the expression of fundamental human aspirations, it relies for that expression on culturally specific iconography. Siberian Crown's social media pages are no exception to this rule; as we shall see, they make full use of Russia's 'distinctive cultural tradition' (Slotkin 1973: 14) in their selection both of metaphor and of metonymy to encourage consumers' pride in their country.

On the brand's Facebook page, launched in April 2012, one finds a number of different types of post. Of the several hundred posts, fewer than ten focus explicitly on beer. On 10 September 2013, for example, one can see a collection of pre-1917 beer labels from Vladivostok, while two weeks later one finds a post showing three early-nineteenth century Russian beer bottle seals. Another post makes the unsubstantiated, and difficultly verifiable, claim that the world's first brewers were eastern Slavs in the fifth century BC. Generally speaking, however, references to beer – and indeed to the Siberian Crown brand – are conspicuous by their absence. Instead, one finds topics such as:

- Photographs of, and quotations by, Russian and Soviet military heroes, artists, writers, scientists, cosmonauts and politicians, all praising some aspect of Russianness. Soviet dissident Aleksandr Solzhenitsyn waxes lyrical about the greatness of the Russian soul, while on 26 August 2013, the nineteenth-century novelist Ivan Turgenev celebrates the 'great, powerful, truthful and free Russian language'. On 17 February 2013, there is a quotation from nineteenth-century Russo-Ukrainian writer Nikolay Gogol', laconically urging readers to 'thank God you're Russian';
- Quotations by various notable foreign figures. On 5 August 2013, for example, the Dalai Lama himself is quoted, praising Russians' 'generosity'. Most of the time, however, these foreign figures are French, reflecting the fact that for many Russians France remains the land of good taste and refinement. De Gaulle praises French courage, in July 2012, while in August 2013, Gérard Depardieu, the ink on his new Russian passport still wet, could be read claiming 'one needs to be very strong to be a Russian';[15]
- Numerous images of the country's natural features, such as Lake Baikal (located in Siberia, this is the world's largest freshwater lake);
- Several photographs of man-made structures, ranging from the fountains at Peterhof, just outside St Petersburg, to the Sochi 2014 Winter Olympics stadium. No opportunity is lost to compare Russia favourably with the West; we learn, for example, that Moscow's Ostankino TV tower is much higher than New York's Empire State Building;
- The summer of 2013 saw the launch of several mini-series, such as

    a   *Only in Russia*, in which we learn for example that Mariya (Tatyana) Pronchisheva was the first woman to explore the Arctic, in the eighteenth century;

    b   *Sporting Pride*, where we may read all about the exploits of various Russian sporting heroes, such as champion wrestler and three times Olympic-gold medallist, Alex Karelin;

    c   *A Hero of Our City*, detailing various acts of heroism from supposedly ordinary Russian citizens. These range from the story of how a ten-year-old boy from an isolated village saved another boy from drowning, to the tale of an orthodox priest bravely defying his captors during the first Chechen War, and losing his life as a consequence (this last story prompts two comments from the brand's followers, one of whom urges the brand to 'send [the story] to Putin!', while the other declares simply 'A real Russian! May his memory live on forever!');

- These were followed in autumn 2013 by a series of unconnected posts celebrating heroic moments or facts from Soviet and Imperial history. These include: the claim (28 September) that press freedom in Imperial Russia was greater than that in many Western countries at the time (a post which neatly sidesteps the fact that the press in Imperial Russia underwent a cyclical pattern of brutal repression and relative freedom); a photograph showing the construction of the Turkestan–Siberia railway, built between 1926 and 1931 and covering 1,442 km; and mention of the first Soviet climbers to conquer Everest, in 1982.

During 2013, the brand added a series of sub-pages to its social media sites, each one closely associated with one particular aspect of Russian, or Soviet, national identity. In April, a special subsidiary page was created to commemorate Cosmonauts' Day (12 April).[16] On this page one can learn a wealth of information about the history of the space race of the 1960s and 1970s. If, to paraphrase Yurchak (1999: 92), the conquest of space was central to the Soviet mythology of the Bright Future, then another of the brand's sub-pages is very much focussed on the country's glorious military past. The page in question is devoted to the Russian Navy Day, celebrated on the last Sunday in July ever since it was inaugurated in 1939. The choice of the navy, rather than another branch of the Russian military such as the paratroopers (who have their own 'day', on 23 August), is of course far from neutral. For one thing, it provides a link with the 'greatest' tsar of all, Peter the Great, who founded the Russian navy at the end of the seventeenth century (a fact celebrated on a number of the Krupskaya brand's chocolate wrappers and boxes, as we saw in our previous chapter). It was with Peter that began Russian leaders' historical obsession to capture and maintain the ice-free ports without which mastery of the seas would remain a pipedream (a trend which can be seen even today, in the recent annexation of the Crimea peninsula). Then there is the fact that the country's nuclear-powered submarines helped it maintain the balance of power during the Cold War. Not surprisingly, then, Soviet-era submarines feature here, as do many other aspects of the country's navy, past and present – flags, ships, battles, technological innovations, even the cost of a sailor's rations in the Soviet era. Whereas the brand's logo and slogan were prominently displayed above each Cosmonauts' Day post, now each Navy Day image is topped with the Russian tricolour, the flag of St Andrew (the Russian navy's emblem), two gold anchors and a double-headed eagle with St George (the patron saint of Moscow) in the middle, slaying the dragon. The only reference to Siberian Crown beer is the green and gold crown (now somewhat diminished in size) in the top left-hand corner.

The most extensive, and interactive sub-page appeared in May 2013 when, to coincide with the 68th anniversary of the victory over Nazi Germany, the company launched an application entitled 'A victory to feel proud about' ('Pobeda, kotoroi my gordimsya').[17] A post on the application's main page explains the principle behind it:

> Thank you for your victory! The Great Patriotic War [World War II] tou- ched every family. For each 'like' on the page http://pomnim-pobedu.ru/ we will donate one rouble to the monument renovation fund! Share the post with your friends and help renovate these monuments to a great Russian victory, the victory of our forefathers!

The monuments in question are in St Petersburg, Nizhny Novgorod, Volgograd and Moscow (in this last case, the tank barriers erected in 1966 alongside the main highway leading from Moscow to Sheremetevo airport to the north of the city, which mark the nearest point that Hitler's troops reached in their attempt to take the Russian capital). One of the most emotive pages concerns the monument in Volgograd to Mikhail Panikhaka. Here we can read the gruesome details of Panikhaka's heroic deed, which involved personally stopping an enemy advance by throwing a petrol bomb – and his own burning body – onto a German tank. This interactive application – thanks to which more than one million roubles (approximately £20,000) were collected for each of the monuments in ques- tion – is no longer viewable now the brand's Facebook page has been closed. An application with a similar name can still be found on its VKontakte page, however (with 79 registered users at the time of writing). This time, there is no interactivity, no appeal to restore Soviet monuments, rather an endless string of facts about the War – tanks, heroes, key battles, etc. – presented as if straight from a Soviet encyclopaedia. The final section has just one page. Entitled 'The lib- erated ones' ('osvobozhdennye'), it presents a list of regions and countries 'partially or totally liberated by the Red Army'. The list in full: Romania, Poland, Bulgaria, eastern areas of Yugoslavia, eastern Austria and eastern Germany, Czechoslo- vakia, Hungary, Norway (the province of Finmark), Demark (Bornholm), north-eastern provinces of China, and Korea (up to the 38th parallel). As we have noted elsewhere (Roberts 2014a), in the dual process of brand mythologisation and state sacralisation in Putin's Russia, all countermemories that might not concord with the hegemonic view of the Great Russian Past are neatly effaced.[18]

The Ukraine crisis, which began in November 2013, saw a moderate, but nevertheless perceptible, change in the kinds of post appearing on the page. Already, on 30 April 2013, the brand's Facebook page had featured a quotation by Russian aphorist Konstantin Koushner (born 1944), suggesting that Russia, Ukraine and Belorussia shared a common cultural heritage. On 31 October 2013, a post was published containing a photograph of a Soviet anti-aircraft battery defending the Crimean port of Sebastopol from 'the German-fascist invaders' (this post attracted a mere 14 likes and a single share). At around this time, posts commemorating days devoted to various wings of the Russian armed forces began to appear, such as the 'Day of Strategic Missile Forces' on 17 December 2013 (28 likes, and one comment). This particular post came barely eight days after another celebrating the 'Day of Heroes of the Fatherland', on which one could see an array of Imperial and Soviet military medals, including the Cross of St George, complete with (the now ubiquitous) orange and black ribbon. On 23 December 2013, another post announced the death of Mikhail Kalashnikov, describing the machine gun which he invented as 'a symbol of the reliability and glory of Russian weaponry, and pride in one's country'.

This military theme continued briefly into 2014. On 6 January came a quotation from one of the most tyrannical of nineteenth-century tsars, Nicholas I, claiming 'Wherever the Russian flag has been raised, it should never be taken down' (50 likes and 40 shares, although no comments). Eight days later, another post referred to the recent launch of Russia's latest nuclear submarine (15 likes and a single comment). However, this theme was soon replaced by sport, which became virtually the only topic in the first half of the year – although the two do briefly overlap in a post featuring ice hockey star Il'ya Koval'chuk, entitled 'Russian Character', in which he claims that 'when the going gets tough, and we have no strength left, we show our Russian character, and emerge victorious'.[19] In early 2014, a number of posts highlighted national success at the Sochi Winter Olympics. Later in the same year (25 May), there appeared a post celebrating the victory of the Russian national ice hockey team over Sweden.[20] This was immediately followed by a post containing a link to the YouTube page featuring the official Russian World Cup song. A competition in which the brand's followers were invited to come up with the official rhyming-couplet chant for fans following the national team at the World Cup in Brazil prompted a huge response, with over 60 entries in just four days (6–10 June). Many of these were accompanied by photo or video selfies of fans in bars brandishing the Russian team scarf alongside Siberian Crown's very own banner. During the competition itself, Siberian Crown posted a number of short videos of Russian fans waving the Russian flag emblazoned with the brand's logo, either in the stands during matches or simply on one of Brazil's many beaches. As Tungate (2008) has noted, exploiting the popularity of football can be a useful marketing tool for brands aimed primarily aimed at men, provided the alliance is credible.

Shortly after the World Cup, on 25 July 2014, the brand's social media strategy entered a new phase. On that day, it published on its Facebook and VKontakte pages a link to a YouTube video featuring the American actor David Duchovny – in what was to become virtually the last post on its Facebook page. In the video, Duchovny (echoing Sylvester Stallone in the Russian Ice ad discussed in chapter two) explains that while he was born and raised in the US, his family name comes from Russia. 'Sometimes I wonder, what if things had turned out differently?', he confides, gazing out over an unidentified US city from a rooftop cocktail bar on a balmy summer's evening, 'What if I were Russian?'. This crucial question is the cue for a remarkable sequence in which Duchovny imagines himself in a number of 'iconic' Russian guises, as a Russian film director, ballet master, ice hockey star, and even as a cosmonaut. 'How would I surround myself with beauty?', he asks himself, 'what role would I play?' 'What path would I choose', we hear him ponder, as he backpacks through a meadow on a beautiful summer's day. 'Or would I make my own?', he continues, now staring out over a frozen sea from the deck of an icebreaker. 'What song would turn my life around?', he muses, driving along a shallow river in a Russian-made jeep before morphing into the moustachioed bass player of a Soviet pop-rock combo. This voyage through one man's highly personalised 'social memory' (Olick 1999) and 'imaginary geography' lasts just under two minutes, before we return to the 'reality' of Duchovny on his rooftop US bar. At this point, he asks perhaps the most important question of all: 'And being Russian,[21] if I had something important to say, how would I say it?' At this point, he begins to recite a poem. The verse in question is by official Soviet poet Vladimir Orlov (1930–99),[22] learnt by heart by generations of Soviet schoolchildren: 'I understood that I belong to a huge family: there's the footpath, and the copse, every ear of corn in the meadow, the stream, and the sky above me – all this is my native land!'

At the end of the clip, which also features an orchestral version of a song by cult Soviet rock band Kino,[23] Duchovny reaches out to pick up a glass of Siberian Crown beer brought to him on a tray by the barman (he's black, which may be a coincidence, or may on the contrary be a subtle way of highlighting racial inequality in the US, a feature of much Soviet cinema). As he raises his glass, he turns to face the camera, and says simply 'To You' ('Za Vas'). This remarkable post broke all records on Siberian Crown's social media pages in terms of likes, shares and comments. While in the overwhelming majority of cases the number of likes that the brand's posts attract is in single figures, this particular ad attracted 394 likes, 39 comments and 456 shares on the brand's Facebook page. On VKontakte, it has so far attracted 128 likes, 43 shares, and eight comments (including a 1'30" parody in which a pair of down-and-out alcoholics feature prominently). One can speculate as to the reasons for the post's popularity. First, this is a particularly well-made video (one VKontakte fan calls it, in English, 'the beuatifulest [sic] advert ever!'). Then there is the popularity in Russia both of the actor himself and of *The X-Files*, the TV series which made him famous, to say nothing of the gentle self-deprecating humour with which he presents himself (at one point, dressed as an ice hockey star, he opens his mouth to smile and reveals a gaps in his teeth), and which is so conspicuous by its absence from the rest of these pages. There is also the nod towards Kino, one of the most popular Soviet rock groups, as well as the recital of Orlov's poem, which is not only famous in its own right, but also serves as an intertextual reference to Aleksey Balabanov's blockbuster gangster movie *Brat 2* (*Brother 2*, 2000), in which several characters recite it (the rock song that David sings towards the end of the clip is from the first *Brother* movie, another blockbuster, released in 1997). Most importantly of all, however, there is the context in which the clip was produced, namely the ongoing military conflict between Russia and Ukraine. In such a context, the fact that such a big-name Hollywood star as Duchovny should publicly affirm his Russian roots – just a few months after declaring himself to be Ukrainian on his Twitter account (*Le Monde* 2014) – was bound to strike a chord among Russian consumers. Indeed, it is in the reaction by the brand's fans to this post that one can most clearly see the emergence of the kind of 'shared consciousness' that Muñiz Jnr and O'Guinn describe as fundamental to all brand communities.

On the very day of the post, a certain Yuliya Narkevich remarks:

> There should be more of these clips, so that people are made aware of just what kind of country they're living in. [...] And the video is not about beer [this in response to a comment from another fan]. IT'S ABOUT OUR COUNTRY!

The brand's community manager, eager to impose the official meaning of the clip, and by extension of the brand itself, immediately backs her up: 'Yuliya, we're delighted you interpreted the video in that way! You're absolutely right that the main point it's making is that we should be proud of our country.' The following day, a certain Aleksandr Smoke backs her up:

> Yuliya, I totally agree with you, the ad is great, [and] the ending is [...] very upbeat, since he drinks to Russia, 'to You'. [...] This is a country in which a single beer advertisement can contain more spirituality than all the films produced in it over an entire year!

When the same fan suggests making such films with certain Russian actors, another fan, a certain Sergey Golitsyn, points out that this would be difficult to square with the 'if I were a Russian' premise at the heart of the clip. Smoke replies:

> Sergey, [...] I entirely agree with you, I just wish there were more videos like this, it really hits the spot! We just can't make decent films in our country, and yet we can make patriotic advertisements like this! That you can watch again and again.

Like Smoke, few fans appear to lose sight of the fact that this is, after all, an ad. A certain Aleksandr Cheglakov even goes so far as to extend 'my congratulations to Siberian Crown's brand managers'. This makes no difference however to Smoke, who argues that if more of this type of film were made, it would 'raise the level of patriotism in our country', before adding 'who cares if it's an ad? The director deserves total respect!'. None of those who make comments mention the self-deprecating humour in the ad, although one or two fans express a degree of cynicism at the allusion to Duchovny's supposedly Russian heritage. A certain Pavel Kabanov sarcastically claims that the Hollywood star, Leonard di Caprio, has recently said his grandparents lived in the USSR. Only one fan, Elena Mosina, mentions that Duchovny had previously tweeted about his Ukrainian heritage: arguing that the film is very well made, she mentions the tweet in question, and wonders whether Duchovny changes his story 'depending on who's paying him', before accusing him of hypocrisy. Another fan, Fedir French, immediately leaps to Duchovny's defence, posting a link to an interview with Russian TV magazine *7 Dnei*, in which the actor said he had always felt half Russian, and expressed regret that his New-York-born father had never visited the country. In the end, and perhaps inevitably, the exchange peters out; there are no comments at all between 6 September 2014, the day on which Maksim Mullin comments wryly that 'it would be a brilliant ad, if it weren't for beer', and 2 December, on which Elena Leonova first makes the enigmatic comment 'Omsk…' – presumably in reference to the beer's home city, before repeating the brand's advertising slogan, 'we've got something to be proud of' (this is the last comment to date related to the Duchovny video on either platform).

On Siberian Crown's social media pages, Russia emerges as a spatial and temporal 'elsewhere', a heady mix of the past, the present and indeed the future, like so many other brands (Heilbrunn 2006a). It is a mythical land of heroes great and small, which excels in seemingly every branch of human endeavour. It is a land of immense vastness – a constant theme not just of contemporary Russian consumer culture, but also of Soviet culture, both highbrow and more popular (Stites 1992; Widdis 2004). Indeed, Siberian Crown's social media pages at times function like the crudest Soviet propaganda, except that this time it is not the future that is bright, but rather the past. This message is conveyed by the utopian, 'restorative' nostalgia (Boym 1994, 2001) that with one or two exceptions takes itself very seriously indeed – in stark contrast to the ironic, 'reflective' nostalgia that so many beer brands in countries such as the UK use to brand themselves (Roberts 2014a). Siberian Crown's particular 'marketplace mythology' (Thompson 2004), like all myth, ultimately reinforces the interests of the country's ruling elite. It does so, moreover, in a way which seeks to present those interests, and the vision on which those interests depend, as natural, 'transforming history into nature', as it were (Barthes 1973: 139; quoted in McFall 2004: 13). The brand's social media pages present a dazzling array of 'mediascapes' (Appadurai 1996) for its fans to experience and transform in order to construct their own social identity narrative – or what Belk (2013), in his study of how consumers engage with brands via Web 2.0 technology, refers to as their 'aggregate identity' (see also Wallace, Buil, de Chernatony and Hogan 2014). If Hamouda and Gharbi (2013), quoting Firat and Venkatesh (1995) observe that individuals create an identity (however fragmentarily 'postmodern') by their acts of consumption, then they do so not only by the products and services that they purchase, but also by the images they consume (Schroeder 2002). Siberian Crown's Facebook and VKontakte pages demonstrate that there are some images at least capable of 'hold[ing] consumers captive', as Schroeder and Borgerson (2003: 3) put it. Those that do so most effectively – that go towards generating a shared consciousness – are those that appeal to consumers' collective sense of self (Hollenbeck and Kaikati 2012), such as the David Duchovny video, which contains so many different tropes of 'Russianness' that there is room (almost literally) for virtually everyone. Ironically, this supports the findings of Marzocchi, Morandin and Bergami (2013), who suggest that many brand community members may ultimately be more interested in each other than in the brand in question (see also Croft 2014; Wallace, Buil, de Chernatony and Hogan 2014).

The fragmentary structure of the Duchovny video, with its array of competing life styles and tropes, might be said to function as a metaphor for what Bauman (2000) calls 'liquid modernity', that state of permanent chaos and uncertainty in which identity is always fluid, and the individual changes persona to fit the moment (see also Clarke 2003). To extend this point a little further, one could argue that Siberian Crown's social media pages encapsulate the 'dialectic of mutual creation' that Miller sees as central to material culture in general (Miller 2010: 114). Indeed, 'The Map of Russian Pride' demonstrates that Web 2.0, like all manifestations of material culture, may be thought of as a form of 'objectification' (Miller 1987); its dematerialised nature notwithstanding, it 'objectifies' social relations (Fehérváry 2009: 429) and thereby social identity. 'The Map of Russian Pride' functions as a 'technology of the self' (Foucault 1985); offering the user the opportunity to fix his identity (however temporarily), it forms a reassuring island of certainty in the otherwise chaotic world of late modernity (Giddens 1991; Bauman 2000). To make this claim is to extend and refine the more general point Miller (2010: 118) makes about the Internet:

> [T]he Internet [is] a form of objectification. At first [users] strive largely to become the selves they hadn't previously been able to achieve. Later, they gain a new imagination of themselves as people they were not aware they could even become.

The principal difference between the objectification of social relations via packaging (as discussed in chapter three) and via social media, is that the latter involves an element of performance on the part of the consumer who (rather like Duchovny himself) 'puts on his show "for the benefit of other people" [as a function of] the impression of reality that he attempts to engender in those among whom he finds himself' (Goffman 1990: 28; see also Belk 2013; Wallace, Buil, de Chernatony and Hogan 2014).

As Peñaloza (2001: 372) has pointed out, 'several researchers have argued that performance is central to many consumption behaviors' (see for example Sherry Jnr 1998; Moisio, Arnould and Gentry 2013). Indeed, an interesting parallel could be drawn between the spectacle offered by Siberian Crown's social media pages, and the Mid-West rodeo and stock show discussed by Peñaloza in the article from which this quotation is taken. As Peñaloza demonstrates, spectating is a central aspect of consumer behaviour at this show, in which, as she puts it, 'consumers actively make cultural meanings in blending fantasy with reality as they stroll and spectate at the various elements of this cattle trade show' (Peñaloza 2001: 389). There is an important analogy with the way in which Peñaloza's Mid-West rodeo visitors negotiate the various exhibition stands, and the manner in which Siberian Crown's fans navigate the 'Map of

Russian Pride'; in both cases, consumers are invited to 'make cultural meanings' based on the collective memories and imaginary geographies evoked by the mediascapes presented to them (offered for their 'spectacular consumption', to paraphrase Schroeder 2002). This is precisely what happens, for example, when Yuliya Narkevich exclaims that the series of clichés contained in the David Duchovny video are 'ABOUT OUR COUNTRY' – a 'cultural meaning' which, as we saw, the brand's community manager was quick to endorse. It is also what happens when the brand's fans are invited to compose a football chant for the national team's supporters at the World Cup – an invitation that prompted a relatively high number of responses. The various chants proposed by the brand's fans reinforce the 'meaning' of the national football team, and its on-field performance, as both metonymy and metaphor for the nation itself.

In our introduction to this chapter, we mentioned the nationalistic branding of beer in the former Soviet republic of Georgia, and we should like to return to this point before drawing our conclusions. Manning (2012: 206) makes the following point:

> Georgian beer marketers have domesticated and 'traditionalized' both 'beer' and 'brand', founding their domestic brands of beer in ethnographic images of the Georgian nation inherited from socialist and pre-socialist ethnography, using ethnographic images of Georgian tradition.

In a similar way, the primary function of Siberian Crown's Facebook and VKontakte pages is to help reposition the brand from obscure provincial brew to nothing less then a – *the* – national brand. Enlisting a seemingly endless range of Russian cultural icons, Siberian Crown wants in effect to turn *itself* into a cultural icon. There are very interesting parallels with US whiskey brand Jack Daniel's here. In his work on 'iconic' brands (Holt 2002, 2004, 2006), Holt shows the different ways in which certain brands draw on cultural imagery, myths, and history to create identity (see also Holt and Cameron 2010). Over time, through the use of a variety of cultural intermediaries, such as pop stars or TV shows, brands become associated with specific values. In other words, they exploit the politics of identity to generate legitimacy and build brand image. In so doing, they both construct collective memories, and co-opt them. As Holt (2004: 3–4) puts it, Coca-Cola, Budweiser, Nike and Jack Daniel's 'are imbued with stories that consumers find valuable in constructing their identities'. In a subsequent article, specifically on Jack Daniel's, Holt argues that it is typical of brands which not only reflect dominant ideology in society, but also actively disseminate that very ideology. In other words, brands are not passive reflectors of societal change; they also contribute to that change. They do so precisely through their reproduction of myth. As Holt puts it, in a comment about the US which could just as easily refer to today's Russia:

> Social and political problems in the USA have been increasingly managed through mythmaking and consumption, rather than through democratic

debate. […] Mythmaking has expanded from a more delimited role as one mode of cultural expression to the country's foundational cultural architecture, a myth society if you will. Iconic brands play a specialized role in this myth society. […] While other types of icons [such as John Wayne or Michael Jordan] serve as the nation's ideological artists, crafting myths to fit the ideological needs of the day, iconic brands are the tireless proselytizers, diffusing these myths into every nook and cranny of everyday life. (Holt 2006: 375)

The parallels between the mythical branding of Jack Daniel's and the social media marketing of Siberian Crown are, we would suggest, too obvious to overlook here – especially since, as Holt (2006: 360) himself points out, the US whiskey brand has itself undergone a transition from obscure regional beverage to national drink. Having examined how a nondescript regional brand has used social media to try to transform itself into an 'iconic' national brand, we will now analyse how a brand that is already 'iconic' – and indeed global – has used Web 2.0 to attempt to impose itself in the Russian market.

Levi's on VKontakte: Branding's final frontier?

Siberian Crown's strategy is, we have argued, to enlist Russian and Soviet cultural iconography, thereby encouraging consumers (inter)actively to produce cultural memory (Peñaloza 2001), in an attempt to reinvent itself as an 'iconic brand' (Holt 2004) for the new Russia. In effect, by seeking to transform itself from obscure regional brew to national tipple, it wants nothing less than to become the 'Jack Daniel's' of Russia. Jack Daniel's is just one of a number of such brands singled out as 'iconic' by Holt (2004). Another indisputably iconic US brand is Levi's (Holt 2002, 2004). To quote Solomon (1986: 619), 'the unique stature of Levi's as a cultural emblem becomes apparent when one considers that [a pair of 501 jeans] is represented in the American collection of the Smithsonian Institution'. As Solomon's observation makes clear, Levi's has a long and rich history (see Downey 2007). In 2013, the company celebrated its 160th anniversary, an event on which it actively communicated online, both on its corporate website and on its social media.

The brand's history would on its own makes Levi's a particularly interesting 'iconic brand' to look at in the context of Russia's emergent consumer culture. What makes it especially appropriate, however, is the marketplace mythology that has grown up around the brand, both in general, and more specifically in Russia itself. For many years, the Soviet authorities equated wearing jeans with treason (Chernyshova 2013: 145). As late as 1970, a woman wearing jeans in Moscow might be arrested and accused of prostitution (Chernyshova 2013: 157). Things began to change in 1973, however, when the Soviet Union launched production of its own jeans (output had reached 16.8 million pairs by 1975; Chernyshova 2013: 141). Jeans nevertheless remained a fundamental component in the image the last Soviet generation in particular constructed of the West as an imaginary, exotic 'elsewhere'; as Yurchak eloquently puts it, they were first and foremost desirable not as material objects in themselves, but rather as 'links to imaginary worlds that were spatially, temporally, and meaningfully "distant", as "fingerprints" of these imaginary worlds on the surface of Soviet life' (Yurchak 2005: 203–4; see also Caldwell 2002: 296). While they were by no means the only denim on Leningrad's Nevsky Prospect or Moscow's Gorky Street, Levi's nevertheless had a special place in the hearts of Soviet youth (Yurchak 2005: 304).[24] In recent years, however, Levi's in Russia has had to deal with competition both from other foreign brands, and from local ones, such as Gloria (on the fashion industry in today's Russia, see Gurova 2015). More importantly, however, it has been forced to negotiate the transition both of itself as a brand and of jeans as a category from forbidden fruit to something far more banal. To paraphrase Miller (1998a), Levi's, like Coca-Cola, once served in Russia as a meta-symbol of capitalism itself (on the political symbolism of jeans in socialist Hungary, see Hammer 2008). Fehérváry (2009: 427) argues that for Soviet citizens, Western goods such as jeans became the very embodiment of a 'political–economic system that allows for creative productivity, social relationships, aesthetic pleasures, and expression without fear of state retribution'. As Kravets and Örge wryly observe, however, once Western goods became generally available in post-Soviet Russia, the inevitable realisation that they did not possess such 'magical powers' was bound to lead to mass disillusionment (Kravets and Örge 2010: 212; see also Veenis 1999; Humphrey 2002; Yurchak 2005). Furthermore, as fast fashion clothing chains sprout up on city centre streets and out-of-town outlet villages all over the country, the product that made Levi's so famous – the blue jean – has become virtually invisible in what Caldwell (2002: 296) calls 'Russia's increasingly globalized consumption practices'. In addition, the brand is finding in Russia what it has found throughout the world since the 1990s, namely that it has come to occupy a no-man's-land between the very cheap jeans on the one hand, and 'designer' jeans on the other (such as Diesel, or G-Star), as well as specialised online designers of 'customised' jeans, such as Getwear. Once at the very top of the 'cultural capital' tree (Bourdieu 1984), Levi's now finds itself lost in the soft underbelly of this ever-expanding sector – in Russia as indeed elsewhere.

The challenges facing Levi's in Russia, then, are as much existential as they are commercial. Levi's has another, even knottier conundrum to deal with in the country, however, one that goes to the heart of the company's branding strategy. To examine this, we need to return once again to Holt's concept of the 'iconic' brand, a concept of which, as we have seen, Levi's is an exemplar. The point about 'iconic brands' as defined by Holt (2004, 2006) is their cultural specificity (see also Foster 2007; Moor 2007; Allen, Fournier and Miller 2008; Lury 2011).[25] For Holt, brands acquire symbolic – 'iconic' – status by mining popular culture and exploiting historical memory in order to tell stories (see also Thompson and Tian 2008; Maclaran 2009; Brown, McDonagh and Schultz II 2013). In so doing, they generate myths which address, and ultimately ease tensions in society. So, for example, Mountain Dew offers an alternative model of masculinity for post-war American society (Cayla and Eckhardt 2008: 217), while Snapple arose as part of the 1980s 'nihilist' backlash against Ronald Reagan's vision of American ideals (Holt 2003). Yet it is their very status as 'myth' which underlines these brands' cultural specificity; if, as Holt reminds us with a nod towards Lévi-Strauss (1963), 'myths are stories people rely on to organise their understanding of themselves and the world' (Holt 2003: 36), the 'world' in question is very much their own.

In a sense, the problem confronting brands such as Levi's which try to cross (cultural) boundaries/frontiers is a rehearsal of the now familiar global/local/glocal debate (see for example de Mooij 1998; Thompson and Arsel 2004; Mansvelt 2005; Foster 2007). Back in 1983, Levitt may well have cited the fact that Levi's were sold 'everywhere' (and indeed that Pepsi was now available on the streets of Moscow) as conclusive proof that the problem had been blown away by 'the sweeping gale of globalization' (Levitt 1983: 93). The fact remains, however, that the cultural and ideological specificity of iconic brands such as Levi's is at once their strength, and their Achilles heel. In today's increasingly globalised economy, as Hackley (2013: 70) pithily puts it, referring specifically to Holt, 'global brands have to negotiate a different kind of consciousness that extends beyond national borders'. This is especially true of brands such as Levi's which are, as Smart (2010: 14–15) notes, seen by many as an integral part of the 'global consumer brand' that is America itself, 'promot[ing] a consumerist way of life'.

As we saw in the previous section on Siberian Crown, there is indeed a very 'different kind of consciousness' within Russia's national borders – one that is at once fiercely patriotic and deeply suspicious both of the West and of Western brands (Hashamova 2004). If brands do indeed 'live in culture', as Holt (2004) suggests, the question is, then, how can a brand such as Levi's successfully gain iconic status in a context in which, to use Holt's terms, both the 'ideological turf wars' and the 'expressive culture' are very different? How, to be more precise, can it maintain control over the meaning-making process on which it rests, and on which it depends, when the culture driving that process is very different? Any brand which simply seeks to impose its own 'brand culture' (Schroeder and Salzer-Mörling 2006) in a different cultural context runs the risk of meeting either incomprehension, or re-appropriation by consumers who actively resist the brand's meaning, and seek to impose their own, radically different meaning on it (Miller 1998a; Askegaard and Csaba 2000; Thompson and Arsel 2004). The Internet lends itself particularly well to such resistance (see for example Hollenbeck and Zinkhan 2006; Krishnamurthy and Kucuk 2009; Albinsson and Perera 2013; Handelman 2013; Odou, Roberts and Bonnin 2014). This is especially true of brands which have developed such a distinctive, culturally specific iconographic tradition (in the case of Levi's, this is the Wild West frontier). As Schroeder (2002: 167) has cogently argued, 'images exist within cultural and historical frameworks that inform their production, consumption, circulation, and interpretation'. So how will these images be consumed and interpreted in what is likely to be a radically different cultural and historical framework?

In a key article, Holt, Quelch and Taylor (2004) address the challenges facing iconic US brands such as Levi's in today's global economy. Pointing out that the American myths with which US brands have for so long seduced the rest of the world have today lost their sheen, they maintain that there now exists a new global popular culture, generated essentially by global communication (newspapers, TV, films, etc.). In this global culture, global brands (by which the authors generally mean US brands) act as 'shared symbols', becoming the 'lingua franca' that enables people from different nations and with at times radically different viewpoints, to communicate with each other. As they put it: 'consumers [...] use brands to create an imagined global identity that they share with like-minded people. Transnational companies therefore compete not only to offer the highest value products but also to deliver cultural myths with global appeal' (Holt, Quelch and Taylor 2004: 71).

The article by Holt, Quelch and Taylor begs a number of questions, not least the central tenet about the emergence of a global popular culture, which is a rehearsal both of Levitt's article of 1983 and more recently of Ritzer's (1993) 'McDonaldization' thesis (see Sassatelli 2007). What is perhaps most interesting, however, is the role that the authors see new media playing in the way consumers come to negotiate the meaning of global brands. As they put it (Holt, Quelch and Taylor 2004: 74): 'Consumer understandings of global brands are framed by the mass media and the rhizome-like discussions that spread over the Internet'. Levi's is very practised in using the potential of digital technology to manage how consumers in different cultures perceive not just it as a brand, but also the world in which they live (Askegaard 2006). In recent years, the company has invested heavily in new media and virtual-world marketing (see for example Elkin 2003). In October 2007, for instance, it launched Levi's World, the first social networking and public chat branded virtual world in Hong Kong and China, aimed at the 15- to 24-year-old age group (Anfuso 2007). As well as changing identity, playing games and chatting to each other, members could buy the latest Levi's collections, earning and spending virtual money in both the virtual world and real-world stores. They could also participate in a range of online events, including DJ music nights. Differentiating itself thanks to the possibilities offered by Web 2.0 is also the cornerstone of Levi's competitive strategy in the new Russia.

Levi's is present in Russia on Facebook, VKontakte and (since February 2014) Instagram. Unlike Siberian Crown, its most creative use of social media can be found on its VKontakte page, which will be the focus of our study here. This page was created some time between September 2006 (the month in which VKontakte was launched) and March 2011 (the date of the earliest remaining post on the page, beyond which it is impossible to go). Initially entitled 'Levi's Club', it was renamed simply 'Levi's' in January 2014. A number of Western brands have exploited VKontakte to create brand communities. Adidas, for example, use the page as a way of encouraging consumers to participate in specially organised sports events (Ghedin 2013b). Coca-Cola's VKontakte page, on the other hand, serves among many other things as a forum on which members can arrange to swap various branded merchandise (special bottle tops, glasses, etc.), online or off. Levi's, like Siberian Crown, and indeed so many brands, uses VKontakte to tell a story – or rather stor*ies* – about itself as a brand (on brands and storytelling, see Bough and Agresta 2011; Smith, Fischer and Youngjian 2012).[26] For Holt, brand stories emerge from popular culture and cultural memory (Holt 2003; see also Maclaran 2009; Brown, McDonagh and Shultz II 2013: 596). Stories are important for brands' mythmaking, since they can 'connec[t] the consumer and the brand in a kind of existential bond' (Vincent 2002: 19; quoted in Maclaran, Otnes and Fischer 2008: 68). On VKontakte, the Levi's myth emerges out of two stories in particular, or two 'mediascape' strands if you will, each of which has its roots in either popular culture, or cultural memory, or both. First, there is a particularly strong 'Anglo-Saxon' strand – what one might call Levi's 'home' culture. Second, one finds a less prominent, distinctly Russian thread. Despite their undoubted cultural specificities, each strand, as we shall see, is designed to convey precisely the kind of 'cultural myths with global appeal' in which Holt, Quelch and Taylor (2004: 71) lay such store.

The references to Anglo-Saxon (largely, but not exclusively white) popular culture are all designed to reinforce the myth – a myth which as we have seen goes back to the Soviet era – of the West as the supreme locus of creativity, not just of the musical variety (Yurchak 2005; Zhuk 2010) but in a general aesthetic sense (Fehérváry 2009). These start with the playlist that one finds at the beginning of Levi's VKontakte page, immediately after the main header/description of the site and the list of 27 'Discussion Boards'.[27] A high proportion of VKontakte sites, both commercial and personal, contain such lists, and the interface of VKontakte itself is designed so as to make them very easy to find, reflecting the fact that many Russians use VKontakte as a way to share audio and video files. Of the 118 rock and pop songs listed and available at the time of writing either to listen to or to download (via VKontakte's own dedicated application), the overwhelming majority are by US or UK bands. These include relatively young bands, such as Arctic Monkeys and The Vaccines, as well as more established groups, such as Oasis or Fleetwood Mac. The list also contains much older songs featured in previous Levi's ad campaigns, such as The Ronettes' 'Be My Baby', further reinforcing the association between the brand and popular Western music.

The brand's centenary year of 2013, on which we have chosen to focus, saw a number of posts containing references to Western popular culture. These include current music stars such as US DJ and rapper Will.i.am, who appears in a video (posted on 19 April 2013) promoting the brand's range of 'Waste<Less' jeans. There are also numerous iconic groups from the past, some of whom have no obvious link to Levi's; on 2 January 2013, for example, a photograph of Paul McCartney and Mick Jagger sharing a cup of tea during the late 1960s can be seen above a brief text explaining that one of these ageing stars may appear on the new British £10 note. Alongside pop stars, one also finds a high number of Hollywood actors. These include a number of contemporary stars

(all pictured wearing Levi's), such as Clements Schick, who appeared in the recent James Bond film *Casino Royale* (11 June 2013).[28] Hollywood cinema stars from yesteryear also appear, such as Marilyn Monroe, James Dean and John Wayne in one of his countless westerns (one of only a very small number of references to that once iconic Levi's image, the cowboy). Alongside these references to mainstream US culture, one also finds allusions to various aspects of counter-culture, including a video featuring clips of illegal hot rod races in the US in the 1950s. Interviews with several (unidentified) participants in these races serve to underline the link between jeans and rebelliousness; one of the interviewees comments wistfully, '[the hot rod drivers] dressed a different way, there was a lot of classic jeans, ducktail haircuts and flat tops'. Finally, there are references to contemporary art, such as the 'What Moves You?' performance in London's Oval Space given by contemporary artists Ghostpoet, Koreless and Alex Turvey, together with links to excerpts of the performance itself and interviews with the three artists on YouTube. Much space is also given to the (interactive) public art project and music festival, 'Station to Station', in collaboration with US contemporary artist Doug Aitken, which saw various artists' 'happenings' all over the US in autumn 2013.[29]

All of these images can be found on the brand's social media outside Russia. However, alongside these allusions to Anglo-Saxon popular culture, one also finds a smaller number of specifically Russian references, anchored in very different cultural codes, and reproducing a very different type of myth. These include:

- references to contemporary Russian pop artists, such as the announcement of a forthcoming concert in Saint Petersburg by Mujuice, accompanied by the video of one of his most famous tracks;
- two black–and–white images from a photo exhibition of Leningrad rock in the Lumière museum in Moscow (including a photograph of the most famous group from the Leningrad rock scene of the late 1980s, Akvarium);
- four images from an exhibition in Moscow's Petrovsky Passage devoted to anti-Western propaganda posters from the Soviet era (ironically, given Levi's extensive use of Wild West iconography in the past, one such image is of a man dressed in cowboy hat and suit, about to light the fuse of a huge bomb atop of which he is perched);
- visual references to Russian fashion bloggers, such as Evgeniya Appelbaum and Anna Midday, wearing Levi's outfits, with links to their blogs.

Levi's are not the only US jeans brand to juxtapose Anglo-Saxon and Russian cultural references on their Russian social media. Another is the online designer of 'customised' jeans, Getwear, whose VKontakte page includes both the story of how Harley Earl came to work as chief designer for Cadillac after World War II ('because the cars of the fifties are another symbol of freedom-loving America, just as jeans are'), and a 1 hour 17 minute documentary video about Moscow street art collective 'Zachem?' ('Why?'). Perhaps the most remarkable thing about Levi's is the sheer quantity and range of images used. This 'mix and match' approach to brand culture is typical of an increasing number of transnational companies who seek to manage their national identities while embracing globalisation (Holt, Quelch and Taylor 2004: 75). Many would-be global Asian companies, for example, draw on multiple and extremely varied cultural sources to build brand identity (Cayla and Eckhardt 2008; Zhiyan, Borgerson and Schroeder 2013). Levi's objective, too, is to extract 'cultural capital' (Bourdieu 1984) from as many different sources as possible in order appeal to Russia's new, young and increasingly cosmopolitan consumers, who are both patriotic and well-travelled.

Their cultural specificity notwithstanding, the numerous allusions to Western and Russian popular culture evoke various kinds of 'cultural myt[h] with global appeal' of which Holt, Quelch and Taylor (2004: 71) speak. One such is the generic myth of individuality, individual agency, and freedom, for so long at the heart of Levi's brand story. This particular myth emerges thanks to the ad, released in 2011 as the latest instalment in the brand's 'Go Forth' series, which appeared at the very top of its VKontakte page during 2013. The soundtrack to this ad, featuring images of inner city riots, is provided by US poet Charles Bukowski. Bukowski can be heard reciting his poem 'The Laughing Heart', which contains the lines 'you can't beat death, but you can beat death in life, sometimes, and the more you learn to do it, the more light there will be'. Then there is what one might call the myth of the democratisation of glamour. The main vehicle for this myth is the series of dozens – and at times hundreds – of photographs of customers taken in makeshift studios (so-called 'Revel Rooms'[30]) set up in universities and shopping malls in autumn 2012 in the cities of Moscow, St Petersburg, Rostov-on-Don, Yekaterinburg and Novosibirsk. The most frequently recurring global myth on Levi's VKontakte page, however, is that of the frontier, and the frontier pioneer. This is the founding myth, not just of America (Slotkin 1973; Peñaloza 2001), but of the Levi's brand itself, which emerged around the time of the California Gold Rush (Downey 2007). If anything, however, the recent history of Levi's branding has been about reinventing – one might say 'de-Americanising' – the chronotope (Bakhtin 1981) of the frontier, divesting it of anything that might connote it with the American West. Not insignificantly, the show by Ghostpoet, Koreless and Turvey in the London Oval, embedded on the page in October 2013, is entitled 'A Journey to the Modern Frontier'.

Each of these 'global' myths is likely to strike a chord with Russian consumers, even if (or perhaps *because*) the vehicle for each of them is still predominantly Anglo-Saxon popular culture. As Goscilo and Strukov (2011: 4) note regarding glamour, for example, 'glamour in Russia is a new utopia, having replaced both the late Soviet project of building a radiant future and the early-1990s vision of a democratic state'. And as for the frontier, Russia – a vast land stretching over eleven time zones – has two natural frontiers. There are the Urals, separating 'European' Russia in the west from the vast expanse of Siberia – 'Russia's Wild East' (Thubron 1999: 18). Then there are the Caucasus, the region to the south which saw two bloody wars in the 1990s (Lieven 1998), and which occupies a special place in the Russian collective imagination, as the dividing line between civilisation and chaos (Figes 2002: 384–90). Furthermore, the Russian state's own frontier has historically been extremely fluid (Widdis 2004) – a pattern which has recently repeated itself with the annexation of Crimea (Dullin, Thorez and Boutkevitch 2015).

The mobilisation of such myths – which one can find on Levi's social media throughout the world – is not, however, the most interesting aspect of Levi's Web 2.0 strategy in Russia. To see what is, we need to look first at the platform it uses, namely VKontakte. There are three important distinctions between VKontakte and the social medium which it most closely resembles, both in terms of the richness of content and its interface, namely Facebook. First, VKontakte has a far greater reach in Russia – it has more than 190 million accounts and 45 million daily users, whereas Facebook has just 4.5 million accounts. It is also extremely popular in the former Soviet republics of Ukraine, Kazakhstan, Moldova and Belarus (Ghedin 2013a). Second, account holders regularly use it to do something one cannot do with Facebook, namely download and share audio and video files thanks to VKontakte's special application (Golynko-Vol'fson 2009; Ghedin 2011). While this activity is not illegal in Russia, which takes a radically different approach to intellectual property rights from that in many other countries, it nevertheless fits in with Levi's historic positioning as an iconically 'counter-culture' brand worn by society's more rebellious elements (Holt 2006).[31] Levi's VKontakte provides access to literally millions of audio files. Third, and most importantly, when one opens a brand's page on VKontakte, one is not invited to 'like' the page (as on Facebook), but rather to 'Join [the brand's] Community' – a point reinforced by the Discussion Boards one frequently finds on a number of brands' pages.

Levi's has shown itself to be particularly good at creating brand communities *off*line – as for example among gay consumers in the US (Kates 2004). But how exactly are the specificities of VKontakte exploited by Levi's in Russia to create a brand community *on*line? As we saw earlier, Muñiz Jnr and O'Guinn (2001) argue that communities are characterised by, first, shared consciousness, second, rituals and traditions, and third, a sense of moral responsibility. The first of these, shared consciousness, emerges in the numerous discussions about taste that appear. In these exchanges, the brand's followers attempt to display what McQuarrie, Miller and Phillips (2013: 139) define, following Gronow (1997) as 'th[e] ability to discriminate stylish, fashionable clothing from merely acceptable dress'.

Some of the discussions on taste emerge in response to posts about new collections. So for example, on 27 December 2013, one user, a certain Alenka Sukhanova, vaunts the merits of Levi's jeans made in Japan. The brief exchange which follows is a typical display of taste (it also demonstrates both how savvy and how brazen Russian consumers are, and how tolerant Levi's social media moderators can be)

ALENKA SUKHANOVA: Jeans made in Japan are the coolest.
EVDOKIA TETERINA: I agree, Alenka. Only jeans from Japan are made from a single piece of material.

ALENKA SUKHANOVA: Well, that's not really the point. The fact is, they're made to very high quality standards and they feature original and exclusive styles. The orange tab, for example, unless I'm mistaken.

NATAL'YA CHERNICHKINA: Do you know where I can get them, Alenka (Japanese ones, I mean)?

ALENKA SUKHANOVA: I know you can get them on ebay, Natal'ya, or in Japan.

NATAL'YA CHERNICHKINA: Thanks, Alenka! They might sell fakes, though, what do you think?

ALENKA SUKHANOVA: It depends on which ebay you buy them. If it's the Russian ebay, they may well be.

Sometimes, consumers exercise their taste to criticise Levi's clothing. The following exchange occurs following a post on 13 December 2013 announcing the arrival of the company's new 'Levi's Commuter' range (an exchange which for all its brevity reveals much about the dangers the brand runs of appearing to reject the heritage on which it positions itself so aggressively elsewhere):

ANDREY SUKHANOV: The new LEVIS [sic] collection just isn't interesting. Where's the spirit of the Wild West, or the Dockers? They [the trousers in the picture] remind me of something Benetton might do....

DENIS KURYATOV: Andrey, Levi's has gone all 'glamour'.

[At this point, the brand community manager intervenes:] LEVI'S CLUB: Thanks for sharing your thoughts, Andrey, but we completely disagree with you. Levi's advances in step with the times, and follows the trends, [design] innovations and new technologies, but the brand is true to its history, which is why our classic range is still around, and always will be.

Dialogue about matters of taste are most actively encouraged, however, not on the main page, but rather on a number of discussion boards. Topics include: 'What Levi's items do you own?' (the second most popular thread, with 188 posts to date); 'What do you think about Levi's Curve ID jeans?'; or 'which famous fashion designers do you think should work for Levi's?'. Other threads touch on fashion in the general sense. Consumers are asked, for example, to define their ideal pair of jeans, to give their opinion as to what kinds of shoes go best with jeans, or even to say at what moment they begin to think about buying a new pair of jeans. Of course, threads such as these can be a valuable market research tool for the brand (Bough and Agresta 2011). From the point of view of the consumer, however, they serve a very different function. Posting a photograph of oneself online, or holding forth on what kind of shoes go best with what style of jeans are precisely the kind of 'authenticating acts and authoritative performances' of which Arnould and Price (2000), following Giddens (1991) and Bauman (1992), speak.[32] As Arnould and Price in particular suggest, such acts are fundamental in the struggle not just to affirm personal agency and thereby establish one's own identity, but also to create a community in which to embed that sense of self (since, as they argue, identity emerges from community: Arnould and Price 2000: 151).[33]

The numerous references to popular music are also part of Levi's attempts to generate a sense of shared consciousness – that of belonging to the same generation, with common interests (and, once again, tastes; see Thornton 1996). They also serve, however, to create a sense of common rituals and tradition – the second characteristic of a brand community in Muñiz Jnr and O'Guinn's (2001) definition. In effect, they construct for community members a common history (since the overwhelming majority of these references are to bands from the past, rather than the present). This is the function of the song playlist at the top of the page, for example, and of the numerous embedded pop videos and related trivia. Users frequently comment on these audio and video posts, even on occasion posting them specifically for other users. Encouraging this kind of peer-to-peer exchange among consumers is also the main objective of the music-related discussion threads. While some of these threads attract considerable interest from consumers ('guess the group' has 244 posts, for example), others prove less inspiring; the thread 'what's the best concert you've ever been to?', for example, elicits a mere five responses, from just two individuals, who appear to have conducted much of the conversation on their private pages in any case.

The third characteristic of a brand community as defined by Muñiz Jnr and O'Guinn is a shared sense of moral responsibility. The most likely place on Levi's VKontakte page where one might expect this to emerge is the discussion thread entitled the 'truth booth' ('budka glasnosti'), where brand followers are invited to 'just say hello to everybody or say what's bugging you'. The 'truth booth' is one of the longest-running threads on Levi's VKontakte page, having been started in March 2011. We could find no equivalent thread on any other official brand page on VKontakte. Essentially, the thread functions as a customer feedback forum, designed to create the impression of consumer empowerment and thereby pre-empt any anti-Levi's consumer groups emerging unofficially, in a manner reminiscent of Dell's online strategy in the US in the mid-2000s (Kaplan and Haenlein 2010). It can also be seen as an attempt to 'channel' brand criticism, by keeping it off the main page. Many of the posts on this thread contain questions relating to Levi's products – the different kinds of cotton, thread or cut which distinguish modern jeans from their vintage equivalent, for example, in which shops one can find a particular model or size of jean, or the differences between 501s and 506s, 'Skinny Fit' and 'Tapered Leg', etc. At times brand managers provide the responses, while at other times, the reply may come from a fellow consumer (in answer to questions on, for example, how to tell a fake pair of jeans from the real thing, the difference the country of manufacture makes, or where to buy cheap jeans online). We found two examples, however, of individuals appearing to demonstrate the kind of 'moral responsibility' to which Muñiz Jnr and O'Guinn refer On each occasion, a consumer demonstrates solidarity with another, coming to his or her aid on an issue relating to consumer rights ('assisting in the use of the brand' is discussed by Muñiz Jnr and O'Guinn specifically as an example of moral responsibility:

Muñiz Jnr and O'Guinn 2001: 425–26). On June 30 2011, for example, a discussion arises around the issue of what consumers are entitled to expect from a brand such as Levi's. It is initiated by a certain Pavel Gavrilov, in response to a post about consumer rights which has since been deleted:

PAVEL GAVRILOV: Valery, that was a very strange reply you got from the defenders of consumer rights. If the store refused to give you a refund, you could have gone to an independent adjudicator, and if they confirm the damage to the article, then you'll be entitled to a refund including compensation. Buy things like that in the States, they're cheaper and better quality. […] Levi's has a lot of long-time, faithful fans, but everybody I know is unhappy with their quality. If people desert the brand, and sales fall, the brand will react. I think in general that the heads of giant corporations are only bothered about the bottom line. If sales decline, they'll keep a closer watch on quality, you can be sure about that.

When one of Levi's official spokespersons (a certain 'Dima She') intervenes to defend the brand's product strategy, Gavrilov continues:

PAVEL GAVRILOV: I'm talking about the fact that today's Levi's Red Tab wear out after just two washes. […] It's a disgrace. People no longer believe that Levi's make strong, durable, hard-wearing jeans […] It's clear to me that famous brands are no longer a guarantee of quality. One needs to check for oneself the quality of the denim, the stitching, etc.

This exchange ends as abruptly as it had started. A similar discussion occurs on 22 September 2013, when a consumer named Sergey Kuznetsov complains about a problem returning a belt that he had bought in a Levi's store, but which turned out to be too big for him. The store manager refused to exchange it, on the grounds that the customer had worn it. Kuznetsov's post prompts the following exchange:

KRISTINA KANAKOVA: […] You will find support in article 25 of the law on the protection of consumer rights! It's all in there, there's even a discussion of precisely your kind of problem!
SERGEY KUZNETSOV: Thanks. I just don't understand why the staff stood their ground and refused to exchange [my belt]. I mean, in our country, I would have thought Levi's are used to refunding and exchanging goods. […]

At this point Dima She intervenes to explain that Sergey is not entitled to a refund. He supports his point with a photograph of the relevant page of Russian consumer law, before adding: '[T]he company always tries to demonstrate loyalty to its customers. Best wishes.' With that, the discussion ends.

This kind of exchange, when one consumer intervenes in order to give advice to another, is remarkably rare, however. As this suggests, the kind of brand community that emerges on Levi's VKontakte page is very fragile. The overwhelming majority of the brand's 56,541 followers on VKontakte[34] take little or no part in any of the discussions. When they do so, moreover, it is usually in order not to engage with other community members, but rather to seek answers to questions of a practical nature which interest them specifically. Beyond gripes about high prices, or enquiries about how to spot counterfeit goods or claim one's money back, there is little real evidence of a shared moral responsibility, despite the opportunities for the expression of such that the clothing industry readily affords (delocalisation, worker exploitation, etc.: Klein 2000). And there is not a single exchange in which any of the brand's followers arrange to meet offline (Amine and Sitz 2007; see also Bough and Agresta 2011: 43). So can we talk about a 'brand community' here in any meaningful sense?

One way to answer this question might be to point out, *pace* Kozinets (2015), that online communities are inherently unstable. To ask this question, however, is to miss the point. For Levi's VKontakte page represents nothing less than a paradigm shift for online brand community formation – a shift, furthermore, intimately connected with its marketplace mythology as the ultimate US counter-culture 'non-brand' (Holt 2006; Quinton 2013). To understand precisely the kind of community Levi's is encouraging its fans to imagine, we need to go back to the most important theorist of imagined communities, namely Benedict Anderson. A historian, Anderson traced the development of what one might call the 'reference community', from religious brotherhood through dynastic empire to nation state. Two points are crucial to bear in mind. First, for Anderson, what distinguishes communities is not whether they are imagined or not (since they all are), but rather '*the style in which they are imagined*', as he puts it (Anderson 2006: 6, our emphasis; see also Muñiz Jnr and O'Guinn 2001: 413). Second, communities are imagined by signs (see also Appadurai 1996). For Anderson, sign systems do not merely reflect imagined communities, however; they actually participate in their construction. As he puts it:

> It is always a mistake to treat languages in the way that certain nationalist ideologues treat them – as *emblems* of nation-ness, like flags, costumes, folk-dances, and the rest. Much the most important thing about language is its capacity for *generating* imagined communities. (Anderson 2006: 133, our emphasis)

In the eighteenth and nineteenth centuries, this process of community generation comes in the form of print-capitalism, the novels and the newspapers that speak to their (middle-class) readers in the new vernaculars, and which 'provid[e] the technical means for "re-presenting" the *kind* of imagined community that is the nation' (Anderson 2006: 25; original emphasis). Subsequently, modern information technology, in particular radio and television, performs the role once played by the printed page (Anderson 2006: 135). In much the same way, the Internet, and more specifically social media, have now taken the place of radio and television in community imagination and formation (Appadurai 1996;

Roberts 2014b). Whatever the medium, however, for Anderson the kind of community that emerges is determined not just by the images mobilised, but also by the way in which those images circulate; it is just as much a question of form as it is of content.

So what exactly is the new kind of brand community that Levi's use of Web 2.0 technology generates (or encourages us to imagine, to paraphrase Anderson)? It is one in which the barrier between brand and consumers becomes so blurred that it eventually all but disappears. It is in this sense that Levi's VKontakte page represents a new 'brand community' paradigm. This is achieved in two complementary ways. First, apparently 'ordinary' consumers are empowered to generate online brand content. In effect, the brand uses individuals who have no apparent affiliation with it, but who are empowered to intervene in certain ways. Individuals named Rano Salieva and Ekaterina Sitnikova, for example, both initiate a number of discussion threads. In doing so, they both help to shape the brand's meaning. Yet neither Rano nor Ekaterina ever explicitly mentions working in an official capacity for Levi's. However, alongside their discussion thread activity, they both also embed ads for the brand – both recent ones and examples from the company's archives – on their respective personal VKontakte pages. Alongside Rano and Ekaterina there is another contributor, a certain 'Dmitry Novikov' (whose avatar is a Red Indian chief), who neither starts threads nor appears to have any official connection with the brand on his personal page, but who makes a number of extended pronouncements on Levi's, its history and its products, which hint at deep expertise and knowledge of the brand, and leads one to question his relation to it. While he plays no official role on Levi's VKontakte page, his personal page contains a number of Levi's-related posts (including four for 2015), suggesting that he too may be more than a run-of-the-mill brand follower.

Rano, Ekaterina and Dmitry's online activity – both on Levi's VKontakte page and on their own personal pages – effectively marks them out as 'brand ambassadors' (on the role of Facebook users as brand ambassadors, see for example Smith 2013). 'Brand ambassadors' (sometimes referred to as 'brand advocates') are individuals who collaborate with a given brand, behaving in such a way as to reinforce that brand's values, enhance its reputation, and improve brand performance (see for example Harris and de Chernatony 2001). Since the arrival of Web 2.0 interest in the marketing potential of online 'brand ambassadors' has grown exponentially (Wallace, Buil and de Chernatony 2012). In an increasingly competitive market, brands in a wide variety of sectors are now turning to all kinds of 'ambassadors', as consumers are trusting less and less traditional 'top-down' marketing communication channels such as advertising (Andersson and Eckman 2009). Alongside celebrities (Muzellec and Lambkin 2006), company employees (Xiong, King and Piehler 2013) and consumers (Martin and Todorov 2010), this may include individuals hired by third-party agencies (indeed, in a private online exchange via VKontakte, Ekaterina confirmed that she had been officially employed in this capacity by an (unnamed) agency working for Levi's). The practice has become so widespread that in November 2014 the UK government announced its intention to introduce legislation to force video bloggers – so-called 'vloggers' – who endorse a particular brand to declare if they have been paid to do so (BBC 2014).

The use of 'brand ambassadors' to 'co-create' the brand (Singh and Son-nenburg 2012) is not, then, exclusive to Levi's in Russia. Rano and Ekaterina's 'collaborative content' (Percy 2014: 80) needs to be seen in its broader context, however. This brings us to the second of the two ways in which the boundary between brand and consumer is blurred by Levi's. On a number of occasions, we are given free and open access to what look very much like the personal VKontakte pages of certain employees. These pages contain virtually no reference to the brand, but appear instead to afford a glimpse into these individuals' private lives. So, for example, on 4 December 2013 a certain Vladimir Stepanov announces that there is only one Levi's Sherpa jacket left in the store he's working in, before signing off with, 'We're waiting for you – mention this post, and you'll get a 10 per cent discount!' Clicking through to his page in early 2014 revealed the kinds of images typical for 27-year-olds on social media throughout much of the world. These include a considerable number of photo-graphs of Vladimir himself, many of which featured him in his swimming trunks on a beach in the arms of a girlfriend. A number of posts were of rather dubious taste. On 1 January 2014, for example, one could see an image of two young women sitting at a Parisian terrace, accompanied by a particularly sexist caption. Other posts for late 2013 include a photograph of a clearly drunk individual gulping down a tumblerful of vodka as two of his friends look on, above the caption 'InSTOgramm' (this is a pun on 'Instagram', as 'sto gramm' means '100 grams' (of vodka) in Russian). We have to scroll down several weeks' worth of posts on Vladimir's page before receiving apparent confirmation that Vladimir is in fact an employee of Levi's; we eventually see him posing at the counter of a Levi's store, sporting a t-shirt with 'Levi's' emblazoned across his chest.

Vladimir is by no means the only Levi's store employee to feature on the brand's VKontakte page and provide free and open access to their highly personal pages. We counted two others for 2013, identified respectively as Ivan Stogny and Gayk Mkrtchyan.[35] When accessed in early 2014, Gayk's account con-tained various pictures of him with his friends, the audio tracks of entire albums by bands such as Sigur Ros and Linkin Park, as well as several posts containing what appear to be professionally drawn colour illustrations of SF and comic characters such as the eponymous hero of the *Alien* films and Spiderman. One had to go back to 30 October 2013 to see any link with Levi's; on this day, Gayk posts a photo of himself posing in one of the brand's 'Revel Rooms'.

Alongside Vladimir, Ivan and Gayk, employees responsible for managing some aspect of Levi's VKontakte page itself also let us see into their private worlds. In 2013 there were four such individuals altogether, listed at the beginning of the page: Dima She ('HR' – a role which in reality included defending the brand on VKontakte against consumers' criticism, as we have already seen), Varvara Korogodskaya ('Administrator'), Kseniya Gleserova

('Editor') and Liza Vtornik (her function is not specified). There was also (and indeed still is) an anonymous avatar called 'Mr Levis' (sic), who is described as the 'Moderator'. At the time of writing, his personal page, on which he is described as a 'commuter born in San Francisco on 8 July 1928', contains a total of just 27 items, all posted between 18 April and 27 June 2012. These include 11 posts in English detailing the early history of the brand, and 14 posts in Russian, shared from the official Levi's page.

Of these individuals, the most active on Levi's VKontakte page is Dima She. The precise nature of Dima's role becomes clear in one of his responses to a consumer, on 28 June 2011, in reply to a negative comment (since deleted) about the brand:

> [T]hat's a shame... that's precisely why this group [i.e. Levi's followers on VKontakte] exists. [...] Unfortunately, misunderstandings always arise, no matter what the topic. And our job is to help clarify things. In future, before buying something, get a second opinion about the quality or the product's characteristics and I will try to give you an exhaustive response. I'll even find the article myself and arrange for you to examine it yourself. [Levi's] is after all an excellent brand, and it has earned its good reputation thanks to quality and attention to detail over a very long time.

While comments such as this appear to confirm Dima's status as a company representative, his personal page gives away even less than Vladimir's. Gone are the latter's snapshots taken on the beach and the jokes of dubious taste. Instead, Dima's page contains a rather eclectic mix of Russian and US, 'high' and 'low' cultural references, in what is a microcosmic analogy of the Levi's VKontakte page as a whole. One finds for example, a lengthy quotation from a poem by Russian Noble Prize winner Joseph Brodsky (the theme of which – 'be yourself!' – recalls the global myth of individual freedom conveyed by Levi's own VKontakte page). In stark contrast, another post is about a cat in New Orleans, who has begun visiting one of the city's bars ever since his owners disappeared after Hurricane Katrina. References to Levi's are few and far between. The very first post by Dima, on 22 May 2013, is a Russian translation of the poem by Charles Bukowski featured in the brand's global 'Go Forth' ad (although it is not signposted as such by Dima). The second, and only explicit allusion to Levi's on Dima's page comes in the shape of a post shared from the brand's own VKontakte account in March 2015. On its own, however, this post does not tell us very much about Dima's possible professional affiliation, coming as it does immediately after a post on the history of UK clothing company Barbour, and just before another post, on US shoe brand Vans.

On Levi's VKontakte page, then, individuals masquerading as ordinary consumers – such as Rano and Ekaterina – seem to be working for the brand, while employees – including Vladimir and Dima – present themselves as ordinary consumers. Indeed, the very distinction – the very 'frontier' – between the two sets, employees and consumers, breaks down, as it becomes difficult to tell them apart. Since he is no longer listed as 'HR' in spring 2015, can we be sure that Dima She is still working as community manager? Is Dmitry Novikov really a 'brand ambassador', as his extensive knowledge of the brand might suggest, or just an obsessive fan? And what about the so-called 'moderator', Mr Levis? What is the relationship between his page (the avatar for which is the brand's logo), and the 'Levi's' page itself? Why does his activity cease so abruptly? Once one begins to ask this sort of question, it becomes difficult to trust anything one sees on these pages; Vladimir Stepanov's new, early-2015 avatar may well have shown him standing proudly at the counter of a Levi's store in front of a giant neon '501' sign, but is he really a Levi's employee? Perhaps he is an actor employed merely in order to 'personalise' the brand? We may have our suspicions, but we can answer none of these questions with a categorical 'yes' or 'no'. In short, the dividing line between 'us' and 'them' becomes so blurred that we can no longer tell where one ends and the other begins. As a consequence, the 'meaning' (Christodoulides 2009) of Levi's VKontakte page itself begins inexorably to slip through the viewer's fingers.

This blurring of the distinction between the brand's official page and the personal pages of its employees (or at least those masquerading as such) illustrates particularly well Bauman's point that with the emergence of social media we are now

> living in a confessional society – a society notorious for effacing the boundary which once separated the private from the public, for making it a public virtue and obligation to expose the private, and for wiping away from public communication anything that resists being reduced to private confidences, together with those who refuse to confide them. (Bauman 2007: 3)

More importantly, however, it also takes us back to the notion of the frontier, a trope at the heart of the Levi's myth, as we have already noted. We should like to conclude this chapter by re-examining this trope, since it is central to the kind of 'brand community' we believe Levi's is aiming to generate on VKontakte. The importance of the frontier (and indeed of its erasure) for the way social media branding works was first evoked by Singh and Sonnenburg (2012). As they argued, if social media have revolutionised branding, it is because brand storytelling is transformed into theatrical performance, a performance in which consumers participate just as much as the brand's community managers. As they put it:

> [I]n social media, the roles of the narrator and the listener are unclear because both the brand owner and consumers can play either the role of a narrator or that of a listener, which results in an interactive co-creation driven by the participants. This is very similar to an improv theater performance that allows an interactive relationship as audience suggestions are used to create the content and direction of the performance by the actors on stage. (Singh and Sonnenburg 2012: 191)

On Levi's VKontakte page, the audience are indeed at times 'used to create the content'; on 2 October 2013, a certain Yaroslav Binchev even posts his own parodies of two Levi's ads. But in this particular case at least, we are aware that this is a parody (rather like the parody of the Duchovny ad on Siberian Crown's VKontakte page); we know, in other words, where to place the boundary between 'brand' and 'consumer'. At other moments, as we have seen, the role playing that Rano, Dima and the others indulge in makes it is far less easy to distinguish between Levi's 'brand owner(s)' and its 'consumers', between 'us' and 'them'. Challenging this very distinction, Levi's VKontakte page resembles not so much Singh and Sonnenburg's 'improv theatre', however, as Mikhail Bakhtin's carnival. Bakhtin developed the concept of the carnival most notably in his work on Rabelais (Bakhtin 1984). For Bakhtin, the essence of carnival is the suspension of all social hierarchies, all borders and frontiers – a suspension based on what he describes as 'free and familiar contact'. There are significant homologies between Bakhtin's concept of carnival and the paradigm of social media branding – and brand community – at the heart of Levi's VKontakte page, not least in the way that both blur perhaps the ultimate ontological boundary, that between 'representation' and 'participation' (Jefferson 1989). In this respect, Levi's VKontakte page functions like Firat and Dholakia's new theatres of consumption – or as they put it, 'new [consumer] playgrounds' (Firat and Dholakia 1998: 156) – in which all social, cultural, economic and indeed political interactions take place on the same stage, as it were.

Carnival, and specifically carnival laughter, is deeply subversive, since it 'builds its own world in opposition to the official world' (Bakhtin 1984: 88, see Clark and Holquist 1984: 308). By the way in which it blurs (or 'liquifies', to paraphrase Bauman 2000) ontological boundaries, carnival threatens the clear separation of spheres and roles, and the maintenance of distinct power structures – the very things that Habermas (1984, 1987) sees as the foundation of modern society (Fuchs 2014: 61). This makes it a particularly apt trope for Levi's, which has positioned itself since the US counter-culture revolution of the 1960s as the ultimate brand for freedom-loving rebellious youth (Holt 2002). The most important point about carnival however – as Bakhtin is at pains to point out – is that it is not the utopia it may first seem to be, since this suspension, this opposition to officialdom is temporary; at the end of carnival, order is restored, normal service, as it were, is resumed (see Brown 1998: 141). Indeed, as we have seen, if Levi's may at times give the impression of relinquishing control over the brand's meaning, there is nevertheless always a moderator lurking in the background to invite members to continue their exchange off air, to defend vigorously the brand against criticism, or even to delete such criticism if necessary. The brand, however fuzzy its edges, ultimately remains in control. Indeed, recently Levi's appears to have sought to take more control, to 'clarify things', as Dima She puts it in his comment of 28 June 2011, cited above; when we revisited its VKontakte page in mid-2015, we were able to observe that all posts by the 'expert fan' Dmitry Novikov had been deleted, as had the post containing Bukowski's poem on Dima She's page. And clicking on Vladimir Stepanov's avatar now merely gives access to a blank page, on which one can read 'Vladimir has restricted access to his profile'. Just as the marketplace mythology on which the brand ultimately rests – the history of the American West – brooks no countermemories (Slotkin 1973), so in the final analysis must the brand (re)assert absolute authority over the marketplace heteroglossia of its social media pages (what Thompson and Arsel (2004) call its 'brandscape') – even as it appears to revel in, and even encourage, that very heteroglossia.

One should not exaggerate the degree to which the boundary between 'employees' and 'consumers' is blurred on Levi's VKontakte page – particularly given the evolution of the page itself between early 2014 and mid-2015. We are not claiming that what Brown (1998: 141) refers to as 'the irreverence, inversion, diversion and perversion' of carnival is a constant feature here – indeed, if anything it appears to have diminished since the brand's anniversary year of 2013. Nevertheless, what fuzziness there is begs the question: why erase the boundary at all? One possible scenario is of course that the community manager for Levi's in Russia was an inexperienced loose cannon whose mismanagement was eventually discovered – and rectified – by Head Office back in the US. But if that were the case, why not close down Vladimir Stepanov's account immediately, rather than in stages, why is Mr Levis' page still accessible after all this time, why is Dima She still sharing Levi's posts on his personal page, and why are Yaroslav Binchev's parodies still visible on Levi's own page? Most importantly of all, perhaps, it is highly unfeasible that a company with such a well-established and carefully managed Web 2.0 presence around the world should lose sight of what was happening in a key market – especially in its centenary year when its official biographer, Lynn Downey, actually visited that market to deliver a well-publicised lecture about the history of the brand (images from which were posted on Levi's VKontakte page, moreover). We believe the answer to the question lies elsewhere. In order to see precisely where, it should be remembered that Bakhtin's fundamental point about carnival is that since the temporary suspension of boundaries (and thereby hierarchies) is not spontaneous but rather sanctioned by traditional power structures, it ultimately *reinforces* those very structures (Stallybrass and White 1986). If carnival, as Bakhtin conceived it and as we have already noted, was designed to stage the spectacle of a great democratic free-for-all, the freedom from repression it offers is a mere illusion, to be brutally cut short at a moment's notice. So, while the access we are afforded to employees' personal pages, and the apparent impunity with which consumers parody the Levi's ads or even give each other tips on how to circumvent the brand's official distribution channels, creates the impression that Levi's is ceding power to the consumer (the power to make meaning: Christodoulides 2009), the reality is very different. The various role reversals and profanities are aimed not at ceding authority to the brands' fans, but are instead carefully (stage-)managed in order to create an aura of transparency, which in turn reinforces the image of the brand itself as authentic. Authenticity is essential for brands on social media, in Russia as elsewhere, as Bough and Agresta (2011), Yan (2011) and Aaker (2013) among others have argued. Or rather, to paraphrase Holt (2002: 83), the resources with which brands provide consumers via social media to further their own personal identity-construction project must be perceived by those consumers as authentic.

There is more to this than a mere attempt to appear 'authentic', however. All social media blur the distinction between the public and the private, as Bauman (2007), Fuchs (2014) and many others have observed. In so doing, they resemble what Bauman refers to as 'liquid modern carnivals', whose force, as he puts it, 'lies in the momentary resuscitation of the togetherness that [in late modernity] has sunk into chaos' (Bauman 2007: 76). Levi's VKontakte page exploits precisely this feature of social media, but in a very particular manner; erasing the boundary between producer and consumer, transforming one into the other, giving each voice equal weight as it were, it not only reproduces the very essence of Bauman's (2000) 'liquid modernity', but presents us with that modernity's ultimate 'global myth', namely liberal democracy. On Levi's VKontakte account, it is liberal democracy that emerges as the Ur-myth encapsulating all the other myths present – the idea that no matter who you are, you can 'go forth' and be whoever you want, that you can be as glamorous as a Hollywood celebrity, or even that you can make a genuine contribution to a creative artistic initiative on the other side of the planet. A product of Bauman's (2007: 115) 'carnivalesque game of identities', the global myth of liberal democracy emerges here as precisely that 'innovative cultural expression' (Holt and Cameron 2010: 173), with which Levi's aims to exploit the social disruption and ideological tension at the heart of Putin's increasingly autocratic Russia. Such innovation is vital, as Holt and Cameron (2010: 173) have argued, if brands are to 'leapfrog the competition', either at home or abroad. And what better global myth to choose? After all, liberal democracy has emerged as the ultimate global myth in recent years, used as it has been to justify military interventions by Western powers in countries from Afghanistan to Iraq, from Libya to Mali. Not only that, but democracy is, as Appadurai (1996: 36) notes, the 'master term', the central element in the chain of ideas underpinning Western states' 'ideoscapes', the concept which encapsulates within it all the other ideas to be found in those states' 'concatenations of images', such as 'freedom, welfare, rights, sovereignty [and] representation.'

Our reading of Levi's VKontakte page, then, underlines the brand's ambition to be the ultimate 'global ideoscape' (Askegaard 2006). Whether Levi's succeeds in its mission, of course, remains to be seen – especially now that it appears to have re-established a kind of order, to have gone some way to 'reclarifying things', to paraphrase Dima She. What its social media carnival reveals, however, is that even today, more than 160 years after it was founded, Levi's is still 'going forth' – not in the real world of the American West, but the virtual one of Russian cyberspace. The promise of authorised transgression, constrained by both time and space, remains central to the brand's 'meaning' (Christodoulides 2009). Social media is an ideal form with which the brand can experiment with that meaning, and indeed its limits, and invite its fans to participate in that experiment. In so doing, it creates, or rather co-creates, nothing less than a new brand community paradigm. In that crucial sense, Levi's VKontakte page really does represents branding's final frontier.

Notes

1 On community membership as a source of reassurance in the modern, insecure, 'liquid' world, see also Bauman (2001).
2 Similarly, Cova (2006) remarks a certain slippage between the concept of 'brand community' and that of 'consumer tribe'. He suggests that one is likely to find a number of different 'tribes' in a single 'community', while at the same time noting that the originator of the notion of 'tribe' in modern sociology, Michel Maffesoli (1996), is less categorical on the difference between the two. Elliott and Davies (2006: 156), for their part, claim that a tribe is 'a more temporary [sic] and frag-mented form of social grouping [than a community]'). For Cova and Kim (2013: 140), consumer tribes have three main features, namely 'collective identification – shared experiences; passions and emotions; and the ability to engage in collection [sic] action'. As they themselves note, this definition underlines the conceptual overlap with 'brand communities' as defined by Muñiz Jnr and O'Guinn (2001; see also Fournier and Lee 2009). Cova and Kim (2013) suggest, however, that con-sumer tribes form primarily around lifestyles, rather than specific brands, and that consequently tribe members may have a greater tendency to meet in the physical world. On 'consumer tribes', see also Cova, Kozinets and Shankar (2007).
3 Aaker (2013) uses the expression 'customer community' rather than 'brand community'.
4 We follow the definition of 'Web 2.0' as 'a collection of open-source, interactive and user-controlled online applications expanding the experiences, knowledge and market power of the users as participants in business and social processes [... sup-porting] the creation of informal users' networks facilitating the flow of ideas and knowledge by allowing the efficient generation, dissemination, sharing and editing/refining of informational content' (Constantinides and Fountain 2008, quoted in Brennan and Croft 2012: 113).
5 For a useful review of the ever expanding literature on social media branding, see Tsimonis and Dimitriadis (2014).
6 On Russians' use of Twitter, see Kelly *et al.* (2012). For a broader discussion of social media in Russia, see Alexanyan (2009).
7 For a discussion of how state airline Aeroflot is using social media to try to become a global brand, see Roberts (2015).
8 Another beer of the same name, sold exclusively by the Monetka retail chain, features a very different image from AB–Inbev's brew, namely that of a 1950s-style pin-up girl sunbathing on a beach: see Da Vinci Design Studio (2013). The problem of 'copycat' names is particularly rife in Russia. For example, Spanish fashion retailer Zara has had to compete with local rival 'Zarina', whose stores can often be found just a few hundred metres away in the same mall. And alongside IKEA's 'Mega Mall' chain, one also finds the completely separate online store 'Meggymall': see MeggyMall.ru [n.d.].
9 On nostalgia and new media, see Niemeyer (2014).
10 As should be clear from our concluding discussion in chapter three, we would not necessarily agree with Manning's point about the world alluded to on gin bottles as being 'nostalgic'. The important thing, rather, is that that world is now 'lost'. It is in this sense that it inevitably constitutes an 'imaginary' geography.

11 The original url was: www.facebook.com/gordostrossii?fref=ts (last accessed 21 January 2015).

12 See Siberian Crown VKontakte account [n.d.]. Since relaunching on 12 June 2015 ('Russia Day') after a six-month hiatus, the page has been renamed 'Sibirskaya korona. Bezalkogol'noe' ('Siberian Crown. Non-alcoholic'). This renaming both reflects the current legal crackdown on beer in Russia, and suggests an explanation as to why the Facebook page was discontinued. Since we began working on this book, the 'Siberian Crown' website has also been closed.

13 'Rossiiskii' ('Russian') is the adjective formed from the noun 'Rossiyanin' (see chapter three, note 5). As Ambrosio (2001: 204) notes, whereas the adjective 'russkii' refers to Russianness in the ethnic sense, 'rossiiskii' on the other hand is 'nonethnic, inclusive and civic'. The concept of Russianness promoted on Siberian Crown's social media pages is indeed highly 'inclusive' – a point eloquently illustrated by the use of Hollywood actor David Duchovny (see below).

14 This may reflect the fact that most Russians, especially those who do not travel abroad, tend to use VKontakte rather than Facebook: Ghedin (2013a). Russian-based brands, on the other hand, tend to prefer Facebook, first, as VKontakte is notorious as a platform for spam, and second, since the majority of its users are teenagers and young adults, who have below-average spending power: Ghedin (2013b). One notable exception to this rule is Levi's, as we shall see below.

15 A well-known and very popular figure in Russia, Depardieu has been involved in a number of marketing campaigns both for Russian brands and indeed for foreign brands targeting the Russian market. At the end of 2014, he appeared in a commercial for Swiss watchmaker Cvstos, in which, speaking in at times barely comprehensible Russian, he invited viewers (to whom he referred as 'my compatriots') to attend the unveiling ceremony for the brand's new collection of 'Proud to Be Russian' watches: FemmePlus.fr (2014).

16 As Yurchak (1999), Makarenko and Borgerson (2009) and others have pointed out, cosmonaut iconography has long been enlisted for marketing purposes (on the use of such iconography in Soviet-era consumer culture, see Roche-Nye 2013).

17 The Ribbon of Saint George featured prominently on the application's home page. It should be noted that celebrating victory over Nazi Germany is widely celebrated in Russia, where 9 May is a public holiday. On this day in 2012, for example, even the Russian Benetton blog featured a photograph of Red Army soldiers disdainfully throwing down Nazi military standards in Red Square in May 1945 (underneath an image of the same Ribbon of Saint George): see United Blogs of Benetton, Russia (2012).

18 On Putin's revisionist policy towards World War II, see Thom (2015).

19 The use of the adjective 'russkii', rather than 'rossiiskii', when referring to 'Russian character' here is extremely interesting, since it implies a clear distinction between 'real', ethnic Russians – men and women of 'character' – and other, inferior types with whom they happen to share a common home. The notion of 'Russianness' featured on Siberian Crown's social media pages is clearly a very moveable feast indeed.

20 As we saw with the case of Gillette in chapter two, a number of foreign brands have used ice hockey as part of their brand positioning strategy in Russia. The Czech firm Škoda, closely associated with the sport in Russia for a number of years, launched an ice-hockey game application, called 'Ice Battle' – yet another allusion to the famous victory on Lake Peipus in 1242 – on its Russian Facebook page in late 2012.

21 The choice of words is important here; depending on the context, the English-language phrase 'being Russian' can mean either 'if I were Russian' or 'since I am Russian'. Duchovny's transformation into an authentic Russian is complete here, thanks to this linguistic sleight of hand.

22 In a neatly ironic twist, Orlov was actually born in the Crimean city of Simferopol.
23 The original song 'A Star Called the Sun' ('Zvezda po imeni solntse'), can be found at: YouTube (2012a).
24 The brand has itself sought to reinforce this myth, thanks to the story 'Levi's® Jeans Go to Moscow' on its corporate website: LeviStrauss.com [n.d.].
25 A useful discussion, and highly persuasive critique of Holt's concept of 'iconic brands' is provided by Kravets and Örge (2010), who analyse the popularity of certain Soviet brands in the post-Soviet era.
26 At the time of writing, the trope of the story is introduced at the very top of Levi's VKontakte page, where one can read: 'Millions of jeans. Each pair has its own story to tell' ('Milliony dzhinsov. U kazhdykh svoya istoriya').
27 VKontakte enables brands to place such threads at the top of its page, thereby creating a dedicated discussion space – a feature that a number of brands use. These include both foreign brands such as Puma, McDonald's and Philips (this last has 556 such boards at the time of writing, August 2015), and domestic brands such as fashion retailer Savage and online shopping site Ozon.
28 This photo is one of several hundred which appear on the dedicated Levi's 501 web page: Levi.com [n.d.]. This page features hundreds of photos from around the world of celebrities, artists, fashion designers, boutique owners and 'ordinary' consumers posing in their 501s. On the growing importance of 'snapshot' photography in advertising, see Schroeder (2012).
29 Not for the first time in its history, Levi's is in the vanguard of what Frank (1997) refers to as 'hip consumerism'.
30 'Revel' is the name of the jean for women launched worldwide by Levi's in 2013. The product, and the 'Revel Rooms' designed to promote them, are examples of the recent 'feminisation' of the brand, a source of discontentment among some of Levi's male fans on VKontakte.
31 As Ghedin (2011) notes, this features of VKontakte has made many Western brands wary of it. Many Western-based majors are also increasingly unhappy with what they see as VKontakte's encouragement of piracy (Dowling 2014).
32 As Bauman (1992: 680) famously puts it, modernity 'lift[s] identity to the level of awareness, making it into a task'.
33 For an eloquent counter-argument to Arnould and Price's point, see Warde (1994).
34 This figure is rather less than the number of followers on VKontakte of Russian jeans brand Gloria (331,441), German sportswear brand Puma (271,084), Adidas (440,093), Gillette (525,634), Nivea (693,885), or other 'iconic' US brands such as Coca-Cola (703,757) (all figures correct at the time of writing, 19 August 2015).
35 Gayk's account (88 followers) is no longer active.

Afterword, or the cautionary tale of Diana, Lada, Myusya – and Vlad

Levi's carnival, Moscow's highly colourful city-branding initiatives, Putin's Hitchcockesque vanishing act, the Vegas mall's Museum of Show Business, IKEA's circus, Louis Vuitton's giant-sized steamer trunk – there is, it would seem, no end to the spectacle at the heart of modern Russia's consumer culture. A spectacle of a rather different sort – but nevertheless intimately linked to this new culture – occurred in August 2015, when a group of individuals masquerading as Cossacks burst into the Auchan hypermarket in one of St Petersburg's Mega Malls. Claiming he merely wanted to ensure the French chain were not selling any of the EU produce still under embargo, one of the men – performance artist Stas Baretsky – seized a can of Tuborg lager, unceremoniously biting it open and spraying the contents all over the floor. Why do you sell foreign brands like this, he asked a bemused Auchan employee, when we make all this here in Russia? In one sense, this incident underlines the point we made in chapter four, about the new political and social symbolism that beer has acquired in post-socialist Russia. It has far broader resonance than this, however. For it points to a growing disenchantment among certain sections of Russian society, not with the new consumer culture per se, but rather with the way foreign brands help shape that culture. This comes at a time when relations between the West and post-Soviet Russia are at an all-time low. Indeed, many commentators, not least the millions who saw the Auchan incident on social media, have drawn comparisons between the xenophobic antics of the 'Cossacks' in St Petersburg and the anti-Western rhetoric now coming from Vladimir Putin in Moscow. Whether or not they are right to do so, the current Russian embargo on EU foodstuffs nevertheless illustrates the harsh truth – not just for Western retailers, but also for Russian brands, and indeed for Russian consumers as well – that what the Kremlin gives, the Kremlin can also take away. This theme is central to a short story entitled 'One Vogue', written by contemporary Russian author Viktor Pelevin in the 1990s. In this remarkably short text, made up of a single sentence of 372 words, three prostitutes, Diana, Lada and Myusya, find themselves in the toilets of one of Moscow's swankiest eateries. As they gaze into the mirror, they focus their attention on each other's possessions, the white lizard-skin Armani handbag, the Gucci watch, the Prada suit, the Burberry dress, even the white Mercedes saloon in which Myusya is driven around by her pimp. Just as they are comforting themselves with the thought that they all possess more or less the same amount of glamour, they suddenly feel a chill wind, blowing from the direction of the Kremlin. At this point the text comes to an abrupt, and rather pregnant end. The brands with which these three women appear to construct their identity offer nothing but an illusion, a simulacrum, liable to be swept away at any moment. With the wind from the Kremlin comes the chilling realisation that their world of 'Vogue' ('Vog') counts for nothing next to the will of the omnipresent, omniscient 'God' ('Bog') lurking just across Red Square. Pelevin's text is of course a grotesque caricature, a piece of self-referential fantasy written at a time when the Kremlin was occupied not by Vladimir Putin, but rather by his predecessor, Boris Yeltsin. Nevertheless, it alludes to a very concrete historical reality in Russia, namely the perennial unpredictability of the political tide, and the remarkably precarious nature of property rights. Auchan and other European brands may well survive the current cooling of political relations between Russia and the West, and the country's economic downturn. Just how those brands, and the consumer culture of which they are a part, develop in Putin's new Russia in the future, remains to be seen.

References

4×4Club.ru [n.d.]:www.club4x4.ru/info/english-version (last accessed 21 August 2015).

Aaker, D. (2013) 'Find the shared interest: A route to community activation and brand building', *Journal of Brand Strategy*, 2, 2: 134–145.

Adams, J. S. (2008) 'Monumentality in urban design: The case of Russia', *Eurasian Geography and Economics*, 49, 3: 280–303.

Adme.ru [n.d.] 'Istoriya obertki shokolada "Alenka"': www.adme.ru/tvorchestvo-reklama/istoriya-obertki-shokolada-alenka-402755 (last accessed 25 November 2015).

AdsOfTheWorld.com (2013) 'Philips body groomer before and after': http://adsoftheworld.com/media/print/philips_body_groomer_before_after (last accessed 21 August 2015).

Afisha.ru (2012) 'Klassik sots-arta Erik Bulatov sdelal spetsial'nyi znak dlya prazdnika', 10 August: http://gorod.afisha.ru/archive/bulatov-sdelal-znak-dlja-dnya-goroda (last accessed 21 August 2015).

Albinsson, P. A. and Perera, B. Y. (2013) 'Consumer activism 2.0: Tools for social change', in Belk, R. W. and Llamas, R. (eds) *The Routledge Companion to Digital Consumption*, Abingdon and New York: Routledge, 356–366.

Alexanyan, K. (2009) 'Social networking on Runet', *Digital Icons: Studies in Russian, Eurasian and Central European New Media*, 1, 2: 1–12, available at: www.digitalicons.org/issue02/karina-alexanyan (last accessed 21 August 2015).

Allen, C. T., Fournier, S. and Miller, F. (2008) 'Brands and their meaning makers', in Haugtvedt, C. P., Herr, P. and Kardes, F. R. (eds) *Handbook of Consumer Psychology*, New York and London: Lawrence Erlbaum Associates, 781–822.

Allnutt, L. (2012) 'How the Kremlin is using sex to sell Putin', 22 February: www.rferl.org/content/how_the_kremlin_is_using_sex_to_sell_putin/24492979.html (last accessed 18 August 2015).

Althanns, L. (2009) *McLenin: Die Konsumrevolution in Russland*, Bielefeld: Transcript Verlag.

Althusser, L. (1969) *For Marx*, Harmondsworth: Allen Lane.

Aman, A. (1992) *Architecture and Ideology in Eastern Europe during the Stalin Era: An Aspect of the Cold War*, Cambridge, MA: MIT Press.

Ambrose, G. and Harris, P. (2011) *Packaging the Brand: The Relationship between Packaging Design and Brand Identity*, Lausanne: AVA Publishing.

Ambrosio, T. (2001) *Irredentism: Ethnic Conflict and International Politics*, Westport, CT: Praeger.

Amine, A. and Sitz, L. (2007) 'Émergence et structuration des communautés de marque en ligne', *Décisions Marketing*, 46, April–June: 63–75.

Anderson, B. (2006) *Imagined Communities: Reflections on the Origin and Spread of Nationalism*, 2nd edn, London and New York: Verso.

Andersson, M. and Eckman, P. (2009) 'Ambassador networks and place branding', *Journal of Place Management and Development*, 2, 1: 41–51.

Anfuso, D. (2007) 'Levi's launches international virtual worlds', 23 October: www.im ediaconnection.com/news/17092.asp (last accessed 21 August 2015).

Angé, O. and Berliner, D. (eds) (2014) *Anthropology and Nostalgia*, Oxford: Berghahn.

Ankist, M. (ed.) (1987) *Soviet Commercial Design of the Twenties*, London: Thames and Hudson.

Antéblian, B., Filser, M. and Roederer, C. (2013) 'L'expérience du consommateur dans le commerce de détail: Une revue de littérature', *Recherche et Applications en Marketing*, 28, 3: 84–113.

Apel, D. (2006) 'The allure of Nazi imagery in Russia': www.opendemocracy.net/globa lization-institutions_government/nazi_russia_3511.jsp (last accessed 21 August 2015).

Appadurai, A. (1990) 'Disjuncture and difference in the global cultural economy', *Theory, Culture and Society*, 7, 2: 295–310.

Appadurai, A. (1996) *Modernity at Large: Cultural Dimensions of Globalization*, Minneapolis, MN and London: University of Minnesota Press.

Arnould, E. J. (2000) 'A theory of shopping/shopping, place, and identity', *Journal of Marketing*, 64, 1: 104–106.

Arnould, E. J. (2005) 'Animating the big middle', *Journal of Retailing*, 81, 2: 89–96.

Arnould, E. J. (2007) 'Consuming experience: Retrospects and prospects', in Carù, A. and Cova, B. (eds) *Consuming Experience*, Abingdon and New York: Routledge, 185–194.

Arnould, E. J. and Price, L. L. (2000) 'Authenticating acts and authoritative performances: Questing for self and community', in Ratneshwar, S., Mick, D. G., and Huffman, C. (eds) *The Why of Consumption: Contemporary Perspectives on Consumer Motives, Goals, and Desires*, London and New York: Routledge, 140–163.

Arnould, E. J. and Thompson, C. J. (2005) 'Consumer Culture Theory (CCT): Twenty years of research', *Journal of Consumer Research*, 31, 4: 868–882.

Artz, N. and Venkatesh, A. (1991) 'Gender representation in advertising', in Holman, R. H. and Solomon, M. R. (eds) *Advances in Consumer Research*, 18, Provo, UT: Association for Consumer Research, 618–623.

Arvedlund, E. E. (2004) 'A mix of beer, free speech and home-grown hip', 15 June: www.nytimes.com/2004/06/15/business/a-mix-of-beer-free-speech-and-home-grown-hip.html (last accessed 28 August 2015).

Arvidsson, A. (2006) *Brands: Meaning and Value in Media Culture*, Abingdon and New York: Routledge.

Askegaard, S. (2006) 'Brands as a global ideoscape', in Schroeder, J. E. and Salzer-Mörling, M. (eds) *Brand Culture*, Abingdon and New York: Routledge, 91–102.

Askegaard, S. and Csaba, F. (2000) 'The good, the bad, and the jolly: Taste, image, and the symbolic resistance to the Coca-Colonization of Denmark', in Brown, S. and Patterson, A. (eds) *Imagining Marketing*, London and New York: Routledge, 214–231.

Axenov, K., Brade, I. and Bondarchuk, E. (2006) *The Transformation of Urban Space in Post-Soviet Russia*, Abingdon and New York: Routledge.

Babin, B. J., Darden, W. R. and Griffin, M. (1994) 'Work and/or fun: Measuring hedonic and utilitarian shopping value', *Journal of Consumer Research*, 20, 4: 644–656.

Bach, J. (2002) 'The taste remains: Consumption (n)ostalgia, and the production of East Germany', *Public Culture*, 14, 3: 545–556.

Backes, N. (1997) 'Reading the shopping mall city', *Journal of Popular Culture*, 31, 3: 1–17.

Badinter, E. (1992) *XY: De l'Identité Masculine*, Paris: Odile Jacob.

Badot, O. and Filser, M. (2007) 'Re-enchantment of retailing: Towards utopian islands', in Carù, A. and Cova, B. (eds) *Consuming Experience*, Abingdon and New York: Routledge, 166–181.

Baer, J. (2009) *Other Russias: Homosexuality and the Crisis of Post-Soviet Identity*, Basingstoke: Palgrave Macmillan.

Baer, J. (2013a) 'Now you see it: Gay (in)visibility and the performance of post-Soviet identity', in Fejes, N. and Balogh, A. P., *Queer Visibility in Post-Socialist Cultures*, Bristol and Chicago, IL: Intellect, 35–55.

Baer, J. (2013b) 'Post-Soviet self-fashioning and the politics of representation', in Goscilo, H. (ed.) *Putin as Celebrity and Cultural Icon*, Abingdon and New York: Routledge, 160–179.

Baker, J., Grewal, D. and Parasuraman, A. (1994) 'The influence of store environment on quality influences and store image', *Journal of the Academy of Science*, 22, 4: 328–339.

Bakhtin, M. M. (1981) *The Dialogic Imagination*, Austin, TX: University of Texas Press.

Bakhtin, M. M. (1984/[1965]) *Rabelais and His World*, Bloomington and Indianapolis, IN: Indiana University Press.

Bakhtin, M. M. (1989) 'Discourse in life and discourse in art [concerning sociological poetics]', in Davis, R. C. and Schleifer, R. (eds) *Contemporary Literary Criticism: Literary and Cultural Studies*, New York: Longman, 392–410.

Bal, M., Crewe, J. and Spitzer, L. (1999) *Acts of Memory: Cultural Recall in the Present*, Hanover, NH: University Press of New England.

Balina, M. and Dobrenko, E. (eds) (2011) *Petrified Utopia: Happiness Soviet Style*, London and New York: Anthem Press.

Ballantyne, D. and Aitken, R. (2007) 'Branding in B2B markets: Insights from the service-dominant logic of marketing', *Journal of Business and Industrial Marketing*, 22, 6: 363–371.

Banet-Weiser, S. (2013) 'Rate your knowledge: The branded university', in McAllister, M. and West, E. (eds) (2013) *The Routledge Companion to Advertising and Promotional Culture*, Abingdon and New York: Routledge, 298–312.

Bardhi, F. and Arnould, E. J. (2005) 'Thrift shopping: Combining utilitarian thrift and hedonic treat benefits', *Journal of Consumer Behaviour*, 4, 4: 223–233.

Barnett, A. and Bielski, N. (1998) *Soviet Freedom*, London: Picador.

Barshak, L. (2011) 'The constituent power of architecture', *Law, Culture and the Humanities*, 7, 2: 217–243.

Barthals, D. (1988) *Putting on Appearances: Gender and Advertising*, Philadelphia, PA: Temple University Press.

Barthes, R. (1973) *Mythologies*, London: Paladin.

Barthes, R. (1984) 'The Eiffel Tower', in *The Eiffel Tower and Other Mythologies*, New York: Hill and Wang, 3–18.

Bartmanski, D. (2013) 'How to practice visual and material culture studies?', *Sociologica*, 1, available at: www.sociologica.mulino.it/doi/10.2383/73714 (last accessed 28 August 2015).

Bassin, M. and Kelly, C. (eds) (2012) *Soviet and Post-Soviet Identities*, Cambridge: Cambridge University Press.

Baudrillard, J. (1981) *For a Critique of the Political Economy of the Sign*, St Louis, MO: Telos.

Baudrillard, J. (1994) *Simulacra and Simulation*, Ann Arbor, MI: University of Michigan Press.

Baudrillard, J. (1996) *The System of Objects*, London: Verso.

Baudrillard, J. (1998) *The Consumer Society: Myths and Structures*, London: Sage.

Bauman, Z. (1992) *Mortality, Immortality and Other Life Strategies*, Cambridge: Polity.

Bauman, Z. (2000) *Liquid Modernity*, Cambridge: Polity.

Bauman, Z. (2001) *Community: Seeking Safety in an Insecure World*, Cambridge: Polity.

Bauman, Z. (2007) *Consuming Life*, Cambridge: Polity.

BBC (2004) 'Alcopops are "losing their cool"', 30 July: http://news.bbc.co.uk/2/hi/business/3937381.stm (last accessed 18 August 2015).

BBC (2011) 'Russia classifies beer as alcoholic', 21 July: www.bbc.com/news/world-europe-14232970 (last accessed 24 June 2015).

BBC (2014) 'Vloggers warned over unclear adverts', 26 November: www.bbc.co.uk/newsround/30195641 (last accessed 21 August 2015).

Beckett, A. (2011) 'Habitat, design of the times', *The Guardian*, 28 July: www.theguardian.com/business/2011/jul/28/habitat-furniture-high-street (last accessed 21 July 2015).

Begout, B. (2003) *Zeropolis: The Experience of Las Vegas*, London: Reaktion Books.

Belk, R. W. (1988) 'Possessions and the extended self', *Journal of Consumer Research*, 15, 2: 139–168.

Belk, R. W. (1990) 'The role of possessions in constructing and maintaining a sense of past', in Goldberg, M. E., Gorn, G. and Pollay, R. W. (eds) *Advances in Consumer Research*, 17, Provo, UT: Association for Consumer Research, 669–676.

Belk, R. W. (2004) 'Men and their machines', in Kahn, B. E. and Luce, M.F. (eds) *Advances in Consumer Research*, 31, Valdosta, GA: Association for Consumer Research, 273–278.

Belk, R. W. (2013) 'Extended self in a digital world', *Journal of Consumer Research*, 40, 3: 477–500.

Belk, R. W. and Bryce, W. (1993) 'Christmas shopping scenes: From modern miracle to postmodern mall', *International Journal of Research in Marketing*, 10, 3: 277–296.

Belk, R. W. and Costa, J. A. (1998) 'The mountain man myth: A contemporary consuming fantasy', *Journal of Consumer Research*, 25, 3: 218–240.

Belk, R. W., Ger, G. and Askegaard, S. (2000) 'The missing streetcar named desire', in Ratneshwar, S., Mick, D. G. and Huffman, C. (eds) *The Why of Consumption: Contemporary Perspectives on Consumer Motives, Goals, and Desires*, London and New York: Routledge, 98–119.

Belk, R. W., Price, L. and Peñaloza, L. (eds) (2014) *Consumer Culture Theory (Research in Consumer Behaviour, Volume 15)*, Bingley: Emerald Group Publishing Limited.

Belk, R. W., Wallendorf, M. and Sherry, J. F., Jnr (1989) 'The sacred and the profane in consumer behaviour: Theodicy on the Odyssey', *Journal of Consumer Culture*, 16, 1: 1–38.

Bell, E., Warren, S. and Schroeder, J. E. (eds) (2013) *The Routledge Companion to Visual Organization*, Abingdon and New York: Routledge.

Bellelli, G. (1991) 'Une emotion ambiguë: La nostalgie', *Cahiers Internationaux de Psychologie Sociale*, 11: 59–76.

Belot, L. (2013) 'Ikea: La mondialisation vue de l'intérieur', *Le Magazine du Monde*, 27 July, 21–27.

Bengtsson, A. and Ostberg, J. (2008) 'Researching the cultures of brands', in Belk, R. W. (ed.) *Handbook of Qualitative Research Methods in Marketing*, Cheltenham: Edward Elgar, 83–93.

Benjamin, W. (2002/[1969]) *The Arcades Project*, Cambridge, MA: Belknap.

Benwell, B. (ed.) (2003) *Masculinity and Men's Lifestyle Magazines*, Oxford: Basil Blackwell.

Berdahl, D. (1999) '"(N)Ostalgie" for the present: Memory, longing, and East German things"', *Ethnos: Journal of Anthropology*, 64, 2: 192–211.

Berdahl, D. (2010) *On the Social Life of Postsocialism: Memory, Consumption, Germany*, Bloomington and Indianapolis, IN: Indiana University Press.

Bérélowitch, W., Blum, A., Cohen, Y., Daucé, F., Gousseff, C. and Koustova, E. (2014) 'Demain, la justice russe liquidera-t-elle Memorial?', *Libération*, 12 November: 20.

Berezkin, L. (2010) 'Flora vmesto vokzala', 13 October: http://old.spbvedomosti.ru/a rticle.htm?id=10270204@SV_Articles (last accessed 21 July 2015).

Berger, J. (1972) *Ways of Seeing*, Harmondsworth: Penguin.

Bernstein, J. (2011) *Food For Thought: Transnational Contested Identities and Food Practices of Russian-Speaking Jewish Migrants*, Chicago, IL: University of Chicago Press.

Beumers, B. (2005) *Pop Culture Russia! Media, Arts, and Lifestyle*, Santa Barbara, CA, Denver, CO and London: ABC-CLIO.

Bitner, M. J. (1992) 'Servicescapes: The impact of physical surroundings on customers and employees', *Journal of Marketing*, 56, 2: 57–71.

Blasi, J. R., Kroumova, M. and Kruse, D. (1997) *Kremlin Capitalism: Privatizing the Russian Economy*, Ithaca, NY, and London: Cornell University Press.

Bloch, P. H., Ridgway, N. M., and Nelson, J. E. (1991) 'Leisure and the shopping mall', in Holman, R. H. and Solomon, M. R. (eds) *Advances in Consumer Research*, 18, Provo, UT: Association for Consumer Research, 445–452.

Blum, M. (2000) 'Remaking the East German past: Ostalgie, identity, and material culture', *The Journal of Popular Culture*, 34, 3: 229–253.

Bonnell, V. E. (1997) *Iconography of Power: Soviet Political Posters under Lenin and Stalin*, Berkeley, CA: University of California Press.

Bordo, S. (1999) *The Male Body: A New Look at Men in Public and in Private*, New York: Farrar, Straus and Giroux.

Borenstein, E. (1999a) 'Masculinity and nationalism in contemporary Russian men's magazines', in Levitt, M. and Toporkov, A. (eds) *Eros and Pornography in Russian Culture*, Moscow: Ladomir: 605–621.

Borenstein, E. (1999b) 'Public offerings: MMM and the marketing of melodrama', in Barker, A. M. (ed.) *Consuming Russia: Popular Culture, Sex, and Society since Gorbachev*, Durham, NC: Duke University Press, 49–75.

Borenstein, E. (2007) *Overkill: Sex and Violence in Contemporary Russian Popular Culture*, Ithaca, NY and London: Cornell University Press.

Borgerson, J. L. (2005) 'Judith Butler: On organizing subjectivities', *The Sociological Review*, 53, s1: 63–79.

Borgerson, J. L. (2014) 'The flickering consumer: New materialities and consumer research', in Belk, R. W., Price, L. and Peñaloza, L. (eds) *Consumer Culture Theory (Research in Consumer Behaviour, Volume 15)*, Bingley: Emerald Group Publishing Limited, 125–144.

Borgerson, J. L., Schroeder, J. E., Bloomberg, B. and Thorssén, E. (2006) 'The gay family in the ad: Consumer responses to non-traditional families in marketing communications', *Journal of Marketing Management*, 22, 9/10: 955–978.

Borghini, S., Diamond, N., Kozinets, R. V., McGrath, M. A., Muñiz, A. M. Jnr and Sherry, J. F. Jnr (2009) 'Why are themed brandstores so powerful? Retail brand ideology at American Girl Place', *Journal of Retailing*, 85, 3: 363–375.

Bough, B. B. and Agresta, S. (2011) *Perspectives on Social Media Marketing*, Boston, MA: Course Technology.

Bourdieu, P. (1977) *Outline of a Theory of Practice*, Cambridge: Cambridge University Press.

Bourdieu, P. (1984) *Distinction: A Social Critique of the Judgement of Taste*. Cambridge, MA: Harvard University Press.

Bourdieu, P. (1998) *La Domination Masculine*, Paris: Seuil; (2001) *Masculine Domination*, Stanford, CA: Stanford University Press.

Bowlby, R. (2000) *Carried Away: The Invention of Shopping*, London: Faber and Faber.

Boyer, D. (2006) 'Ostalgie and the politics of the future in Eastern Germany', *Public Culture*, 18, 2: 361–381.

Boyle, M. (2013) 'Yes, real men drink beer and use skin moisturizer', *Bloomberg Business*, 3 October: www.bloomberg.com/bw/articles/2013-10-03/men-now-spend-more-on-toiletries-than-on-shaving-products (last accessed 24 July 2015).

Boym, S. (1994) *Common Places: Mythologies of Everyday Life in Russia*, Cambridge, MA: Harvard University Press.

Boym, S. (2001) *The Future of Nostalgia*, New York: Basic Books.

Boym, S. (2007) 'Nostalgia and its discontents', *The Hedgehog Review*, 1, available at: www.virginia.edu/iasc/eNews/2007_10/9.2CBoym.pdf (last accessed 28 August 2015).

Brauer, G. (ed.) (2002) *Architecture as Brand Communication*, Basel: Birkhäuser.

Bren, P. and Neuburger, M. (eds) (2012) *Communism Unwrapped: Consumption in Cold War Eastern Europe*, Oxford and New York: Oxford University Press.

Brennan, R. and Croft, R. (2012) 'The use of social media in B2B marketing and branding: An exploratory study', *Journal of Customer Behaviour*, 11, 2: 101–115.

Brewer, J. and Trentmann, F. (eds) (2006) *Consuming Cultures, Global Perspectives: Historical Trajectories, Transnational Exchanges*, Oxford: Berg.

Bristor, J. M. and Fischer, E. (1993) 'Feminist thought: Implications for consumer research', *Journal of Consumer Research*, 19, 4: 518–536.

Brod, H. and Kaufman, M. (eds) (1994) *Theorising Masculinities*, London: Sage.

Brodie, R. J., Ilic, A., Juric, B. and Hollebeek, L. (2011) 'Consumer engagement in a virtual brand community: An exploratory analysis', *Journal of Business Research*, 61, 1: 105–114.

Brown, R. L. (1958) 'Wrapper influence on the perception of freshness in bread', *Journal of Applied Psychology*, 42, 4: 257–260.

Brown, S. (1995) *Postmodern Marketing*, London and New York: Routledge.

Brown, S. (1998) *Postmodern Marketing Two: Telling Tales*, London: International Thompson Business Press.

Brown, S., Kozinets, R. V. and Sherry, J. F. Jnr (2003) 'Teaching old brands new tricks: Retro branding and the revival of brand meaning', *Journal of Marketing*, 67, 3: 19–33.

Brown, S., McDonagh, P. and Schultz, C. J., II (2013) 'Titanic: Consuming the myths and meanings of an ambiguous brand', *Journal of Consumer Research*, 40, 4: 595–614.

Brown, S., Stevens, L. and Maclaran, P. (1999) 'I can't believe it's not Bakhtin! Literary theory, postmodern advertising, and the gender agenda', *Journal of Advertising*, 28, 1: 11–24.

Brownlie, D. and Hewer, P. (2007) 'Prime beef cuts: Culinary images for thinking men', *Consumption, Markets and Culture*, 10, 3: 229–250.

Brundny, Y. M. (2013) 'Myths and national identity choices in post-communist Russia', in Bouchard, G. (ed.) *National Myths: Constructed Pasts, Contested Presents*, Abingdon and New York: Routledge, 133–156.

Buckler, J. (ed.) (forthcoming) *Cultural Properties: The Afterlife of Imperial Objects in Soviet and Post-Soviet Russia*.

Bush, J. (2004) 'More Russians are saying "Charge it"', *Newsweek*, 4 October, 56: www.bloomberg.com/bw/stories/2004-10-03/more-russians-are-saying-charge-it (last accessed 21 July 2015).

BusinessGazeta.ru (2014) '"Tandem-galeriya" – novyi format torgovli v Kazani', 16 April: www.business-gazeta.ru/article/101899 (last accessed 21 August 2015).

Butler, J. (2007/[1990]) *Gender Trouble: Feminism and the Subversion of Identity*, Abingdon and New York: Routledge.

Butler, J. (2011/[1993]) *Bodies That Matter: On The Discursive Limits of 'Sex'*, Abingdon and New York: Routledge.

Cairns, G. (2010) *Deciphering Advertising, Art and Architecture: New Persuasion Techniques for Sophisticated Consumers*, Faringdon: Libri.

Caldwell, M. L. (2002) 'The taste of nationalism: Food politics in post-socialist Moscow', *Ethnos: Journal of Anthropology*, 67, 3: 295–319.

Caldwell, M. L. (2004) 'Domesticating the French fry: McDonald's and consumerism in Moscow', *Journal of Consumer Culture*, 4, 1: 5–26.

Caldwell, M. L. (2006) 'Tasting the worlds of yesterday and today: Culinary tourism and nostalgia foods in post-Soviet Russia', in Wilk, R. (ed.) *Fast Food/Slow Food: The Cultural Economy of the Global Food System*, Lanham, MD: Altamira, 97–112.

Caldwell, M. L. (2007) 'Feeding the body and nourishing the soul: Natural foods in postsocialist Russia', *Food, Culture and Society*, 10, 1: 43–71.

Caldwell, M. L. (2009) 'Introduction: Food and everyday life after state socialism', in Caldwell, M. L. (ed.) *Food and Everyday Life in the Postsocialist World*, Bloomington and Indianapolis, IN: Indiana University Press, 1–28.

Campbell, C. (1995) 'The sociology of consumption', in Miller, D. (ed.) *Acknowledging Consumption: A Review of New Studies*, London: Routledge, 96–126.

Carah, N., Brodmerkel, S. and Hernandez, L. (2014) 'Brands and sociality: Alcohol branding, drinking culture and Facebook', *Convergence*, 20, 3: 259–275.

Carù, A. and Cova, B. (eds) (2007) *Consuming Experience*, Abingdon and New York: Routledge.

Cassiday, J. A. and Johnson, E. D. (2013) 'A personality cult for the postmodern age: Reading Vladimir Putin's public persona', in Goscilo, H. (ed.) *Putin as Celebrity and Cultural Icon*, Abingdon and New York: Routledge, 37–64.

Cathelat, B. (2001/[1968]) *Publicité et Société*, Paris: Payot.

Cayla, J. and Eckhardt, G. M. (2008) 'Asian brands and the shaping of a transnational imagined community', *Journal of Consumer Research*, 35, 2: 216–230.

Champoux, V., Durgee, J. and McGlynn, L. (2012) '"Corporate Facebook pages: When "fans attack"', *Journal of Business Strategy*, 33, 2: 22–30.

Charters, S. (2006) 'Aesthetic products and aesthetic consumption: A review', *Consumption, Markets and Culture*, 9, 3: 235–255.

Chernyshova, N. (2013) *Soviet Consumer Culture in the Brezhnev Era*, Abingdon and New York: Routledge.

Chesnokova, E. (2012) 'Cutting malls down to size', 15 March: http://themoscownews.com/realestate/20120315/189538120.html (last accessed 21 August 2015).

Chester, P. (1997) 'Strawberries and chocolate: Tsvetaeva, Mandelshtam, and the plight of the hungry poet', in Glants, M. and Toomre, J. (eds) *Food in Russian History and Culture*, Bloomington and Indianapolis, IN: Indiana University Press, 146–161.

Chocolate Wrappers Museum [n.d.]: www.chocolatewrappers.info/museum.htm (last accessed 21 August 2015).

Chramtchenko, T. (2014) '"Notre culture est européenne": Un héritage partagé' [interview with Erik Bulatov, *Rossiyskaya Gazeta* supplement] *Le Figaro*, 17 September, 7.

Christodoulides, G. (2009) 'Branding in the post-internet era', *Marketing Theory*, 9, 1: 141–144.

Christodoulides, G., Jevons, C. and Bonhomme, J. (2012) 'Memo to marketers: Quantitative evidence for change. How user-generated content really affects brands', *Journal of Advertising Research*, 52, 1: 53–64.

Ciochetto, L. (2011) *Globalisation and Advertising in Emerging Economies: Brazil, Russia, India and China*, Abingdon and New York: Routledge.

Clare, A. (2000) *On Men: Masculinity in Crisis*, London: Chatto and Windus.

Clark, K. (2000) *The Soviet Novel: History as Ritual*, 3rd edn, Bloomington and Indianapolis, IN: Indiana University Press.

Clark, K. and Holquist, M. (1984) *Mikhail Bakhtin*, Cambridge, MA and London: Belknap.

Clarke, D. (2003) *The Consumer Society and the Postmodern City*, Abingdon and New York: Routledge.

Clarke, P. (2010) 'Understanding the historic heritage of Russian packaging': http://popsop. com/2010/06/understanding-the-historic-heritage-of-russian-packaging (last accessed 7 October 2014).

Climo, J. and Cattell, M. G. (2002) *Social Memory and History: Anthropological Perspectives*, Lanham, MA: Rowman and Littlefield.

Clock Shout Photo (2010) 'A busy decade', 12 December: http://clockshoutphoto. blogspot.fr/2010/12/busy-ten-years.html (last accessed 21 August 2015).

Clowes, E. W. (2011) *Russia on the Edge: Imagined Geographies and Post-Soviet Identity*, Ithaca, NY and London: Cornell University Press.

Cockburn, P. (2000) 'Have roubles, want sofa-bed', *The Independent* [The Monday Review], 10 April, 7.

Cogan, H. (2014) 'Russia chocolate company's new product The Crimea bar has shocking slogan', 6 June: http://planetivy.com/russian-chocolate-companys-new-product-crimea-bar-shocking-slogan (last accessed 18 August 2015).

Cohen, L. (2003) *A Consumers' Republic: The Politics of Mass Consumption in Postwar America*, New York: Vintage Books.

Cohon, G. [with McFarlane, D.] (1997) *To Russia with Fries*, Toronto: McClelland and Stewart.

Cole, S. (2010) *The Story of Men's Underwear*, New York: Parkstone International.

Condee, N. and Padunov, V. (1995) 'The ABC of Russian consumer culture: Readings, ratings, and real estate', in Condee, N. (ed.) *Soviet Hieroglyphics: Visual Culture in Late Twentieth-Century Russia*, Bloomington and Indianapolis, IN: Indiana University Press/London: BFI Publishing, 130–172.

Connell, R. W. (2005) *Masculinities*, 2nd edn, Berkeley and Los Angeles, CA: University of California Press.

Connell, R. W. and Messerschmidt, J. W. (2005) 'Rethinking hegemonic masculinity', *Gender and Society*, 19, 6: 829–859.

Constantinides, E. and Fountain, S. J. (2008) 'Web 2.0: Conceptual foundations and marketing issues', *Journal of Direct, Data and Digital Marketing Practice*, 9: 231–244.

Conway, H. and Roenisch, R. (1994) *Understanding Architecture*, London and New York: Routledge

Coskuner, G. (2006) 'Exploring masculine ideologies', in Pechman, C. and Price, L. (eds) *Advances in Consumer Research*, 33, Duluth, MN: Association for Consumer Research, 63–66.

CosmeticsBusiness.com (2014) 'Intercharm 2014': www.cosmeticsbusiness.com/events/a rticle_page/Intercharm_2014/93758 (last accessed 21 August 2015).

Costlow, J. T., Sandler, S. and Vowles, J. (eds) (1993) *Sexuality and the Body in Russian Culture*, Stanford, CA: Stanford University Press.

Cougénas, N. (2005) 'Du pack au pack: Pour une sémiotique du packaging', in Cougénas, N. and Bertin, É. (eds) *Solutions Sémiotiques*, Paris: Lambert-Lucas, 49–66.

Courtney, A. and Whipple, T. (1983) *Sex Stereotyping in Advertising*, Lexington, MA: Lexington Books.

Cova, B. (2006) 'Développer une communauté de marque autour d'un produit de base: L'exemple de my nutella The Community', *Décisions Marketing*, 42, April–June: 53–62.

Cova, B. and Dalli, D. (2009) 'Working consumers: The next step in marketing theory?', *Marketing Theory*, 9, 3: 315–339.

Cova, B. and Kim, T. Y. (2013) 'Luxury consumer tribes in Asia: Insights from South Korea', in Hoffmann, J. and Coste-Manière, I. (eds) *Global Luxury Trends: Innovative Strategies for Emerging Markets*, Basingstoke: Palgrave Macmillan, 138–154.

Cova, B., Kozinets, R. V. and Shankar, A. (eds) (2007) *Consumer Tribes*, Oxford: Butterworth-Heinemann,

Cova, B. and Pace, S. (2006) 'Brand community of convenience products: New forms of customer empowerment – The case "My Nutella the community"', *European Journal of Marketing*, 40, 9/10: 1087–1105.

Cox, R. (2003) 'All this can be yours! Soviet commercial advertising and the social construction of space', in Dobrenko, E. and Naiman, E. (eds) *The Landscape of Stalinism: The Art and Ideology of Soviet Space*, Seattle, WA and London: University of Washington Press, 125–162.

Cox, R. (2006) '"NEP without nepmen!" Soviet advertising and the transition to socialism', in Kiaer, C. and Naiman, E. (eds) *Everyday Life in Early Soviet Russia: Taking the Revolution Inside*, Bloomington and Indianapolis, IN: Indiana University Press, 119–152.

Credit Suisse (2013) 'Global Wealth Report, 2013': http://resistir.info/varios/global_ wealth_report_2013.pdf (last accessed 21 August 2015).

Creed, B. (1993) *The Monstrous-Feminine: Film, Feminism, Psychoanalysis*, London and New York: Routledge.

Crocus City [n.d.]: http://crocusgroup.com/objects/crocus-city (last accessed 21 August 2015).

Crocus Expo [n.d.]: http://eng.crocus-expo.ru/index.php?lang=change (last accessed 21 August 2015).

Crocus Group [n.d.]: http://crocusgroup.com (last accessed 21 August 2015).

Croft, R. (2014) 'Blessed are the geeks: An ethnographic study of consumer networks in social media, 2006–2012', *Journal of Marketing Management*, 29, 5/6: 545–561.

Crossick, G. and Jaumain, S. (1999) 'The world of the department store: distribution, culture and social change', in Crossick, G. and Jaumain, S. (eds) *Cathedrals of Consumption: The European Department Store 1850–1939*, Aldershot: Ashgate, 1–45.

Csaba, F. F. and Askegaard, S. (1999) 'Malls and the orchestration of the shopping experience in a historical perspective' in Arnould, E. J. and Scott, L. M. (eds) *Advances in Consumer Research*, 26, Provo, UT: Association for Consumer Research, 34–40.

Cushman and Wakefield (2015) 'Russia becomes Europe's largest shopping centre market for first time', 19 April: www.cushmanwakefield.com/en/news/2015/04/ european-shopping-centre-development-april-2015 (last accessed 21 August 2015).

Dahlgren, L. (2010) *Vopreki absurda: Kak ya pokoryal Rossiyu, a ona – menya*, Moscow: Al'pina Biznes.

Dann, K. (2015) 'Small business in the spotlight ... Corker's crisps', 25 April: www.theguardian.com/small-business-network/2015/apr/25/small-business-spotlight-corkers-crisps (last accessed 18 August 2015).

Dano, F. (1996) 'Packaging: Une approche sémiotique', *Recherche et Applications en Marketing*, 11, 1: 23–35.

Dano, F. (1998) 'Contribution de la sémiotique à la conception des conditionnements: Application à deux categories de produits', *Recherche et Applications en Marketing*, 13, 2: 9–29.

Daucé, F., Laruelle, M., Le Huérou, A. and Rousselet, K. (2015). 'Introduction: What does it mean to be a patriot?', *Europe–Asia Studies*, 67, 1: 1–7.

Da Vinci Design Studio (2013) 'Dizain etiketki – pivo Zhigulevskoe', 18 April: www.studiodv.ru/news/archiv/2013/167 (last accessed 21 August 2015).

Davis, F. (1979) *Yearning for Yesterday: A Sociology of Nostalgia*, New York: The Free Press.

de Boise, S. (2015) *Men, Masculinity, Music and Emotions*, Basingstoke: Palgrave Macmillan.

Debord, G. (1992/[1967]) *La Société du Spectacle*, Paris: Gallimard; (1994) *The Society of the Spectacle*, New York: Zone Books.

Debray, R. (1992) *Vie et Mort de l'Image: Une Histoire du Regard en Occident*, Paris: Gallimard.

de Certeau, M. (1984) *The Practice of Everyday Life*. Berkeley, CA: University of California Press.

Deighton, J. (1992) 'The consumption of performance', *Journal of Consumer Research*, 19, 3: 362–372.

de Lauretis, T. (1984) *Alice Doesn't: Feminism, Semiotics, Cinema*, London: Macmillan.

de Mooij, M. (1998) *Global Marketing and Advertising: Understanding Cultural Paradoxes*, London: Sage.

Denegri-Knott, J., Zwick, D. and Schroeder, J. E. (2006) 'Mapping consumer power: An integrative framework for marketing and consumer research', *European Journal of Marketing*, 40, 9/10: 950–971.

Dinwoodie, G. (1997) 'Reconceptualizing the inherent distinctiveness of product design trade dress', *North Carolina Law Review*, 75: 471–606.

Divard, R. and Robert-Demontrond, P. (1997) 'La nostalgie: Un thème récent dans la recherche marketing', *Recherche et Applications en Marketing*, 17, 2: 131–144.

Dixon, M. L. (2015) 'The southern square in the Baltic pearl: Chinese ambition and "European" architecture in St Petersburg, Russia', in Diener, A. C. and Hagen, J. (eds) *From Socialist to Post-Socialist Cities: Cultural Politics of Architecture, Urban Planning, and Identity in Eurasia*, Abingdon and New York: Routledge.

Dmitriev, D. and Yurev, O. (1997) 'Sovetskaya ideya "Russkogo Bistro"', *Ogonek*: www.ogoniok.com/archive/1997/4523/40-04-06 (last accessed 21 July 2015).

Dorozhkin, E. (1997) 'Russkaya ideya "Russkogo Bistro"', *Kommersant*, 5 February: www.kommersant.ru/doc/171829 (last accessed 21 July 2015).

Douglas, M. and Isherwood, B. (1996/[1979]) *The World of Goods: Towards an Anthropology of Consumption*, 2nd edn, London: Routledge.

Dovey, K. (2008/[1998]) *Framing Places: Mediating Power in Built Form*, 2nd edn, Abingdon and New York: Routledge

Dowling, K (2014) 'VKontakte case puts Russian music piracy into spotlight', 11 August: www.bbc.com/news/business-28739602 (last accessed 21 August 2015).

Downey, L. (2007) *Levi Strauss and Co. [Images of America]*, Charleston, SC: Arcadia Publishing.

Dullin, S., Thorez, J. and Boutkevitch, M. (2015) 'La fabrique des frontières (post) soviétiques', unpublished round table discussion, Paris, 22 June.

Ebrahim, A. [n.d.] '40 rapper stars and their performance cars': www.carthrottle.com/40-rapper-stars-and-their-performance-cars (last accessed 21 August 2015).

Eckhardt, G. M. (2015) 'Commentary: The cultural approach to branding', in Schroeder, J. E. (ed.) *Brands: Interdisciplinary Perspectives*, Abingdon and New York: Routledge, 107–115.

The Economist (1997) 'The cashless society', 13 May: www.economist.com/node/369396 (last accessed 21 July 2015).

Edwards, T. (2006) *Cultures of Masculinity*, Abingdon and New York: Routledge.

Elam, K. (1980) *The Semiotics of Theatre and Drama*, London and New York: Methuen.

Elder, M. (2011) 'Moscow museum celebrates sex', *The Guardian*, 12 July: www.guardian.co.uk/artanddesign/2011/jul/12/moscow-sex-museum-sparks-controversy (last accessed 28 August 2015).

Elkin, T. (2003) 'Nike, Levistrauss [sic] test virtual world marketing', 27 October: http://adage.com/article/digital/nike-levi-strauss-test-virtual-world-marketing/38676 (last accessed 21 August 2015).

Elliott, R. and Davies, A. (2006) 'Symbolic brands and authenticity of identity performance', in Schroeder, J. E. and Salzer-Mörling, M. (eds) *Brand Culture*, Abingdon and New York: Routledge, 155–170.

Elliott, R. and Elliott, C. (2005) 'Idealised images of the male body in advertising: A reader-response exploration' *Journal of Marketing Communications*, 11, 1: 3–9.

Etgar, M. (2008) 'A descriptive model of the consumer co-production process', *Journal of the Academy of Marketing Science*, 36, 1: 97–108.

Etiket Konditerskikh Fabrik [n.d.a]: http://etiket-kf.narod.ru (last accessed 21 August 2015).

Etiket Konditerskikh Fabrik [n.d.b]: http://etiket-kf.narod.ru/541.htm (last accessed 21 August 2015).

Etlin, R. (1991) *Modernism in Italian Architecture, 1890–1940*, Cambridge, MA: MIT Press.

Euromonitor (2014a) 'Fast food in Russia', October: www.euromonitor.com/fast-food-in-russia/report (last accessed 21 July 2015).

Euromonitor (2014b) 'Chocolate confectionery in Russia', December: www.euromonitor.com/chocolate-confectionery-in-russia/report (last accessed 21 August 2015).

Evans Clements, B. (2002) 'Introduction', in Evans Clements, B., Friedman, R. and Healey, D. (eds) *Russian Masculinities in History and Culture*, Basingstoke: Palgrave Macmillan, 1–14.

Faludi, S. (2000) *Stiffed: The Betrayal of Modern Man*, London: Vintage.

Feasey, R. (2008) *Masculinity and Popular Television*, Edinburgh: Edinburgh University Press.

Featherstone, M. (1982) 'The body in consumer culture', *Theory, Culture and Society*, 1, 2: 18–33.

Featherstone, M. (1991) *Consumer Culture and Postmodernism*, London: Sage.

Federigan, B. (2014) 'Largest shopping malls in the world', 25 November: http://insights.colliers.com/largest-shopping-malls-in-the-world (last accessed 21 August 2015).

Fehérváry, K. (2009) 'Goods and states: The political logic of state-socialist material culture', *Comparative Studies in Society and History*, 51, 2: 426–459.

FemmePlus.fr (2014) 'Gérard Depardieu, "fier d'être russe", étonne dans une publicité', 9 December: www.femmesplus.fr/actu-people-gerard-depardieu-fier-detre-russe-etonne-dans-une-publicite-video.745962.1181.html?xtor=EPR-51-745775[FemmesPlus-a-la-Une]-20141210 (last accessed 21 August 2015).

Figes, O. (2002) *Natasha's Dance: A Cultural History of Russia*, London: Allen Lane.

Fine, B. (2002) *The World of Consumption: The Material and Cultural Revisited*, 2nd edn, Abingdon and New York: Routledge.

Fine, B. (2006) 'Addressing the consumer', in Trentmann, F. (ed.) *The Making of the Consumer: Knowledge, Power and Identity in the Modern World*, Oxford: Berg, 291–310.

Firat, A. F. and Dholakia, N. (1998) *Consuming People: From Political Economy to Theaters of Consumption*, London and New York: Routledge.

Firat, A. F. and Venkatesh, A. (1995) 'Liberatory postmodernism and the reenchantment of consumption', *Journal of Consumer Research*, 22, 3: 239–267.

Fitzpatrick, S. (2012) 'Things under socialism: The Soviet experience', in Trentmann, F. (ed.) *The Oxford Handbook of the History of Consumption*, Oxford and New York: Oxford University Press: 451–466.

Floch, J.-M. (1995) *Identités Visuelles*, Paris: Presses Universitaires de France.

Fontanka (2012) 'Yamu smenit galereya s basseinom', 22 January: www.fontanka.ru/2009/01/22/038 (last accessed 21 August 2015).

Foster, R. J. (2007) 'The work of the new economy: consumers, brands, and value creation', *Cultural Anthropology*, 22, 4: 707–731.

Foucault, M. (1979) *Discipline and Punish: The Birth of the Prison*, New York: Vintage.

Foucault, M. (1985) *The History of Sexuality Vol. 2: The Uses of Pleasure*, Harmondsworth: Penguin.

Fournier, S. and Avery, J. (2011) 'The uninvited brand', *Business Horizons*, 54, 3: 193–207.

Fournier, S. and Lee, L. (2009) 'Getting brand communities right', *Harvard Business Review*, April, 105–111.

Frank, T. (1997) *The Conquest of Cool: Business Culture, Counterculture, and the Rise of Hip Consumerism*, Chicago, IL: University of Chicago Press.

Franklin, S. (2004) 'Identity and religion', in Franklin, S. and Widdis, E. (eds) *National Identity in Russian Culture*, Cambridge: Cambridge University Press, 95–115.

Fuchs, C. (2014) 'Social media and the public sphere', *tripleC*, 12, 1: 57–101.

Fukuyama, F. (1992) *The End of History and the Last Man*, New York: Free Press.

Gamman, L. and Marshment, M. (eds) (1988) *The Female Gaze: Women as Viewers of Popular Culture*, London: The Women's Press.

Gee, M. (2013) 'Art and advertising – circa 1880 to the present', in Wharton, C. (ed.) *Advertising as Culture*, Bristol and Chicago, IL: Intellect, 127–142.

Gee, S. (2009) 'Mediating sport, myth, and masculinity: The national hockey league's "Inside the Warrior" advertising campaign', *Sociology of Sport Journal*, 26, 4: 578–598.

Genette, G. (1982) *Palimpsestes: La Littérature au Second Degré*, Paris: Seuil; (1997) *Palimpsests: Literature in the Second Degree*, Lincoln, NE: University of Nebraska Press.

Ghedin, G. (2011) 'Social media in Russia: Why is VKontakte better than Facebook?', 19 October: www.digitalintheround.com/social-media-russia-vkontatke (last accessed 28 August 2015).

Ghedin, G. (2013a) 'Marketing on VKontakte: How to engage the Russian audience', 1 February: www.digitalintheround.com/vkontakte-marketing (last accessed 28 August 2015).

Ghedin, G. (2013b) 'Social media marketing in Russia: Facebook vs. VKontakte' [interview with Christina Pavlova, of Moscow-based social media agency, NLO Marketing], 29 March: www.digitalintheround.com/social-media-russia-facebook-v kontakte (last accessed 28 August 2015).

Ghodsee, K. (2011) *Lost in Transition: Ethnographies of Everyday Life after Communism*, Durham, NC: Duke University Press.

Gibbons, J. (1999) 'The male body in advertising' (unpublished manuscript, in author's possession).

Gibbons, J. (2005) *Art and Advertising*, London and New York: I. B. Tauris.

Giddens, A. (1990) *The Consequences of Modernity*, Cambridge: Polity.

Giddens, A. (1991) *Modernity and Self-Identity: Self and Society in the Late Modern Age*, Stanford, CA: Stanford University Press.

Giddens, A. (1994) 'Living in a post-traditional society', in Beck, U., Giddens, A. and Lash, S. (eds) *Reflexive Modernization: Politics, Tradition and Aesthetics in the Modern Social Order*, Cambridge: Polity, 56–109.

Gillespie, D. (forthcoming) *Masculinity, Violence and Power in Modern Russia: Men, Guns and Identity*, Abingdon and New York: Routledge.

Gilmour, J. and Evans Clements, B. (2002) '"If you want to be like me, train": The contradictions of Soviet masculinity', in Evans Clements, B., Friedman, R. and Healey, D. (eds) *Russian Masculinities in History and Culture*, Basingstoke: Palgrave Macmillan, 210–222.

Girin, N. (2015) 'Kioski zabirayut, chtoby ostavit'', 4 April: www.novayagazeta.ru/economy/67115.html (last accessed 28 August 2015).

Glancey, J. (2014) 'The death of the US shopping mall', 21 October: www.bbc.com/culture/story/20140411-is-the-shopping-mall-dead (last accessed 21 July 2015).

Glaser, J. (2014) 'Choices, assessments and judgements: How graphic designers account for typographic selections and choices in branding', unpublished paper presented at 2nd International Colloquium on Design, Branding and Marketing, December, Nottingham Trent University.

Goffman, E. (1979) *Gender Advertisements*, New York: Harper and Row.

Goffman, E. (1990/[1959]) *The Presentation of Self in Everyday Life*, Harmondsworth: Penguin.

Goldman, M. I. (1960) 'Retailing in the Soviet Union', *Journal of Marketing*, 24, 4: 9–15.

Goldman, M. I. (2003) *The Piratization of Russia: Russian Reform Goes Awry*, London and New York: Routledge.

Goldman, R. (1992) *Reading Ads Socially*, London and New York: Routledge.

Goldman, R. and Papson, S. (1996) *Sign Wars: The Cluttered Landscape of Advertising*, New York: Guilford.

Goldschmidt, P. W. (1999) 'Pornography in Russia', in Barker, A. M. (ed.) *Consuming Russia: Popular Culture, Sex, and Society since Gorbachev*, Durham, NC: Duke University Press, 318–336.

Goldstein, D. (2011) 'Hot prospekts: Dining in the new Moscow' in Goscilo, H. and Strukov, V. (eds) *Celebrity and Glamour in Contemporary Russia*, Abingdon and New York: Routledge, 255–278.

Golec, M. J. (2008) *The Brillo Box Archive: Aesthetics, Design, and Art*, Dartmouth, MA: Dartmouth College Press.

Golynko-Vol'fson, D. (2009) 'Sotsiyal'nye seti v nesetovom sotsiume (O biopolitike, istorizme i mifologii russkikh sotsial'nykh setei)', *Digital Icons: Studies in Russian, Eurasian and Central European New Media*, 1, 2: 101–113, available at: www.digitalicons.org/issue02/dmitry-golynko (last accessed 28 August 2015).

Gombrich, E. H. (1999) *The Uses of Images: Studies in the Social Function of Art and Visual Communication*, London: Phaidon.

Gorbachev, O. (2015) 'The Namedni project and the evolution of nostalgia in post-Soviet Russia', *Canadian Slavonic Papers*, 57, 3/4: 180–194.

Goscilo, H. (2000) 'Style and s(t)imulation: Popular magazines, or the aestheticization of postsoviet Russia', *Studies in Twentieth Century Literature*, 24, 1: 7–14.

Goscilo, H. (2011) 'Zurab Tsereteli's exegi monumentum, Luzhkov's largesse, and the collateral rewards of animosity', in Goscilo, H. and Strukov, V. (eds) *Celebrity and Glamour in Contemporary Russia*, Abingdon and New York: Routledge, 221–254.

Goscilo, H. (2013a) (ed.) *Putin as Celebrity and Cultural Icon*, Abingdon and New York: Routledge.

Goscilo, H. (2013b) 'Introduction' in Goscilo, H. (ed.) *Putin as Celebrity and Cultural Icon*, Abingdon and New York: Routledge, 1–5.

Goscilo, H. (2013c) 'Russia's ultimate celebrity: VVP as VIP *objet d'art*', in Goscilo, H. (ed.) *Putin as Celebrity and Cultural Icon*, Abingdon and New York: Routledge, 6–36.

Goscilo, H. (2013d) 'Putin's performance of masculinity: The action hero and macho sex-object' in Goscilo, H. (ed.) *Putin as Celebrity and Cultural Icon*, Abingdon and New York: Routledge, 180–207.

Goscilo, H. and Hashamova, Y. (2010) *Cinepaternity: Fathers and Sons in Soviet and Post-Soviet Film*, Bloomington and Indianapolis, IN: Indiana University Press.

Goscilo, H. and Strukov, V. (2011) 'Introduction: Surface as sign, or the cultural logic of post-Soviet capitalism', in Goscilo, H. and Strukov, V. (eds) *Celebrity and Glamour in Contemporary Russia*, Abingdon and New York: Routledge, 1–26.

Gottdiener, M. (1995) 'Recapturing the center: A socio-semiotic analysis of shopping malls', in Gottdiener, M. (ed.) *Postmodern Semiotics: Material Culture and the Forms of Postmodernism*, Oxford: Basil Blackwell, 81–98.

Gramsci, A. (1971) *Selections from the Prison Notebooks*, New York: International Publishers.

Gray, C. (1986) *The Russian Experiment in Art, 1863–1922*, 2nd edn, London: Thames and Hudson.

Grayson, K. (1999) 'The dangers and opportunities of playful consumption', in Holbrook, M. B. (ed.) *Consumer Value: A Framework for Analysis and Research*, London and New York: Routledge, 105–125.

Gronow, J. (1997) *The Sociology of Taste*, London and New York: Routledge.

Gronow, J. (2003) *Caviar with Champagne: Common Luxury and the Ideals of the Good Life in Stalin's Russia*, Oxford and New York: Berg.

Gross, E. (1990) 'The body of signification', in Fletcher, J. and Benjamin, A. (eds) *Abjection, Melancholia and Love: The Work of Julia Kristeva*, London and New York: Routledge, 80–103.

Groys, B. (1992) *The Total Art of Stalinism: Avant-Garde, Aesthetic Dictatorship, and Beyond*, Princeton, NJ: Princeton University Press.

Grozny, P. (2010) 'Konets epokhi lar'kov: Fastfood kak zerkalo russkoi politiki', *Afisha*, 11 November: www.afisha.ru/article/7908 (last accessed 28 August 2015).

Guedel, W. G. (2006) 'Soviet secrets of success: Why Eastern Europe rules the heavyweight division', 24 May: www.boxing247.com/weblog/archives/108216 (last accessed 28 August 2015).

Gummerus, J., Liljander, V., Weman, E. and Pihlström, M. (2010) 'Customer engagement in a Facebook brand community', *Management Research Review*, 35, 9: 857–877.

Gurova, O. (2015) *Fashion and the Consumer Revolution in Contemporary Russia*, Abingdon and New York: Routledge.

Guy, K. M. (2003) *When Champagne Became French: Wine and the Making of a National Identity*, Baltimore, MD, and London: Johns Hopkins University Press.

Habermas, J. (1984) *The Theory of Communicative Action, Vol. 1*, Boston, MA: Beacon Press.

Habermas, J. (1987) *The Theory of Communicative Action, Vol. 2*, Boston, MA: Beacon Press.

Habibi, M. R., Laroche, M. and Richard, M.-O. (2014) 'Brand communities based in social media: how unique are they? Evidence from two exemplary brand communities', *International Journal of Information Management*, 34, 2: 123–132.

Hackley, C. (2001) *Marketing and Social Construction: Exploring the Rhetorics of Managed Consumption*, London and New York: Routledge.

Hackley, C. (2002) 'The panoptic role of advertising agencies in the production of consumer culture', *Consumption, Markets and Culture*, 5, 2: 211–229.

Hackley, C. (2013) *Marketing in Context: Setting the Scene*, Basingstoke: Palgrave Macmillan.

Halbwachs, M. (1966) *The Collective Memory*, New York: Harper and Row.

Halbwachs, M. (1992/[1925]) *On Collective Memory*, Chicago, IL: University of Chicago Press.

Hall, S. (1996) 'Introduction', in Hall, S. and du Gay, P. (eds) *Questions of Cultural Identity*, London: Sage, 1–11.

Hammer, F. (2008) 'Sartorial manoeuvres in the dusk: Blue jeans in socialist Hungary', in Soper, K. and Trentmann, F. (eds) *Citizenship and Consumption*, Basingstoke: Palgrave Macmillan, 51–68.

Hamouda, M. and Gharbi, A. (2013) 'The postmodern consumer: An identity constructor?', *International Journal of Marketing Studies*, 5, 2: 41–49.

Handelman, J. M. (2013) 'Online consumer activism', in Belk, R. W. and Llamas, R. (eds) *The Routledge Companion to Digital Consumption*, Abingdon and New York: Routledge, 386–395.

Hanson, P. (1974) *Advertising and Socialism: The Nature and Extent of Consumer Advertising in the Soviet Union, Poland, Hungary and Yugoslavia*, London: Macmillan.

Harris, F. and de Chernatony, L. (2001) 'Corporate branding and corporate brand performance', *European Journal of Marketing*, 35, 3/4: 441–456.

Hashamova, Y. (2004) 'Post-Soviet Russian film and the trauma of globalization', *Consumption, Markets and Culture*, 7, 1: 53–68.

Hashamova, Y. (2007) *Pride and Panic: Russian Imagination of the West in Post-Soviet Film*, Bristol and Chicago, IL: Intellect.

Haynes, J. (2003) *New Soviet Man: Gender and Masculinity in Stalinist Soviet Cinema*, Manchester and New York: Manchester University Press.

Healey, D. (2010) 'Active, passive, and Russian: The national idea in gay men's pornography', *The Russian Review*, 69, 2: 210–230.

Healey, P. (2002) 'On creating the "city" as a collective resource', *Urban Studies*, 39, 10: 1777–1792.

Healy, J. C., and McDonagh, P. (2013) 'Consumer roles in brand culture and value co-creation on virtual communities', *Journal of Business Research*, 66, 9: 1528–1540

Hearn, J. (2012) 'Male bodies, masculine bodies, men's bodies: The need for a concept of gex', in Turner, B. S. (ed.) *The Routledge Handbook of Body Studies*, Abingdon and New York: Routledge, 307–320.

Hede, A.-M. and Watne, T. (2013) 'Leveraging the human side of the brand using a sense of place: Case studies of craft breweries', *Journal of Marketing Management*, 29, 1/2: 207–224.

Hegel, G. (1975) *Aesthetics*, Oxford: Clarendon Press.

Heilbrunn, B. (2006a) 'Brave new brands: Cultural branding between utopia and a-topia', in Schroeder, J. E. and Salzer-Mörling, M. (eds) *Brand Culture*, Abingdon and New York: Routledge, 103–117.

Heilbrunn, B. (2006b) *Le Logo*, 2nd edn, Paris: Presses Universitaires de France.

Heilbrunn, B. and Barré, B. (2012) *Le Packaging*, Paris: Presses Universitaires de France.

Hellebust, R. (2003) *Flesh to Metal: Soviet Literature and the Alchemy of Revolution*, Ithaca, NY and London: Cornell University Press.

Herlihy, P. (2012) *The Alcoholic Empire: Vodka and Politics in Late Imperial Russia*, Oxford and New York: Oxford University Press.

Herszenhorn, D. M. (2013) 'New beer law draws cautious support, with notes of pessimism', January 6: www.nytimes.com/2013/01/07/world/europe/russian-beer-law-draws-support-and-some-pessimism.html?_r=0 (last accessed 21 August 2015).

Hessler, J. (2004) *A Social History of Soviet Trade*, Princeton, NJ: Princeton University Press.

Hewson Group (2012a) 'Women, sex and shopping': www.womensexandshopping.com (last accessed 21 August 2015).

Hewson Group (2012b) 'Global sex toy index', 27 May: www.womensexandshopping.com/blog/global-sex-toy-index (last accessed 21 August 2015).

Hilton, M. L. (2012) *Selling to the Masses: Retailing in Russia, 1880–1930*, Pittsburgh, PA: University of Pittsburgh Press.

Hine, T. (1995) *The Total Package: The Secret History and Hidden Meanings of Boxes, Bottles, Cans, and Other Persuasive Containers*, Boston: Black Bay Books.

Hirschman, E. C. (1993) 'Ideology in consumer research, 1980 and 1990: A Marxist and feminist critique', *Journal of Consumer Research*, 19, 4: 537–555.

Hirschman, E. C. (2003) 'Men, dogs, guns, and cars: The semiotics of rugged individualism', *Journal of Advertising*, 32, Spring: 9–22.

Hirschman, E. C. (2014) 'Branding masculinity: Tracing the cultural foundations of brand meaning', in Cotte, J. and Wood, S. (eds) *Advances in Consumer Research*, 42, Duluth, MN: Association for Consumer Research, 324–329.

Holak, S. L. and Havlena, W. J. (1992) 'Nostalgia: An exploratory study of themes and emotions in the nostalgic experience', in Sherry, J. F. Jnr and Sternthal, B. (eds) *Advances in Consumer Research*, 19, Provo, UT: Association for Consumer Research, 380–387.

Holak, S. L., Matveev, A. L. and Havlena, W. J. (2008) 'Nostalgia in post-socialist Russia: Exploring applications to advertising strategy', *Journal of Business Research*, 61, 2: 172–178.

Holbrook, M. B. and Hirschman, E. C. (1982) 'The experiential aspects of consumption: Consumer fantasies, feelings, and fun', *Journal of Consumer Research*, 9, 2: 132–140.

Holbrook, M. B. and Schindler, R. M. (1991) 'Echoes of the dear departed past: Some work in progress on nostalgia', in Holman, R. H. and Solomon, M. R. (eds) *Advances in Consumer Research*, 18, Provo, UT: Association for Consumer Research, 330–333.

Hollenbeck, C. R. and Kaikati, A. M. (2012) 'Consumers' use of brands to reflect their actual and ideal selves on Facebook', *International Journal of Research in Marketing*, 29, 4: 395–405.

Hollenbeck, C. R. and Zinkhan, G. M. (2006) 'Consumer activism on the internet: The role of anti-brand communities', in Pechmann, C. and Price, L. (eds) *Advances in Consumer Research*, 33, Duluth, MN: Association for Consumer Research, 479–485.

Holt, D. B. (2002) 'Why do brands cause trouble? A dialectical theory of consumer culture and branding', *Journal of Consumer Research*, 29, 1: 70–90.

Holt, D. B. (2003) 'How to build an iconic brand', *Market Leader*, 21: 35–42.

Holt, D. B. (2004) *How Brands Become Icons: The Principles of Cultural Branding*, Boston, MA: Harvard Business School.

Holt, D. B. (2006) 'Jack Daniel's America: Iconic brands as ideological parasites and proselytizers', *Journal of Consumer Culture*, 6, 3: 355–377.

Holt, D. B. and Cameron, D. (2010) *Cultural Strategy: Using Innovative Ideologies to Build Breakthrough Brands*, Oxford: Oxford University Press.

Holt, D. B., Quelch, J. A. and Taylor, E. L. (2004) 'How global brands compete', *Harvard Business Review*, September, 68–75.

Holt, D. B. and Thompson, C. J. (2004) 'Man-of-action heroes: The pursuit of heroic masculinity in everyday consumption', *Journal of Consumer Research*, 31, 2: 425–440.

Hopkins, J. (1990) 'West Edmonton Mall: Landscape of myths and elsewhereness', *The Canadian Geographer*, 34, 1: 2–17.

Howard, E. (2007) 'New shopping centres: Is leisure the answer?', *International Journal of Retail and Distribution Management*, 35, 8: 661–672.

Hubbs, J. (1993) *Mother Russia: The Feminine Myth in Russian Culture*, Bloomington and Indianapolis, IN: Indiana University Press.

Hudgins, T. (1997) 'Onions with no bottoms and chickens with no tops: Shopping for food in the emerging market economies of Siberia and the Russian Far East', in Walker, H. (ed.) *Food on the Move: Proceedings of the Oxford Symposium on Food and Cookery, 1996*, Totnes: Prospect Books: 157–176.

Huffington Post (2012a) 'Vladimir Putin ad: "First time" voting campaign stirs controversy', 27 February: www.huffingtonpost.com/2012/02/27/vladimir-putin-first-time-ad_n_1304462.html (last accessed 21 August 2015).

Huffington Post (2012b) 'Vladimir Putin ad: Creepy video promotes "first time" with doctor approval', 29 February: www.huffingtonpost.com/2012/02/29/vladimir-putin-ad-campaign_n_1310611.html (last accessed 21 August 2015).

Huffington Post (2014) 'Conchita Wurst gagne l'Eurovision: En Russie aussi on a aimé le travesti autrichien … et l'Ukraine', 11 May: www.huffingtonpost.fr/2014/05/11/conchita-wurst-eurovision_n_5303844.html (last accessed 21 August 2015).

Hughes, L. (1998) *Russia in the Age of Peter the Great*, New Haven, CT and London: Yale University Press.

Hughes, L. (2004) 'Monuments and identity', in Franklin, S. and Widdis, E. (eds) *National Identity in Russian Culture*, Cambridge: Cambridge University Press, 171–196.

Humphrey, C. (2002) *The Unmaking of Soviet Life: Everyday Economies after Socialism*, Ithaca, NY and London: Cornell University Press.

Hutchings, S. and Rulyova, N. (2009) *Television and Culture in Putin's Russia: Remote Control*, Abingdon and New York: Routledge.

Huxtable, A. L. (1997) *The Unreal America: Architecture and Illusion*, New York: The New Press.

Idov, M. (2011) *Made in Russia: Unsung Icons of Soviet Design*, New York: Rizzoli.

Ilicic, J., Baxter, S. and Kulczynski, A. (2015) 'Names versus faces: Examining spokesperson-based congruency effects in advertising', *European Journal of Marketing*, 49, 1/2: 62–81.

I Love Moscow [n.d.]: http://moscowiloveyou.ru/page/about.html (last accessed 14 January 2014).

Interfax (2014) '"Edinuyu Rossiyu" vozmutila pobeda "borodatogo transvestita" na "Evrovidenii"', 12 May: www.interfax.ru/russia/375798 (last accessed 21 August 2015).

Ioffe, D. G. and White, F. H. (2014) 'Taxi blues: The anxiety of Soviet masculinity', *Journal of European Studies*, 44, 3: 263–280.

Izakowski, Ł. (2014) 'Russia: Vegas Crocus City opened its doors for customers', 18 June: retailnet.eu/2014/06/18/72032-russia-vegas-crocus-city-opened-doors-customers (last accessed 21 August 2015).

Jackson, S. J. and Andrews, D. L. (eds) (2005) *Sports, Culture and Advertising: Identities, Commodities and the Politics of Representation*, Abingdon and New York: Routledge.

Jacobs, J. (1986) *The Mall: An Attempted Escape from Everyday Life*, Long Grove, IL: Waveland Press

Jahn, H. F. (2004) '"Us": Russians on Russianness', in Franklin, S. and Widdis, E. (eds) *National Identity in Russian Culture*, Cambridge: Cambridge University Press, 53–73.

Jameson, F. (1984) 'Postmodernism, or the cultural logic of late capitalism', *New Left Review*, 146, July/August: 59–92.

Jarski, V. M. (2014) 'How product packaging affects buying decisions', 6 September: www.marketingprofs.com/chirp/2014/25957/how-product-packaging-affects-buying-decisions-infographic?adref=nl090814 (last accessed 18 August 2015).

Jefferson, A. (1989) 'Bodymatters: Self and other in Bakhtin, Sartre and Barthes', in Hirschkop, K. and Shepherd, D. (eds) *Bakhtin and Cultural Theory*, Manchester: Manchester University Press, 152–177.

Jeffords, S. (1989) *The Remasculinisation of America: Gender and the Vietnam War*, Bloomington and Indianapolis, IN: Indiana University Press.

Johansson, U. and Holm, L. S. (2006) 'Brand management and design management: A nice couple or false friends?', in Schroeder, J. E. and Salzer-Mörling, M. (eds) *Brand Culture*, Abingdon and New York: Routledge, 136–151.

Johar, G. V., Holbrook, M. B., and Stern, B. B. (2001) 'The role of myth in creative advertising design: Theory, process and outcome', *Journal of Advertising*, 30, 2: 1–26.

Judah, B. (2013) *Fragile Empire: How Russia Fell in and out of Love with Putin*, New Haven, CT and London: Yale University Press.

Julier, G. (2005) 'Urban designscapes and the production of aesthetic consent', *Urban Studies*, 42, 5/6: 869–887.

Kaganovsky, L. (2004) 'How the Soviet man was (un)made', *Slavic Review*, 63, 3: 577–596.

Kalinina, E. (2014) 'Multiple Faces of the Nostalgia Channel in Russia', *View: Journal of European Television, History and Culture*, 3, 5; available at: www.viewjournal.eu/index.php/view/article/view/JETHC061/124 (last accessed 18 August 2015).

Kapferer, J.-N. (2012) *The New Strategic Brand Management*, London: Kogan Page.

Kaplan, A. E. (1983) *Women and Film: Both Sides of the Camera*, London: Methuen.

Kaplan, A. M. and Haenlein, M. (2010) 'Users of the world, unite! The challenges and opportunities of social media', *Business Horizons*, 53, 1: 59–68.

Kaplan, A. M. and Haenlein, M. (2012) 'The Britney Spears universe: Social media and viral marketing at its best', *Business Horizons*, 55, 1: 27–31.

Kates, S. M. (1999) 'Making the ad perfectly queer: Marketing "normality" to the gay men's community?', *Journal of Advertising*, 28, 1: 25–37.

Kates, S. M. (2002) 'The protean quality of subcultural consumption: An ethnographic account of gay consumers', *Journal of Consumer Research*, 29, 3: 383–399.

Kates, S. M. (2004) 'The dynamics of brand legitimacy: An interpretive study in the gay men's community', *Journal of Consumer Research*, 31, 2: 455–464.

Kates, S. M. and Goh, C. (2003) 'Brand morphing: Implications for advertising theory and practice', *Journal of Advertising*, 32, 1: 59–68.

Keane, W. (2003) 'Semiotics and the social analysis of material things', *Language and Communication*, 23, July: 409–425.

Keane, W. (2005) 'Signs are not the garb of things: On the social analysis of material things', in Miller, D. (ed.) *Materiality*, Durham, NC and London: Duke University Press, 182–205.

Keller, K. L. (2012) *Strategic Brand Management: Building, Measuring, and Managing Brand Equity*, 4th edn, Upper Saddle River, NJ: Prentice Hall.

Kelly, C. (1998) 'Creating a consumer: Advertising and commercialization', in Kelly, C. and Shepherd, D. (eds) *Russian Cultural Studies: An Introduction*, Oxford and New York: Oxford University Press: 223–246.

Kelly, C. and Volkov, V. (1988) 'Kul'turnost' and Consumption', in Kelly, C. and Shepherd, D. (eds) *Constructing Russian Culture in the Age of Revolution: 1881–1940*, Oxford and New York: Oxford University Press, 291–313.

Kelly, J. *et al.* (2012) 'Mapping Russian Twitter', Berkman Center for Internet and Society at Harvard University, 20 March, available at: http://cyber.law.harvard.edu/publications/2012/mapping_russian_twitter (last accessed 21 August 2015).

Kent, A., Warnaby, G. and Kirby, A. (2009) 'Architecture and the marketing of urban shopping destinations', unpublished paper delivered at UK Academy of Marketing conference, July, Leeds Metropolitan University: http://ualresearchonline.arts.ac.uk/2405 (last accessed 21 July 2015).

Kessous, A. and Roux, E. (2008) 'A semiotic analysis of nostalgia as a connection to the past', *Qualitative Market Research: An International Journal*, 11, 2: 192–212.

Kiaer, C. (2005) *Imagine No Possessions: The Socialist Objects of Russian Constructivism*, Cambridge, MA, and London: MIT Press.

KidsReview.ru [n.d.] 'Torgovo-razvlekatel'nye kompleksy vo Vladivostoke': www.kidsreview.ru/vladivostok/catalog/magaziny/torgovo-razvlekatelnye-kompleksy (last accessed 21 August 2015).

Kietzmann, J. H., Hermkens, K., McCarthy, I. P. and Silvestre, B. S. (2011) 'Social media? Get serious! Understanding the functional building blocks of social media', *Business Horizons*, 54, 3: 241–251.

Kilambi, A., Laroche, M. and Richard, M.-O. (2013) 'Constitutive marketing: Towards understanding brand community formation', *International Journal of Advertising*, 32, 1: 45–64.

Kirk, T. (2005) *The Architecture of Modern Italy, vol. 2 Visions of Utopia, 1900–the Present*, New York: Princeton Architectural Press.

Klein, N. (2000) *No Logo*, London: Flamingo.

Klingmann, A. (2007) *Brandscapes: Architecture and the Experience Economy*, Cambridge, MA: MIT Press.

Kniazeva, M. and Belk, R. W. (2007) 'Packaging as a vehicle for mythologizing the brand', *Consumption, Markets and Culture*, 10, 1: 51–69.

Kniazeva, M. and Charters, S. (2014) 'Authenticity in the mirror of consumer memories, or drinking champagne in Russia', in Wang, C. L. and He, J. (eds) *Brand Management in Emerging Markets: Theories and Practices*, Hershey, PA: IGI Global, 121–136.

Knoll, S., Eisend, M. and Steinhagen, J. (2011) 'Gender roles in advertising: Measuring and comparing gender stereotyping on public and private TV channels in Germany', *International Journal of Advertising*, 30, 5: 867–888.

Kobrin, K. (2015) 'Vseobshchee pomeshatel'stvo na "istorii"', 1 June: www.vedomosti.ru/opinion/articles/2015/06/01/594513-vseobschee-pomeshatelstvo-na-istorii (last accessed 19 August 2015).

Koch, N. (2010) 'The monumental and the miniature: Imagining "modernity" in Astana', *Social and Cultural Geography*, 11, 8: 769–787.

Kochan, L. (1962) *The Making of Modern Russia*, London: Jonathan Cape.

Kolbe, R. H. and Albanese, P. J. (1996) 'Man to man: A content analysis of sole-male images in male-audience magazines', *Journal of Advertising*, 25, 4: 1–20.

Kommersant' (2014) 'Pivnaya reanimatsiya', 4 September: www.kommersant.ru/doc/ 2545287 (last accessed 21 August 2015).

Kon, I. (2002) 'Muzhskoe telo kak eroticheskii ob'ekt', in Oushakine, S. (ed.) *O Muzhe (n)stvennosti*, Moscow: Novoe literaturnoe obozrenie, 43–78.

Kon, I. and Riordan, J. (eds) (1997) *Sex and Russian Society*, Bloomington and Indianapolis, IN: University of Indiana Press.

Kondakov, E. (2008) *Russkaya seksual'naya revolyutsiya*, Moscow: Octopus.

Kostyakova, E. (2009) '"V kazhdom brende est' uspeshnye produkty" – Thomas Hausch' [interview with DaimlerChrysler CEO, Thomas Hausch], 1 October: www. advertology.ru/article52651.htm (last accessed 21 August 2015).

Kotler, P. (1973) 'Atmospherics as a marketing tool', *Journal of Retailing*, 49, 4, 48–88.

Kotler, P. and Armstrong, G. (2015) *Principles of Marketing*, 16th edn, Upper Saddle River, NJ: Pearson Prentice Hall.

Kozinets, R. V. (2006) 'Netnography 2.0', in Belk, R. W. (ed.) *Handbook of Qualitative Research Methods in Marketing*, Cheltenham: Edward Elgar, 129–142.

Kozinets, R. V. (2015) *Netnography: Redefined*, 2nd edn, London: Sage.

Kozinets, R. V., Sherry, J. F., Jnr, Storm, D., Duhachek, A., Nuttavuthisit, K. and Deberry-Spence, B. (2004) 'Ludic agency and retail spectacle', *Journal of Consumer Research*, 31, 3: 658–672.

Krainova, N. (2013) 'Giant Louis Vuitton suitcase on Red Square causes outrage', *Moscow Times*, 27 November: www.themoscowtimes.com/news/article/giant-louis-vuitton-suitcase-on-red-square-causes-outrage/490292.html (last accessed 21 July 2015).

Kramer, A. E. (2008) 'New Russian wealth sets off mall development boom', *New York Times*, 16 May: www.nytimes.com/2008/05/16/business/worldbusiness/16iht-mall. 4.12971272.html?pagewanted=1&_r=0 (last accessed 28 August 2015).

Kramer, A. E. (2013a) 'Malls blossom in Russia, with a middle class', *New York Times*, 1 January: www.nytimes.com/2008/05/16/business/worldbusiness/16iht-mall.4. 12971272.html?pagewanted=2&_r=0 (last accessed 21 July 2015).

Kramer, A. E. (2013b) 'Chocolate factory, trade war victim', *New York Times*, 29 October: www.nytimes.com/2013/10/30/business/international/ukrainian-chocolates-caught-in-trade-war-between-europe-and-russia.html?pagewanted=all&_r=0 (last accessed 22 August 2015)

Kramer, A. E. (2015) 'Russian consumers reflect the pinch of economic sanctions', *New York Times*, 9 April: www.nytimes.com/2015/04/10/business/international/in-moscow-economic-sanctions-rattle-malls.html (last accessed 21 July 2015).

Kravets, O. (2012) 'Russia's "pure spirit": Vodka branding and its politics', *Journal of Macromarketing*, 32, 4: 361–376.

Kravets, O. and Örge, Ö. (2010) 'Iconic brands: A socio-material story', *Journal of Material Culture*, 15, 2: 205–232.

Kremlin.ru (2014) 'Vstrecha s molodymi uchenymi i prepodavatelyami istorii', 5 November: http://news.kremlin.ru/transcripts/46951 (last accessed 21 August 2015).

Kreml' v Izmailovo [n.d.]: www.kremlin-izmailovo.com/o-kremle/istorija-sozdanija (last accessed 21 August 2015).

Krishnamurthy, S. and Kucuk, S. U. (2009) 'Anti-branding on the internet', *Journal of Business Research*, 62, 11: 1119–1126.

Kristeva, J. (1982) *Powers of Horror: An Essay on Abjection*, New York: Columbia University Press.

Kuhn, A. (1993) *Women's Pictures: Feminism and Cinema*, London and New York: Verso.

Kulikova, I. and Godart, F. (2014) 'How history, culture, and demography drive luxury consumption in Russia', in Atwal, G. and Bryson, D. (eds) *Luxury Brands in Emerging Markets*, Basingstoke: Palgrave Macmillan: 49–62.

Lally, K. (2012). 'Russian doctor declares war on McDonald's "gamburgers"', 24 July: http://articles.washingtonpost.com/2012-07-24/world/35486371_1_russians-gambur gers-mcchicken (last accessed 28 August 2015).

Langer, R. (2007). 'Marketing, prosumption and innovation in the fetish community', in Cova, B., Kozinets, R. V. and Shankar, A. (eds) *Consumer Tribes*, Oxford: Butterworth-Heinemann, 243–259.

Langrehr, F. W. (1991) 'Retail shopping mall semiotics and hedonic consumption', in Holman, R. H. and Solomon, M. R. (eds) *Advances in Consumer Research*, 18, Provo, UT: Association for Consumer Research, 428–433.

Larsen, S. (2003) 'National identity, cultural authority and the post-soviet blockbuster: Nikita Mikhalkov and Aleksei Balabanov', *Slavic Review*, 62, 3: 491–511.

Laruelle, M. (2009) *In The Name of the Nation: Nationalism and Politics in Contemporary Russia*, Basingstoke: Palgrave Macmillan.

Lavrientiev, A. (2006) *Rodtchenko et le Groupe Octobre*, Paris: Hazan.

Ledeneva, A. V. (1998) *Russia's Economy of Favours: Blat, Networking and Informal Exchange*, Cambridge: Cambridge University Press.

Lehman, P. (2007) *Running Scared: Masculinity and the Representation of the Male Body*, Detroit, MI: Wayne State University Press.

Lemon, A. (1998) '"Your eyes are green like dollars": Counterfeit cash, national substance, and currency apartheid in 1990s Russia', *Cultural Anthropology*, 13, 1: 22–55.

Lemon, A. (2009) 'The emotional lives of Moscow things', *Russian History*, 36, 2: 201–218.

Le Monde (2014) 'David Duchovny, une bière russe et la crise ukrainienne', 27 July: www.lemonde.fr/europe/article/2014/07/27/david-duchovny-une-biere-russe-et-la-crise-ukrainienne_4463445_3214.html#xtor=AL-32280270 (last accessed 28 August 2015).

Levi.com [n.d.]: www.levi.com/501-series (last accessed 28 August 2015).

Levinskaya, A. (2014) 'Pishchevaya nostal'giya', 24 April: http://rbcdaily.ru/market/ 562949991278368 (last accessed 27 November 2015).

Lévi-Strauss, C. (1963) *Structural Anthropology*, New York: Basic Books.

Lévi-Strauss, C. (2014/[1978]) *Myth and Meaning*, Abingdon and New York: Routledge.

LeviStrauss.com [n.d.]: http://www.levistrauss.com/about/heritage/archives/tales-a rchives (last accessed 12 January 2015).

Levitas, R. (1990) *The Concept of Utopia*, New York: Philip Allen.

Levitt, T. (1983) 'The globalization of markets', *Harvard Business Review*, May–June, 92–102.

Levy, M., Grewal, D., Peterson, R. A. and Connolly, B. (2005) 'The concept of the "Big Middle"', *Journal of Retailing*, 81, 2: 83–88.

Liechty, M. (2005) *Suitably Modern: Making Middle-Class Culture in a New Consumer Culture*, Princeton, NJ: Princeton University Press.

Lieven, A. (1998) *Chechnya: Tombstone of Russian Power*, New Haven, CT and London: Yale University Press.

Lipman, M. (1999) 'Fade to red: Letter from Moscow', *New Yorker*, 21 September, 107.

Lipovetsky, G. (2006) *Le Bonheur Paradoxal: Essai sur la Société d'Hyperconsommation*, Paris: Gallimard.

Lotman, Yu. M. (2000) *The Semiotics of Russian Cultural History*, Ithaca, NY and London: Cornell University Press.

Lotman, Yu. M. (2001/[1990]) *Universe of the Mind: A Semiotic Theory of Culture*, London and New York: I. B. Tauris.

Louyest, A. and Roberts, G. H. (2015) 'Guest editors' introduction: Nostalgia, culture and identity in Central and Eastern Europe', *Canadian Slavonic Papers*, 57, 3/4: 175–179.

Loveland, K. E., Smeesters, D. and Mandel, N. (2010) 'Still preoccupied with 1995: The need to belong and preference for nostalgic products', *Journal of Consumer Research*, 37, 3: 393–408.

Luchshii Gorod Zemli [n.d.]: www.lgz-moscow.ru (last accessed 4 November 2014).

Luhn, A. (2015) 'The latest explanation for Vladimir Putin's mystery disappearance … flu', 15 March: www.theguardian.com/world/2015/mar/15/vladimir-putins-mystery-disappearance-seems-to-have-been-flu (last accessed 18 August 2015).

Lury, C. (2004) *Brands: The Logos of the Global Economy*, Abingdon and New York, Routledge.

Lury, C. (2011) *Consumer Culture*, 2nd edn, Cambridge: Polity.

L'vov, Y. (2014) 'V "Luzhnikakh" moshenniki neredko prodayut otrestavrirovannye starye shuby', *Den'gi*, 1 September, 16–17.

L'vova, V. (2004) 'The cloning of shopping centers', *Commercial Real Estate/Kommercheskaya Nedvizhimost'*, 18 June: 22–23.

Lyotard, J.-F. (1984) *The Postmodern Condition: A Report on Knowledge*, Manchester: Manchester University Press.

McAlexander, J. H., Schouten, J. H. and Koenig, H. F. (2002) 'Building brand community', *Journal of Marketing*, 66, 1: 38–54.

McCarthy, J., Rowley, J., Ashworth, C. J. and Pioch, E. (2014) 'Managing brand presence through social media: The case of UK football clubs', *Internet Research*, 24, 2: 181–204.

McCracken, G. (1988) *Culture and Consumption: New Approaches to the Symbolic Character of Consumer Goods and Activities*, Bloomington and Indianapolis, IN: Indiana University Press.

McCracken, G. (2005) *Culture and Consumption II: Markets, Meaning, and Brand Management, vol. 2*, Bloomington and Indianapolis, IN: Indiana University Press.

McDaniel, C. and Baker, R. C. (1977) 'Convenience food packaging and the perception of product quality', *Journal of Marketing*, 41, 4: 57–58.

McFall, L. (2004) *Advertising: A Cultural Economy*, London: Sage.

McIntyre, C. (2014) 'The physical embodiment of retail brand value within the local social capital of city facades: Creating a meaningful visitor experience via the store exterior', unpublished paper presented at 2nd International Colloquium on Design, Branding and Marketing, December, Nottingham Trent University.

Maclaran, P. (2009) 'Building brand cultures', in Parsons, E. and Maclaran, P. (eds) *Contemporary Issues in Marketing and Consumer Behaviour*, Oxford: Butterworth-Heinemann, 73–88.

Maclaran, P. and Brown, S. (2005) 'The center cannot hold: Consuming the utopian marketplace', *Journal of Consumer Research*, 32, 2: 311–323.

Maclaran, P., Otnes, C. and Fischer, E. (2008) 'Maintaining the myth of the monarchy: How producers shape consumers' experiences of the British royal family', in Lee, A. Y. and Soman, D. (eds) *Advances in Consumer Research*, 35, Duluth, MN: Association for Consumer Research, 67–71.

McQuarrie, E. F. and Mick, D. G. (1999) 'Visual rhetoric in advertising: Text-interpretive, experimental, and reader-response analyses', *Journal of Consumer Research*, 26, 1: 37–54.

McQuarrie, E. F., Miller, J. and Phillips, B. J. (2013) 'The megaphone effect: Taste and audience in fashion blogging', *Journal of Consumer Research*, 40, 1: 136–158.

Maffesoli, M. (1996). *The Time of the Tribes: The Decline of Individualism in Mass Society*, London: Sage.

Mail.ru [n.d.] 'Chto za gorod izobrazhen na pochtovoi kartochke?': http://otvet.mail.ru/question/30811926 (last accessed 21 August 2015).

Makarenko, K. and Borgerson, J. (2009) 'Ice Cream and "CCCP": Evoking nostalgia in post-Soviet packaging': www.materialworldblog.com/2009/05/ice-cream-and-cccp-evoking-nostalgia-in-post-soviet-packaging (last accessed 27 November 2015).

Makhrova, A. and Molodikova, I. (2007) 'Land market, commercial real estate, and the remolding of Moscow's urban fabric', in Stanilov, K. (ed.) *The Post-Socialist City: Urban Form and Space Transformations in Central and Eastern Europe after Socialism*, Dordrecht: Springer, The GeoJournal Library, 92, 101–116.

Malls.com (2014) 'IKEA set to expand across Russia', 25 September: www.malls.com/news/news/ikea-set-to-expand-across-russia.shtml (last accessed 21 August 2015).

Mangan, J. A. (2012) *'Manufactured' Masculinity: Making Imperial Manliness, Morality and Militarism*, Abingdon and New York: Routledge.

Manning, P. (2010) 'The semiotics of brand', *Annual Review of Anthropology*, 39: 33–49.

Manning, P. (2009) 'The epoch of Magna: Capitalist brands and postsocialist revolutions in Georgia', *Slavic Review*, 68, 4: 924–945.

Manning, P. (2012) *The Semiotics of Drink and Drinking*, London: Continuum.

Manning, P. and Uplisashvili, A. (2007) '"Our beer": Ethnographic brands in postsocialist Georgia', *American Anthropologist*, 109, 4: 626–641.

Mansvelt, J. (2005) *Geographies of Consumption*, London: Sage.

Marsh, R. (2007) *Literature, History and Identity in Post-Soviet Russia, 1991–1996*, Bern: Peter Lang.

Martin, K. and Todorov, I. (2010) 'How will digital platforms be harnessed in 2010, and how will they change the way people interact with brands?', *Journal of Interactive Advertising*, 10, 2: 61–66.

Marzocchi, G., Morandin, G. and Bergami, M. (2013) 'Brand communities: Loyal to the community or the brand?', *European Journal of Marketing*, 47, 1/2: 93–114.

Mazur, L. (2015) 'Golden Age mythology and nostalgia of catastrophes in post-Soviet Russia', *Canadian Slavonic Papers*, 57, 3/4: 213–238.

Mazzarella, W. (2003) *Shovelling Smoke: Advertising and Globalization in Contemporary India*, Durham, NC: Duke University Press.

MeggyMall.ru [n.d.]: www.meggymall.ru (last accessed 21 August 2015).

Merck, M. (2007) 'Mulvey's manifesto', *Camera Obscura*, 66, 22, 3: 1–23.

Merridale, C. (2000) *Night of Stone: Death and Memory in Russia*, London: Granta Books.

Merz, M. A., He, Y. and Vargo, S. L. (2009) 'The evolving brand logic: A service-dominant logic perspective', *Journal of the Academy of Marketing Science*, 37, 3: 328–344.

Mick, D. G. (1986) 'Consumer research and semiotics: Exploring the morphology of signs, symbols, and significance', *Journal of Consumer Research*, 13, 2: 196–213.

Mick, D. G. and Buhl, C. (1992) 'A meaning based model of advertising experiences', *Journal of Consumer Research*, 19, 3: 317–338.

Mickiewicz, E. (1997) *Changing Channels: Television and the Struggle for Power in Russia*, Oxford and New York: Oxford University Press.

Mikhel, D. [n.d.] 'Body politics in post-Soviet Russia': http://scan.net.au/scan/journal/display.php?journal_id=41 (last accessed 28 August 2015).

Miles, S. (2010) *Spaces for Consumption: Pleasure and Placelessness in the Post-industrial City*, London: Sage.

Miller, D. (1987) *Material Culture and Mass Consumption*, Oxford: Basil Blackwell.

Miller, D. (1998a) 'Coca-Cola: A sweet black drink from Trinidad', in Miller, D. (ed.) *Material Culture: Why Some Things Matter*, Chicago, IL: University of Chicago Press, 169–187.

Miller, D. (1998b) *A Theory of Shopping*, Cambridge: Polity.

Miller, D. (2005) (ed.) *Materiality*, Durham, NC and London: Duke University Press.

Miller, D. (2008) *The Comfort of Things*, Cambridge: Polity.

Miller, D. (2010) *Stuff*, Cambridge: Polity.

Miller, D. (2011) *Tales from Facebook*, Cambridge: Polity.

Miller, D., Jackson, P., Thrift, N., Holbrook, B. and Rowlands, M. (1998) *Shopping, Place and Identity*, Abingdon and New York: Routledge.

Miller, J. (2014) 'Making up is masculine: The increasing cultural connections between masculinity and make-up', *Critical Studies in Men's Fashion*, 1, 3: 241–253.

Moisio, R., Arnould, E. J., and Gentry, J. W. (2013) 'Productive consumption in the class-mediated construction of domestic masculinity: Do-it-yourself (DIY) home improvement in men's identity work', *Journal of Consumer Research*, 40, 2: 216–298.

Moor, L. (2007) *The Rise of Brands*, Oxford: Berg.

Moore, R. (2012) *Why We Build*, London: Picador.

Moore, R. E. (2003) 'From genericide to viral marketing: On "brand"', *Language and Communications*, 23: 331–357.

Moran, M. (2015) *Identity and Capitalism*, London: Sage.

Morenkova, E. (2012) '(Re)creating the Soviet past in Russian digital communities: Between memory and mythmaking', *Digital Icons: Studies in Russian, Eurasian and Central European New Media*, 7: 39–66, availbale at: www.digitalicons.org/issue07/elena-morenkova (last accessed 21 August 2015).

Morris, J. (2005) 'The empire strikes back: Projections of national identity in contemporary Russian advertising', *The Russian Review*, 64, 4: 642–660.

Morris, J. (2007) 'Drinking to the nation: Russian television advertising and cultural differentiation', *Europe–Asia Studies*, 59, 8: 1387–1403.

Morrison, E. (2012) *Tales from the Mall*, Glasgow: Cargo.

Mort, F. (1988) 'Boy's own? Masculinity, style and popular culture', in Chapman, R. and Rutherford, J. (eds) *Male Order: Unwrapping Masculinity*, London: Lawrence and Wishart, 193–224.

Moskovskaya Pravda (2012) '"Luchshii gorod Zemli" otmetit den' rozhdeniya', 30 August: http://mospravda.ru/home/article/lychshii_gorod_zemli_otmetit_den_rojdeniya (last accessed 21 August 2015).

Moss, K. (2013) 'Straight eye for the queer guy: Gay male visibility in post-soviet Russian films', in Fejes, N. and Balogh, A. P., *Queer Visibility in Post-Socialist Cultures*, Bristol and Chicago, IL: Intellect, 197–220.

Moss, M. (2007) *Shopping as an Entertainment Experience*, Lanham, MD and Plymouth: Lexington Books.

Motor1.com (2006) 'Hummer H3 production start in Russia', 6 April: www.worldcarfans.com/10604067365/hummer-h3-production-start-in-russia (last accessed 21 August 2015).

Mullen, A. (2013) 'Selling politics: The political economy of political advertising', in Wharton, C. (ed.) *Advertising as Culture*, Bristol and Chicago, IL: Intellect, 161–189.

Mulvey, L. (1999/[1975]) 'Visual pleasure and narrative cinema', in Braudy, L. and Cohen, M. (eds) *Film Theory and Criticism: Introductory Readings*, 5th edn, Oxford and New York: Oxford University Press, 833–844.

Mulvey, L. (2009/[1989]) 'Afterthoughts on "Visual pleasure and narrative cinema" inspired by King Vidor's Duel in the Sun', in *Visual and Other Pleasures*, 2nd edn, Basingstoke: Palgrave Macmillan, 31–40.

Mumford, E. (2009) 'CIAM and the Communist bloc, 1928–1959', *The Journal of Architecture*, 14, 2: 237–254.

Muñiz, A. M., Jnr and O'Guinn, T. C. (2001) 'Brand community', *Journal of Consumer Research*, 27, 4: 412–432.

Muñiz, A. M., Jnr and Schau, H. J. (2005) 'Religiosity in the abandoned Apple Newton brand community', *Journal of Consumer Research*, 31, 4: 737–747.

Muthar, N. (ed.) (2013) *Consumer Culture, Modernity and Identity*, London: Sage.

Muzellec, L. and Lambkin, M. (2006) 'Corporate rebranding: Destroying, transferring or creating brand equity?', *European Journal of Management*, 40, 7/8: 803–824.

My Sex Toys [n.d.]: www.mysextoys.ru (last accessed 21 August 2015).

MyTradeGroup.com (2015) 'Rynok piva v Rossii sokratilsya na 9%, a dolya "Baltika" ostalas' stabil'noi', 13 May: http://my-trade-group.com/index.php/novosti/item/2189-rynok-piva-v-rossii-sokratilsya-na-9-a-dolya-baltika-ostalas-stabilnoj/2189-rynok-piva-v-rossii-sokratilsya-na-9-a-dolya-baltika-ostalas-stabilnoj (last accessed 21 August 2015).

Nadkarni, M. and Shevchenko, O. (2004) 'The politics of nostalgia: A case for comparative analysis of post-socialist practices', *Ab Imperio*, 2: 487–519.

Neidhart, C. (2003) *Russia's Carnival: The Smells, Sights, and Sounds of Transition*, Lanham, MD: Rowman and Littlefield.

Neiger, M., Meyers, O. and Zandberg, E. (2011) *On Media Memory: Collective Memory in a New Media Age*, Basingstoke: Palgrave Macmillan.

Nelson, M. R. and Paek, H.-J. (2008) 'Nudity of female and male models in primetime TV advertising across seven countries', *International Journal of Advertising*, 27, 5: 715–744.

Neprikosnovennyi Zapas (2010) http://magazines.russ.ru/nz/2010/6 (last accessed 21 August 2015).

Nérard, F.-X. (2015) 'Manger dans les cantines staliniennes: "Consommateurs" soviétiques à l'époque des premiers plans quinquennaux', *La Revue Russe*, 44: 131–142.

Neumeyer, J. (2012) 'Russian chocolate unwrapped', 26 March: http://themoscow news.com/arts/20120326/189563834.html (last accessed 18 August 2015).

Nguyen, B., Melewar, T. C. and Chen, J. (2013) 'The brand likeability effect: Can firms make themselves more likeable?', *Journal of General Management*, 38, 3: 25–50.

Nieburg, O. (2014a) 'Candy counterstrike: Ukraine bans chocolate from Russia's United Confectioners', 7 April: www.confectionerynews.com/Regulation-Safety/Candy-counterstrike-Ukraine-bans-chocolate-from-Russia-s-United-Confectioners (last accessed 18 August 2015).

Nieburg, O (2014b) 'Slavyanka to acquire Orkla brands Russia', 2 December: www.confectionerynews.com/Manufacturers/Slavyanka-buys-Orkla-Brands-Russia (last accessed 18 August 2015).

Niemeyer, K. (ed.) (2014) *Media and Nostalgia: Yearning for the Past, Present and Future*, Basingstoke: Palgrave Macmillan.

Nixon, S. (1996) *Hard Looks: Masculinities, Spectatorship and Contemporary Consumption*, London and New York: Routledge.

Nostalgia TV [n.d.]: www.nostalgiatv.ru (last accessed 21 August 2015).

Nove, A. (1984/[1969]) *An Economic History of the U.S.S.R.*, Harmondsworth: Penguin.

O'Brien, L. G. and Harris, F. W. (2013/[1991]) *Retailing: Shopping, Society, Space*, Abingdon and New York: Routledge.

O'Donohoe, S. (2000) 'Women and advertising: Reading the relationship', in Catterall, M., Maclaran, P. and Stevens, L. (eds) *Marketing and Feminism: Current Issues and Research*, London and New York: Routledge, 75–93.

Odou, P., Roberts, G. H. and Bonnin, G. (2014) 'The co-production of protest: The pivotal role of webzines in the framing of an advertising counter-campaign', Proceedings of ICAR conference on Anti-Consumption and Consumer Wellbeing, Kiel University, July, 92–96.

Olick, J. (1999) 'Collective memory: The two cultures', *Sociological Theory*, 17, 3: 333–348.

O'Mahoney, M. (2006) *Sport in the USSR: Physical Culture – Visual Culture*, London: Reaktion Books.

O'Shaughnessy, J. and O'Shaughnessy, N. J. (2004) *Persuasion in Advertising*, London and New York: Routledge.

Östberg, J. (2013) 'Masculine self-presentation', in Ruvio, A. A. and Belk, R. W. (eds) *The Routledge Companion to Identity and Consumption*, Abingdon and New York: Routledge, 129–136.

O'Sullivan, S. R., Richardson, B. and Collins, A. (2011) 'How brand communities emerge: The Beamish conversion experience', *Journal of Marketing Management*, 27, 9/10: 891–912.

Otnes, C. and Zayer, L. T. (eds) (2013) *Gender, Culture and Consumer Behaviour*, Abingdon and New York: Routledge.

Oushakine, S. A. (2000) 'The quantity of style: Imaginary consumption in the new Russia', *Theory, Culture and Society*, 17, 5: 97–120.

Oushakine, S. A. (2001) 'The fatal splitting: Symbolizing anxiety in post-Soviet Russia', *Ethnos: Journal of Anthropology*, 66, 3: 291–319.

Oushakine, S. A. (2007) '"We're nostalgic but we're not crazy": Retrofitting the past in Russia', *The Russian Review*, 66, 3: 451–482.

Oushakine, S. A. (2013) 'Remembering in public: On the affective management of history', *Ab Imperio*, 1: 269–302.

Padgett, A. (2002) 'Coca-Cola, MTV and the laboratory of culture in the new Russia', *The Soviet and Post-Soviet Review*, 29, 3: 277–289.

Papadopoulos, A. G. and Axenov, K. (2006) 'St. Petersburg: Kiosks as mediators of the new market economy', in Schneider-Sliwa, R. (ed.) *Cities in Transition: Globalization, Political Change and Urban Development*, Dordrecht: Springer, The GeoJournal Library, vol. 83: 147–173.

Parker, I. (2004) *Slavoj Žižek: A Critical Introduction*, London and Sterling, VA: Pluto Press.

Parr, M. and Healey, A. (2010) 'Photographer Martin Parr's best shot', 28 July: www.guardian.co.uk/artanddesign/video/2010/jul/28/photographer-martin-parr (last accessed 21 August 2015).

Patico, J. (2002) 'Chocolate and cognac: Gifts and the recognition of social worlds in post-Soviet Russia', *Ethnos: Journal of Anthropology*, 67, 3: 345–368.

Patico, J. (2008) *Consumption and Social Change in a Post-Soviet Middle Class*, Washington, DC: Stanford University Press.

Patico, J. and Caldwell, M. L. (2002) 'Consumers exiting socialism: Ethnographic perspectives on daily life in post-communist Europe', *Ethnos: Journal of Anthropology*, 67, 3: 285–294.

Patterson, M. and Elliott, M. (2002) 'Negotiating masculinities: Advertising and the inversion of the male gaze', *Consumption, Markets and Culture*, 5, 3: 231–249.

Patterson, P. H. (2011) *Bought and Sold: Living and Losing the Good Life in Socialist Yugoslavia*, Ithaca, NY and London: Cornell University Press.

Pechenkin, G. (2015) 'Mikhalkov i Konchalovskii prosyat u Putina milliard na obshchepit Vysotskoi', 9 April: www.mk.ru/economics/2015/04/09/utomlyon nye-mcdonalds-mikhalkov-i-konchalovskiy-prosyat-u-putina-milliard-na-fastfud.html (last accessed 21 July 2015).

Peñaloza, L. (1998) 'Just doing it: A visual ethnographic study of spectacular consumption behaviour at Nike Town', *Consumption, Markets and Culture*, 2, 4: 337–400.

Peñaloza, L. (2001) 'Consuming the American West: Animating cultural meaning and memory at a stock show and rodeo', *Journal of Consumer Research*, 28, 3: 369–398.

Percy, L. (2014) *Strategic Integrated Marketing Communications*, 2nd edn, Abingdon and New York: Routledge.

Phillips, B. J. and McQuarrie, E. F. (2008) 'Beyond visual metaphor: A new typology of visual rhetoric in advertising', *Marketing Theory*, 4, 1/2: 113–136.

Pikabolo [n.d.]: http://pikabolo.ru (last accessed 21 August 2015).

Podesta, S. and Addis, M. (2007) 'Converging industries through experience' in Carù, A. and Cova, B. (eds) *Consuming Experience*, Abingdon and New York: Routledge, 139–153.

Pongsakornrungslip, S. and Schroeder, J. (2011) 'Understanding value co-creation in a co-consuming brand community', *Marketing Theory*, 11, 3: 303–324.

Popov, M. (2014) 'Russia is using McDonald's to exact revenge on America', 23 October: www.businessinsider.com/afp-russia-takes-bite-out-of-mcdonalds-with-us-ties-in-deep-freeze-2014-10?IR=T (last accessed 21 July 2015).

Prahalad, C. K., and Ramaswamy, V. (2004) 'Co-creation experiences: The next practice in value creation', *Journal of Interactive Marketing*, 18, 3: 5–14.

Pulju, R. J. (2011) *Women and Mass Consumer Society in Postwar France*, Cambridge: Cambridge University Press.

Putin Shop [n.d.]: http://putinshop.ru (last accessed 28 May 2015).

Putnam, R. D. (1995) 'Tuning in, tuning out: The strange disappearance of social capital in America', *PS*, 28, 4: 664–683.

Puzakova, P., Kwak, H. and Larsen Andras, T. (2010) 'Mitigating consumer ethno-centrism via advertising and media consumption in a transitional market: A study from Russia', *International Journal of Advertising*, 29, 5: 727–764.

Quam-Wickham, N. (1999) 'Rereading man's conquest of nature: Skills, myths and the historical construction of masculinity in Western extractive industries', *Men and Masculinities*, 2, 2: 135–151.

Quinton, S. (2013) 'The community brand paradigm: A response to brand manage-ment's dilemma in the digital era', *Journal of Marketing Management*, 29, 7/8: 912–932.

Rabikowska, M. (ed.) (2013) *The Everyday of Memory: Between Communism and Post-Communism*, Bern: Peter Lang.

Rainsford, S. (2015) 'Brand Putin: Russia's president still fashion 15 years on', 27 March: www.bbc.com/news/world-europe-32076836 (last accessed 18 August 2015).

Rancière, J. (2004) *The Politics of Aesthetics*, London: Continuum.

Randall, A. E. (2008) *The Soviet Dream World of Retail Trade and Consumption in the 1930s*, Basingstoke: Palgrave Macmillan.

Redclift, M. (2004) *Chewing Gum: The Fortress of Taste*, London and New York: Routledge.

Reddy-Best, K. L. and Howell, A. (2014) 'Negotiations in masculine identities in the Utilikilts brand community', *Critical Studies in Men's Fashion*, 1, 3: 223–240.

Reichart, T. and Lambiase, J. (eds) (2012/[2003]) *Sex in Advertising: Perspectives on the Erotic Appeal*, Abingdon and New York: Routledge.

Remnick, D. (1997) *Resurrection: The Struggle for a New Russia*, New York: Random House.

Riordan, J. (1999) 'The impact of communism on sport', in Riordan, J. and Krüger, A. (eds) *The International Politics of Sport in the 20th Century*, London and New York: E and FN Spon, 48–66.

Ritzer, G. (1993) *The McDonaldization of Society*, Newbury Park, CA: Pine Forge Press.

Ritzer, G. (2010) *Enchanting a Disenchanted World: Continuity and Change in the Cathedrals of Consumption*, 3rd edn, Thousand Oaks, CA: Pine Forge Press.

Ritzer, G. and Jurgenson, N. (2010) 'Production, consumption, prosumption: The nature of capitalism in the age of the digital "prosumer"', *Journal of Consumer Culture*, 10, 1: 13–36.

Roberts, G. H. (1999) 'Different for girls? Language, the gaze and power in film', *Essays in Poetics*, 24: 232–249.

Roberts, G. H. (2005) 'Auchan's entry into Russia: Prospects and research implications', *International Journal of Retail and Distribution Management*, 33, 1: 49–68.

Roberts, G. H. (2008) 'Palimpsestes ou âmes mortes? La russification des marques européennes de grande consommation': http://institut-est-ouest.ens-lsh.fr/spip.php?article129 (last accessed 24 July 2015).

Roberts, G. H. (2013a) 'I love theatre! Branding Russia's "Mega Mall" shopping centres', *The Marketing Review*, 13, 3: 255–269.

Roberts, G. H. (2013b) 'Revolt into style: Consumption and its (dis)contents in Valery Todorovsky's film *Stilyagi*', *Film, Fashion and Consumption*, 2, 2: 187–200.

Roberts, G. H. (2014a) 'Message on a bottle: Packaging the Great Russian Past', *Consumption, Markets and Culture*, 17, 3: 295–313.

Roberts, G. H. (2014b) 'Rebranding Russia's capital city on selected social media', in Morris, J., Rulyova, N. and Strukov, V. (eds) *New Media in New Europe–Asia*, Abingdon and New York: Routledge, 286–304.

Roberts, G. H. (2014c) 'On the Trans-Siberian with Sylvester Stallone: National identity and brand identity in post-socialist Russia', *Quaestio Rossica*, 3, 2: 197–208.

Roberts, G. H. (2015) '"A Russian airline for an English club … F★★★★★★ joke": Aeroflot, Manchester United and corporate reputation (mis)management on social media', Working Paper no. 5–2015: www.univ-reims.fr/site/laboratoire-labellise/laboratoire-d-economie-et-gestion-de-reims-regards-ea-6292/working-papers,15890,27266.html (last accessed 29 August 2015).

Roche-Nye, L. (2013) 'Représentations de l'homme dans le cosmos, projections d'une identité collective? Objets usuels et ésthetique spatiale en URSS de 1961 à 1991', unpublished paper presented at Material Culture in Russia since Peter the Great conference, May, Nanterre University.

Rosenfield, J. (1987) 'Packaging wraps up sales', *Marketing Communications*, 12, 9: 43–48.

Rossi, A. (1982) *The Architecture of the City*, Cambridge, MA and London: MIT Press.

Roxburgh, A. (2012) *The Strongman: Vladimir Putin and the Struggle for Russia*, London and New York: I. B. Tauris.

Russian Ice [n.d.]: icapturemarketing.com/russianice/about-us (last accessed 22 May 2015).

Russia Today (2014) '12 McDonald's restaurants temporarily closed in Russia, 100 inspections underway', 29 August: www.rt.com/business/183740-12-mcdonalds-close-russia (last accessed 21 July 2015).

Ruvio, A. A. and Belk, R. W. (eds) (2013) *The Routledge Companion to Identity and Consumption*, Abingdon and New York: Routledge.

Ryan, N. (2007) 'Vegas at the tipping point', in Aitchison, C., Richards, G. and Tallon, A. (eds) *Urban Transformations: Regeneration and Renewal through Leisure and Tourism*, Eastbourne: Leisure Studies Association, 141–159.

Ryazanova-Clarke, L. (2013) 'The discourse of spectacle at the end of the presidential term', in Goscilo, H. (ed.) *Putin as Celebrity and Cultural Icon*, Abingdon and New York: Routledge, 104–132.

Rybak, S. (2003) '"Tin'koff" nanyal Oliv'ero Toskani', 20 November: www.advertol ogy.ru/article1445.htm (last accessed 21 August 2015).

Ryklin, M. (2003) '"The best in the world": The discourse of the Moscow metro in the 1930s', in Dobrenko, E. and Naiman, E. (eds) *The Landscape of Stalinism: The Art and Ideology of Soviet Space*, Seattle, WA and London: University of Washington Press, 261–276.

Sabonis-Chafee, T. (1999) 'Communism as kitsch: Soviet symbols in post-Soviet society', in Barker, A. M. (ed.) *Consuming Russia: Popular Culture, Sex, and Society since Gorbachev*, Durham, NC and London: Duke University Press, 362–382.

Said, E. (1978) *Orientalism*, London and New York: Routledge and Kegan Paul.

Sandomirskaya, I. (2000) 'Ikea i Moskva', *Moderna Tider*, 121, November: 54–57; for a slightly different version of this article, published in English, see: http://artmargins. com/index.php/2-articles/370-ikea-in-moscow (last accessed 23 November 2015).

Sassatelli, R. (2007) *Consumer Culture: History, Theory and Politics*, London: Sage.

Schapiro, L. (1984) *1917: The Russian Revolution and the Origins of Present-Day Communism*, Harmondsworth: Penguin.

Scharoun, L. (2012) *America at the Mall: The Cultural Role of a Retail Utopia*, Jefferson, NC: McFarland and Co.

Schau, H. J. and Gilly, M. C. (2003) 'We are what we post? Self-presentation in personal web space', *Journal of Consumer Research*, 30, 3: 385–404.

Schau, H. J., Muñiz, A. M. Jnr and Arnould, E. J. (2009) 'How brand community practices create value', *Journal of Marketing*, 73, 5: 30–51.

Schouten, J. W. (1991) 'Selves in transition: Symbolic consumption in personal rites of passage and identity reconstruction', *Journal of Consumer Research*, 17, 4: 412–425.

Schouten, J. W. and McAlexander, J. H. (1995) 'Subcultures of consumption: An ethnography of the new bikers', *Journal of Consumer Research*, 22, 1: 43–61.

Schouten, J. W., Martin, D. M. and Belk, R. (2014) *Consumer Culture Theory (Research in Consumer Behaviour, Vol. 16)*, Bingley: Emerald Group Publishing Limited.

Schrad, M. L. (2014) *Vodka Politics: Alcohol, Autocracy, and the Secret History of the Russian State*, Oxford and New York: Oxford University Press.

Schroeder, J. E. (2002) *Visual Consumption*, Abingdon and New York: Routledge.

Schroeder, J. E. (2005) 'The artist and the brand', *European Journal of Marketing*, 39, 11/12: 1291–1305.

Schroeder, J. E. (2009) 'The cultural codes of branding', *Marketing Theory*, 9, 1: 123–126.

Schroeder, J. E. (2012) 'Style and strategy: Snapshot aesthetics in brand culture', in Puyou, F.-R., Quattrone, P., McLean, C. and Thrift, N. (eds) *Imagining Organizations: Performative Imagery in Business and Beyond*, Abingdon and New York: Routledge, 129–151.

Schroeder, J. E. (2015a) 'Introduction', in Schroeder, J. E. (ed.) *Brands: Interdisciplinary Perspectives*, Abingdon and New York: Routledge, 1–10.

Schroeder, J. E. (2015b) 'Communicating identity/consuming difference', *Consumption, Markets and Culture*, 18, 6: 485–489.

Schroeder, J. E. and Borgerson, J. L. (1998) 'Marketing images of gender: A visual analysis', *Consumption, Markets and Culture*, 2, 2: 161–201.

Schroeder, J. E. and Borgerson, J. L. (1999) 'Packaging paradise: Consuming Hawaiian music', in Arnould, E. J. and Scott, L. M. (eds) *Advances in Consumer Research*, 26, Provo, UT: Association for Consumer Research, 46–50.

Schroeder, J. E. and Borgerson, J. L. (2003) 'Identity and iteration: Marketing images and the constitution of consuming subjects', Proceedings of CMS conference, University of Waikato, NZ, 2003: www.mngt.waikato.ac.nz/ejrot/cmsconference/2003/proceed ings/criticalmarketing/Schroeder.pdf (last accessed 27 November 2015).

Schroeder, J. E. and Borgerson, J. L. (2012) 'Packaging paradise: Organizing repre-sentations of Hawaï', in Prasad, A. (ed.) *Against the Grain: Advances in Postcolonial Organization Studies*, Copenhagen: Copenhagen Business School Press, 32–53.

Schroeder, J. E. and Salzer-Mörling, M. (eds) (2006) *Brand Culture*, Abingdon and New York: Routledge.

Schroeder, J. E. and Zwick, D. (2004) 'Mirrors of masculinity: Representation and identity in advertising images', *Consumption, Markets and Culture*, 7, 2: 21–52.

Schultz, E. J. (2012) 'Beer-ad ban hits Russia as nation boosts sobriety', 2 January: http://adage.com/article/global-news/beer-ad-ban-hits-russia-nation-boosts-sobriety/ 231864 (last accessed 21 August 2015).

Schwirtz, M. (2010) 'Revolution? Da. Sexual? Nyet', *New York Times*, 14 July: www. nytimes.com/2010/07/15/fashion/15sex.html?_r=1& (last accessed 21 July 2015).

Scott, L. M. (1994a) 'Images in advertising: The need for a theory of visual rhetoric', *Journal of Consumer Research*, 21, 2: 252–273

Scott, L. M. (1994b) 'The bridge from text to mind: Adapting reader-response theory to consumer research', *Journal of Consumer Research*, 21, 3: 461–480.

See-To, E. W. K. and Ho, K. K. W. (2014) 'Value co-creation and purchase intention in social network sites: The role of electronic word-of-mouth and trust: A theoretical analysis', *Computers in Human Behavior*, 31, 1: 182–189.

Seiler, C. (2008) *Republic of Drivers: A Cultural History of Automobility in America*, Chicago, IL: University of Chicago Press.

Shaburova, Zh. (2002) 'Muzhik ne suetitsya, ili pivo s kharakterom', in Oushakine, S. (ed.) *O Muzhe(n)stvennosti*, Moscow: Novoe literaturnoe obozrenie, 532–555.

Shanks, M. and Tilley, C. Y. (1992) *Re-constructing Archaeology*, London and New York: Routledge.

Sheresheva, M. Y. and Antonov-Ovseenko, A. A. (2015) 'Advertising in Russian periodicals at the turn of the communist era', *Journal of Historical Research in Marketing*, 7, 2: 165–183.

Sherry, J. F. Jnr (1998) *Servicescapes: The Concept of Place in Contemporary Markets*, Lincolnwood, IL: NTC Business Books.

Sherry, J. F. Jnr and Fischer, E. (2007) *Explorations in Consumer Culture Theory*, Abing-don and New York: Routledge.

Shevchenko, E. (2013) 'V metro poyavitsya kioski v stile "stalinskii ampir"', 22 January: http://izvestia.ru/news/543349 (last accessed 21 July 2015).

Shevchenko, O. (2002) '"Between the holes": Emerging identities and hybrid patterns of consumption in post-socialist Russia', *Europe Asia Studies*, 54, 6: 841 866.

Shklovski, I. (2013) 'The internet, that's where you find people! Reconnecting with lapsed ties online in post-Soviet countries of Russia and Kazakhstan', unpublished paper delivered at Post-Socialism Playing Global: Computer Gaming Industries and Digital Media Culture conference, November, Birmingham University.

Shleifer, A. and Treisman, D. (2000) *Without a Map: Political Tactics and Economic Reform in Russia*, Cambridge, MA: MIT Press.

ShopandMall.ru [n.d.] 'Torgovyi-razvklekatel'nyi tsentr Murmansk Moll, g. Murmansk': www.shopandmall.ru/torgovye-centry/murmansk_moll-murmansk-pr-t_lenina_dom_34 (last accessed 21 August 2015).

Shterin, M. (forthcoming, 2016) *Religion in the Remaking of Russia*, Oxford: Oxford University Press.

Siberian Crown VKontakte account [n.d.]: vk.com/sibirskayakorona (last accessed 21 August 2015).

Siegelbaum, L. H. (2008) *Cars for Comrades: The Life of the Soviet Automobile*, Ithaca, NY and London: Cornell University Press.

Simonson, A. and Schmitt, B.H. (1997) *Marketing Aesthetics: The Strategic Management of Brands, Identity and Image*, New York: Free Press.

Singh, S. and Sonnenburg, S. (2012) 'Brand performances in social media', *Journal of Interactive Marketing*, 26, 4: 189–197.

Sit, J. K. and Birch, D. (2014) 'Entertainment events in shopping malls – profiling passive and active participation behaviors', *Journal of Consumer Behaviour*, 13, 6: 383–392.

SkyscraperCity.com [n.d.a]: www.skyscrapercity.com/showthread.php?t=1147975 (last accessed 21 August 2015).

SkyscraperCity.com [n.d.b]: www.skyscrapercity.com/showthread.php?t=604213 (last accessed 21 August 2015).

Slater, D. (1997) *Consumer Culture and Modernity*, Cambridge: Polity.

Slotkin, R. (1973) *Regeneration through Violence: The Mythology of the American Frontier, 1600–1800*, Middletown, CT: Wesleyan University Press.

Smart, B. (2010) *Consumer Society: Critical Issues and Environmental Consequences*, London: Sage.

Smecker, F. (2014) *Night of the World: Traversing the Ideology of Objectivity*, Alresford: Zero Books.

Smirennyi, I. N. (2007) *Moskva Na Upakovkakh i Etiketkakh*, Moscow: UpakGrafika.

Smirnova, L. (2012) 'Outlet malls springing up in Moscow', 20 June: www.themoscowtimes.com/news/article/outlet-malls-springing-up-in-moscow/460667.html (last accessed 21 July 2015).

Smith, A. N., Fischer, E. and Youngjian, C. (2012) 'How does brand-related user-generated content differ across YouTube, Facebook and Twitter?', *Journal of Interactive Marketing*, 26, 2: 102–113.

Smith, S. (2013) 'Conceptualising and evaluating experiences with brands on Facebook', *International Journal of Market Research*, 55, 3: 357–374.

Smith, S. and Kelly, C. (1998) 'Commercial Culture and Consumerism' [with additional material by McReynolds, L.], in Kelly, C. and Shepherd, D. (eds) *Constructing Russian Culture in the Age of Revolution: 1881–1940*, Oxford and New York: Oxford University Press, 106–164.

Sokolov, M. (2014) 'Desyat' let Naval'nomu. SSSR vozvrashchaetsya?', 19 December: www.svoboda.org/content/transcript/26752402.html (last accessed 3 July 2015).

Solomon, M. R. (1986) 'Deep-seated materialism: The case of Levi's 501 jeans', in Lutz, R. J. (ed.) *Advances in Consumer Research*, 13, Provo, UT: Association for Consumer Research, 619–622.

Sostav.ru (2001) 'Dolya rynka piva "Baltika" neuklonno snizhaetsya', 24 July: www.sostav.ru/news/2001/07/24/mark5 (last accessed 21 August 2015).

Sostav.ru (2009) '"Einem" rodilsya vtoroi raz', 18 March: www.sostav.ru/news/2009/03/18/r4 (last accessed 21 August 2015).

Sostav.ru (2013a) 'Ovechkin prinyal vyzov Gillette', 23 January: www.sostav.ru/news/2013/01/23/gillette_ovechkin (last accessed 21 August 2015).

Sostav.ru (2013b) '"Zhigulevskie" stilyagi', 14 February: www.sostav.ru/news/2013/02/14/zhigulyavskie_stilyagi (last accessed 21 August 2015).

Sostav.ru (2013c) '"San Inbev" registriruet novyi dizain "Zhigulevskogo"', 19 April: www.sostav.ru/publication/san-inbev-registriruet-novyj-dizajn-zhigulevskogo-2694.html (last accessed 21 August 2015).

Sostav.ru (2015) '"Konfael" sozdal "Politicheskii shokolad"', 24 February: www.sostav.ru/publication/konfael-sozdala-politicheskij-shokolad-15129.html (last accessed 28 August 2015).

Soviet Is in the Details [n.d.]: http://sovietdetails.tumblr.com (last accessed 21 August 2015).

Sperling, V. (2015) *Sex, Politics and Putin: Political Supremacy in Russia*, Oxford: Oxford University Press.

Stallybrass, P. and White, A. (1986) *The Poetics and Politics of Transgression*, London: Methuen.

Starks, T. (2008) *The Body Soviet: Propaganda, Hygiene and the Revolutionary State*, Madison, WI: University of Wisconsin Press.

Stern, B. B. (1992) 'Historical and personal nostalgia in advertising text: The fin de siècle effect', *Journal of Advertising*, 21, 4: 11–22.

Stern, B. B. (1996) 'Textual analysis in advertising research: Construction and deconstruction of meanings', *Journal of Advertising*, 25, 3: 61–73.

Stern, B. B. (2012/[2003]) 'Masculinism(s) and the male image: What does it mean to be a man?', in Reichart, T. and Lambiase, J. (eds) *Sex in Advertising: Perspectives on the Erotic Appeal*, Abingdon and New York: Routledge, 215–228.

Stern, B. B. and Holbrook, M. B. (1994) 'Gender and genre in the interpretation of advertising text', in Costa, J. A. (ed.) *Gender Issues and Consumer Behaviour*, London: Sage, 11–41.

Stern, B. B. and Schroeder, J. E. (1994) 'Interpretive methodology from art and literary criticism: A humanistic approach to advertising imagery', *European Journal of Marketing*, 28, 3: 114–132.

Stites, R. (1992) *Russian Popular Culture: Entertainment and Society since 1900*, Cambridge: Cambridge University Press.

Stokburger-Sauer, N. (2010) 'Brand community: Drivers and outcomes', *Psychology and Marketing*, 27, 4: 347–368.

Strate, L. (1991) 'The cultural meaning of beer commercials', in Holman, R. H. and Solomon, M.R. (eds) *Advances in Consumer Research*, 18, Provo, UT: Association for Consumer Research, 115–119.

Strukov, V. (2012) 'Spatial imagining and ideology of digital commemoration (Russian online gaming)', *Europe–Asia Studies*, 64, 8: 1584–1604.

Sturken, M. and Cartwright, L. (2001) *Practices of Looking: An Introduction to Visual Culture*, Oxford and New York: Oxford University Press.

Sturken, M. and Cartwright, L. (2009) *Practices of Looking: An Introduction to Visual Culture*, 2nd edn, Oxford and New York: Oxford University Press.

SunInBev.ru [n.d.]: www.suninbev.ru/brands/sibkor (last accessed 23 August 2015).

Supphellen, M. and Grønhaug, K. (2003) 'Building foreign brand personalities in Russia: The moderating effect of consumer ethnocentrism', *International Journal of Advertising*, 22, 2: 203–226.

Taranova, A. (2010) '500 kiosks closed, more to follow', *Russia and India Report*, 17 November: http://in.rbth.com/articles/2010/11/17/500_kiosks_closed_more_to_follow04899.html (last accessed 21 July 2015).

Tasker, Y. (1993) *Spectacular Bodies: Gender, Genre and the Action Film*, London and New York: Routledge.

Tass.ru (2014) 'U uchastnikov proekta "Skolkovo" budet svoya poliklinika', 21 June: http://tass.ru/skolkovo/1331469 (last accessed 21 August 2015).

Thil, É. (2000/[1966]) *Les Inventeurs du Commerce Moderne: Des Grands Magasins aux Bébés-requins*, Paris: Jouwen.

Thom, F. (2015) 'La "Grande Guerre patriotique: Les ingrédients d'un mythe', *Histoire et Liberté*, 57, June: 33–38: http://www.est-et-ouest.fr/revue/HL057_articles/057_033.pdf (last accessed 27 November 2015).

Thomas, K. D. (2013) 'Endlessly creating myself: Examining marketplace inclusion through the lived experience of black and white male millenials', *Journal of Public Policy and Marketing*, 32, Spring special issue: 95–105.

Thompson, C. J. (2000) 'Postmodern consumer goals made easy!!!!', in Ratneshwar, S. Mick, D. G. and Huffman, C. (eds) *The Why of Consumption: Contemporary Perspectives on Consumer Motives, Goals, and Desires*, London and New York: Routledge, 120–139.

Thompson, C. J. (2004) 'Marketplace mythology and discourses of power', *Journal of Consumer Research*, 31, 1: 162–180.

Thompson, C. J. (2006) 'The McDonaldization of enchantment and consumers' practices of re-enchantment: A dialectic view of transformative consumption [Special Session Summary]', in Pechman, C. and Price, L. (eds) *Advances in Consumer Research*, 33, Duluth, MN: Association for Consumer Research, 352–354.

Thompson, C. J. and Arsel, Z. (2004) 'The Starbucks brandscape and consumers' (anticorporate) experiences of glocalization', *Journal of Consumer Research*, 31, 3: 631–642.

Thompson, C. J. and Holt, D. B. (2004) 'How do men grab the phallus? Gender tourism in everyday consumption', *Journal of Consumer Culture*, 4, 3: 313–338.

Thompson, C. J. and Tian, K. (2008) 'Reconstructing the south: How commercial myths compete for identity value through the ideological shaping of popular memories and countermemories', *Journal of Consumer Research*, 34, 5: 595–613.

Thornhill, J. (1997) 'Ivan the terribly lost', *Financial Times*, 29–30 November, Weekend Section, 1: www.business-standard.com/article/specials/ivan-the-terribly-lost-197121001073_1.html (last accessed 21 July 2015).

Thornton, S. (1996) *Club Cultures: Music, Media, and Subcultural Capital*, Middletown, CT: Wesleyan University Press.

Thubron, C. (1999) *In Siberia*, Harmondsworth: Penguin.

Tisseron, S. (1996) *Le Mystère de la Chambre Claire: Photographie et Inconscient*, Paris: Flammarion.

Tochka-G [n.d.]: www.tochkag.net (last accessed 21 August 2015).

Toderian, B. (2008) 'Does Vancouver need (or want) iconic architecture?' 21 January: www.planetizen.com/node/29385 (last accessed 28 August 2015).

Todorova, M. and Gille, Z. (eds) (2012) *Post-Communist Nostalgia*, Oxford: Berghahn.

Tolstikova, N. (2000) 'Reading *Rabotnitsa*: Fifty years of creating gender identity in a socialist economy', in Catterall, M., Maclaran, P. and Stevens, L. (eds) *Marketing and Feminism: Current Issues and Research*, London and New York: Routledge, 160–182.

Toner, D. (2015) *Alcohol and Nationhood in Nineteenth-Century Mexico*, Lincoln, NE and London: University of Nebraska Press.

Trading Economics (2015) 'Russian Consumer Credit, 2006–2015': www.tradingeco nomics.com/russia/consumer-credit (last accessed 21 August 2015).

Tsimonis, G. and Dimitriadis, S. (2014) 'Brand strategies in social media', *Marketing Intelligence and Planning*, 32, 3: 328–344.

Tuncay, L. (2006) 'Men's responses to depictions of ideal masculinity in advertising', in Pechman, C. and Price, L. (eds) *Advances in Consumer Research*, 33, Duluth, MN: Association for Consumer Research, 64.

Tungate, M. (2008) *Branded Male: Marketing to Men*, London and Philadelphia: Kogan Page.

Turner, B. (1987) 'A note on nostalgia', *Theory, Culture and Society*, 4, 1: 147–156.

Twitchell, J. B. (1999) *Lead Us into Temptation: The Triumph of American Materialism*, New York: Columbia University Press.

Underwood, R. L. (2003) 'The communicative power of product packaging: Creating brand identity via lived and mediated experience', *Journal of Marketing Theory and Practice*, 11, 1: 62–76.

Underwood, R. L. and Ozanne, J. L. (1988) 'Is your package an effective communicator? A normative framework for increasing the communicative competence of packaging', *Journal of Marketing Communications*, 4, 4: 207–220.

United Blogs of Benetton, Russia (2012) 'Vazhnyi den'', 28 April: http://blog.benetton. com/russia/page/2 (last accessed 21 August 2015).

United Confectioners [n.d.]: www.uniconf.ru (last accessed 21 August 2015).

Upakovano.ru [n.d.]: www.upakovano.ru (last accessed 21 August 2015).

Upakovano.ru (2008): http://upakovano.ru/interviews/166 (last accessed 21 August 2015).

Urde, M., Greyser, S. A. and Balmer, J. M. T. (2007) 'Special issue papers: Corporate brands with heritage', *Journal of Brand Management*, 15, 1: 4–19.

Vaissié, C. (2014) 'Black robe, golden epaulettes: From the Russian dissidents to Pussy Riot', *Religion and Gender*, 4, 2: 166–183.

Vale, L. J. (2008) *Architecture, Power and National Identity*, 2nd edn, Abingdon and New York: Routledge.

Varese, F. (2001) *The Russian Mafia: Private Protection in a New Market Economy*, Oxford and New York: Oxford University Press.

Veblen, T. (1925/[1899]) *The Theory of the Leisure Class: An Economic Study of Institutions*, London: George Allen and Unwin.

Veenis, M. (1999) 'Consumption in East Germany: The seduction and betrayal of things', *Journal of Material Culture*, 4, 1: 79–112.

Vegas City [n.d.a]: www.vegas-city.ru (last accessed 21 August 2015).

Vegas City [n.d.b]: http://kashirskoe.vegas-city.ru/ginza (last accessed 21 August 2015).

Verdery, K. (1992) *The Transition from Socialism: Anthropology and Eastern Europe*, Cambridge: Cambridge University Press.

Vincent, L. (2002) *Legendary Brands*, Chicago, IL: Dearborn Trade Publications.

Walker, J., Ursitti, C. and McGinnis, P. (1991) *Photo Manifesto: Contemporary Photography in the USSR*, New York: Stewart, Tabori and Chang.

Walker, S. (2011) 'End of a drinking culture? Russia accepts that beer is alcoholic', 21 July: www.independent.co.uk/life-style/health-and-families/health-news/end-of-a-drinking-culture-russia-accepts-that-beer-is-alcoholic-2317798.html (last accessed 21 August 2015).

Walker, S. (2015) 'Is the "Moscow experiment" over?', *The Guardian*, 8 June: www. theguardian.com/cities/2015/jun/08/is-the-moscow-experiment-over-gorky-park-sergei-kapkov-alexei-navalny (last accessed 3 July 2015)

Wallace, E., Buil, I. and de Chernatony, L. (2012) 'Facebook "friendship" and brand advocacy', *Journal of Brand Management*, 20, 2: 128–146.

Wallace, E., Buil, I., de Chernatony, L. and Hogan, M. (2014) 'Who "likes" you … and why? A typology of Facebook fans. From "fan"-atics and self-expressives to utilitarians and authentics', *Journal of Advertising Research*, 54, 1: 92–109.

Wallendorf, M. and Arnould, E. J. (1991) 'We gather together: The consumption rituals of Thanksgiving Day', *Journal of Consumer Research*, 18, 1: 13–31.

Wang, J. (2008) *Brand New China: Advertising, Media, and Commercial Culture*, Cambridge, MA, and London: Harvard University Press.

Warde, A. (1994) 'Consumption, identity-formation and uncertainty', *Sociology*, 28, 4: 877–898.

Warde, A. (2005) 'Consumption and theories of practice', *Journal of Consumer Culture*, 5, 2: 131–153.

Warrington, P. T. and Gourgova, A. (2006) 'Beauty, brains, or brawn: Idealized male images in advertising', in Pechman, C. and Price, L. (eds) *Advances in Consumer Research*, 33, Duluth, MN: Association for Consumer Research, 344–345.

Weaver, C. (2013) 'Russia sees surge in consumer credit', *Financial Times*, 13 February: www.ft.com/intl/cms/s/0/14d3091c-7477-11e2-b323-00144feabdc0.html#axzz3d7 tqU8G0 (last accessed 2 July 2015).

Weber, M. (1978/[1922]) *Economy and Society*, Berkeley, CA: University of California Press.

West, S. (2011) *I Shop in Moscow: Advertising and the Creation of Consumer Culture in Late Tsarist Russia*, DeKalb, IL: Northern Illinois University Press.

Whannel, G. (2007) 'Mediating masculinities: The production of media representations in sport', in Aitchison, C. C. (ed.) *Sport and Gender Identities: Masculinities, Femininities, and Sexualities*, Abingdon and New York: Routledge, 7–21.

Wharton, C. (ed.) (2013) *Advertising as Culture*, Bristol and Chicago, IL: Intellect.

Whitaker, J. (2006) *Service and Style: How the American Department Store Fashioned the Middle Class*, New York: St Martin's Press.

Whitaker, J. (2011) *The Department Store: History, Design, Display*, London: Thames and Hudson.

White, L. (2009) 'Foster's lager: From local beer to global icon', *Marketing Intelligence and Planning*, 27, 2: 177–190.

White, P. G. and Gillett, J. (1994) 'Reading the muscular body: A critical decoding of advertisements in *Flex* magazine', *Sociology of Sport Journal*, 11, 1: 18–39.

Whitehead, S. M. (2002) *Men and Masculinities*, Cambridge: Polity.

Widdis, E. (2004) 'Russia as space', in Franklin, S. and Widdis, E. (eds) *National Identity in Russian Culture*, Cambridge: Cambridge University Press, 30–49.

Williams, R. H. (1982) *Dream Worlds: Mass Consumption in Late Nineteenth-Century France*, Berkeley, CA: University of California Press.

Williamson, J. (1978) *Decoding Advertisements: Ideology and Meaning in Advertising*, London and New York: Marion Boyars.

Wilson, A. and Bachkatov, N. (1988) *Living with Glasnost: Youth and Society in a Changing Russia*, Harmondsworth: Penguin.

Winter, J. and Sivan, E. (eds) (1999) *War and Remembrance in the Twentieth Century*, Cambridge: Cambridge University Press.

Wirtz, J. *et al.* (2013) 'Managing brands and customer engagement in online brand communities', *Journal of Service Management*, 24, 3: 223–244.

Wolin, L. D. (2003) 'Gender issues in advertising – an oversight. Synthesis of research: 1970–2002', *Journal of Advertising*, 43, 1: 111–129.

Woodward, I. (2007) *Understanding Material Culture*, London: Sage.

Woodward, K. (2007) *Boxing, Masculinity and Identity: The 'I' of the Tiger*, Abingdon and New York: Routledge.

Wrigley, N. and Lowe, M. (2014/[1998]) *Reading Retail: A Geographical Perspective on Retailing and Consumption Spaces*, Abingdon and New York: Routledge.

Xiong, L., King, C. and Piehler, R. (2013) '"That's not my job": Exploring the employee perspective in the development of brand ambassadors', *International Journal of Hospitality Management*, 35: 348–359.

Yampolsky, M. (1995) 'In the shadow of monuments: Notes on iconoclasm and time', in Condee, N. (ed.) *Soviet Hieroglyphics: Visual Culture in Late Twentieth-Century Russia*, Bloomington and Indianapolis, IN: Indiana University Press/London: BFI Publishing, 93–112.

Yan, J. (2011) 'Social media in branding: Fulfilling a need', *Journal of Brand Management*, 18, 9: 688–696.

Yasinskaya, A. (2012) 'TTS "Galeriya" stala prichinoi probok v Peterburge', 26 March: www.vedomosti.ru/realty/articles/2012/03/26/psevdoklassika_na_milliard (last accessed 21 July 2015).

YouTube (2008a) 'One like Putin': www.youtube.com/watch?v=zk_VszbZa_s (last accessed 28 August 2015).

YouTube (2008b) 'Sylvester Stallone in Russian Ice vodka commercial': www.youtube.com/watch?v=mXDNzA8UaOg (last accessed 21 August 2015).

YouTube (2010) 'Bruce Willis vodka': www.youtube.com/watch?v=2xL0MOIgtig (last accessed 21 August 2015).

YouTube (2011) 'Gillette: Alexandr Ovečkin': www.youtube.com/watch?v=1xgRMiRQfn4 (last accessed 21 August 2015).

YouTube (2012a) 'Viktor Tsoi i gruppa Kino – Zvezda po imeni solntse': www.youtube.com/watch?v=3MuH2ITFGpc (last accessed 21 August 2015).

YouTube (2012b) 'Otkroveniya devushki pro ee pervyi raz': www.youtube.com/watch?v=MbIzj21X0tU (last accessed 21 August 2015).

YouTube (2013a) 'Gillette TVC with Alexander Ovechkin': www.youtube.com/watch?v=NoSzwqo4T-g (last accessed 21 August 2015).

YouTube (2013b) 'Ovechkin i spetsial'naya seriya Gillette Fusion ProGlide k Olimpiiskim igram v Sochi 2014': www.youtube.com/watch?v=0_2zubabFgI (last accessed 21 August 2015).

YouTube (2014a) 'Lionel Messi and Roger Federer trading places Gillette': www.youtube.com/watch?v=Hc7oa-e3Blg (last accessed 21 August 2015).

YouTube (2014b) 'Olympian John Tavares this is my game face commercial Gillette Canada YouTube': www.youtube.com/watch?v=c9oW8Ou2f4A (last accessed 21 August 2015).

Yurchak, A. (1997) 'Mif o nastoyashchem muzhchine i nastoyashchei zhenshchine v Rossiiskoi televizionnoi reklame', in Tishkov, V. (ed.) *Sem'ya, Gender, Kul'tura*, Moscow: Institut Etnologii i Antropologii Akademii Nauk i Etnologicheskii Tsentr Rossiiskogo Gosudarstvennogo Gumanitarnogo Universiteta, 389–399.

Yurchak, A. (1999) 'Gagarin and the rave kids: Transforming power, identity, and aesthetics in post-Soviet nightlife', in Barker, A. M. (ed.) *Consuming Russia: Popular Culture, Sex, and Society since Gorbachev*, Durham, NC: Duke University Press, 76–109.

Yurchak, A. (2000) 'Po sledam zhenskogo obraza: Simvolicheskaya rabota novogo reklamnogo diskursa', in Al'chuk, A. (ed.) *Zhenshchina i vizual'nye znaki*, Moscow: Ideya-Press, 65–78.

Yurchak, A. (2005) *Everything Was Forever, Until It Was No More: The Last Soviet Generation*, Princeton, NJ: Princeton University Press.

Yurchak, A. (2011) 'Aesthetic politics in Saint Petersburg: Skyline at the heart of political opposition', National Council for Eurasian and East European Research Working Paper: www.ucis.pitt.edu/nceeer/2011_824-15_Yurchak.pdf (last accessed 18 August 2015).

Yurchak, A. (2015) 'Bodies of Lenin: The hidden science of communist sovereignty', *Representations*, 129, 1: 116–157.

Zaglia, M.E. (2013) 'Brand communities embedded in social networks', *Journal of Business Research*, 66, 2: 216–223.

Zdravomyslova, E. and Temkina, A. (2002) 'Krizis maskulinnosti v pozdnesovetskom diskurse', in Oushakine, S. (ed.) *O Muzhe(n)stvennosti*, Moscow: Novoe literaturnoe obozrenie, 432–451.

Zeruvabel, Y. (1995) *Recovered Roots: Collective Memory and the Making of Israeli National Tradition*, Chicago, IL: University of Chicago Press.

Zhao, X. and Belk, R. W. (2008) 'Appropriation of political ideology in China's social transition', *Journal of Consumer Research*, 35, 2: 231–244.

Zhelnina, A. (2009) 'From Barakholka to shopping malls: Transformation of retail spaces in St. Petersburg', *Anthropology of East Europe Review*, 27, 1: 51–64.

Zhiyan, W., Borgerson, J. L. and Schroeder, J. E. (2013) *From Chinese Brand Culture to Global Brands: Insights from Aesthetics, Fashion, and History*, Basingstoke: Palgrave Macmillan.

Zholkovsky, A. (1983) 'The semiotics of a Soviet cooker wrapper', *Wiener Slawistischer Almanach*, 11: 341–354.

Zhou, Z., Zhang, Q., Su, C. and Zhou, N. (2012) 'How do brand communities generate brand relationships? Intermediate mechanisms', *Journal of Business Research*, 65, 7: 890–895.

Zhuk, S. (2010) *Rock and Roll in the Rocket City: The West, Identity, and Ideology in Soviet Dniepropetrovsk, 1960–1985*, Baltimore, MD: Johns Hopkins University Press.

Žižek, S. (1992) *Looking Awry: An Introduction to Jacques Lacan through Popular Culture*, Cambridge, MA and London: MIT Press.

Zukin, S. (2004) *Point of Purchase: How Shopping Changed American Culture*, Abingdon and New York: Routledge.

Zukin, S. and Maguire, J. S. (2004) 'Consumers and consumption', *Annual Review of Sociology*, 30: 173–197.

Index

'4 "P"s' of marketing 7
4x4 vehicles 54–5, 59 *see also* Dodge
    Caliber advertisement

AB-InBev 7, 120, 122 *see also* Siberian
    Crown case study
'abject' other 66
Accessorize 27
Addis, M. 39
Adidas 135
advertising 52–4; Dodge Caliber case
    study 54–9; four mythic orientations of
    53; male grooming products case study
    67–72; and masculinity 49–51; and
    masculinity in Russia 45–7, 50, 52–78;
    and Putin's presidential campaign of
    2012 74–8; Russian Ice case study
    60–3; Tinkoff's Zooom case study 63,
    64–7
Agresta, S. 117
alcopops: Zooom advertisement 63, 64–7
Ambrose, G. 99
Amine, A. 116
Anderson, B. 7, 110, 111, 143–4
androcentric vision 48–9
Angé O. 104
Anglo-Saxon popular culture 136, 137,
    138 *see also* Western popular culture
Appadurai, A. 7, 24, 86–7, 109, 110, 111,
    150
Appelbaum, E. 137
Apple, Newton personal assistant 117
Arbat, the 96, 97, 102
Archangel's Cathedral 97–8
architecture 34–6
Arnaud, Antoine 10
Arnould, E. J. 3, 118, 140–1
Arsel, Z. 118
Aser'yants, A. 93

Askegaard, S. 86, 87
Auchan 30, 40, 43n27, 154, 155
authenticity 149–50
Avery, J. 118
Avia Park, Moscow 32
Axenov, K. 19
Azerbaijan 23

Babaevsky 95, 97, 99
Bachkatov, N. 16
Backes, N. 31
Badinter, É. 49
Badot, O. 11, 13–14, 20, 25, 27, 29, 30,
    32, 39, 40–1
Bakhtin, M. M. 52, 53, 148, 149
Balina, M. 36
Balmer, J. M. T. 101
Banania 87
Barré, B. 86
Barthes, R. 8, 108
Baskin-Robbins 23
Batalina, O. 47
Baudrillard, J. 3, 5, 12, 19, 32
Bauman, Z. 4, 130, 140, 147, 150
beer 48, 63, 119–20, 154 *see also* Siberian
    Crown case study; Tinkoff's Zooom
    advertisement
Belarus 139
Belk, R. W. 29, 85–6, 129
Benetton 27
Benjamin, W. 28–9
Bergami, M. 130
Berliner, D. 104
'Big Middle' 28
Bitner, M. J. 35
black markets 16, 18
Bloch, P. H. 28
Bluewater mall, London 27
Blyton, E. 87

body, the: in Russian culture 47–8
bodybuilding: popularity of in Russia 56, 57
Bolshoi Theatre 99
Bondarchuk, E. 19
Bordo, S. 53–4, 56
Borgerson, J. L. 52, 86
Borgerson, J.L. 106
Boucicaut, A. 15
Bough, B. B. 117
Bourdieu, P. 3, 18, 48–9
Bowlby, R. 25, 26, 89
boxing: in the Dodge Caliber advertisement 55–6; in Russia 62; Russian Ice advertisement 60–3
Boym, S. 92, 96, 103–4, 105, 107, 110–11
Brade, I. 19
'brand ambassadors' 144–5
brand communities 7, 115–17, 139–45, 147, 151n2
brand culture 8, 134
brand loyalty 99
'brand morphing' 59
brands: co-creation of 117–18, 145; increasing visibility of 7; mythical function of 88; and packaging 83, 84, 86–7; perspectives on in literature 7–8
brands and social media 115–21; Levi's case study 132–51; Siberian Crown case study 122–32
Brezhnev, L. 16
'bricolage' 3, 13
Brodsky, Joseph 146
Brown, S.. 32
Brown, S. 53, 78, 104, 110, 149
Brundny, Y. M. 9
Bryce, W. 29
Budweiser 131
Bukberi 28
Bukowski, C. 138, 146
Bulatov, E. 93
Burger King 23
Butler, J. 47, 48, 50, 66–7, 78
Buy Russian campaign 22, 97

Caldwell, M. L. 22, 26, 91, 133
Calvin Klein advertisements 56
Cameron, D. 150
carnival 148–50
Cartwright, L. 56
Carù, A. 12–13
Cassiday, J. A. 74, 103
Cathedral of Christ the Saviour 92, 97, 102, 103, 108

Chapman Taylor 33
Chernyshova, N. 16, 26
Chester, P. 95
chocolate: packaging 81–3, 89–91, 94–101, 102, 107–9, 110; in Russian society 82–3, 89, 95
Chocolate Traditions 82
Christian Dior 15
Christodoulides, G. 118
Clark, K. 65
Clarke, D. 2–3, 28
Clarke, P. 88–9
co-creation of brands 117–18, 145
Coca-Cola 131, 135–6
Cockburn, P. 26
Cohon, G. 21
collective memory 106, 120–1, 122
comic (orientation of advertising) 53
Connell, R. W. 56–7
conspicuous consumption 4
consumer agency 118
consumer culture: definition and scope of 2–3; and packaging 84; political influence on 10–11; and social identity 4
Consumer Culture Theory (CCT) 6
consumer ideology 52
consumer perspective on brands 8
consumer society, definition of 2–3
consumer tribes 151n2
consumers: co-creation of brands 117–18, 145; emotional experience of 12; as producers 13
contingent and conspicuous strategy for re-enchantment of retailing 14, 40
contingent and street corner strategy for re-enchantment of retailing 14, 25, 27, 30, 40
Conway, H. 35
corporate perspective on brands 8
Cosmonauts' Day 124
Cova, B. 12–13, 39, 115–16, 117, 151n2
Covent Garden, London 32
credit, availability of 26
critical perspective on brands 8
Crocus City 30–1, 40
Crocus Expo 31
cultural perspective on brands 8

Dalai Lama 123
Dano, F. 85
Danone Actimel advertisement 67
Davis, F. 104
de Certeau, M.3, 13
de Gaulle, C. 123

de Laurentis, T. 54
Debenhams 27
Debord, G. 11, 12, 73
Debray, R. 52
Depardieu, G. 123
department stores 30; in Russia 15, 29
Derrida, J. 50
Dholakia, N. 35, 148
di Caprio, L. 128
disenchantment 13
Dobrenko, E. 36
Dodge Caliber advertisement 54–9
Dormition Cathedral 97, 108
Dorozhkin, E. 24
Douglas, M. 3
Dovey, K. 34
Downey, L. 149
Duchovny, D. 126–30, 131
Dunkin' Donuts 23
Durkheim, É. 120

e-commerce 29
'edutainment' 39
Einem' 95, 99–100, 101, 107–8, 110
Elki-Palki 25
Elliott, M. 51
empty signs 108
Etlin, R. 35
EU foodstuffs, Russian embargo on 154
Evans Clements, B. 47, 57, 62

Facebook 139; AB-InBev's 'Siberian
    Crown' beer 7; Levi's case study 135;
    Tochka-G 38, 44n44 *see also* social
    media
Faludi, S. 62–3
fast food 21–5, 40
Federer, R. 72
Fehérváry, K. 133
Ferrero 95
Figes, O. 91, 98
Filser, M. 11, 13–14, 20, 25, 27, 29, 30,
    32, 39, 40–1
Firat, A. F. 12, 32, 35, 118, 129, 148
Floch, J.-M. 85
FMCG packaging in Russia 88–91
football 126
Ford, 'Fiesta Angels' 117
foreign goods 18–19, 20–1
Foster, R. 84
Foucault, M. 47, 51
Fournier, S. 118
Freud, S. 47
frontier image 138, 147

Frye, N. 53
Fuchs, C. 116

Gagarin, Yu 83
Galeriya mall, St Petersburg 33–6, 40, 110
    change to: St Petersburg
gaze, the 50–1, 66, 67, 75
Gee, S. 70
gender: and advertising 49–50; and the
    androcentric vision 48–9; and
    performativity 5
General Motors, Hummer 55
Genette, G. 52
Georgia 131
Getwear 133, 137
Gharbi, A. 129
Gibbons, J 69
Giddens, A. 3, 140
Gillespie, D. 48
Gillett, J. 56
Gillette Fusion ProGlide razor
    advertisement 69–72
Gilmour, J. 57, 62
Ginza 31
glasnost (openness) 17
Glavobshchepit 21
Gleserova, K. 145
global popular culture 134
Goffman, E. 5, 49
Gogol', N. 123
Goh, C. 59
Goldman, R. 21
Goldschmidt, P. W. 37
Goldstein, D. 24
golliwog figure 87
Gorbachev, M.17, 63
Gorky Park, Moscow 1–2
Goscilo, H. 48, 73, 74, 138
Gourgova, A. 56
Gramsci, A. 56
grand narratives 7
Great Russian Past 7, 11, 103
Greimas, A. J. 85
Greyser, S. A. 101
Gronow, J. 139
Grozny, P. 23
Guerlain 86
GUM 10, 15, 28
Gurova, Olga 2

Habermas, J. 148
Habibi, M. R. 117
Habitat 27
Hackley, C. 134

Halbwachs, M. 120
Hallmark 27
Hamouda, M. 129
Harley Davidson 116, 117
Harris, P. 99
Hashamova, Y. 48
Havlena, W. J. 104–5, 106
Haynes, J. 54
Hearn, J. 49
Hede, A. M. 82
hegemonic brandscape 118
hegemonic masculinity 56–7, 58, 62,
    73, 78
Heilbrunn, B. 86, 93
Hellebust, R. 58
Hilton, M. L. 15, 36
Hine, T. 84, 85, 110
hip consumerism 153n29
Hirschman, E. C. 12, 52, 67
Hitchcock, A. 75–6
Holak, S. L. 104–5, 106
Holbrook, M. B. 12, 53
Holocaust, the 120
Holt, D. B. 7, 58, 131–2, 133–4, 135,
    136, 150
homosexuality in Russia 38, 44n44,
    47, 78n2
HP brown sauce 108
Hughes, L. 90–1, 95–6
Hummer (General Motors) 55
Humphrey, C. 21
Huxtable, A. L. 2
hyperinflation 18
hypermarkets 30

ice hockey 69–70
iconic brands 7, 118, 131–2, 133–4, 135
iconic buildings 36
identity 3–4; and packaging 85;
    performative aspects of 5
ideoscape 7, 86–7, 109, 150
Idov, M. 90
IKEA 25–7, 29, 40
imaginary geographies 120, 121–2
Imperial Russia: political influence on
    consumer culture 11 *see also* Romanov
    dynasty
income inequality in Russia 10
Instagram: Levi's case study 135
ironic (orientation of advertising) 53
Isherwood, B. 3

Jack Daniels 131, 132
Jahn, H. F. 107–8

Jarski, V. M. 84
jeans *see* Levi's case study
Johar, G. V. 53
Johnson, E. D. 74, 103

Kalashnikov, M. 126
Kapkov, S. 93, 101
Kaplan, A. E. 50
Kates, S. M. 50, 59
Kazakhstan 139
Keane, W. 8
Keller, K. L. 84
Kelly, C. 54
Kent, A. 28
Kessous, A. 104
KFC 28
Khrushchev, N. 16
Kiev 91
Kino 127
Kirby, A. 28
Kniazeva, M. 85–6
Komar, V. 113n19
Konfael', 'Political Chocolates' 81
Korogodskaya, V. 145
Kotler, P. 7, 12
Koushner, K. 125
Koval'chuk, I. 126
Kozinets, R. V. 39, 104, 110, 119, 143
Kraft 95
Kramer, A. E. 14–15, 29, 30
Kravets, O. 60, 88, 104, 133
Kremlin: representations of on packaging
    98, 108
Kristeva, J. 66
Krosha Kartoshka 23

labels 84 *see also* packaging
Lacan, J. 47, 50, 52, 75–6, 77
Lacoste 54
Lady Vanishes, The (Hitchcock) 75–6
Laroche, M. 117
Lehman, P. 47
Lenin, V. 76
Leroy Merlin 27
Lévi-Strauss, C. 85, 86, 119, 134
Levi's case study 7, 132–51
Levi's World 135
Levitt, T. 134, 135
LGBT communities in Russia 38,
    44n44
liberal democracy 150
Lipman, M. 16
logos 93
Lotman, Yu. 8

Louis Vuitton steamer trunk, Red Square, Moscow 10–11, 94
Lury, C. 7, 84
luxury brands 11, 31
Luzhkov, Yu. 20, 23–4, 97

M-video 27
Maclaran, P. 32, 53, 77–8
mafia, and street kiosks 19
Makarenko, K. 106
make-up products for men 67
Malevich, K. 113n20
Mall of America 27
malls 27–36
Manning, P. 8, 63, 84, 86, 87, 119, 121, 131
Mansvelt, J. 14
Marks and Spencer 27
Mars 95
Marzocchi, G. 130
masculinity 48–9; in/and advertising 49–51; and Russian advertising 45–7, 50, 52–78; and Russian culture/identity 5–6, 47–8
Matveev, A. L. 104–5, 106
Mayakovsky, V. 89–90
McCracken, G. 39
McDonald's, in Russia 21–2, 25, 28
'McDonaldization' 13, 22–3, 135
McIntyre, C. 35
McQuarrie, E. F. 139
'mediascapes' 109–10, 111, 120
Mega Mall 27, 28–9, 40
Melamid, A. 113n19
MEMORIAL 107
men's grooming product advertisements 67–72
Messi, L. 72
Midday, A. 137
Mikhalkov-Konchalovsky, A. 43n22
Mikhalkov, N. 43n22
Miles, S. 32, 36, 38
Miller, D. 4, 5
Miller, J. 67, 110, 130, 133, 139
Millionaire's Fair 31
modern era 12
Moldova 139
Moore, R. 36
Moore, R. E. 84
moral responsibility, in brand communities 141–2
Moran, M. 3–4
Morandin, G. 130
Morris, J. 48, 63, 104, 106, 109, 122

Moscow: city branding 6, 93–4; and myth 91–5; representations of in packaging 6, 83, 94–101, 102–4, 107–9, 110; street kiosks 19–20, 23–4
Moscow Motor Show 31
Moss, M. 29
Mothercare 27
Mountain Dew 133–4
Muir and Merrilies (TsUM) 15, 28, 101
Mulvey, L. 50, 51
Muñiz Jnr., A. M. 115, 116, 117, 128, 139, 141–2
Museum of Erotic Art 38
Museum of Show Business 31
'muzhik' figure 48
myths: and brands 122, 132, 133–4, 136, 138–9; and Levi's 132; and Moscow 91–5

nationalism, and packaging 90–1
Navy Day 124
Neidhart, C. 16, 18, 26
Nelson, J. E. 28
neoclassical architecture 34–5
Nestlé 95
netnographic research 119
Neumeyer, J. 95
new man imagery 69
Nike 131; Nike Town 40
Nivea for Men advertisement 68
Nixon, S. 51, 69
non-contingent and conspicuous strategy for re-enchantment of retailing 14, 39, 40
non-contingent and street corner strategy for re-enchantment of retailing 14, 20, 40
nostalgia 101, 103–7, 109, 111
Nutella 115–16, 117

O'Guinn, T. C. 115, 116, 128, 139, 141–2
OBI 27
Ogilvy and Mather 68
Okhudzhava, B. 96–7
Olick, J. 121
One Vogue (Pelevin) 154–5
Onishchenko, G. 23
Örge, O. 104, 133
Orkla 95
Orlov, V. 127
Ostankino brewery 106

Oushakine, S. A. 108–9, 121
outlet villages 43n31
Ovenchkin, A. 69–71

Pace, S. 117
packaging 6, 84–8; as branding/ideology/
    marketing 6; chocolate products
    81–3, 89–91, 94–101, 102,
    107–9, 110; in Russia 81–3, 87–9,
    94–111
palimpsests 52
Palmetta 28
Panikhaka, M. 125
Panopticon 51
Park of the Arts 92
Parker, I. 75
Patico, J. 2, 26, 82
patriotism 106, 107, 108, 109; patriotic
    consumerism 90
Patterson, M. 51
Peirce, C. S. 8, 85
Pelevin, V. 154–5
Peñaloza, L. 130
Penthouse 37
perestroika ([economic] reconstruction) 17
performativity, and gender 5
Peter the Great 14, 92, 113n18, 124
Petersson-Lind, K. 26
Philips' male grooming advertisements
    68–9
Phillips, B. J. 139
Pizza Hut 23, 24, 28
Podesta, S. 39
political influence on consumer culture
    10–11
Pongsakornrungslip, S. 117, 118
popular music 141
pornography 37
Poroshenko, P. 81–2
postmodern era 12
possessions, and identity 3
postmodern branding 7
postmodernism 12
Powerscourt Townhouse Centre,
    Dublin 32
Prahalad, C. K. 117–18
Price, L. L. 3, 118, 140–1
privatisation 18
Pussy Riot 78n1, 97
Putin, V. 9, 21; advertisements for
    presidential campaign of 2012 74–8;
    anti-Western rhetoric 154; imagery
    of on products 81; and masculinity
    5–6, 47, 48, 57; personality cult

of 51, 73; political influence on
    consumer culture 11
Putnam, R. D. 35

Quelch J. A. 135, 136

Ramaswamy, V. 117–18
Randall, A. E. 15
re-enchanting consumption 12
re-enchantment of retailing 10–15,
    17–41; four strategies for 13–14, 40
reader-response theory 53
Red October (chocolate brand) 80, 89,
    95, 101, 110; Einem' 95, 99–100, 101,
    107–8, 110; Tretyakov Gallery series
    98, 99–100
Red Square, Moscow 102; as a 'space for
    consumption' 11; Louis Vuitton stea-
    mer trunk 10–11, 94
reflective nostalgia 105
restorative nostalgia 105
retail architecture 34–5
retailing in Russia: Imperial and USSR
    periods 4–5, 15–17; re-enchantment of
    10–15, 17–41
retro packaging 106
Richard, M.-O. 117
Ridgway, N. M. 28
Riordan, J. 57
Ritzer, G. 13, 14, 19, 22, 25, 29, 32, 135
Robertson's jams 87
Rodchenko, A. 89–90, 93
Roenisch, R. 35
romance (orientation of advertising) 53
Romanov dynasty 10, 11, 89 *see also*
    Imperial Russia
Roshen 81–2
Rot Front 6, 83, 95, 97, 101, 102
Roux, E. 104
Russia: chocolate in Russian society 82–3,
    89, 95; desire to outdo the West 14;
    income inequality 10; national identity
    121 *see also* Imperial Russia; USSR
Russian Chocolate 97–8, 102
Russian Ice advertisement 60–3
Russian Orthodox faith 48, 97, 99
Russkoe Bistro 24–5

Sabonis-Chafee, T. 106
sacrifice, and shopping 4, 5
Said, E. 121
Sakharov, A. 107
Sandomirskaya, I. 25
Sassatelli, R. 3, 5, 14, 19

Savage advertisement 45–7
Schau, H. J. 117
Schick, C. 137
Schroeder, J. E. 3, 7–8, 35, 51, 52, 54, 73–4, 86, 88, 117, 118, 134
Scott, L. M. 52, 53, 88
Seiler, C. 54
semiotics: and packaging 85; 'semiotic ideology' 8
service quality: and McDonald's 22; poor service 16
'servicescape' 35
sex museums 38
sex shop market in Russia 36–40
Shaburova, Zh. 50
Shankar, A. 39
Shanks, M. 119
She, D. 145, 146, 149
Sherry, Jnr., J. F. 104, 110
Shevchenko, O. 18
shopping: and identity construction 4; and sacrifice 4, 5; theatricality of 29
shopping malls 27–36
shortages 16, 17
shuttle trading 18
Siberian Crown case study 122–32
Siegelbaum, L. H. 54
signification 3, 9
signs 8
'simulacrum' 4
Singh, S. 117, 147, 148
Sitz, L. 116
Sivan, E. 121
Slater, D. 3
Slotkin, R. 122
Smart, B. 5, 134
Smirennyi, I. N. 6
Snapple 134
Sobyanin, S. 23
Socchi, Winter Olympics 2014 34, 71, 126
social capital, and retail architecture 35
social identity 4
social media and brands 7, 111, 115–21; Levi's case study 132–51; Siberian Crown case study 122–32
Socialist Realism 65
Solomon, M. R. 132
Solzhenitsyn, A. 123
Sonnenburg, S. 117, 147, 148
Sony 27
Southdale Mall, Minneapolis 29
Sperling, V. 48, 73, 75

Sport-master 27
St Basil's Cathedral 90, 97, 108
St George Ribbon 9, 111n4
St Petersburg 91, 92
Stalin, J. 15
Stallone, S.: Russian Ice advertisement 60–3
Stardog!s 23
Starks, T. 57
Stepanov, V. 145, 147, 149
Stern, B. B. 53
Stevens, L. 53
Stockmann 27
storefront design 35
'stores trial' 17
Strate, L. 64, 65
street kiosks 18–20, 23–4, 40, 41
Strukov, V. 138
Sturken, M. 56
SUN-InBev 122
super-hero 6
Symbolic Order 47, 52, 66, 75, 76, 77

Taranova, A. 23–4
Tavares, J. 71–2
Taylor, E. L. 135, 136
Tekhno-sila 27
theatricality of shopping 29
themed environments 38, 40
Thil, É. 16
Thompson, C. J. 5, 58, 118
Tilley, C. Y. 119
Tinkoff, O. 63–4
Tinkoff's Zooom advertisement 63, 64–7
Tochka-G 38–40, 41, 96
Toderian, B. 36
Toscani, O. 63, 64
Toyota advertisements 50
tragic (orientation of advertising) 53
Tungate, M. 126
Turgenev, I. 123
Twitchell, J. B. 14, 29

Ukraine 9, 82, 107, 125–6, 139
Underwood, R. L. 85, 101
United Confectioners 82, 95, 96, 98; Babaevsky 95, 97, 99; Rot Front 6, 83, 95, 97, 101, 102; Russian Chocolate 97–8, 102
'Upper Trading Rows', Moscow 15
Urde, M. 101
Urgant, I. 67
USSR: architecture 34; ban on sex shops and pornography 37; and bodybuilding

57–8; chocolate packaging 89–90; political influence on consumer culture 11; Socialist Realism 65 *see also* Russia
utopias 32

Varese, F. 19
Veblen, T. 4
Vegas mall 31–3, 40
Venkatesh, A. 12, 32, 118, 129
Verdery, K. 16
'visual consumption' 3
visual culture 50–1
Vitorgan, M. 10
VKontakte: Coca-Cola 135–6; Levi's case study 132–51; Siberian Crown case study 122, 125, 126, 127, 129 *see also* social media and brands
vloggers (video bloggers) 145
vodka 60; label imagery 88; Russian Ice advertisement 60–3
Vodyanova, N. 10
Vtornik, L. 146

Wal-Mart 14
Warnaby, G. 28
Warrington, P. T. 56
Watne, T. 82

Web 2.0 116, 118
Weber, M. 13
Western popular culture 136–7, 138 *see also* Anglo-Saxon popular culture
White, P. G. 56
Widdis, E. 92
Will.i.am 136
Wilson, A. 16
Winter Olympics 2014 34, 71, 126
Winter, J. 121
women: and advertising 49; role in Russian society 78n1
World Cup, Brazil 126
Wurst, C. 47

Yakobashvili, D. 21
Yampolsky, M. 98
Yasinskaya, A. 34
Yeltsin, B. 9, 17, 22, 72, 111n4, 155
Yurchak, A. 87–8, 124, 133

Zara 27
Zeruvabel, Y. 121
Zhigulevskoe brewery 106
Žižek, S.75–6, 77
Zooom advertisement 63, 64–7
Zwick D. 51, 73–4